FREEDOM AT RISK

Secrecy, Censorship, and Repression in the 1980s

FREEDOM

AT

RISK

Secrecy, Censorship, and Repression in the 1980s

Edited by RICHARD O. CURRY

TEMPLE UNIVERSITY PRESS   Philadelphia

Temple University Press, Philadelphia 19122
Copyright © 1988 by Temple University. All rights reserved
Published 1988
Printed in the United States of America

The paper used in this publication meets the minimum
requirements of American National Standard for Information
Sciences—Permanence of Paper for Printed Library Materials,
ANSI Z39.48-1984

Library of Congress Cataloging-in-Publication Data
Freedom at risk: secrecy, censorship, and repression in the 1980s /
edited by Richard O. Curry.

    p.   cm.

  Bibliography: p.

  Includes index.

  ISBN 0-87722-543-5 (alk. paper)

    1. Freedom of speech—United States. 2. Freedom of the press—
United States. 3. Freedom of information—United States.
4. Censorship—United States. 5. Official secrets—United States.
6. United States—National security—Law and legislation.
I. Curry, Richard Orr.
KF4770.F76 1988
342.73'0853—dc19   87-30343
[347.302853]   CIP

For Patti and our children, Michael, Kim, Becky, and Jon

Contents

Contents

Acknowledgments

Anyone who writes or edits a book owes debts of gratitude to other people. First of all, I want to thank Lawrence I. Kiern, my former graduate student, for making available the transcript of the proceedings of a conference on "The Reagan Administration and the First Amendment" held at the University of Michigan Law School in 1984. This transcript acquainted me with the views of Diana M. T. K. Autin, Richard Delgado, and Geoffrey R. Stone, who later agreed to contribute essays to this collection. My colleague, Thomas G. Paterson, first called my attention to Donna Demac's book on censorship. Demac, in turn, not only agreed to contribute an essay on the Office of Management and Budget, but recommended the inclusion of Professor Thomas I. Emerson's essay on the First Amendment. Demac also read portions of the manuscript and made a number of useful suggestions and incisive comments. Other contributors, especially Richard Delgado, Martin Garbus, Michael Ratner, Athan Theoharis, and Stephen Unger, also provided assistance in a variety of important ways. Selecting an appropriate title is often an elusive process. When Steven Burkholder came up with the phrase "Freedom at Risk," it met with universal acclaim. Burkholder, along with Diana Autin, also provided a number of tips about using the Freedom of Information Act effectively—an important skill in this amazing era.

My greatest intellectual IOU's in this project belong to my friends, colleagues, and associates, Vincent A. Carrafiello and Lawrence B. Goodheart. Numberous conversations with both, ofttimes on a daily basis, helped to define the parameters of the book. In addition, both read portions of the manuscript, and their criticisms on matters relating to organization, style, and content were helpful. I am especially grateful to Goodheart for his careful reading of the introduction, and to Carrafiello for sharing his knowledge of constitutional and legal issues, which is truly impressive. My colleagues, Bruce Stave and Howard Reiter, and Karl Valois, a doctoral candidate at the University

xii of Connecticut, also made useful comments and observations that helped to improve the introduction. Valois, in addition, prepared the index with funds provided by the University of Connecticut Research Foundation.

Barry Morrill, my editor at Temple University Press, whose enthusiasm and support for this book never faltered, provided much needed advice and criticism and an infectious sense of humor.

I also want to thank my congressman, Representative Sam Gejdenson, for his assistance and support over a long period of time. His former staffer, Susan Quinn, not only brought enthusiasm to her work but provided information that I was able to use in writing one of the essays on the U.S. Information Agency included here. Moreover, I appreciate the moral support provided by former Senator J. William Fulbright, who expressed the view, at a critical juncture, that my analysis of USIA policies was right on target. Moreover, a timely letter from U.S. Senator Christopher Dodd prompted a response from USIA officials that was long overdue. I also want to thank former Congressman Toby Moffett for reprinting one of my early essays in the *Congressional Record*.

Ellen Embardo, curator of the Alternative Press Collection at the University of Connecticut, provided several useful bibliographies. In addition, her presentation to my undergraduate seminar on civil liberties during the Reagan era facilitated student access to and use of alternative press materials. I also want to thank Professor J. R. "Dick" Bennett of the University of Arkansas, Fayetteville, for making his annotated bibliography on "Disinformation, Deceit, and Doublespeak" available. Walter Schneir and Miriam Schneir provided an extended bibliography dealing with right-wing attacks on the media. Several other contributors also provided important bibliographic materials. Moreover, Elizabeth Brauer, currently a law student at Dickinson College, provided much needed assistance in tracking down important essays published in the Alternative Press.

A special note of thanks goes to Audrey Stewart, who typed much of the manuscript with extraordinary accuracy and a sharp eye for deletions, mistakes, or oversights. Moreover, the University of Connecticut chapter of the American Association of University Professors deserves thanks for making some funds available for typing services.

I want to thank my wife, Patricia Montenegro Curry, and my daughter, Kimberly, for reading the introduction in a sympathetic but critical way. Moreover, Patti's patience in dealing with the uncertain joys involved in meeting a deadline is a virtue worth commending.

One final note—our German shepherd, Cleo, and our Australian shepherd, Lil' Bear, let me know at appropriate moments that it was time to take a run.

About the Contributors

Richard O. Curry is a professor of American history at the University of Connecticut. He specializes in nineteenth-century political and intellectual history. He is the author, coauthor, or editor of six other books including *A House Divided* (1964); *The Abolitionists* (1965 and 1973); *Radicalism, Racism, and Party Realignment* (1969); *Conspiracy: The Fear of Subversion in American History* (1972); and *The Shaping of America* (1972). He is the contributing coeditor of a forthcoming collection of original essays on individualism. Curry was a postdoctoral fellow at Harvard Divinity School in 1965–1966 and in 1986 he received a Distinguished Alumnus Award from Marshall University. In 1981 he served as a senior Fulbright lecturer in New Zealand, and was a USIA lecturer in the Philippines (1978) and Australia (1981).

Diana M. T. K. Autin, formerly executive director of the Fund for Open Information and Accountability, is the deputy general counsel of the New York City Bureau of Labor Services. She is also an adjunct professor in labor law and labor history at the Cornell School of Industrial and Labor Relations. In 1987 she was awarded a Charles Revson Fellowship on the future of New York City for her outstanding contributions to the city. She has written and lectured extensively on a variety of public-interest legal issues and is the author of *Young People and the Law*, a book on the rights of young people and students.

Steven Burkholder, a staff writer for the *Hartford Courant*, also has reported for the *Milwaukee Journal* and the *Advocate* of Stamford, Connecticut. His articles have appeared in the *Progressive*, the *New York Times*, and other publications, and in 1983 he reported from Panama for Pacific News Service and the *Journal*. He worked in 1977–1978 for the Congressional Research Service. He received a B.A. degree from Oberlin College and an M.A. in public policy from the University of Wisconsin–Madison.

xiv **Richard Delgado** is professor of law at the University of California at Davis, where he teaches civil procedure, law and medicine, and civil rights. Professor Delgado earned his J.D. degree from the University of California, Berkeley (Boalt Hall) School of Law, where he served as Notes & Comments editor on the law review. Delgado has written extensively about legal issues of civil rights and law and medicine.

Donna A. Demac is a communications lawyer, writer, and educator living in New York City. She teaches graduate-level courses in telecommunications regulation, copyright law, and international media at New York University's Interactive Telecommunications Program. She has written numerous articles on government information policy and satellite communications, is the editor of *Tracing New Orbits: Cooperation and Competition in Global Satellite Development*, and the author of *Keeping America Uninformed: Government Secrecy in the 1980s*.

Thomas I. Emerson is Sterling Professor Emeritus of public law at Yale Law School. Emerson is one of America's leading authorities on First Amendment law, history, and theory. His books include *Toward a General Theory of the First Amendment*; *The System of Freedom of Expression*; and *Political and Civil Rights in the United States*. Professor Emerson is a past president of the National Lawyers Guild, and his numerous honors and awards include Guggenheim and Ford Foundation fellowships. He also served as legal adviser for the Connecticut Civil Liberties Union as well as the American Civil Liberties Union (ACLU).

Martin Garbus is a partner in the New York law firm of Frankfurt, Garbus, Klein & Selz. He has taught at the law schools of Columbia University and Yale and has served as an associate director of the ACLU. He is the author of two books: *Ready for the Defense* and *Traitors and Heroes*. His articles have appeared in the *Nation, Publishers Weekly*, the *New York Times, Harper's Magazine*, and elsewhere.

Renny Golden is a professor in the Criminal Justice Department at Northeastern Illinois University. She is actively involved in the Sanctuary movement and is coauthor (with Michael McConnell) of *Sanctuary: The New Underground Railroad*.

Nat Hentoff is a free-lance writer who has published a book on the history of the First Amendment and numerous articles on contemporary First Amendment issues. His columns appear regularly in the *Village Voice* and the *Progressive*.

Jamie Kalven is a journalist who writes frequently about First Amendment xv matters. He is the editor of *A Worthy Tradition: Freedom of Speech in America* by Harry Kalven, Jr.

Judith Schenck Koffler currently teaches law at Pace University School of Law, as well as at Sing-Sing Prison. She has published articles on Shakespeare and Dante as well as on constitutional law and bankruptcy, and does *pro bono* work for the homeless. Professor Koffler has an L.L.M. degree from Harvard, and is a Fellow of the Society for the Humanities at Cornell University.

Harry G. Levine is associate professor of sociology at Queens College, City University of New York. He has published many journal articles on the sociology and history of alcohol and drugs. He has held fellowships from the National Institute of Alcohol Abuse and Alcoholism and the National Endowment for the Humanities, and he won the Keller Award for his article "The Discovery of Addiction." He is currently completing a book on the history of the alcohol question in America.

Michael McConnell is a minister in the United Church of Christ. He is actively involved in the Sanctuary movement and is coauthor (with Renny Golden) of *Sanctuary: The New Underground Railroad.*

Thomas G. Paterson is a professor of diplomatic history at the University of Connecticut. He is the author, coauthor, or editor of ten books. They include *The Origins of the Cold War; Containment and the Cold War; American Imperialism and Anti-Imperialism; Soviet-American Confrontation;* and *Cold War Critics.* Paterson has published numerous articles in journals and magazines such as the *Nation,* the *Journal of American History,* and the *American Historical Review.* He is a past president of the Society for Historians of American Foreign Relations (SHAFR). His many awards have included grants from the National Endowment for the Humanities (NEH), the American Philosophical Society, and the Harry S. Truman Institute. In the summer of 1987 he lectured at four universities in the People's Republic of China.

William Preston, Jr., formerly the head of the History Department of John Jay College, College of the University of New York, is the author of *Aliens and Dissenters: Federal Suppression of Radicals, 1930–1933.* He currently serves as president of the Fund for Open Information and Accountability, Inc., in New York City. It has expedited numerous FOIA requests by scholars and researchers.

xvi **Janet Raloff** has been a staff writer for *Science News* for the past ten years. She has written extensively on the connections between science, technology, and public policy issues.

Margaret Randall lived in Latin America (Mexico, Cuba, Nicaragua) for twenty-three years before returning to her native United States in early 1984. She has been fighting an ongoing battle with the Immigration and Naturalization Service (INS), which attempted to deport her because of the critical content of her writings. Randall's most recent books are *Albuquerque: Coming Back to the USA*; *The Coming Home Poems*; *This is About Incest*; and *Memory Says Yes* (coming soon from Curbstone Press, Willimantic, Connecticut). She is a visiting professor in the English Department at Trinity College, Hartford.

Michael Ratner is presently the legal director of the Center for Constitutional Rights in New York City. He was formerly the president of the National Lawyers Guild. Presently, Mr. Ratner is litigating cases challenging U.S. intervention in Central America and cases seeking to end Federal Bureau of Investigation (FBI) spying on groups engaged in domestic dissent. He has written numerous articles in these areas and has testified on these subjects before Congress.

Ellen Ray is editor of *Our Right to Know*, which is published by the Fund for Open Information and Accountability, Inc., in New York City. She is also coeditor (with Louis Wolf) of *Covert Action Information Bulletin*.

Craig Reinarman is assistant professor of sociology at Northeastern University in Boston. He has been a postdoctoral Fellow at the Alcohol Research Group, University of California, Berkeley, and has taught at the University of California, at Santa Barbara and at Santa Cruz. Accounts of his research on drug problems have appeared in numerous scholarly journals. His book on political beliefs, *American States of Mind*, was published in 1986 by Yale University Press.

Mark Schapiro, formerly a free-lance writer, is currently European editor of "InterNation"—a new monthly series of international investigative articles appearing in the *Nation* magazine. He is the coauthor of *The Circle of Poison*, which deals with pesticides, and has published in journals and magazines such as the *New Republic*, the *Washington Monthly*, and *New Age*. He is currently based in Paris, France.

Walter Schneir and Miriam Schneir covered the Westmoreland-CBS libel trial and wrote about it for the *Nation* and the *New York Times* Op-Ed page. He

also edited an 80,000-page microfiche collection on the case, *VIETNAM: A* **xvii**
Documentary Collection, Westmoreland v. CBS. Their writings on a wide variety
of subjects have appeared in magazines, newspapers, and anthologies. They are
coauthors of a study of the Rosenberg case, *Invitation to an Inquest*. She writes
frequently for *Ms* and is the editor of *Feminism: The Essential Historical Writings*.
He is a winner of the 1987 PEN Syndicated Fiction Competition.

John Shattuck is vice president of Harvard University (government, community, and public affairs). He also holds appointments as lecturer at the Harvard Law School and senior research associate in the Program on Science,
Technology, and Public Policy at Harvard's John F. Kennedy School of Government. He received an LL.B. degree from the Yale Law School, where he
was an editor of the *Yale Law Journal*. A former national counsel and legislative
director of the American Civil Liberties Union, Mr. Shattuck has taught at
Princeton. He has authored, edited, or contributed to *Privacy: Cases, Materials
and Questions*; *Endangered Rights*; *Constitutional Government in America*; *Rights of
Privacy*; and *Government Secrecy in America*.

Eleanor Stein is an attorney who, until recently, was a staff legal worker at
the Center for Constitutional Rights.

Geoffrey R. Stone is dean and Harry Kalven, Jr., Professor of Law at the
University of Chicago Law School. He has taught constitutional law for fifteen years. He is the coauthor of a new casebook on constitutional law and
has written a wide range of articles on such subjects as freedom of expression,
privacy, undercover investigations, and freedom of religion.

Athan Theoharis is a professor of history at Marquette University. He is
the author, coauthor, or editor of several books including *Spying on Americans: Political Surveillance from Hoover to the Huston Plan* and *Beyond the Hiss
Case: The FBI, Congress, and the Cold War*. He is also the coauthor of a forthcoming biography of J. Edgar Hoover. He has served as a consultant to various congressional committees (most notably the Senate Select Committee on
Intelligence Activities in 1975). His numerous awards include the Binkley-
Stephenson Award from the Organization of American Historians and a Gavel
Award from the American Bar Association.

Stephen H. Unger is currently professor of computer science, Columbia
University. Prior to 1961 he was a member of the technical staff at Bell Telephone Laboratories. He has served as a consultant to IBM, RCA, Western
Electric, and other organizations. He is the author of more than forty technical publications in the field of computer science, including a book on se-

quential switching circuits. He is also a past president of Institute of Electrical and Electronic Engineers, which deals with the social implications of technology. He has presented over seventy papers on engineering ethics and technology policy and is the author of *Controlling Technology: Ethics and the Responsible Engineer*. A member of A A A S (the American Association for the Advancement of Science) Committee on Scientific Freedom and Responsibility between 1981 and 1984, he chaired a subcommittee on National Security and Scientific Communication.

Louis Wolf is a journalist who has done extensive research on American intelligence activities throughout the world. He is cofounder and coeditor of *Covert Action Information Bulletin*. He is also coeditor of *Dirty Work: The CIA in Western Europe* and *Dirty Work II: The CIA in Africa*. Wolf has lived and worked in Laos, the Philippines, and Europe in a variety of capacities. In Laos, he did conscientious objector work as a rural development volunteer; in Laos and the Philippines, he was a correspondent for Dispatch News Service International, 1966–1972. Between 1972 and 1976 he was a free-lance writer and researcher in London; and between 1976 and 1986 he was a correspondent for Transnational Feature Service/Research Associates International.

FREEDOM AT RISK

Secrecy, Censorship, and Repression in the 1980s

[Richard O. Curry]

INTRODUCTION

Perhaps it is a universal truth that the loss of liberty at home is to be charged to provisions of danger, real or pretended, from abroad.

—James Madison

The greatest dangers to liberty lurk in insidious encroachment by men of zeal, well-meaning, but without understanding.

—Justice Louis Brandeis

Most Americans like to think of the United States as an enlightened and progressive society. It is difficult to minimize the influence of the American Revolution, Enlightenment ideas, the protections afforded by the Bill of Rights, the advance of political democracy, attacks upon monopoly and special privilege, the destruction of slavery, and the implications of some social reform movements. Indeed, there is much to admire about American politics, life, and culture.

Yet, there is a darker side to American history as every informed person knows. We are not referring here to the truism that social progress is inevitably accompanied by conflict—bitterly contested encounters with conservative or traditionalist forces opposed to innovation and change. We are speaking, rather, of a reactionary and authoritarian tradition that is as deeply ingrained in American society and politics as is the spirit of light and progress.

This is not to say that American history is little more than a perpetual struggle between forces of light and darkness. Life is far too complex to be explained by simplistic exaggerations. Yet, this is precisely what some of our leaders, past and present, would have us believe. President Reagan for example, has portrayed the Soviet Union as an "evil empire"—a godless, atheistic octopus extending its tentacles everywhere in remorseless efforts to destroy the "free world." Moreover, Mr. Reagan not only has maintained that the nuclear freeze movement in the United States has been infiltrated by KGB agents, but argued (before the onset of "Irangate") that opponents of his Central American policies, if not outright subversives, were "soft on communism." The administration has also denied visas to distinguished foreign visitors under the ideo-

4 logical exclusion sections of the McCarran-Walter Act, and has labeled two Canadian films, one on nuclear energy and the other on acid rain, as "political propaganda." The Soviet-American summit in December 1987 has resulted in the modification of anti-Soviet rhetoric by the president and other administration officials. However, the future course of Russo-American relations is by no means clear. A rapprochement, if it occurs, will be a long and arduous process. Moreover, the effects of a "thaw" on domestic policies are likely to be minimal within the forseeable future.

In *one* sense, there is nothing remarkable about President Reagan's use of conspiracy rhetoric to justify a repressive "national security" program. From the colonial era to the present, many Americans, including prominent national leaders, have attributed the disruptions produced by war, labor upheavals, economic depression, and wrenching social change to subversives. At various times, Roman Catholics, Jews, anarchists, international bankers, labor organizers, Japanese-Americans, Communists, and others have served as convenient scapegoats for those groups and individuals who are unwilling or unable to understand the realities of a fragmented and complex world. In part, therefore, the Reaganite belief that "individual liberties are secondary to the requirements of national security" is part of a continuum that needs to be placed in historical perspective.

Nevertheless, the policies of the Reagan administration also reflect *radical departures* from the past. This is revealed not only by the comprehensive scope of the administration's policies but by its ability to *institutionalize* secrecy, censorship, and repression in ways that will be difficult, if not impossible, to eradicate. This is true not because Mr. Reagan's perceptions and convictions reflect greater passion and zeal than those held by earlier countersubversive crusaders. The Reagan administration's success stems, rather, from *major structural and technological changes* that have occurred in American society during the twentieth century—especially the emergence of the modern bureaucratic state and the invention of sophisticated electronic devices that make surveillance possible in new and insidious ways. Although Mr. Reagan has made effective use of "antistatist" rhetoric throughout his presidency in regard to domestic policy, he has, in fact, expanded the power of the national bureaucracy for "national security" purposes in systematic and unprecedented ways.

The major objectives of this essay, therefore, are threefold: to place the policies of the Reagan administration in historical perspective, to analyze the implications of the president's policies themselves, and to explain why Mr. Reagan's policies have the potential to become a permanent part of the American institutional and bureaucratic structure.

If fears of subversion are omnipresent throughout American history, this fact is not nearly so important as their virulence at a given point in time. The first important point to note is that such fears are most intense during times of national crisis—whether caused by international conflicts, domestic disruptions, or a combination of both. During World War I, for example, American citizens of German ancestry were treated as a potential fifth column. German language courses were abolished in some American colleges and universities, and the famed violinist, Fritz Kreisler, was not allowed to perform in Carnegie Hall. After the Japanese attack on Pearl Harbor, the West Coast was gripped by panic, and the government imprisoned thousands of Japanese-American citizens in internment camps in California, Colorado, and elsewhere. Senator Joseph R. McCarthy's erroneous but widely believed charges that government agencies, especially the State Department, were infested by Communist agents were, in part, a response to the tensions and frustrations generated by the Cold War.

Domestic crises, especially severe social and economic dislocations, have also produced conspiratorial interpretations that blamed foreign agents or alien ideologies rather than internal problems for social conflicts. The Populists, impoverished by the agricultural depression of the 1890s, believed that international bankers were engaged in a secret plot to reduce American farmers to peonage. Labor leaders, in the wake of the Haymarket Square riot and violent strikes that attended the rise of unions, were denounced as anarchists or agents of the Comintern. The Great Crash of 1929 was also blamed by some observers on the intrigues of international Jewish bankers.

A prime example of conspiracy fears resulting from a combination of pressures in both foreign and domestic affairs occurred during the 1790s. The Federalists and Jeffersonians took turns accusing one another of subversion. Jefferson's followers were denounced by Federalists as Jacobins who planned to bring the French Revolution's Reign of Terror to American shores. Conversely, Jeffersonians declared that the Federalists, who enacted the Alien and Sedition Acts, were monarchists bent on destroying the Bill of Rights.

Major examples of countersubversive crusades directed against purely domestic enemies are reflected in abolitionist attacks on the "great slave power conspiracy," Southern fears of abolitionist-inspired slave rebellions during the antebellum period, and the repressive measures directed by the Lincoln administration against conservative Northern Democrats or "Copperheads" during the Civil War. Even here it must be noted that the mounting sectional crisis during the 1850s caused many Americans to regard both North and South virtually as foreign nations; and during the war itself, "Copperheads" were wrongly regarded by Republicans as traitors who favored Southern independence.

Scholars have also noted that conspiracy rhetoric, accompanied by political, social, or religious repression, is also quite intense during periods when

6 traditional social and moral standards are being transformed by rapid changes in the social order. Historian David Brion Davis has written two illuminating essays on the nineteenth-century American experience ("Some Ideological Functions of Prejudice" and "Some Themes of Counter-Subversion"), which deal primarily with anti-Catholic, anti-Mormon, and anti-Masonic rhetoric.

In part, Davis argues that the open and competitive nature of American society inevitably bred anxiety and political insecurity. The very fact that the United States had democratic ideals and liberal institutions led, in times of foreign or domestic crisis, to exaggerated fears of subversion or betrayal. Since loyalty in American society could not be compelled, it had to be internalized. In sum, it had to be based on voluntary compliance since the United States did not have an elaborate national security apparatus until the mid-twentieth century which could, if deemed necessary, take extraordinary steps to maintain "public order" or protect "national security."

In the nineteenth century, therefore, "outsiders"—foreigners, Jews, Roman Catholics, Mormons, Masons, and other "subversive" or potentially traitorous groups—were often subjected to harassment and violence not by government agents or prosecutors but by vigilantes. These groups justified their actions by using the vocabulary of demonology to protect their visions of public morality, public safety, or, indeed, democratic principles themselves. In fact, the reverse was true. Countersubversive mobs succeeded only in assaulting the very principles they professed to revere.

It may be objected that there were exceptions to the rule—for example, the passage of the Alien and Sedition Acts by the Federalists in the 1790s, and the arbitrary imprisonment of "Copperheads" by overzealous officials of the Lincoln administration during the Civil War. But even in these instances, considering the absence of a highly centralized, bureaucratic state, the effects of political repression proved to be temporary aberrations that established no long-range precedents.

Some scholars, in attempting to gauge the significance of countersubversive movements in American politics, believe that attacks on "conspiracy" in high places is little more than a sham, a crude tactic designed to discredit political opponents whose domestic policies are the real target. Thus, Federalists who opposed Jefferson's social and economic ideas tried to link him with atheism and the French Reign of Terror. More recently, Republican opponents of the New Deal hoped to drive the Democrats from power by accusing them of advocating "creeping socialism," selling out Nationalist China, or appointing avowed Communists to high public office.

The cynical use of conspiracy rhetoric by unscrupulous politicians provides a partial explanation for its public appeal in some instances. Obviously, such tactics cannot succeed unless large numbers of people fervently believe that

Jewish bankers, Roman Catholics, Mormons, anarchists, or "evil empires" constitute a clear and present danger to American security and ideals.

In an effort to explain why these fears are endemic, many writers have utilized sociological and psychological theories as analytic tools. Franz Neumann, Gordon Allport, and Erich Fromm, for example, emphasize the importance of societal disruption, alienation, and personality disorders in accounting for the success of demonic appeals in both the United States and Europe. Whether or not demagogues believe in the reality of the subversive activities they excoriate is not as important as their role as catalysts. In short, attributing personal or societal defects to scapegoats provides a psychological defense mechanism that allows individuals to rationalize failure by externalizing it. Germany, so the story goes, did not lose World War I because its armies were overwhelmed by superior forces. To the contrary. The nation was "stabbed in the back" by Jews!

The concept of status politics is another theory used by some scholars to explain the appeal of countersubversive crusades. Seymour Martin Lipset, a leading proponent of this approach, argues that status-oriented rhetoric "appeals . . . not only [to] groups which have risen in the economic structure, who may be frustrated in their desire to be accepted socially by those who hold status, but [to] groups possessing status as well, who feel that various social groups threaten their own claims to high social position, or enable previously lower-status groups to claim equal status with them." As a result, such groups relieve their anxieties and frustrations by concluding that conspiratorial groups occupy or are attempting to seize the bastions of power in government, the churches, the press, and the universities.

It must be kept in mind, however, that these sociological and psychological explanations of conspiracy fears are theoretical propositions that do not come to grips with all the variables required to provide comprehensive analysis. Such theories of behavior are open to the objection that they associate conspiracy rhetoric almost exclusively with right-wing extremism, and ideology is reduced to little more than subconscious rationalization, which is not always the case.

For example, the abolitionists before the Civil War and the Republican party during the war itself were groups that not only used conspiracy rhetoric effectively, but occupied the cutting edge in promoting revolutionary change. Moreover, many leaders of the American Revolution, as Bernard Bailyn has cogently argued, were convinced that the policies pursued by George III and his ministers were part of a gigantic plot to destroy the "rights of Englishmen" not only in the American colonies but at home. Thus, fears of subversion are not the exclusive domain of charlatans, crackpots, and the disaffected.

In conclusion: Countersubversive movements are pervasive in American

8 society and have wreaked havoc on the lives of some groups and individuals at least once during every generation since the 1790s. At the same time, we have argued that attacks on alleged subversives have been sporadic and have not resulted, therefore, in any systematic effort to transform the United States into a "barracks state." If this is true, why then should President Reagan's pronouncements on the Soviet Union and the dangers of international communism be viewed in an even more forbidding light than the exaggerated appeals of earlier groups who viewed historical processes through a conspiratorial lens?

Earlier on, we mentioned the fact that the Reagan administration's "thirst for autocracy" (to use Walter Karp's phrase) benefits not only from excessive zeal, but from *major structural changes* that have occurred in American society during the twentieth century. The most important of these changes is, of course, the emergence and growth of a highly centralized bureaucratic state.

Powerful government bureaucracies have administered the liberal domestic reform programs associated with the New Deal, Fair Deal, and Great Society programs; but the emergence of the United States as a superpower during the Second World War has also had major consequences. The advent of the Cold War, and ongoing conflicts with the Soviet Union and the "international Communist conspiracy" (e.g., Vietnam) have created what President Eisenhower called a "military-industrial complex" that has placed the American economy on a permanent "war footing." Equally important, the Cold War and America's role as the acknowledged leader of the "free world" have resulted in the creation of an elaborate national security apparatus in the United States. This has come about through congressional enactments, a myriad of executive orders and national security directives, and a series of Supreme Court decisions which, collectively, have downgraded First Amendment values whenever the government has invoked that magical concept called "national security."

Many of the functions of the FBI, the CIA, and other government intelligence agencies are legitimate; but the Watergate revelations, numerous congressional hearings, and information released under the terms of the Freedom of Information Act have revealed indefensible patterns of abuse that, if allowed to continue, threaten the existence of democratic institutions themselves.

The central point, therefore, is that the growth of institutionalized governmental power carried out by impersonal but entrenched bureaucracies has created the potential for implementing reactionary as well as beneficent policies. Governmental power can be used not only to promote social change, but to prevent it; and it can be used not only to safeguard the rights and liberties of Americans but to attack, undermine, and destroy them.

The Reagan administration, obviously, did not create the modern bureaucratic state, but its officials clearly understand how to use the enormous power at their disposal to promote their own domestic and foreign policy agendas.

One of the ironies involved here is that the Reagan administration clearly understands that antistatist rhetoric has enormous popular appeal—and it exploits it to the fullest.

Mr. Reagan struck a responsive chord by promising, among other things, to cut taxes, eliminate waste and inefficiency in government, bring escalating costs for social services under control, restore "free enterprise" to the marketplace through deregulation ("getting government off our backs"), close alleged "windows of vulnerability," and, at the same time, eliminate deficits and balance the federal budget.

The contradictions in the Reagan program have long been recognized by foe and friend alike—for example, by former OMB Director David Stockman and Vice President George Bush. The latter once described the Reagan agenda as "voodoo economics." Taxes and social services have been cut, but military spending has reached unprecedented proportions. Mr. Reagan's "Star Wars" or SDI initiatives if pursued will not simply escalate the arms race and increase mounting deficits, but reflect an attempt *to escape history*—an effort to achieve total military security which, in the thermonuclear age, appears to be an impossible dream. The president's policies have, in fact, produced $200 billion a year deficits which, combined with ever-increasing trade imbalances, threaten economic disaster. In sum, the Reagan administration, mired in its own contradictions, has thus far provided only short-range illusions, not long-range solutions to the complex problems encountered in both the domestic and foreign policy spheres.

It may be objected that the president's policies, whatever their apparent contradictions, reflect the existence of a coherent ideology—a desire to dismantle the New Deal and Great Society programs, combined with a commitment to the most massive military buildup the world has ever known. If this is true, then Mr. Reagan's attacks on "big government" are highly selective ones. The present administration has granted such enormous power to the Office of Management and Budget under David Stockman and his successor, James T. Miller, that it has become the most powerful government agency in history. Moreover, the powers exercised by the FBI, the CIA, and the other intelligence agencies have increased so dramatically as a result of Mr. Reagan's national security directives, it becomes increasingly clear that it is not highly centralized power that the current administration objects to, but the objectives that governmental power is designed to achieve. The Reagan administration's extraordinary secrecy and censorship policies, combined with its massive assaults on civil liberties in the name of national security, can be attained only by the arbitrary exercise and massive abuse of governmental power.

Even so, it is important to stress that *not all* the policies currently being

10 pursued by the Reagan administration are unprecedented. Many of Mr. Reagan's initiatives represent a continuation of the fears and "national security" concerns of previous administrations and the Supreme Court during the past forty years.

The McCarran-Walter Act, for example, passed in 1952 over President Truman's veto, has been used time and again during the past three and a half decades to deny visas to foreigners whose views are considered dangerous to American ideals and values. Thus, the Reagan administration's decision to deny visas to foreigners such as Gabriel García Márquez, Patricia Lara, Hortensia Allende, and Carlos Fuentes—and indeed, its effort to deport the American-born writer Margaret Randall—should be viewed as part of a continuum although the Reagan administration's primary (if not exclusive) objective is to exclude critics, or potential critics, of its Central American policies.

In December 1987, however, Congress passed an amendment to McCarran-Walter (sponsored by Senator Daniel Patrick Moynihan and Congressman Barney Frank) removing ideological exclusion as grounds for excluding aliens from the United States. The amendment will only be in effect until February 1989; but a Justice Department lawyer announced on February 4, 1988 that the government would no longer oppose Randall's appeal of her deportation order. Whether or not Congress will permanently repeal the ideological exclusion provisions of McCarran-Walter remains to be seen.

Moreover, the development of "balancing tests" by the Supreme Court, whereby the Court purports to balance the security of the state against the First Amendment rights of individuals, is hardly a new phenomenon. The same holds true for the doctrine of "seditious libel" (albeit in disguised form) in such cases as *Haig* v. *Agee, The Progressive*, and the *Snepp* decisions.

Other examples that reflect continuity in American policy since the 1950s include the use of disinformation and psycholinguistic devices such as misleading metaphors and euphemisms to sway public opinion on both domestic and foreign policy issues. Recent examples—for instance, Ali Agca and the alleged KGB plot to kill the pope, the use of "spy dust" (mutagens) by the Russians to keep track of American embassy officials in Moscow, the mysterious Libyan "hit squads" which, somehow, failed to make their appearance in the United States, and President Reagan's public announcements linking Nicaragua with international terrorism, international communism, and the international drug traffic—are merely some of the latest propaganda efforts by the American government to mold public attitudes. In addition, attacks on the media, whether in the form of White House criticism, libel cases brought by Generals Westmoreland and Sharon, or diatribes by right-wing organizations such as the Heritage Foundation and Reed Irvine's Accuracy in Media (AIM), did not suddenly begin to germinate, flower, and bear fruit after Ronald Reagan's election to the presidency. Finally, the new wave of conspiracy trials, which have taken place since the early 1980s, are reminiscent of the conspiracy prosecutions of the Nixon era whereby the Justice Department tried to intimidate or silence critics of the Vietnam War. The Reagan administration, however, has added several new twists: the use of preventive detention, anonymous juries, "the armed courtroom," and the elimination of "justification defenses" which ofttimes led to acquittals in the late 1960s and early 1970s. A justification defense is, of course, testimony that allows defendants to discuss their motives in taking a particular course of action.

The practice of preventive detention has been challenged in the courts, but to no avail. In May 1987 the Supreme Court ruled by a six-to-three majority in *U.S.* v. *Salerno* that the Bail Reform Act of 1984, which mandated preventive detention, was constitutional. Defense attorneys argued that the act violated the Fifth Amendment's prohibition of imprisonment without due process and the Eighth Amendment's guarantee of bail before trial. The Court ruled, however, that "the government's regulatory interest in community safety can, in appropriate circumstances, outweigh an individual's liberty interest." In fact, Chief Justice Rehnquist declared that "we cannot categorically state that pretrial detention offends some principle of justice so rooted in the traditions and conscience of our people as to be ranked as fundamental."

In a scathing dissent, Justice Thurgood Marshall said that preventive detention was "consistent with the usages of tyranny and the excesses of what bitter experience teaches us to call the police state." The majority's decision, he concluded, "applies itself to an ominous exercise in [constitutional] demolition. Theirs is truly a decision which will go forth without authority, and come back without respect."

Conspiracy trials, combined with the new tactics currently being utilized, thus reflect both *continuity with* and *a radical departure from* the history of the recent past. There are, however, numerous other policies implemented by the Reagan administration that are *totally unprecedented*. For example, Mr. Reagan's secrecy and censorship policies are the most sweeping in American history. The most highly publicized measure, the president's National Security Decision Directive 84 (NSDD 84), has required approximately 290,000 government employees and contractors with access to classified information to sign *lifetime* censorship agreements as a condition of employment. Such agreements, until recently, were required only of CIA operatives. As a result of opposition in Congress, President Reagan agreed to suspend, not rescind, this provision; but Mr. Reagan's agreement was nothing more than a subterfuge. The administration is still requiring government employees to sign lifetime nondisclosure agreements under the terms of an earlier 1981 contract, Form 4193, as well as a series of similar agreements prepared by various departments of the ex-

12 ecutive branch. In 1983 alone, more than 28,000 speeches, articles, and books written by government employees were submitted to government censors for clearance!

In addition, President Reagan's Executive Order 12356 reversed President Carter's guidelines for classifying documents which were the most liberal in history—the culmination of a thirty-year trend toward reducing not only the number of documents classified but the levels of classification as well. Not only has President Reagan repudiated this liberalizing trend (which included the declassification of most documents within six years), but has *reclassified* documents made available to researchers by previous administrations. The American Historical Association and the Organization of American Historians have filed suit in federal district court in Washington challenging the legality of this practice, but, as yet, no decision has been rendered.

Even more astonishing is the Reagan administration's efforts to classify research by American professors *based on unclassified information* whether or not such research was funded by the government, and whether or not the research in question is even remotely related to "national security" issues. Beyond this, private companies that collect nonclassified information for sale abroad—including newspaper articles and the transcripts of congressional hearings (in sum, information that is available in public libraries)—are being pressured by government agents not to make such information available to foreign subscribers. These blatant attempts to censor "sensitive, but nonclassified" information may not be legally enforceable; but the ostensible justification for exerting such pressure is based on "mosaic or compilation theory"—the idea that nonclassified data may form part of a puzzle which, when pieced together, could jeopardize "national security."

The Reagan administration has also invoked the provisions of the export control laws—which were designed originally to prevent the export of certain types of technical devices or equipment—to prevent scientists from presenting papers based on *unclassified* information at international conferences, and this despite the fact that many of the papers involved had already been published.

In August 1986 the Reagan administration came up with still another initiative in an effort to control the dissemination of nonclassified information. The administration now requires all government employees with security clearances to sign Standard Form 189, an offshoot of NSDD 84. The form requires employees not to divulge not only classified information but that which is "nonclassified but classifiable." Steven Garfinkel, director of the Information Security Oversight Office, explained: "A party to SF 189 would violate its nondisclosure provisions only if he or she disclosed without authorization classified information *or information that he or she knew, or reasonably could have known, was classified, although it did not yet include required classified markings*" [emphasis added]. In the Fall of 1986 the government also issued SF 189A which required government contractors, including researchers, who handle classified information to sign this form."

This new category, "nonclassified but classifiable," may be as absurd as Catch-22, but employees accused of violating its murky provisions can be fired and prosecuted. Nearly two million federal employees have already signed the form "knowingly or blindly." Only twenty-four people have refused to do so on First Amendment grounds. "Because of their courage and outrage," the Hartford *Courant* editorialized, "Congress will conduct hearings on SF 189" in the Fall of 1987. Equally important, two government employee unions filed suit in federal district court on August 17, 1987, challenging the constitutionality of SF 189. As a result, Garfinkel announced that enforcement of SF 189 was being "temporarily suspended" pending the outcome of litigation.

The Reagan administration has also attempted to destroy the effectiveness of the Freedom of Information Act (FOIA). The FOIA, enacted in 1966 and strengthened as a result of the Watergate revelations, has been an indispensable source in gaining access to information dealing with such questions as toxic wastes (Love Canal), nuclear safety, intelligence agency abuses, FBI abuses, hazards in the workplace, discrimination, civil rights violations, consumer products safety, and much, much more. The Reagan administration has not been able to destroy the FOIA (its original objective); but it has managed to get modifications that deny public access to issues involving the use of nuclear energy (even peaceful uses—for example, nuclear power plant designs), information on consumer products (on the grounds that its release might compromise trade secrets), and matters involving "national security"— including all operational files of the CIA and FBI records pertaining to foreign intelligence, counterintelligence operations, and international terrorism. Some safeguards in these areas are, in fact, necessary; but the past history of abuse demonstrates that the FBI and CIA want to impose the mantle of secrecy on all their activities, especially those illegal operations that have come to light. Recent amendments to the FOIA have liberalized fee waiver restrictions. For example, automatic fee waivers now exist for the media and organizations that can qualify as being "educational or scientific" in nature; but the actual effects of the implementation of these new guidelines by the Office of Management and Budget remain to be seen. Moreover, the new exemptions regarding access—many of which resulted from riders tacked onto the Anti-Drug Abuse Act passed in November 1986—have narrowed the range of information now available to researchers and the public.

We have already observed that the powers of the OMB have grown enormously during the Reagan years. It has become the "nerve center" of the executive branch, a superagency that not only controls the budget but exercises

14 an absolute veto power over the activities of all government regulatory agencies. The OMB has also disregarded the intent of the Paperwork Reduction Act of 1980 by reducing and in some cases eliminating vital statistical information essential for informed public policy debates on the national, state, and local levels. In those instances where statistical information has not been eliminated or reduced, its collection and dissemination have been farmed out to private contractors. Not only has the "commodification" of information greatly increased its cost, but, in the opinion of informed critics, has cast doubt in many instances upon its reliability or accuracy. "Paperwork reduction," as implemented by the Reagan administration, has become, therefore, another form of censorship. The administrations's "information policies," which are based on exaggerated fears of Russian capabilities, and a demonstrated hostility to the concept of an open society, bode ill for the future.

No discussion of the Reagan administration's obsession with secrecy and censorship would be complete without analyzing the implications of the Samuel Loring Morison case. Morison, a strong advocate of a U.S. military buildup, is the first person ever convicted under the terms of the American espionage statutes for *leaking information to the press*. In the past, the espionage laws were directed primarily against persons who provided secret information to foreign enemies.* Morison, however, was convicted of espionage for providing a British magazine, *Jane's Defense Weekly*, with three classified photographs of the Soviet Union's first nuclear aircraft carrier.

Joseph A. Young, the federal district judge who presided at Morison's trial, could have dismissed the charges against Morison by ruling that the espionage laws could not be used to prosecute leakers. Or, he might have instructed the jury that the prosecutors, in order to obtain a conviction, would have to prove, as required by the Espionage Act of 1917, that Morison intended to harm the United States by providing *Jane's* with photographs. Judge Young might also have said, in his charge to the jury, that the prosecutors also had to prove that the damage done to national security was "reasonably foreseeable, not remote or speculative." But Judge Young not only refused to dismiss the charges against Morison, but ruled that anyone who "willfully" transmits information is guilty of espionage "no matter what his motives." Young also ruled that the government did not have to prove that the photographs harmed national security. The transmission of classified information to unauthorized recipients, even if it had no effect on national security at all, was an act of espionage. Thus, Judge Young's interpretations of the espionage laws, however tortured, made Morison's conviction virtually a foregone conclusion since jurors must rely on a judge's rulings as to what laws mean.

---

* Daniel Ellsberg and Anthony Russo were indicted under the espionage statutes in the Pentagon Papers case in 1972, but charges were dismissed because of government improprieties.

But the issue involved here is not simply Judge Young's interpretations of the espionage laws. If Morison's conviction is not reversed by higher courts, the Reagan administration's goal of virtually eliminating all unauthorized leaks will have been achieved by *judicial means* rather than *legislative enactment*. Stated in slightly different terms, the U.S. Congress has consistently refused to pass an American version of Great Britain's Official Secrets Act. This law, as Martin Garbus observes, "nearly gives the [British] government the final, judicially unreviewable right to impose its own definition of what information injures the nation." The implications of the Morison case, therefore, are enormous. If Morison's conviction is allowed to stand, congressional action will no longer be required to give the executive branch almost total control over what information is released to the public. In that event, it is not only future leakers who must beware, but journalists, broadcasters, authors, and publishers who receive such information and dare to use it. The "chilling effects" of such a prospect cannot be exaggerated.★

As things now stand, the government's ability to mold public opinion is enormous. State-imposed secrecy and censorship, combined with disinformation campaigns and psycholinguistic manipulation, ordinarily succeed in drowning out weaker voices. But the Morison case threatens to transform what is now an uneven contest into a rout. Floyd Abrams sums up the problem in eloquent terms when he observes that the Reagan administration "not only focuses on security but equates security with secrecy, and treats information as if it were a potentially contagious disease that must be controlled, quarantined and ultimately cured."

Still another example of the Reagan administration's hostility to free inquiry and the open exchange of ideas is provided by its opposition to international educational and cultural exchanges. In 1981, USIA director Charles Z. Wick recommended that funding for the Fulbright program be cut by 56 percent. This recommendation, had it been approved by Congress, would have eliminated Fulbright lectureships and research fellowships in sixty one countries—primarily in Third World nations. In addition, Mr. Wick recommended that the Hubert H. Humphrey fellowship program be abolished and that drastic cuts be made in the critically important International Visitors Program. Fortunately, these funds were restored by a bipartisan coalition in Congress.

Besides this, the Reagan administration has asked Congress each year since 1981 to eliminate all funding under Title VI of the Higher Education Act. These proposed cuts would have eliminated funding for ninety-one international education and foreign language centers and for seventy-two undergraduate international studies programs at American colleges and universities. The

★ In April 1988 the Fourth Federal Circuit Court of Appeals unanimously upheld Morison's conviction.

16   administration's Title VI proposals would also have cut approximately $5 million each year for Fulbright graduate research fellowships. Conversely, the Reagan administration responded favorably to a Kissinger Commission report that recommended bringing some ten thousand Central American students to the United States to study at American universities at a cost of some $380 million. Congress authorized funding for this initiative for fiscal years 1986 and 1987 but not at the levels requested.

The political and ideological motivations behind these contradictory initiatives are clear. As Hugh M. Hamill, Jr., observes, the administration's efforts to weaken international education are predicated upon the idea that many U.S. educators and students "who do learn about Latin America and other areas of the world are articulate and effective critics" of American foreign policy. On the other hand, the administration apparently believes "that the Salvadorans, Hondurans and Guatemalans who study here will be so impressed by their experiences that they will return home to eschew possible revolutionary solutions to their problems and to inculcate North American values and institutions in place of Hispanic ones." If this is the case, then the administration's efforts appear to be self-defeating. In 1966 Senator J. William Fulbright stated (in terms still relevant today):

> The pervading suspicion of social revolutionary movements on the part of United States policy makers is most unfortunate, because there is a strong possibility of more explosions in Latin America, and insofar as the United States makes itself the enemy of revolutionary movements, communism is able to make itself their friend. The anti-revolutionary bias in United States policy, which is rooted in the fear of communism, can only have the effect of strengthening communism.

Equally disturbing is USIA's politicization of its AMPARTS program—a program that sends some five hundred to six hundred speakers overseas each year. As early as 1983 the House Foreign Affairs Subcommittee on International Operations criticized USIA officials for "violating the letter and spirit of its charter." Not only had USIA attempted to eliminate "educational and cultural affairs programs which have stood the test of time," but had chosen its AMPARTS speakers on the basis of "partisan political ideology." It was not until early 1984, however, that USIA's policies became a national scandal. On January 31, the Washington *Post* revealed that since late 1981 the USIA had been compiling a blacklist. The blacklist included the names not only of prominent academics but of national figures including Coretta Scott King, Congressman Jack Brooks, and former Senator Gary Hart. Other administrations have undoubtedly sent speakers overseas to explain or defend some of their policies; but none has viewed USIA as an "American Propaganda Machine" (to use the Hartford *Courant*'s phrase) whose sole function is to promote a particular president's foreign policy rather than present a balanced view of American life and society mandated by its charter.

The Reagan administration's search for "total security" has not been a piecemeal process. It extends to nearly every aspect of American life. Each policy initiative forms part of a carefully crafted mosaic or tapestry that blends together to form part of a unified whole. It comes as no surprise, therefore, that the administration has also authorized the resumption of "open-ended" domestic security investigations by the FBI. The FBI has a legitimate role to play by investigating organized crime and other groups who use force or violence in efforts to achieve social and political ends; but since 1981, the FBI's investigations have included individuals or groups whose only "crime" is their outspoken opposition to President Reagan's foreign policy.

Before analyzing the Reagan administration's policies, it needs to be emphasized that the history of the FBI's domestic security investigations has been characterized by illegality and abuse. For example, the FBI, during the Red Scare of the 1920s, kept secret files on approximately two hundred thousand Americans. Moreover, former FBI Director J. Edgar Hoover, without authorization from Congress or any president, launched a highly secret operation called COINTELPRO in 1957. Between that year and 1974 the FBI kept files on the activities of nearly five hundred thousand Americans whom Hoover and other FBI officials considered to be "subversives" or potential "national security risks."

The FBI's repertoire of illegal activities included break-ins, bugging, wiretapping, mail-tampering, character defamation, and the use of paid informants or undercover agents to infiltrate "subversive" organizations. Among the organizations infiltrated were the NAACP, the Socialist Workers Party, the Medical Committee for Human Rights, the National Lawyers Guild, and even a Milwaukee Boy Scout troop.

These activities came to light as a result of the Watergate revelations, congressional hearings, and information obtained under FOIA requests. As a result, Attorney General Edward Levi in April 1976 promulgated for the first time "a set of public guidelines governing the initiation and scope of the FBI domestic security investigations."

The Levi guidelines, by establishing a criminal standard for investigations, eliminated FBI surveillance of dissident political groups. They authorized full domestic security investigations only "on the basis of *specific and articulable facts* [emphasis added] giving reason to believe that an individual or group is or may be engaged in [unlawful] activities which involve the use of force or violence." Beyond this, the FBI was instructed to take into consideration the "magnitude

18 of the threatened harm," the "likelihood that it will occur," the "immediacy of the threat," and the "danger to privacy and free expression posed by a full investigation."

The Levi guidelines had a dramatic impact. In March 1976 the FBI was conducting 4,868 domestic security investigations. By December 1981 the number had dropped to only 26 and the organizations being investigated, such as the Jewish Defense League, the Communist Workers Party, and the Arizona chapter of the Ku Klux Klan, were clearly involved in violent criminal activity.

The Reagan administration has eliminated the safeguards against FBI abuse that the Levi guidelines were designed to prevent. It has done so by promulgating two interrelated executive branch initiatives: Executive Order 12333, which was issued in 1981, and Attorney General William French Smith's guidelines, which replaced Levi's in 1983.

The Smith guidelines eliminated the "probable cause" standard contained in the "specific and articulable facts" requirement of the Levi guidelines. They state that the FBI can launch domestic security investigations if the facts "reasonably indicate" that groups or individuals are involved in criminal activity. Moreover, the Smith guidelines apply the "enterprise concept," which has been used in organized crime investigations, to domestic security cases. This permits the FBI to investigate the activities of groups and individuals who "knowingly support" terrorist or subversive groups but do not themselves engage in violence. Such an application, Geoffrey Stone argues, is totally inappropriate. Even more important, the new guidelines also authorize the FBI to "anticipate or prevent crime." As a result, the FBI is now permitted to investigate groups or individuals whose statements "advocate criminal activity or *indicate an apparent intent* to engage in crime, particularly crimes of violence" [emphasis added].

The Smith guidelines, therefore, are far more permissive than Levi's. The terminology of the guidelines is specific in some instances but deliberately vague in others. In short, its language provides FBI officials with sufficient interpretive latitude to investigate virtually any group or individual it chooses to target, including political activists who oppose the Reagan administration's foreign policy.

The most permissive aspect of the Smith guidelines, perhaps, is the authorization of domestic security investigations against individuals or groups whose statements "indicate an apparent intent to engage in crime." It assumes that the abstract advocacy of violence, even though it is not accompanied by violence itself, provides sufficient grounds for investigation. This position flies in the face of the Supreme Court's decision in *Brandenburg* v. *Ohio* (1969), which draws a sharp distinction between expression and *conduct*. In *Brandenburg,* the Court ruled that speech is protected except where advocacy of law violation is "directed to inciting or producing imminent lawless action and is likely to **19** incite or produce such action." The Court thus took the position that the premises behind abstract advocacy may contain radical criticisms of government or society that deserve a hearing.

The *Brandenburg* standard, however, has recently come under attack in the courts. Circuit Court Judge Richard Posner, a Reagan appointee, wrote a majority opinion in *Alliance to End Repression* v. *Chicago* which declared that although *Brandenburg* protected proponents of abstract advocacy from criminal prosecution, it did not rule out domestic security investigations if they were "properly motivated." The problem with many past FBI investigations, Professor Stone writes, "was not that they were improperly motivated, but that they were the product of exaggerated fears, bad judgment, and insensitivity to the value of constitutional rights." "The danger of terrorism is real," Stone concludes. "The FBI may and must act to combat it." But the Reagan administration, "in its investigative guidelines and its judicial decisions, is heading in the wrong direction."

The terms of President Reagan's Executive Order 12333, which deals with the permissible activities of the intelligence agencies, are equally reactionary. The order states that the CIA and the other intelligence agencies are authorized to conduct "counterintelligence" activities within the United States so long as they are coordinated with the FBI. It also states that the FBI, when requested by the CIA or another intelligence agency, "can collect foreign intelligence information or support foreign intelligence collection requirements." An earlier draft of the executive order authorized the CIA to directly infiltrate and influence domestic organizations without a warrant. But the terms of the CIA's charter, issued in 1947, specifically prohibit such activity. Thus, the terminology of the final order is little more than a subterfuge. Its wording may comply with the letter of CIA's charter, but clearly not its spirit.

On the surface, the order appears to provide some safeguards against abuse. It states that "no foreign intelligence by such agencies may be taken for the purpose of acquiring information concerning the domestic activities of United States persons." But, as Athan Theoharis and Diana M. T. K. Autin both observe, this prohibition is an inadequate safeguard at best. The fact is that President Reagan and other administration spokesmen have argued that the domestic activities of dissident groups such as the Sojourners, the Sanctuary movement, Quest for Peace, the antinuclear movement, and CISPES (Committee in Solidarity With the People of El Salvador) have been infiltrated and influenced by foreign agents. As Theoharis phrases it, "Reagan's executive order, in effect, authorized the FBI to resume investigating [the] dissident political activities" of American citizens.

Until late January 1988, the scale on which such investigations were occur-

20   ring could not be ascertained; but sufficient evidence had surfaced by the mid-1980s to show beyond question that numerous investigations of groups and individuals are now underway. According to congressional sources, the FBI, in 1985 alone, conducted ninety-six investigations of groups and individuals opposed to the Reagan administration's Central American policies. Furthermore, Frank Varelli, a former FBI informant, testified before a congressional subcommittee that between 1981 and 1984 he succeeded in infiltrating the Dallas chapter of CISPES. During that time he provided the FBI with 3,500 pages of information regarding the activities of CISPES members. In an interview with CBS *Evening News,* Varelli stated that FBI officials instructed him to "find the guns." When Varelli reported that CISPES had no weapons, he was instructed to continue his search until he found them. Furthermore, the FBI admitted to the *National Catholic Reporter* that it was keeping files on Seattle Archbishop Raymond Hunthausen, who is actively involved in the antinuclear movement, and on Detroit's Auxiliary Bishop Thomas Gumbleton, the spokesperson for Quest for Peace, an organization providing humanitarian aid to Nicaragua in the form of food, clothing, and medical supplies.

Then, in late January 1988 the Center for Constitutional Rights in New York released information obtained from the FBI under FOIA requests revealing that in addition to CISPES, the Sanctuary movement, Quest for Peace, and antinuclear groups, the FBI had also targeted the Southern Leadership Conference, the Maryknoll Sisters in Chicago, the American Federation of Teachers, and the United Auto Workers in Cleveland. Moreover, another document obtained by the CCR revealed that an FBI agent in Philadelphia provided FBI headquarters in Washington with the names of another dozen groups "actively involved in demonstrations, seminars, marches, et cetera, regarding U.S. intervention in Central America." In fact, fifty-two of the FBI's fifty-nine regional offices have been involved in open ended domestic security investigations.

On January 29, White House spokesman, Marlin Fitzwater, stated that President Reagan had ordered an internal review of FBI surveillance activities because the president was opposed to "investigations of Americans for their political beliefs." Fitzwater went on to say that "no one in the White House or the National Security Council knew about the five-year surveillance campaign." The responsibility, according to Fitzwater, rested entirely with former FBI Director William Webster.

On February 3, however, the White House changed its position. Mr. Reagan, Fitzwater stated, had accepted current FBI Director Sessions' explanation that the FBI was not involved in "massive" surveillance of groups and individuals opposed to the Administration's Central American policies. Its investigations, Sessions maintained, were confined primarily to CISPES. This investigation, Fitzwater continued, was based on allegations that CISPES had links to leftist rebels in El Salvador who were carrying out terrorist acts. The investigation ended in 1985, Fitzwater maintained, "after investigators determined that CISPES was a legitimate political group."

These White House contradictions were neither surprising nor convincing. The evidence of FBI abuse that has surfaced since the early 1980s appears to be irrefutable. Moreover, in light of the permissive terminology contained in President Reagan's Executive Order 12333 and the replacement of the Levi guidelines by Attorney General William French Smith's in 1983, open-ended domestic security investigations are perfectly legal. Unless and until the terms of E.O. 12333 are challenged in court and declared unconstitutional, or until Congress is willing to pass legislation creating an FBI charter that carefully defines and limits its powers, current FBI abuses can proceed unchecked. In sum, the very activities that were illegal during J. Edgar Hoover's heyday have now been legitimized by Executive branch fiat!

Equally alarming: President Reagan's E.O. 12333 is extremely permissive in permitting the FBI to use warrantless wiretaps. Some critics of the Reagan administration, who have found many provisions of the executive order odious, have denied that it permits unrestricted electronic surveillance of American citizens; but the terms of the executive order are unmistakably clear. In its "counterintelligence" operations, the FBI is permitted to utilize intrusive techniques that otherwise would be illegal—for example, mail and physical surveillance, theft, unconsented physical searches, and the use of infiltrators and informants. And, as Diana M. T. K. Autin observes, the executive order permits the use of warrantless wiretaps if "*the Attorney General has determined in each case that there is probable cause to believe that the technique is directed against a foreign power or an agent of a foreign power*" [emphasis added]. An earlier draft of the executive order actually contained a provision stating that the "inherent powers" of the presidency permitted the use of warrantless wiretaps in "national security" cases. This provision was deleted after objections were raised by members of the congressional intelligence committees who reviewed it. Even so, the order provided Attorney Generals William French Smith and Edwin Meese with carte blanche. Since the FBI's use of other intrusive techniques to monitor the activities of political dissidents is incontestable, the use of warrantless wiretaps appears to be not only likely, but probable.

Congressman Don Edwards, a frequent critic of the FBI, who chairs the House Judiciary Subcommittee on Civil and Constitutional Rights, could issue subpoenas to Smith and Meese in an effort to determine if (and how frequently) they used the counterintelligence provisions of E.O. 12333 to justify

22 the use of warrantless wiretaps to monitor activities of domestic opponents. In such an event, President Reagan would, in all probability, attempt to invoke executive privilege in an effort to block such testimony. In *U.S.* v. *Nixon* (the Watergate tapes case) the Supreme Court ruled unanimously that executive privilege could be invoked only in matters involving foreign or military affairs. Whether or not the Court would uphold executive privilege in a case involving the use of warrantless wiretaps against U.S. citizens opposed to Reagan's Central American policies cannot be predicted. But clearly, the Subcommittee on Civil and Constitutional Rights has an opportunity to find out.

President Reagan's most enduring legacy, perhaps, will be his impact on the federal judiciary. The elevation of William Rehnquist to chief justice, the appointments of Sandra Day O'Connor, Antonin Scalia, and Anthony Kennedy to the Supreme Court (and indeed, the failed nominations of judges Robert Bork and Douglas Ginsburg) reflect President Reagan's efforts to provide a conservative majority that can change the course of constitutional law for the rest of the century. Even so, the impact of the president's appointments to the Supreme Court remains to be seen. Less dramatic, but equally important, is the fact that Mr. Reagan, by the end of his second term, will have appointed nearly half of the nation's seven hundred forty-four federal judges.

The president has gladly appointed qualified conservative ideologues to the federal bench when they are available—for example, Richard Posner, Ralph Winter, Antonin Scalia, and Robert Bork. However, it is not professional competence but ideological purity that is the Reagan administration's primary criterion in selecting judges.

It may be objected that the nature of Mr. Reagan's appointments does not differ drastically from that of other presidents. Presidents, after all, ordinarily prefer judges whose ideology is compatible with their own. Although this argument carries some weight, Jamie Kalven argues that there is a "qualitative difference" that characterizes President Reagan's choice of judges. In the past, Kalven writes, judicial selection processes have had the "saving grace of messiness"—that is, court appointments reflected diversity in terms of values and interests represented. Mr. Reagan's selection process, by contrast, "is unprecedented in its unwavering clarity of purpose, its narrowly ideological criteria, and its single-minded diligence." As the number of judicial appointments mounted, therefore, the professional competence of individuals elevated to the federal bench began to decline. In sum, the Reagan administration has made a concerted effort to achieve its one and only objective: the creation of a federal judiciary "dominated by judges committed to the Reagan constitutional agenda."

What is that agenda? Among other things, it would eliminate procedural protections for criminal defendants; it would reverse *Roe* v. *Wade,* which permits choice on abortion; it would abolish affirmative action, and would adopt "a more relaxed standard" in matters involving the separation of church and state.

Attorney General Edwin Meese has also issued a series of public statements calling for "judicial restraint"—a demand that judges base their opinions on the "original intentions" of the Founding Fathers, not their own subjective values. In addition, Meese has attacked the validity of the "doctrine of incorporation," whereby the Supreme Court, since the 1920s, has applied the Bill of Rights to the states as well as the federal government.

The constitutional views of Mr. Reagan, Edwin Meese, Judge Bork, and other advocates of the doctrine of "judicial restraint" are cast "in the idiom of conservatism"; but Jamie Kalven argues that theirs is actually a radical vision. By downgrading the role of the judiciary in American society, they would promote an unparalleled exercise of power by the executive and legislative branches of government. In short, the Reagan administration would eliminate the traditional system of checks and balances that has been an integral part of the American constitutional system since the 1790s; and they would do so precisely because the Reaganites consider many of the Supreme Court's past decisions intolerable.

Kalven's analysis illuminates the theoretical implications of the Reagan constitutional agenda in clear and unmistakable terms. Even so, there is another way of looking at the Reagan administration's emphasis on "judicial restraint." Some evidence exists to suggest that its position on this issue is not an unalterable commitment. "Judicial activism," after all, is a double-edged sword that can be used to promote conservative as well as liberal constitutional objectives. As we shall see, the commitment of some Reagan appointees to "judicial restraint" has already been downgraded or ignored. If a degree of flexibility exists in the Reagan administration's "game plan," it is surely one of means, not ends.

The Reagan administration is entitled, of course, to take whatever positions it finds congenial on issues such as abortion, school prayer, affirmative action, or the separation of powers. Whether or not one agrees or disagrees with Mr. Reagan's attempts to bring about a fundamental change in constitutional law depends, in some measure, on subjective value judgments.

There is one overriding aspect of Mr. Reagan's constitutional agenda, however, that ought to give pause to all Americans, whatever their philosophical or ethical persuasion. The Reagan administration's policies that we have discussed thus far reveal a mind-set that rejects First Amendment values—for instance, NSDD 84 (lifetime censorship agreements), Executive Order 12356

24   (document classification guidelines), the denial of visas to foreigners, the decision to prosecute Samuel Loring Morison for espionage, and Executive Order 12333 (intelligence agency guidelines).

Unfortunately, a careful analysis of the views of some of Mr. Reagan's judges demonstrates that their commitment to free expression is so cramped and limited that they would rob the First Amendment of most of its meaning. For example, in a 1971 law review article, Judge Robert Bork contended:

> Constitutional protection should be extended only to speech that is explicitly political. There is no basis for judicial intervention to protect any other form of expression, be it scientific, literary or that variety of expression we call obscene or pornographic. Moreover, within that category of speech we ordinarily call political, there should be no constitutional obstruction to laws making criminal any speech that advocates forcible overthrow of the government or the violation of any law.

The implications of these views are extraordinary. As Kalven phrases it, Judge Bork's views reflect, among other things, "a bizarre divorce of political discourse from its social and cultural foundations." Moreover, Bork contends that "political truth" is what "the majority thinks it is at any given moment." Finally, Bork argues that "subversive advocacy" (another phrase for the theoretical "right of revolution") has no value "within a republican system of government." In fact, as we have already observed, the Supreme Court has ruled, most recently in *Brandenburg* v. *Ohio,* that speech is protected "except where advocacy of law violation is directed to inciting or producing imminent lawless action and is likely to incite or produce such action."

If one carries Judge Bork's views to their logical conclusion, it appears that the theoretical foundations on which the American Revolution was based are illegitimate, as are the moral postulates that led Henry David Thoreau and Martin Luther King to advocate civil disobedience. In sum, Mr. Bork's views can only lead, as Justice Brandeis phrased it, to "silence coerced by law."

Judge Bork, responding to an article written by Kalven, maintained that his views on protected speech have been broadened to include "many other forms of discourse" such as "moral and scientific debate." Even so, Bork's reply said nothing about artistic expression (including literature, art, and film) which, arguably, would leave the door open to attacks on "obscenity" and "pornography." More important, Bork made no mention whatever of his views on abstract advocacy even though most of Kalven's analysis of Bork's intellectual universe focused on this issue.

Judge Bork's testimony on *Brandenburg* during his confirmation hearings was contradictory at best. At one point, Bork stated that the Court's decision in *Brandenburg* "is okay. That is a good test." Later on, he told Senator Specter: "[o]n *Brandenburg,* I did not say my mind had changed. . . . I think *Brandenburg* may have gone too far—went too far, but I accept it as a judge and I have no desire to overturn it. . . . Its settled law. That's all I've said. I haven't said these writings [that is, his earlier criticisms of *Brandenburg*] were wrong."

But even if one accepts Bork's view that he now accepts *Brandenburg* as "settled law," Burke Marshall, a Yale law professor, testified that a judge could "accept" precedents "while variously restricting the application of such precedents to their original facts." In short, new cases always deal with new facts involving a change of time, place, and circumstances. A judge, therefore, could reach different conclusions than those contained in *Brandenburg*. In the end, Judge Bork's changing positions led the Senate Judiciary Committee to conclude that "He Might Not Fully Apply This Vital Precedent."

If Bork's views on abstract advocacy have not changed, and there is little basis for thinking otherwise, they are by no means singular. As Geoffrey Stone observes, Circuit Court Judge Richard Posner's decision in the *Alliance* case took exception to part of the Supreme Court's ruling in *Brandenburg*. Moreover, Judge Joseph A. Young's decision in the *Morison* case, as Steven Burkholder and other commentators point out, ignored the legislative history of the espionage statutes. Its framers clearly had no intention of applying it to "leakers." Judge Young also ignored the act's provision requiring federal prosecutors to prove an intent to harm the United States in order to obtain a conviction. Moreover, the opinions by Justices Rehnquist, Scalia, and O'Connor in *U.S.* v. *Salerno* hardly reflect a commitment to the concept of "restraint." The conclusion is inescapable, therefore, that the call for "judicial restraint" by Edwin Meese and others is not so much a principled philosophical position as it is a *weapon to be used or ignored* in promoting the Reagan administration's political objectives.

Even as things now stand, the Supreme Court's record in First Amendment cases during the past fifteen years is equivocal at best—especially in cases where government prosecutors have invoked that magical concept "national security." As Professors Thomas I. Emerson and Judith Schenck Koffler observe, First Amendment rights have been rejected or ignored in cases such as *United States* v. *Marchetti* (1972), *United States* v. *The Progressive, Inc.* (1979), *Snepp* v. *United States* (1980), and *Haig* v. *Agee* (1981). In these cases, however, the Court has treated First Amendment issues on an *ad hoc* basis (that is, the Court has not developed a clearcut or systematic position on First Amendment rights). Whether or not a more conservative Court will do so in the future, and on what basis, remains to be seen.

Thus far, our analysis has centered primarily on the domestic aspects of the Reagan administration's massive assaults on civil liberties in the name of

26 "national security." Yet, the Reagan administration's conduct of foreign policy also has important domestic ramifications. Domestic and foreign policy initiatives are, in fact, inextricably intertwined. Nowhere is the Reagan administration's distrust of openness and democratic processes better reflected than in its Central American policies.

Among other things, the Iran-Contra hearings revealed not only a basic distrust of the American people and of Congress but also an insensitivity to the principle of separation of powers itself. This principle includes, of course, the accountability of executive branch agencies to congressional oversight committees. The president, as commander in chief, is charged with conducting foreign policy. But the Congress, as mandated by the Constitution, does have a critical role to play in the foreign policy sphere. When scholars refer to the growth of the "imperial presidency" since the Second World War, they refer, obviously, to the enormous growth of presidential power in the conduct of foreign affairs. As regards Central America, however, and especially Nicaragua, Congress has reasserted its constitutional powers with vigor. The Boland Amendment provides a case in point.

The Boland Amendment, which is often referred to in the press as a "congressional ban," was in fact a law—a rider attached to the Defense Appropriations Act of 1985 signed by President Reagan. The amendment stated: "During the fiscal year 1985, no funds available to the Central Intelligence Agency, or any other agency or entity of the United States involved in intelligence activities may be obligated or expended for the purpose of supporting, directly or indirectly, military or paramilitary operations" against the Sandinista government.

Although President Reagan admitted that he signed an order authorizing the sale of weapons to Iran, he has consistently denied culpability in the diversion of funds to the Contras. No evidence gathered by the Tower Commission or the congressional Iran-Contra Committee proved otherwise. But President Reagan, in response to charges that the National Security Council had violated the Boland Amendment by secretly supplying the Contras, stated to a group of magazine editors:

> My interpretation was that it [the Boland Amendment] was not restrictive on the National Security Adviser or National Security Council. . . . I believe that the NSC is not an intelligence operation; it's simply advisory to me. And there is nothing in the Boland Amendment that would keep me from asking other people to help [e.g., private individuals, the Sultan of Brunei, Saudia Arabia, and South Africa].

Such a defense, according to congressional critics and many legal experts, is not valid. Even Robert McFarlane, the former National Security adviser, admitted to the Iran-Contra Committee that the NSC was indeed an agency involved in intelligence activities and thus subject to the restrictions imposed by the Boland Amendment. Even more telling are the terms of President Reagan's Executive Order 12333. It designated the NSC "as the highest executive branch entity that provides review of, guidance for, and direction to the conduct of all national and foreign intelligence [and] counterintelligence" operations.

Numerous commentators have observed that President Reagan's lack of knowledge that illegal funds were diverted to the Contras by some of his top aides is a shocking revelation—nearly as shocking as involvement itself. The fact that the president's interpretations of E.O. 12333 reveal ignorance of the contents of his own edict must be placed in the same category. Executive Orders, it must be remembered, have the force of law.

It cannot be too strongly emphasized, moreover, that the Constitution states that the "executive branch shall faithfully execute the laws of the United States." When a president (or members of his administration) unilaterally decides which laws to execute and which to ignore, he places himself above the law which, in turn, degrades and threatens the democratic process itself. As Peter Rodino, chairman of the House Judiciary Committee and a member of the Iran-Contra Select Committee, phrased it:

> The fundamental question posed, just as in the Watergate crisis, has to do with the Executive's misunderstanding of the rule of law. Nothing undermines our representative system of government more than actions taken by officials entrusted with the reins of government, which even for purposes believed to be good, are designed to set aside the law, distort, or ignore it. . . . Only our adherence to the rule of law can, in the end, restore the people's trust which has been so sorely impaired.

Perhaps the most startling disclosure to emerge from the Iran-Contra scandal was the Reagan administration's contingency plan for imposing martial law. Alfonso Chardy, a reporter for the *Miami Herald*, revealed in July 1987 that Lt. Col. Oliver North, while serving on the National Security Council's staff, had worked with FEMA (Federal Emergency Management Agency) on a plan to suspend the Bill of Rights by imposing martial law in the event of "national opposition to a U.S. military invasion abroad." John Russell, a Justice Department spokesperson, denied the charges. Russell stated: "We have the Posse Comitatus Act, part of Title XVIII of the U.S. [Government] Code that bars the military from engaging in law enforcement."

The existence of such a law, in any event, did not deter high ranking Reagan administration officials from proceeding with their secret plans. A Pentagon

28   document, "Department of Defense Directive No. 3025.10," dated July 22, 1981, declared:

> In those areas in which martial law has been proclaimed, military resources may be used for local law enforcement. Normally a state of martial law will be proclaimed by the president.
>
> However, in the absence of such action by the president, a senior military commander may impose martial law in an area of his command where there has been a complete breakdown in the exercise of government functions by local civilian authorities. Military assumption of judicial, law enforcement and administrative functions will continue only so long as necessity of that extreme nature requires interim military intervention.

The author of this document is none other than Frank C. Carlucci, President Reagan's current Secretary of Defense. According to investigative reporter David Lindorff, this martial law directive is still in effect.

Reporter Ron Ridenhour observes that President Reagan has long been fascinated by martial law. Ridenhour secured documents under a 1975 FOIA request which revealed that Mr. Reagan, as governor of California, ran a series of martial law "war games." These "war games" occurred between 1968 and 1972 under the code name "Operation Cable Splicer I, II, and III." They involved California National Guard units, local police, and detachments from the U.S. Sixth Continental Army. The military commander in charge of these operations was National Guard Col. Louis Guiffreda who was named by President Reagan in 1981 to head FEMA. Thus, it was Guiffreda with whom Lt. Col. North worked. The director in charge of Operation Cable Splicer, however, was Governor Reagan's executive secretary, Edwin Meese. At that time, Meese stated that the most important factor in implementing martial law "was advance intelligence gathering to facilitate internment of the leaders of civil disturbances."

As Lindorff phrases it, the Constitution of the United States has no "self-destruct" clause. The only time that martial law can constitutionally be imposed is during war when, and only when, civilian courts are unable to function. But are the Reagan administration's martial law contingency plans anything more than reactionary political fantasies? Under normal circumstances, the answer is no. On at least three occasions in our history, however, the government has, in fact, imposed martial law during times of crisis or "perceived crisis." The one major stain on President Lincoln's otherwise exemplary record was his suspension of the writ of *habeas corpus* in the North. In addition, martial law was imposed in Hawaii after the Japanese attack on Pearl

Harbor and, during the Second World War, the government's illegal and un-justified imprisonment of Americans of Japanese ancestry serves as a reminder that fear and hysteria, in times of crisis, can override normal constitutional guarantees. Barring some unforeseen catastrophe, the Reagan administration's contingency plans will undoubtedly lie dormant. However, the administration's determination to overthrow the Sandinista regime in Nicaragua by military force—regardless of public opinion and congressional opposition—reveals a frightening lack of respect for democratic processes and a willingness to impose its own dark vision on the American people at all costs.

Congressman Don Edwards (D-California), who chairs the House sub-committee on civil liberties and constitutional rights, which is currently investigating domestic break-ins and FBI surveillance, stated: "I'm deeply disturbed by the reports of martial law planning. We should demand that the whole thing be made public. I had no idea that this kind of thing could go on in this country, but that's where secret government leads you. It is very ominous."

Is "freedom at risk" in the United States today? The Reagan administration's obsession with secrecy and censorship and its conclusive and sustained hostility to democratic processes indicate that the nation has reached another crossroads. As a certain Mrs. Powell asked Benjamin Franklin: "What have you given us, doctor—a monarchy or a republic?" Franklin replied: "A republic, if you can keep it."

[Thomas I. Emerson]

I

THE STATE OF THE FIRST

AMENDMENT AS WE ENTER

"1984"

When the First Amendment became a part of the Constitution in 1791 the scope and implications of that provision were by no means clear. Its fundamental purpose was to support the principles of an open and self-governing society. More specifically, it was intended to protect speakers who criticized the government, to forbid censorship of the press, and to permit assemblies in the public halls or demonstrations on the streets. But many questions remained unanswered, such as its effect upon the law of seditious libel, private libel, blasphemy, obscenity, and advocacy of law violation. Even the issue of who was protected by its terms was not beyond dispute. Moreover, the guarantee did not apply to the states. Thus the First Amendment had a vast potential—it was indeed a daring innovation—but its future was uncertain.

For well over a hundred years there was little or no development by the courts of First Amendment doctrine. Some right to freedom of expression existed in practice. But the right was subject to frequent infringement, including prosecutions under the Alien and Sedition Acts, molestation of aboli-

Professor Emerson made these remarks when he accepted the First Amendment Defender Award presented to him by the Institute for Communications Law Studies of the Catholic University School of Law in recognition of his lifelong efforts to preserve and strengthen First Amendment protections. Reprinted from *Communications Lawyer* 2 (Winter 1984), pp. 3–10, by permission of the author and the publishers.

32 tionists, and disruption of I W W meetings. Yet not until World War I did the issues come before the Supreme Court in a serious way. And not until 1925 was the First Amendment made applicable to the states, where most of the abridgements of the right of free expression were occurring.

In the last five or six decades, however, there has been a tremendous development of First Amendment law. Fortunately, the Supreme Court and other courts, despite some argument to the contrary, have interpeted the First Amendment as part of a living constitution. They have broadly accepted the basic principles embodied in the First Amendment and carried the application of those principles far beyond the immediate areas the framers apparently had in mind. The result has been the creation of a constitutional structure that supports a relatively strong system of freedom of expression. That system, flawed as it is in many respects, has had a global impact and constitutes a major contribution to the progress of humankind.

Partly as a result of the First Amendment and its accompanying body of law, George Orwell's *1984* has not come to pass in the United States. Nevertheless, serious dangers to the system exist, and difficult problems remain to be solved. In appraising these dangers it is necessary to explore, in general terms, the extent to which a basic understanding of the First Amendment prevails in our society and the way in which the supporting constitutional doctrines have been developing. It is also important to take note, albeit very briefly, of some of the specific problems that currently require solution.

BASIC UNDERSTANDING OF THE FIRST AMENDMENT

Creation of a healthy system of freedom of expression under the First Amendment does not come without travail. As Justice Holmes has said, majorities are prone "to sweep away all opposition." Governments strongly prefer acquiescence to dissent. The long-term benefits of tolerating the views of others are often not immediately apparent. The system, in short, is a sophisticated one, requiring the education and reeducation of each generation. Ultimately it rests upon a sensitive understanding of the principles at work and a firm commitment to their support.

There are signs in the land that this essential understanding and support are slackening in some quarters. Three areas of concern stand out.

First, the current administration, from the highest levels on down, has taken a series of actions that can only be premised upon ignorance of, or wanton disregard for, First Amendment values. Thus, although the Freedom of Information Act has been one of the major advances in the democratic process over the past several decades, the administration has proposed weakening amendments that would drastically curtail its capacity to give the American people information they need to know. The administration has also denied visas to important foreign visitors, apparently on the theory that their ideas are too dangerous for the American people to hear. It has revised the Foreign Agents Registration Act to require that two Canadian films, one on acid rain and the other on nuclear energy, be labeled "political propaganda"; the point seems to be that the American people must have fatherly advice in order to evaluate materials emanating from foreign sources. In the area of political surveillance, the administration, despite past disclosures of glaring abuse by the intelligence agencies, has not only failed to bring the intelligence agencies under statutory control, but by executive order and revision of the attorney general's guidelines has sought to undo even the feeble reforms instigated by the prior administration. And, contrary to past practice, the administration excluded the press from Grenada during the invasion, thereby leaving the American people without any independent source of information on what was taking place.

The failure of the current administration to comprehend the elementary principles of the First Amendment is revealed most starkly by its efforts to control the dissemination of scientific information on national security grounds. While secrecy on some matters affecting national security is essential, the administration has gone much beyond reasonable precautions. Using the export control laws, it has imposed far-reaching restrictions on the teaching and research activities of American universities and scientists. Thus, it has undertaken to control the publication of research materials, even where they do not deal with classified information, to monitor the study of foreign students in American universities, and generally to hinder communication between American and foreign scientists. One example of the administration's activities occurred in August of last year when, at a conference in San Diego of 2,700 photo–optical engineers, the Department of Defense blocked the presentation of one hundred papers containing nonclassified information. The administration seems totally unaware that the scientific method itself—the hope for scientific progress—depends on full freedom of inquiry, the exposure of fact and theory to testing and criticism, building upon the knowledge uncovered by others, and an atmosphere of open dialogue. The administration's guiding philosophy, to the contrary, leads straight to *1984.*

A second area of weakness in the basic understanding essential to a vigorous First Amendment involves what has been called the "pollution" of the marketplace of ideas. The system of freedom of expression has always operated in a somewhat rowdy fashion. Much that is said is false or misleading,

34   impugns the motives of the opposition, is intemperate, or appeals to prejudice
rather than reason. It is not the province of the government to attempt to pu-
rify the process. That could only be done at the price of destroying the system
altogether.

Nevertheless, participants in the system do have a moral and political
responsibility. Surely there is some obligation to maintain and improve the
quality of the debate. Above all, it is vital that all of us learn from the mistakes
of the past; there should be no need to repeat the blunders of McCarthyism.
Hence one must always hope that the content of the system will become more
meaningful and more useful to society as a whole.

Unfortunately this does not seem to be happening. Indeed there are ominous signs of contrary trends. Traditionalist forces in the nation, basically opposed to innovation and diversity, have become more articulate, better organized, and politically more powerful. And their area of attention has moved
from social issues—the family and religion—to questions of military and foreign policy. Their participation in the system is welcome, but their mode of
operation has tended to undermine the First Amendment in at least two ways.

One is that expression of their particular point of view tends to be accompanied by attempts to suppress the viewpoints of others. As Justice Douglas
once said, they "demand conformity—or else." This attitude has found expression, for instance, in the efforts to ban books from libraries and schools.
Considerable evidence points to the conclusion that the book-banning phenomenon has reached alarming proportions. Thus, last year, according to the
Office for Intellectual Freedom of the American Library Association, more
than 50 percent of high school libraries responding to a national survey reported some form of censorship pressure. And a recent study by People for the
American Way concluded that censorship efforts have been steadily increasing, with "secular humanism" the most frequent target of the attacks. Book
banning is, of course, the essence of *1984*.

The other danger to the First Amendment arises from the practice of substi-
tuting for a discussion on the merits an attack upon motives or an appeal to fear
or prejudice. This mode of exercising First Amendment rights takes the form
of questioning the integrity of the opposition, attributing its information or
ideas to foreign or other sinister sources, suggesting hidden agendas proclaim-
ing guilt by association, and generally equating opposition to official policy
with disloyalty or even treason. Examples of this approach are seen in much
of the response to the nuclear freeze movement, the attack upon the National
Council of Churches, and the campaign against the Institute for Policy Studies.
In all these cases the very real substantive issues raised by the groups involved
were not faced and the public was deprived of an opportunity for national
debate.

A third concern with the basic support for the First Amendment in con- **35** temporary society arises out of some backsliding on the intellectual front, particularly among some constitutional experts. The attempt by the academic community to formulate rules of law that will give realistic protection to First Amendment rights has not moved forward. On the contrary, theories of limitation are being advanced in some quarters. Thus proposals to restrict coverage of the First Amendment to "political expression," that is, participation in the affairs of government, are still being pressed. Ideas for downgrading the importance of the rule against prior restraint are being put forward. And arguments that time, place, and manner restrictions are permissible, so long as the regulation is "content neutral," are being urged. One is, of course, not entitled to ask the legal academic community to accept any one approach to strengthening the First Amendment. But a less constrained, and more generous, attitude toward the problem might not be out of place.

THE SUPPORTING CONSTITUTIONAL FRAMEWORK AS FASHIONED BY THE SUPREME COURT

Under our system of government we rely heavily upon the courts, topped by the Supreme Court, to create and maintain a legal structure that will make the protection of First Amendment rights a reality. We count on our judicial institutions to expound the principles, to formulate the doctrines, to apply the rules in new situations, and generally to enforce the guarantees of the First Amendment against legislative, executive, or popular pressures. The fashioning of an effective body of up-to-date law is a matter of supreme importance in the fortunes of the First Amendment.

In general the Supreme Court has accepted the basic values that underlie the First Amendment and has recognized the functions it was meant to serve in our society. Moreover, in the years since World War I the Court has constructed a substantial set of legal rules, derived from those values and functions that give solid life to the constitutional guarantee. yet the dream of a comprehensive and tight-fitting constitutional structure has not been realized. Not only do important differences of opinion persist among the justices, but the rules remain loose and a gradual dilution of doctrine seems to be taking place.

The most fundamental tenet of First Amendment law is that speech or expression, as distinct from other conduct, occupies a special position in our hierarchy of values and is entitled to special legal protection. In other words,

36   in constitutional adjudication speech or expression must be given a "preferred position." The right to freedom of expression cannot simply be balanced away by being made subordinate to other governmental interests. Rather, the other interests must fit within a structure that protects expression, that is, be achieved by means that do no deny or abridge freedom of speech. Although this is the starting point of First Amendment analysis the Supreme Court has wavered on the matter. It has never flatly repudiated the principle, but more and more it has ceased to pay attention to it. Certain of the justices, and sometimes a majority, treat First Amendment rights as merely of passing concern, readily subordinated to any other substantial governmental interest. The special place accorded freedom of expression in our constitutional law seems to be diminishing.

A second fundamental tenet of First Amendment law is that freedom of speech extends to all forms of expression, whether political, academic, artistic, or other, and that expression is protected regardless of content, whether racist, sexist, totalitarian, or other. Here the Supreme Court has held firm. It has refused to limit the First Amendment to "political speech" and, in the Skokie case, it made clear that even racist speech of the most vitriolic kind came within the protection of the First Amendment.

Beyond this, however, the Supreme Court has not advanced very far in defining just what is expression, and hence entitled to constitutional protection, and what is non-speech or action and not covered by the First Amendment. The Court still adheres to the fiction that obscenity is not expression. It has not found any technique for determining when symbolic speech comes within the purview of the First Amendment. And it has not succeeded in drawing a satisfactory line between militant advocacy and violent action. Hence the question of what conduct is protected by the First Amendment has been left in a state of ambiguity. The result is that expression and action tend to be merged in the Court's analysis and the protection given expression does not rise above that afforded other forms of conduct.

Once having determined that certain conduct is expression within the ambit of the First Amendment, the further question is what degree of protection is constitutionally required. Apart from the advocacy cases, where a test combining clear and present danger and incitement is employed, the Supreme Court relies principally upon the balancing test, attempting to weigh First Amendment values against other interests. The objections to the balancing test have been recounted many times. The difficulties include the fact that there are no comparable factors to weigh against each other, that the formula is so unstructured as to lead to any result, and that the Court tends ultimately to look mainly to the government interest involved and ignore the preferred position which ought to be accorded expression. In addition, as the Supreme Court continues to expand its balancing techniques, it has come to weigh in the balance various factors with which the government, under First Amendment theory, ought not to concern itself. Thus the Court has taken to considering the relative value of different forms and different contents of speech, trying to measure the extent of the abridgement of expression caused by the government's action, and permitting a greater degree of government control where other modes of expression are available to the speaker. In utilizing factors of this sort in the balancing process the Court is permitting the government to make judgments as to the social value of different kinds of expression—matters that should not be the business of the government at all.

On another front, the doctrine of prior restraint has been losing some of its force. The Supreme Court still recognizes the drastic impact of advance censorship and the unique character of a prior restraint. But a majority of the Court has been unwilling to formulate general rules forbidding such controls. The result is that the existence of an invalid prior restraint is determined on an *ad hoc* basis in each case. And the courts have not been adverse to imposing a temporary prior restraint until the final determination can be made. This is what happened in the *Progressive* magazine case, where a prohibition against publication was in effect for nearly seven months until the ultimate issue was resolved.

Nor has the Supreme Court sponsored innovative doctrine in the First Amendment area. Despite the fact that many individuals and groups lack access to the means of communication, the Court has done little or nothing to solve this problem. In fact, on the whole it has narrowed, rather than expanded, the right of access. And, although the Court has acknowledged the existence of a public right to know, it has not developed this doctrine in any substantial way.

All in all, it can be said that the Supreme Court has maintained a significant body of law supporting the First Amendment. But there are loopholes, ambiguities, and other serious weaknesses in the system. It is by no means sure that a sufficiently hard-shelled structure has been developed to withstand the pressures of a crisis. Nor has the Court moved forward to deal with some of the upcoming problems engendered by the times.

THE FIRST AMENDMENT
AND NATIONAL SECURITY

Of the specific First Amendment problems confronting the nation on the eve of 1984, perhaps the most significant, and certainly the most urgent, is the reconciliation of national security interests with the principles of the First Amend-

38 ment. The issues are complex and troublesome. Preservation of national security is, of course, a basic need of any society. Appeals in the name of national security arouse the kind of popular response that tends to "sweep away" all other considerations. The secrecy surrounding most national security claims makes it difficult for the public to obtain the full facts. Yet, if we are to remain a democratic country we must find a way to fit national security concerns into our system of individual rights.

The tightening circle of government restrictions upon freedom of expression, imposed as requirements of national security, has been described by many observers. Some of these measures have been noted above. One more, which dramatically illustrates the direction in which we are traveling, may be added.

On March 11, 1983, the president issued a Directive on Safeguarding National Security Information. This directive, as implemented by Department of Justice regulations, provides that all persons with access to classified information must sign an agreement that they will never disclose classified or classifiable information related to their government employment. In the case of persons with authorized access to special, so-called Sensitive Compartmented Information, estimated at over 290,000 government employees, the agreement would require that future writings related to their government employment, including works of fiction, be presented to the agency for its approval before publication. All classifiable information to which access is made available "is now and will forever remain the property of the United States Government." The agreements are to be enforceable in a civil action for injunction, damages, or other relief. In addition, the directive instructs every government agency to adopt regulations providing that its employees may be required to submit to polygraph examinations in the course of any investigation of the unauthorized disclosure of classified information. The FBI is given jurisdiction to investigate unauthorized disclosures even when no criminal prosecution is anticipated.

The restrictions imposed by the directive would drastically curtail the flow of information concerning government policies and activities. They would, for example, require a former secretary of state writing his memoirs to submit the manuscript for advance approval by the current secretary of state. It is not too much to say that implementation of the directive, which has been temporarily held up by congressional action, would substantially change the balance of power between the government and the citizenry.

Obviously, these developments raise serious First Amendment issues. Before examining the recent Supreme Court decisions in the national security area, however, it is important to sketch the broader constitutional landscape.

The starting point is that governmental efforts to achieve national security, like the exercise of all other government powers, must operate within the constitutional structure. More specifically, the goal of national security must be sought by methods that do not infringe First Amendment rights. The government has increasingly contended otherwise. But that position has been consistently rejected by the Supreme Court. Thus, when President Truman attempted to take over the steel mills during the Korean War, on the ground that seizure was necessary to our national defense, the Court ruled that "we cannot with faithfulness to our constitutional system" uphold such action. In *New York Times* v. *United States* the Court refused to grant an injunction against publication of the Pentagon Papers even though the government claimed it would cause "grave and irreparable injury" to national security. And in *United States* v. *United States District Court,* decided in 1972, the Court rejected the government's claim that the Fourth Amendment did not apply to wiretapping in domestic security cases. "We recognize the constitutional basis of the President's domestic security role," said a unanimous Court, "but we think it must be exercised in a manner compatible with the Fourth Amendment."

It must be recognized, of course, that national security considerations continue to play a significant role in constitutional adjudication. In the application of constitutional limitations, national security factors are frequently relevant. A strong argument can be made for the proposition that, in certain kinds of cases, national security factors can never justify infringement on freedom of expression. Thus, in most cases of prior restraint, in cases involving the suppression of information in the public domain, and in cases of political surveillance not related to law enforcement, the First Amendment should automatically carry the day. The Supreme Court has not, however, taken this road. In place of giving the full protection of the First Amendment it has adopted a balancing test. Furthermore, there are some situations, such as control over expression by government employees, where full protection is not possible and resort to balancing becomes necessary.

In any event, by balancing or otherwise, the courts retain substantial leeway to determine whether government efforts to achieve national security conform to constitutional limitations. In that contest between national security and First Amendment rights, the cause of freedom of expression tends to be subordinated. The heaviest pressures seem to be on the side of national security, and individual rights are too readily balanced away. Under these circumstances a resolution of the issues that gives adequate weight to First Amendment values can be achieved only if the courts adhere to certain equalizing rules. These rules may be stated as follows:

1. Constitutional principles protecting freedom of expression occupy a preferred position in the heirarchy of democratic values; hence, there is a presumption in favor of the constitutional right.
2. Government claims of injury to national security must be viewed with a healthy skepticism.

40

3. The burden of proof to demonstrate its case for limitation rests upon the government.

4. The government must show a direct, immediate, grave, and specific harm to national security, not just a vague or speculative threat.

5. The restriction sought by the government must be confined to the narrowest possible constraint necessary to achieve the goal, and should not be permitted where methods having a less drastic effect upon First Amendment rights are available.

6. Wherever possible, hard and fast rules, rather than loose balancing tests, should be formulated and applied.

Unfortunately the Supreme Court has not accepted this approach, and its recent record in First Amendment–national security cases gives cause for alarm. In the *Pentagon Papers* case the Court was unable to produce a majority opinion, but the least common denominator of six of the opinions rendered would seem to be that the government could enjoin the publication of information whenever it is shown that dissemination of such information would cause a "direct, immediate, and irreparable damage to our Nation or its people," regardless of the extent of the injury or its impact upon freedom of expression. Moreover, a prior restraint can be imposed while that issue is being determined. In *Laird* v. *Tatum* the Court rules that a wide-ranging program of political surveillance by army intelligence caused only a "subjective chill," insufficient to give the targets of the surveillance standing to challenge the government's action. In *Snepp* v. *United States* the Court upheld a CIA prepublication secrecy agreement against a former employee who had published a book critical of the CIA even though the book was not alleged to contain any classified information. The Court did not bother to wait for briefs on the merits or to hear oral argument. It teated the prepublication agreement as if it were nothing more than a private contract not raising any issue of the public's right to know. And it dealt with the First Amendment only in a casual footnote, saying that the agreement exacted of Snepp was "a reasonable means" of protecting a compelling interest. Finally, in *Haig* v. *Agee* the Court approved a State Department regulation that authorized withdrawal of a passport where the activities of an American citizen abroad "are causing or are likely to cause serious damage to the national security or the foreign policy of the United States." "Matters intimately related to foreign policy and national security," declared a majority of the Court, "are rarely proper subjects for judicial intervention."

Thus, the Supreme Court, far from adopting a set of principles that would give the First Amendment a fighting chance against assertions of national security, has come close to abandoning the effort to assure that constitutional liberties will be taken into account. There is real danger that First Amendment rights will be overwhelmed by national security demands. Such a result need not be. Past experience shows that the dangers to national security from free- **41** dom of expression have been vastly overdrawn and that a democratic accommodation can be made. Our traditions also tell us that it is futile to search for total security. National security achieved at the sacrifice of our system of individual rights is not national security in any true sense.

THE FIRST AMENDMENT AND THE CHANGING TECHNOLOGY

A second major problem—or, rather, series of problems—for the First Amendment arises out of the vast changes taking place in the technology of communication. When the First Amendment was drafted at the end of the eighteenth century the chief form of expression consisted of the printed press, meetings, demonstrations, and the like. During the course of this century radio and television came to play a prominent role. At the present time the system of freedom of expression is being revolutionized by the development of radically new modes of communication. These include cable television, satellites, microwaves, optical fibers, computers, facsimile, videotapes, and many similar devices. Two aspects of this new technology are of paramount importance for the future of the First Amendment. One concerns the breakdown of the traditional differences in First Amendment law between the print media and the electronic media. The other is the potential for wider access, by diverse individuals and groups, to the mass media.

As First Amendment law has developed there has emerged a significant difference in the degree of governmental control allowed over the traditional print media and the newer electronic media. The older forms of communication enjoy, at least in theory, a somewhat higher degree of protection from governmental interference. Restrictions upon the content of the communication, with some exceptions for libel, obscenity, advocacy of law violation, and the like, are forbidden. Time, place, and manner controls are limited, by and large, to those necessary to provide physical accommodation for competing interests. Special procedural doctrines, such as the rule against prior restraint, are applied with some degree of firmness. All in all, the print media are constitutionally well entrenched.

The same does not apply, at least to the same degree, to the electronic media. There the physical scarcity of channels through which to communicate has led to greater government controls. Thus, despite the rule against prior restraint, no radio or television station can operate without first obtaining a license from

42 the government. Some control over content is permitted. A broadcasting station must operate in "the public interest"; various limitations on ownership are imposed, such as prohibition against cross-ownership of newspapers and television stations; broadcasters must comply with the fairness doctrine and grant equal time to candidates for election. Furthermore, in the *Pacifica* case the Supreme Court upheld restrictions on the use of "offensive" language by broadcasting stations, resting its decision in part upon the special capacity of radio and television signals to enter the home.

One impact of the revolution in technology is a merging of the print and electronic modes of communication. Thus a facsimile newspaper may be sent into the home by electronic means. Access to information in a computer is in many ways similar to access to a library. The question has been raised as to whether, under these circumstances, the First Amendment law applicable to the print media or that applicable to the electronic media will be applied to the emerging modes of communication. In the former case government power over the media would be substantially more limited than in the latter case.

It is impossible to foresee how these matters will turn out. On the face of it, however, it would appear that the grounds for invoking First Amendment electronic law—the scarcity of physical facilities for communication—will largely disappear as a consequence of the new technology. If this be true, then First Amendment principles would certainly restrict governmental intervention in the system to matters of engineering and measures to limit monopoly. Unless the *Pacifica* theory prevails, and electronic communication is held to possess a unique character, the result should enhance, not diminish, First Amendment rights.

The other feature of the modern technology is that it creates the physical facilities for virtually unlimited access to the means of communication. Thus, in place of the relatively few channels available for traditional television broadcasting, cable television allows a hundred programs to be broadcast simultaneously over a single wire. Whether this potential for expanding the volume and diversity of expression is realized in practice is one of the urgent open questions of the day. Increased exercise of First Amendment rights will not come about automatically. Positive steps to achieve that result will have to be taken. Thus, legal doctrines to govern the new situation will need to be formulated. For example, common carrier concepts, by which the instruments for communication can be available to all who pay a reasonable cost, have to be modernized. The actual measures necessary to assure that the new potential for expanded communication materializes fall within the province of the legislative and executive branches of government. The courts, however, retain the function of guiding and channeling these measures within the boundaries of the Constitution. The outcome of this process will in large measure determine how effectively the First Amendment will operate in the new technological world.

AFFIRMATIVE GOVERNMENTAL ACTION AFFECTING FIRST AMENDMENT RIGHTS

Most of our First Amendment law deals with the negative force of the First Amendment in preventing the government from prohibiting or interfering with freedom of expression. Yet some governmental conduct of a more affirmative nature may also have an impact upon First Amendment rights. Thus, the government may undertake to promote the system of freedom of expression by assisting speakers in their endeavors to communicate, or it may participate in the system itself as a speaker. Along with other governmental functions, these activities of the government have been increasing at an accelerated rate. Obviously they both confer important benefits and present acute dangers.

First Amendment doctrine concerned with governmental conduct in this area is just beginning to develop. It is likely to become a critical issue for future generations. Some of the problems to be solved are illustrated by the use of government subsidies to finance various forms of expression and by government participation in expression through the operation of school libraries.

Government funding of expression takes place on a widespread scale. It includes giving financial support to public radio and television, providing public money for political candidates, making grants for scientific research, and furnishing financial aid to cultural activities. The principal First Amendment difficulty is that, in carrying out such programs, the government must designate the basic purposes for which public funds are to be made available and it thereby passes judgment on the content of the expression, preferring the subsidized to that not subsidized. Moreover, by the very nature of the relationship, the government is in a position to dictate or influence the message communicated by the beneficiary of the funds. The resolution of this dilemma would seem to rest in part upon developing a distinction between government intervention at the macro level and governmental intervention at the micro level. Thus, the government would be authorized to support expression by selecting a general area for subsidy but prevented from controlling the details of the expression within that area.

A different kind of issue is presented by the government's conduct in maintaining a school library. Questions arise when public officials remove or fail to provide a book because of its ideological content. A persuasive argument

44 can be made that such action violates First Amendment rights. The function of the school, at least above the elementary level, is not only to instill traditional knowledge in its students but to give them the capacity for critical thought and innovative action. The library is a key institution in this process. The student, who frequently is a captive audience because of the compulsory attendance laws, would appear to have a constitutional right to have access to a broad range of information and ideas. The Supreme Court in its recent decision in the *Island Trees School* case has indeed recognized such a right.

On the other hand, translation of the theoretical right into a concrete legal remedy is not without difficulty. In building a school library—adding or removing books—the school authorities must necessarily delve into the worth of the information and ideas contained in the material under consideration. By what standard is a court to decide whether this judgment violates the student's constitutional right? For answers the Court must look to concepts of balanced presentation and the professional judgment of educators as to whether the action of the school officials unduly restricts the space needed by the student for growth and development. Of course, even if the courts can formulate a workable standard they could not supervise every decision made by the school authorities. At most they would be able to keep the pertinent constitutional principles alive and apply them in egregious cases.

Affirmative government support of what is essentially a laissez-faire system and participation by the government in that system present a paradox. Government controls are brought into play, but the controls must in turn be controlled. The working out of this dilemma still remains a major task.

CONCLUSION

To sum up, there is some evidence that basic understanding and support for the system of freedom of expression have lost ground in some quarters. There are some weaknesses in the constitutional structure that has evolved from the decisions of the Supreme Court. The claims being pressed in the name of national security pose a critical issue; adjustment to the new technology demands an immediate solution; and controls over an active government, seeking to promote and participate in the system, have not yet evolved. Nevertheless, on the whole, the First Amendment lives a powerful life. If we can keep basic economic, environmental, and other social conditions from overwhelming us, keep warfare from destroying us, and keep faith in the progress we have made, the symbolic year of 1984 need never arrive.

[John Shattuck]

2

FEDERAL RESTRICTIONS

ON THE FREE FLOW OF

ACADEMIC INFORMATION

AND IDEAS

The freedom of scholars to express ideas and exchange them with colleagues is essential to the operation of universities in the United States and to maintaining the high quality of academic research. Academic freedom is rooted in the First Amendment to the Constitution, the same provision that protects the right of people to speak freely and the freedom of the media to report events as they see them.

Recent actions and proposals by some agencies of the federal government threaten to erode the American tradition of academic freedom. These proposals and actions fall into two broad categories—those restricting dissemination of ideas and those restricting the access of foreign scholars to U.S. classrooms and laboratories.

Reprinted from *Government Information Quarterly* 3 (1986), pp. 5–29, with permission of the author and the publishers. © 1986 by JAI Press, Inc. Portions of this essay have been revised or updated.

46   In most instances, the justification given for these restrictions is the need to protect national security, an area in which technology plays an increasingly important role.

Responding to mounting government concern that technological information with potential military applications may be reaching the Soviet Union and other adversaries through industry and the scientific community, the National Academy of Sciences (NAS) issued a report in September 1982 on *Scientific Communication and National Security*. The study was conducted by an NAS panel chaired by Dale Corson, a former president of Cornell University. The authors expressed the hope that their recommendations would make it possible to "establish within the Government an appropriate group to develop mechanisms and guidelines in the cooperative spirit that the report itself display[ed]."

Universities, which conduct most of the basic scientific research in the United States, were a primary focus of the NAS study. The report found "a substantial transfer" of U.S. technology to the Soviet Union, but concluded that "very little" of the problem resulted from open scientific communication. Moreover, the report took note of the close connections between the American tradition of open communication, scientific and technological innovation, and national security. Despite this conclusion, NAS staff members reported this year that government policymakers are moving to implement new secrecy regulations before a government-wide consensus is reached. The staff also stated that, where regulations already exist, policymakers are aggressively stretching their authority beyond its previous limits.

These secrecy regulations often go far afield of any reasonable definition of national security. Indeed, the requirements of prepublication review now reach several federal departments and agencies and areas of sponsored research that have no relationship to national security matters. Nor is the regulatory scheme limited to research that is federally funded. Instead, it is being extended to broad categories of research and information—such as cryptography and nuclear energy—that are deemed to be so sensitive and important that the federal government must intervene whether or not it is paying for the research.

The movements afoot in Washington to restrict publication and dissemination of scientific research findings are matters of deep concern among members of the academic community. Similar concerns also arise over government restrictions on the activities of foreign scholars.

These concerns are addressed in the pages that follow.

PREPUBLICATION REVIEW AND
CONTRACT RESTRAINTS

Political philosophers have long maintained that the rights of free speech and of a free press are essential to the proper functioning of democracy. The importance of open communication in our society has been so compelling that courts have held that only an overwhelming danger "so imminent that it may befall before there is opportunity for full discussion" provides sufficient grounds for restraining free speech. If the danger or evil is not imminent, then the remedy is "more speech, not enforced silence."

Until very recently, any proposed prior restraint on publication has come under a "heavy presumption against its constitutional validity." This presumption was so dominant that only narrowly focused government claims of national security during wartime could be balanced against it. For example, the Supreme Court held in *Near* v. *Minnesota* that publishing "the sailing dates of transports or the number and location of troops" would be the only kind of publishing activity the government could rightfully prevent in such circumstances.

As technology has come to play an increasingly important role in warfare and national defense, the traditional analysis of prior restraint issues has come into question. Many analysts have argued that U.S. security no longer depends on having "the largest military" or "the best-trained soldiers" but increasingly, rather, on a "technological lead over our military adversaries." This has led to a change in the focus of controls over exports "from goods to the technology used to produce those goods." One technique for achieving this new objective is prepublication review.

In the past, only the CIA has used prepublication review, pursuant to contractual arrangements with its employees that implement its statutory mandate to "protec[t] intelligence sources and methods from unauthorized disclosure." CIA employees involved in covert intelligence operations have routinely had their speeches and writings reviewed for content that might disclose classified information without authorization. The constitutionality of this specialized CIA practice was upheld in 1972 by a United States court of appeals in *United States* v. *Marchetti*. That decision did not, however, address whether prepublication review could be required for *all* material, including unclassified information.

The Supreme Court addressed this issue in 1980, in *Snepp* v. *United States*, a case involving a former CIA agent who published a book criticizing practices of the United States during the Vietnam War. All parties to the litigation agreed "that Snepp's book divulged no classified intelligence." Nevertheless,

48   the Court held that Snepp had violated his agreement with the CIA by not giving "an opportunity to determine whether the material he proposed to publish would compromise classified information or sources." The Court awarded damages to the government in the form of a "constructive trust" into which Snepp was required to "disgorge the benefits of his faithlessness."

The application of this decision has far-reaching consequences for academic research and publication. Two recent developments illustrate the point: (1) National Security Decision Directive 84, a presidential order requiring all government employees (and contractors) with authorized access to certain categories of classified information to sign lifetime prepublication review agreements as a condition of such access; and (2) the trend toward including prepublication review clauses in government-sponsored, university-based basic research contracts.

National Security Decision Directive 84

On March 11, 1983, the White House announced a security program designed to prevent unlawful disclosure of classified information by government employees. Since the date of its release, National Security Decision Directive 84 (NSDD 84) has generated a storm of controversy. Two of its provisions are particularly onerous. The first requires more than 120,000 government employees to sign nondisclosure agreements containing prepublication review clauses as a condition of access to certain categories of classified materials.* The second permits government agencies to order polygraph examinations of agency personnel "when appropriate, in the course of investigations of unauthorized disclosures of classified information." It also requires each agency to promulgate regulations to "govern contacts between media representatives and agency personnel, so as to reduce the opportunity for negligent or deliberate disclosures."

In 1984 Congress reviewed the implications of the directive. Testifying at a Congressional hearing, Thomas Ehrlich, provost of the University of Pennsylvania, described NSDD 84 as "virtually alone among important issues in recent times" in receiving a "completely uniform and completely negative . . . reaction of those in academia." Speaking for his own institution as well as for the Association of American Universities, the American Council on Education, and the National Association of State Universities and Land Grant Colleges, Ehrlich declared that he could not "overstate the dangers I see in the approach it adopts." If fully implemented as issued, NSDD 84 would have "disastrous

---

*The number has risen to 290,000, according to a report by the GAO. [Ed.]

effects on the quality of our government in terms of those who enter and leave public service from academic life," Ehrlich stressed. It would, he said, cast a "deep freeze over any inducement for academics to serve in government by denying them the primary benefit of using government experience and information in scholarly publications and classroom lectures." Government would be deprived of academia's much-needed expertise and insight. More important, the directive would thwart criticism of government, since those "in the best position to provide that criticism"—academics who have served in government and returned—would be enjoined from discussing matters on which they had worked. In view of academia's traditional role of providing a forum for criticism and debate, the restrictions in NSDD 84 would significantly reduce the scope of academic freedom.

Under pressure from the Congress the Administration suspended the prepublication review provision of NSDD 84 in September 1984. Nevertheless, it left in place a 1981 requirement that all government employees with high level security clearance sign Form 4193 which contains a lifetime promise to submit for prepublication review

> all materials, including works of fiction, that I contemplate disclosing to any person not authorized to have [Sensitive Compartmented Information and other classified information], or that I have prepared for public disclosure, which contain or purport to contain: (a) any SCI, any description of activities that produce or relate to SCI, or any information derived from SCI; (b) any classified information from intelligence reports or estimates; or (c) any information concerning intelligence activities, sources of methods.

A 1986 General Accounting Office report on the impact of Form 4193 concluded that suspension of NSDD 84's prepublication review requirement had little effect. For example, in 1984, 21,718 books, articles, speeches, and other materials were reviewed through agency prepublication review processes. In 1985 the number grew to 22,820. The GAO determined that as of December 31, 1985, at least 240,776 individuals had signed Form 4193 in either its original 1981 version or in the 1983 revision. During the same two-year period, there were a total of 15 unauthorized disclosures of information through books, articles, or speeches by current or former employees.

Government Sponsored Research

Most major universities receive funding from the federal government for basic scientific and social research. The funding is generally bestowed through con-

50   tracts and grants between federal agencies and individual institutions. The terms of a contract or grant are subject to the statutory mandate and regulations of the funding agency.

In recent years, a growing number of federal agencies have inserted prepublication review clauses in university contracts, even those involving only unclassified material. For example, publication restrictions have been proposed for unclassified research to be performed under contract with the Department of the Air Force ("Measurement of Lifetime of the Vibrational Levels of the B State of N_2"), the National Institutes of Health ("International Comparison of Health Science Policies"), the National Institute of Education ("Education and Technology Center"), the Department of Housing and Urban Development ("Study on Changing Economic Conditions of the Cities"), the Environmental Protection Agency ("Conference on EPA's Future Agenda"), the Health Resources and Sciences Administration ("Workshop for Staff of Geriatric Education Centers"), and the Food and Drug Administration ("Development of a Screening Test for Photocarcinogenesis on a Molecular Level").

Although prepublication review arose from national security concerns about the illicit transfer of technology to unfriendly governments, some of the most restrictive proposed contract clauses are contained in nontechnological social research contracts. Apparently, federal agencies believe they can in this way ensure that the research they fund is consistent with their view of their mission. The following is a clause from a proposed contract offered by the Department of Housing and Urban Development for university research on the use of housing vouchers:

> Approval or disapproval (in part or in total) of the final report shall be accomplished by the GTR within thirty (30) days after receipt. Disapproved reports shall be resubmitted for review following correction of the cited deficiency unless otherwise directed by the contracting officer.

Consider another clause from a contract offered by the National Institute of Education:

> The contractor shall not disclose any confidential information obtained in the performance of this contract. Any presentation of any statistical or analytical material or reports based on information obtained from studies covered by this contract will be subject to review by the Government's Project officer before publication or dissemination for *accuracy of factual date and interpretation* [emphasis added].

In addition, two other contract provisions referred to commonly as "Technical Direction" and "Changes" clauses are used to alter the outcome of a given project. This is done either by direct participation in the project by a government official (technical direction) or by changing without notice the content and/or scope of the research contract without the researcher's agreement (changes clause).

Harvard's Office of Sponsored Research (OSR) reports success in negotiating changes in all three types of restrictive clauses. These negotiated changes enable the university to accept such contracts and perform them successfully. However, the Environmental Protection Agency in one instance has flatly refused to negotiate, offering a research contract only on a take-it-or-leave-it basis. But what is more important, OSR reports increasing resistance to negotiate deviations from standard agency provisions in all agencies. The university has accordingly refused some contracts.

In sum, the federal government is increasingly asserting an authority to require prepublication review of intellectual work by government employees, research universities, and private citizens. As a result, the imposition of censorship has grown substantially beyond the boundaries of the traditional wartime national security exception to the ban on prior restraints that has long been a fundamental element of First Amendment doctrine.

INCREASED CLASSIFICATION

President Reagan established the current system of security classification in 1982 by Executive Order 12356. To grasp the import of this new system, one must first understand the security systems used by previous administrations.

Although the security classification systems used during the Truman, Eisenhower, Nixon, Ford, and Carter administrations differed in their details, each contributed to a gradual trend toward government recognition of "the public's interest in the free circulation of knowledge by limiting classification authority, by defining precisely the purposes and limits of classification, and by providing procedures for declassification."

The classification system designed by the Carter administration was the culmination of this trend. It required government officials "to balance the public's interest in access to government information with the need to protect certain national security information from disclosure." It stipulated that even if information met one of the seven classification categories, it was not to be classified unless "its unauthorized disclosure reasonably could be expected to cause *at least identifiable damage* to the national security" [emphasis added]. It provided for automatic declassification routinely after six years; only officials with "Top Secret" Security clearance classify a document for more than "twenty years." Finally, it established a presumption such that "[i]f there is a reasonable doubt which designation is appropriate, or whether the information should be classified at all, the less restrictive designation should be used, or the information should not be classified" [emphasis added].

Executive Order 12356 reverses this trend toward openness by significantly altering or eliminating each of the earlier systems' major features. The new order eliminates the balancing test: No longer must classifiers weigh the public's need to know against the need for classification. In addition, the threshold standard for classification has been reduced. Heretofore, the classifier had to show "identifiable damage" to the national security. The new executive order leaves much more room for discretion: It demands only that the classifier have a reasonable expectation of damage to the nation's security. The new order also eliminates automatic declassification, requiring that information remain classified "as long as required by national security considerations." Finally, the presumption in favor of openness is reversed. Now, "if there is a reasonable doubt about the need to classify information, it shall be safeguarded as if it were classified . . . and if there is a reasonable doubt about the appropriate level of classification it shall be safeguarded at the higher level of classification."

Secondary features of the security classification system have also undergone extensive revision in Executive Order 12356. In the areas of basic scientific research and reclassification, changes have taken place. Under both the new and the old executive orders, basic scientific research information unrelated to national security is exempt from classification. However, the initial drafts of the new order did not include the basic research exemption. In addition, the previous order expressly limited the government's interest in nongovernmental sponsored basic research—a matter that the new order leaves to administrative discretion.

Under President Carter's order, "[c]lassification may not be restored to documents already declassified and released to the public." But under the new order, declassified information may be reclassified if "the information requires protection in the interests of national security; and [if] the information may be reasonably recovered." Acting under this clause, the Reagan administration unsuccessfully attempted in 1982 to recover documents previously released to a private researcher about electronic surveillance carried out by the CIA and NSA against antiwar activists in the 1970s. The documents had been provided to author James Bamford, under a Freedom of Information request made in 1979. Executive order 12356 provides that "information may be classified or reclassified after an agency has received a request for it under the Freedom of

Information Act or the Privacy Act." In contrast, the earlier order provided that "no document originated on or after the effective date of this Order may be classified after an agency has received a request for the document under the Freedom of Information Act."

Given the bent toward secrecy exhibited by the many changes in the security classification system, scholars now fear that "[a]cademic research not born classified may, under this order die classified." The new order gives unprecedented authority to government officials to intrude upon academic research by imposing classification restrictions on areas of research after projects have been undertaken in those areas. The new order appears to allow classification to be imposed at any stage of a research project and to be maintained for as long as government officials deem prudent. Thus, the order could inhibit academic researchers from making long-term intellectual investments in nonclassified projects with features that make them likely subjects for classification at a later date.

EXPORT CONTROLS

Regulatory Scheme

In the area of export regulation, both military and civilian, statutory controls have been imposed over scientific communication related to basic research. These controls affect basic research through their definition of the terms "technological data" and "export." Information subject to export controls need not be classified so long as it falls within the definition of "technological data" and is to be "exported."

The Export Administration Regulations (EAR), promulgated under the Export Administration Act of 1979, define "technological data" as "information of any kind that can be used, or adapted for use in the design, production, manufacture, utilization, or reconstruction of articles or materials. The data may take a tangible form, such as a model, prototype, blueprint, or an operating manual; or they may take an intangible form such as technical service." Under the Arms Export Control Act of 1968, the International Traffic in Arms Regulations (ITAR) contain an even more expansive definition of technological data, including anything that "advances the state of the art."

Both sets of regulations target areas of data through the use of lists. EAR creates the Commodity Control List. ITAR creates the U.S. Munitions List. The technological data related to any product that appears on either list are subject to export control. ITAR provides that information is "exported" whenever it is communicated overseas by "oral, visual or documentary means . . .",

54 including "visits abroad by American citizens." Under EAR, export means "(i) an actual shipment or transmission of technical data out of the United States; or (ii) any release of technical data in the United States with the knowledge or intent that the data will be shipped or transmitted from the United States." Data may be released for export through "(i) visual inspection by foreign nationals . . . ; [or] (ii) oral exchanges of information in the United States or abroad of personal knowledge or technical experience acquired in the United States."

Application to Universities

Historically, university researchers have been covered by exemptions (or general licenses) available under each set of regulations. ITAR specifically exempts information "in published form" or "sold at newsstands." EAR gives such data a general license and also specifically allows "correspondence, attendance at or participation in meetings" and "instruction in academic laboratories" to be included under a general license. However, these activities are allowable only so long as they do not relate "directly and significantly to design, production, or utilization in industrial processes." Until recently, routine academic activity has not been interpreted as being controllable under this clause.

In 1981, the Department of State sent a form letter to many universities inquiring into the study programs of certain Chinese foreign-exchange students. The authorities cited for this action were the Arms Export Control Act and the Export Administration Act. In refusing to provide the information requested, Harvard University General Counsel Daniel Steiner characterized the inquiry as "an interference into matters at the very heart of the academic enterprise." Other universities took similar actions.

The universities were not overreacting. Much of the requested information would have required close surveillance of student activities. The government wanted information on "professional trips" taken by students, "specific experiments" conducted on campus, and even information concerning "instruments or specialized equipment (e.g., laser measuring devices, automated analytical equipment, computers, etc.) that may be used during the course of the study program." The State Department made a similar inquiry about a Polish scholar at Harvard in 1982.

The debilitating effects on academic freedom of the new export regulations are dramatically illustrated by a course on Metal Matrix Composites, offered recently at UCLA, that was advertised in the course catalogue as restricted to "U.S. Citizens Only." The restriction was required because the course material

involved unclassified technical data appearing on the Munitions Control List   **55**
(ITAR) and thus subject to export control.

Atomic Energy Research

The government also asserts broad authority to control scientific communication in the area of atomic energy research. The Atomic Energy Act regulates
the "development, utilization and control of atomic energy for military and
all other purposes." In addition, a 1981 amendment to the act authorizes the
Secretary of Energy, with respect to atomic energy defense programs, to "pre-
scribe such regulations . . . as may be necessary to prohibit the unauthorized
dissemination of *unclassified* information" [emphasis added]. Although the act
also authorizes the creation of "a program for the dissemination of unclassified scientific and technical information . . . *so as to encourage scientific and
industrial progress*" [emphasis added], creation of such a program has been constrained by a Department of Energy regulation proposed in April 1983. The
proposed regulation, "Identification and Protection of Unclassified Controlled
Nuclear Information (UCNI)," would require that all UCNI be treated as
"proprietary business information" within the regulated organization. Such
organizations would have to take "reasonable and prudent" steps to protect
UCNI from unauthorized disclosure. In addition, government contractors
would have to assure that potential users have a "need to know," are U.S.
citizens, or meet one of six other criteria.

In commenting on the proposed regulations, Stanford University, joined
by Harvard, suggested a redrafting of the rules because of the major difficulty
that they would cause for research universities. The proposed rules would
require a university to make "known an unclassified information secret." The
Stanford comments pointed out that the proposed regulations would be so
inclusive as to apply to materials used in "all those basic and advanced courses
in fields of physics, electrical engineering, materials science and the like, that
teach the basic information discovered and classified before the early 1950's and
since declassified." Most important, the commentators argued that restrictions
requiring use of business standards in protecting proprietary material would
interfere with basic research because of university policy that "such data be
specifically identified in advance so that [it] can be certain its acceptance is
consistent with . . . research guidelines." Moreover, the regulations made no
statement concerning new research-generated UCNI. Stanford and Harvard
asserted that this ambiguity would conflict with their fundamental policy that
"all new information developed in the course of research be publishable."

On August 3, 1984, a new draft of the UCNI regulations was issued for

56 public comment. As a matter of principle, Harvard and other research universities continue to oppose federal restrictions on the dissemination of unclassified information. However, the new draft does contain improvements over its predecessor. Specifically, Harvard's comments on the new draft noted a "narrowed and better defined scope of application" of the proposed regulations. Also, the new draft contains an exemption for basic scientific information. Nevertheless, university commentators were careful to note the need for defining basic research so as to protect academic freedom. The Harvard comment suggested that basic research, exempt from all regulation, should be defined as: "information resulting from research directed toward increasing knowledge or understanding of the subject under study rather than any practical application of that knowledge."

Current Policy Developments

The debate over federal restrictions on the free flow of information and ideas has been particularly intense in recent years in the area of export control regulations. In October 1983, the House of Representatives adopted an amendment to a bill extending the Export Administration Act which provided that:

> It is the policy of the United States to sustain vigorous scientific enterprise. To do so requires protecting the ability of scientists and other scholars to freely communicate their research findings by means of publication, teaching, conferences, and other forms of scholarly exchange.

However, the Senate version of the extension bill substituted the words "involves sustaining" for "requires protecting." More important, the Senate version inserted the word "non-sensitive" before the words "research findings." This key change substantially altered the meaning and intent of the entire paragraph. The Senate version would have created the very restriction on scholarly exchange that the House version was intended to avoid.

The Export Administration bill died at the end of the 98th Congress in October 1984 because no agreement could be reached in a House-Senate Conference Committee over a wide variety of issues in the bill. In June 1985 the House and Senate finally reached agreement on a subsequent version of the extension legislation. While the final version incorporates the original House declaration of policy "to sustain vigorous scientific enterprise . . . by means of publication, teaching, conferences, and other forms of scholarly exchange," other language broadly defining "technology" and "export" creates considerable ambiguity about the status of this policy declaration.

Another recent development involves the Military Critical Technologies **57** List (MCTL), which has been revised and expanded. This list is similar to the Commodity Control List and the U.S. Munitions list in that it designates sensitive applied technologies that the Defense Department desires to control. The list itself is classified, but a directive describing it states that the list now "covers all newly created technical documents generated by Department of Defense–funded research, development, test, and evaluation programs."

The MCTL is controversial for two reasons. First, it is statutorily incorporated into the Commodity Control List (CCL). Using the MCTL as a base, the Pentagon can propose changes in the CCL. Second, the MCTL is reportedly over seven hundred pages long, and has been described by one Department of Defense official as "really a list of modern technology" and as a document that "could further complicate the use of these regulations as a means of trying to control scientific and technical communications." The MCTL designates as "sensitive" technologies that the Department of Defense desires to restrict.

In the field of export control, the designation of information as "sensitive" arises in part from a "gray area" identified by DoD officials "where controls on unclassified scientific information are warranted." This "gray area" approach, however, encountered opposition within the Defense Department itself. In testimony in May 1984 before the Subcommittee on Science, Research, and Technology, Edith Martin, then deputy undersecretary of defense for research and engineering, stated that the Department of Defense had decided "not to pursue the gray area concept because the option had proved to be more complicated than it had seemed." She told the subcommittee that "it is the policy of this administration that the mechanism for control of fundamental research in science and engineering universities and federal laboratories is classification." This statement was repeated on October 1, 1984, in a memorandum signed by the then under secretary of defense for research and engineering Richard DeLauer, stating that "no controls other than classification may be imposed on fundamental research and its results when performed under a federally "supported contract." The DeLauer memorandum was attached as a cover to a draft national policy on scientific and technical information. In September 1985 the new policy was issued by President Reagan as National Security Decision Directive 189, which provides that "no restrictions may be placed upon the conduct or reporting of a federally-funded fundamental resource that has not received national security classification except as provided in applicable U.S. statutes."

58 RESTRICTIONS ON FOREIGN SCHOLARS

Under the Immigration, Naturalization, and Nationality Act (known as "the McCarran Act"), foreign nationals can be denied entry into the United States because of their political and ideological beliefs. The restrictive provisions apply to "aliens who . . . engaged in activities which would be prejudicial to the public interest"; to "aliens who are members of the Communist Party" or "who advocate the economic, international and government doctrines of world communism."

The leading Supreme Court decision interpreting the McCarran Act involved a Belgian journalist and Marxist theoretician, Ernest Mandel. Although not a member of the Communist party, Mandel described himself as "a revolutionary Marxist." Despite this description on all his visa applications, Mandel had been admitted to the United States temporarily in 1962 and again in 1968 before his first entry denial. In 1969, he was invited to speak at Stanford and he again applied for a six-day temporary visa. The visa was denied on the grounds that his 1963 activities while in the United States went far beyond the stated purposes of his trip . . . represent[ing] a flagrant abuse of the opportunities afforded him to express his views in this country." Mandel and six U.S. citizens, all university professors, sued the United States. The professors claimed that their First Amendment rights to hear and communicate with Mandel were being violated. A closely divided Court rejected the First Amendment claim.

The Mandel decision paved the way for a variety of entry denials or deportation proceedings against foreign-born tenured professors at American universities. Three recent examples:

Dennis Brutus, a poet, writer, and critic of apartheid, banned in South Africa for petitioning the South African Olympic Committee to allow black South Africans to compete on the national team. By attending a meeting of the South African Olympic Committee he violated the ban by being "with more than two people at a time." He was sentenced and served 18 months in prison. He came to the United States in 1970 to accept the teaching position at Northwestern University. His visa expired in 1980. He was required to obtain a permanent visa from outside the U.S. but because he had let his British passport expire this was not possible. He requested asylum. At his asylum hearing in 1983, Immigration Department lawyers used classified documents to make their case denying Brutus' attorneys access. Indirectly it was learned that he was considered deportable under Sec. 212(a) (28) because of membership in the

South African "Colored Peoples Congress." He was ordered deported **59**
but on appeal won asylum in late 1983.

Cosmo Pieterse, who came to Ohio State University in 1970 and was
tenured in 1976. In 1979 he went to London to meet with his publisher
and when attempting to return in 1981 was denied reentry. This denial
was based on classified information. It is believed that he has been denied
entry for being a Communist even though his university colleagues deny
this. He is still in London.

Angel Rama, a native of Uruguay, who made many trips to the U.S.
before 1966. He was admitted on a regular visa until 1969 when he
was apparently classified as a subversive and allowed to enter only on
a waiver basis. In 1980 he earned tenure at the University of Maryland
and applied for permanent residence status. The Immigration Department denied this request stating that the denial was based on "classified
information . . . which [could] not be discussed . . . or made available."
Rama believed his denial was based on a series of articles he had written
in the magazine *Marcha,* in which he reported on attempts by the CIA
to infiltrate Latin American intelligence organizations. He was killed in
a plane crash in Madrid before his case was resolved.

In addition to these university professors, a wide variety of foreign speakers
invited to address university audiences in the United States have been denied
entry from time to time in recent years under the "prejudicial to the public interest" provision of the McCarran Act. Among these are Nobel Prize-winning
authors Gabriel García Márquez and Czeslaw Milosz, as well as author Carlos
Fuentes, playwright Dario Fo, actress Franca Rame, NATO Deputy Supreme
Commander Nino Pasti, and Hortensia Allende, widow of the former Chilean
president, Salvador Allende.

CONCLUSION

The free flow of ideas among scholars and their colleagues is essential to the
fabric of academic life. The foregoing discussion shows the extent to which
federal authority is now being asserted to restrict and disrupt that flow.

[Thomas G. Paterson]

3

THOUGHT CONTROL AND

THE WRITING OF HISTORY

The American people have witnessed in recent years a series of executive branch decisions that, taken together, have put this country in danger of what we must unabashedly call "thought control." No single edict was issued from the highest echelons of Washington, D.C. Rather, a host of seemingly unconnected steps have merged into a discernible trend unbefitting a nation that prides itself on freedom of expression. The United States Information Agency, for example, has selected American speakers for its overseas programs on the basis of their allegiance to Reagan administration policies, and agency officials, at one point, even compiled a blacklist that included Betty Friedan, Walter Cronkite, John Kenneth Galbraith, and McGeorge Bundy. The McCarran-Walter Act of 1952, a legacy of the McCarthyite era, was revitalized to bar foreign speakers from the United States because their "ideology" was unacceptable. The Colombian journalist Patricia Lara, Hortensia Bussi de Allende—the widow of the slain president of Chile—and the Mexican novelist Carlos Fuentes at one time or another have faced ideological exclusion. The attempted control of information has also been evident in the Reagan administration's preparation of legislation making it a crime for government personnel or former government officials to disclose classified information without authorization, and in restrictions on American travel to Cuba.

The writing of history has also suffered from thought control. The historian's access to government documents and information has been blocked by questionable interpretations of the law, by restrictive guidelines and directives that keep documents locked up for longer periods of time, by poor record-keeping methods, and by unsympathetic government bureaucrats whose commitment to secrecy is excessive. Diplomatic historians—of which I am one —particularly have faced obstacles that stem not so much from inadequate budgets or insufficient staffing at the Department of State or National Archives as from definitions of national security that are alarmingly sweeping. The issue is, *what* is being declassified to satisfy the people's right to know and the historian's need for thorough documentation. And the fundamental question is this: What kind of history will we be getting if the current policies of restriction continue? Will historians who teach and write about the recent past have available to them the documents necessary to conduct thorough analyses and draw substantiated conclusions? Surely we need not debate the value of the study of history—that discipline that helps tell us where we are going, and what we are doing, and why—because it charts where we have been. What must be debated are those rules and regulations that poke out the eyes and deafen the ears of the past.

When we speak of "thought control" we are talking not about the burning of books, but about the prevention of books. Information is being controlled and managed as never before. Open-ended definitions of national security elevate secrecy to new levels. Arguably, some materials should be kept security-classified—codes, orders of battle, weapons designs, the names of American spies. But historians are by-and-large not so interested in such details as they are eager to discover who made a decision and why. We would rather see the presidential memorandum authorizing a certain clandestine operation than the list of cloak-and-dagger agents who implemented the plan, and we need to study the briefing papers that helped produce policy. But the Reagan administration has impeded the flow of information about the past, especially in its handling of the Freedom of Information Act. Government officials have apparently seen historical knowledge as a threat to the nation, rather than as a vital component of a functioning democracy in which the people must be informed and their government held accountable. In studying this subject, I found myself descending into a dark cavern of executive orders, legislative acts, executive directives, proposed amendments, letters of explanation, secret guidelines, and court rulings. I am sure I do not understand all of it, and I am assured by archivists and historians in the government that they have not mastered the rules either. But the procedural cloudiness should not obscure the critical question: What kind of history will emerge from our government's current policies?

The pattern of thought control is unmistakably defined. Take several recent examples. The first occurred in early 1983 when the National Security Agency (NSA) ordered the George C. Marshall Library in Virginia to remove letters from the private papers of William F. Friedman. These letters had once before been reviewed by the NSA and had been made open to researchers; indeed,

62   James Bamford's 1982 book on the National Security Agency, titled *The Puzzle Palace,* cited these documents. NSA representatives did not like what they read. In early 1983 they moved into the Marshall Library, rubber-stamped the letters "Secret," and insisted that the correspondence be placed in the library's vault. In February of the next year, with a lawsuit against it filed or about to be filed, NSA decided to hold from public view thirty-one pieces of correspondence. In other words, a federal agency claimed the authority to reclassify private papers in private libraries if the documents are judged to be sensitive under the rubric of "national security." President Ronald Reagan's 1982 Executive Order 12356, in fact, permits agencies to reclassify materials which have already been released to the public. The problem historians face in the future, then, is not simply one of hurrying the declassification process, but of preventing reclassification. Some documents Barry Rubin researched to write his book *Paved with Good Intentions: The American Experience and Iran* (1980) have been reclassified to deny them to future scholars. In 1984, Steven Garfinkel, director of the Information Security Oversight Office (ISOO), upon hearing that the private papers of Senator Frank Church had been deposited at Boise State University in Idaho, offered to send a team of reviewers to survey the collection for classified "national security information" and asked the Boise State library "to safeguard" such materials in the interim. The University's librarian assured Garfinkel that classified documents did not exist in the papers, but agreed to remove any such materials should they turn up and submit them to the ISOO. In the Marshall Library case the American Historical Association and the Organization of American Historians became co-plaintiffs in a suit that seeks to deny NSA's authority to classify or close private papers deposited by individuals in libraries or archives and to restrain NSA from further efforts to block public access to such information. But the worries remain: Which collections will these federal censors move into next? How many times can the government review documents and change its mind about their classification? Can the government control information once it has gotten out of its hands?

Still another example is the "gag rule" the Reagan administration announced in March of 1983 as National Security Decision Directive 84. According to this directive, government personnel who had access to classified materials had to sign a lifetime secrecy pledge. Thereafter all speeches, articles, and books had to be submitted for approval prior to delivery or publication. Because the government heretofore had been unable to demonstrate that enough classified information previously had been released to the detriment of the national interest, this lifetime restriction raised a storm of protest from civil libertarians, members of Congress, and former government officials. The former under-secretary of state George Ball, whose memoirs *The Past Has Another Pattern*

(1982) would have had to be submitted to the censors had the directive been in place when he held office in the 1960s, called it "an appalling document." The public protest forced President Reagan to reconsider; he suspended the offending censorship provision. Even so, more than two hundred thousand government employees have already signed a lifetime prepublication agreement, and in 1983, government censors reviewed 28,364 books, articles, speeches, and other writings. Is a modern-day George F. Kennan to be muzzled for life?

The Central Intelligence Agency has long required its employees to submit their writings for security clearance, and in some cases the government has prosecuted former CIA personnel who violated their contractual agreements. The censorship has been arbitrary and time-consuming. Jimmy Carter's director of central intelligence, Stansfield Turner, discovered how "unreasonable and unnecessary" the system could be when he dutifully filed the manuscript of his autobiographical book, *Secrecy and Democracy: The CIA in Transition* (1985), with the CIA. The CIA, after delays, made more than a hundred deletions; Turner appealed, but could get only three restored. He then threatened to publish two of the deletions to protest the "extreme arbitrariness of the review process." In the end he decided not to include the objectionable material. "Fortunately," he explained in the opening of his book, "the message can still be understood, even though the reader must read through some euphemisms." But what if all the readers do not recognize the "euphemisms"? There is no way to dodge the point: Such a restrictive process produces censored history.

Another example of the problem of thought control sprang from government methods of records-keeping. In this case, the question arose more from the use of the computer than from suspicious government officials. In general, the government has shifted from paper to computerized records. In early 1985, a committee of historians and archivists chaired by Professor Ernest May of Harvard University called upon the president to issue an order to safeguard government records. "The United States is in danger of losing its memory," warned the committee report. What has happened is this: Information stored on disks has often been erased after policy statements or memoranda were rewritten. Historians learn a great deal from *drafts* of speeches or letters; they are able to explain the development of thinking and policy from a close reading of changes from draft to draft. But these drafts are being destroyed. "Without records, there is no understanding of continuity and change," concluded the committee. The computer, perhaps unwittingly, has become another obstacle to the writing of thorough history.

Another instance of thought control involved the Federal Bureau of Investigation. In 1975 or so the FBI began destroying documents in an apparent attempt to render the Freedom of Information Act (see below) ineffective. Substantial FBI holdings were destroyed before a January 1980 court order

64 stopped the destruction and instructed the agency to provide the court with plans and schedules for files retention. Judge Harold Greene of the Federal District Court in Washington, D.C., declared that "perhaps more than those of any other agency" the documents of the FBI "constitute a significant repository of the record of the recent history of this nation. . . . The lessons of history can hardly be learned if the historical record is allowed to vanish." The FBI appealed this injunction. Historical associations lined up to support the court order. In mid-1980 Judge Greene denied the FBI's motion to dissolve the injunction. The FBI persisted. In the Fall of 1983 a U.S. court of appeals rejected the FBI appeal. So Judge Greene's order stands: the National Archives and Records Service and the FBI must initiate plans for archivists to inspect and evaluate FBI records before the agency is permitted to destroy anything. Scholars who know the history of the FBI cannot feel confident that the agency will give its full cooperation, court order or not.

Let us turn next to the status of the Freedom of Information Act (FOIA). Passed in 1966 to "empower individuals to hold government accountable," the FOIA has served scholars well. Although the FOIA exempts from declassification those documents, which, if released, might endanger the national security, reveal company trade secrets, or bring risk to private individuals, many recent books in diplomatic history have utilized the act. But the scholar's use of the FOIA is now threatened in a variety of ways. Long delays—of sometimes two to three years—set back research, and often what is released is heavily sanitized. The government, moreover, has been stingy in granting fee waivers. The act is generous on fee waivers; that is, fees should be waived if the release of the materials is "in the public interest." Fees, which can include both search time and photoduplication costs, can run very high. My own research on Cuban-American relations, 1950s to the present, has become expensive because of FOIA fees. The Department of State, for example, has refused my appeals for fee waivers by arguing that "although the subject of your book is indeed broad, the actual nature of the material in which you are interested is simply too specialized" to be in the public interest. How can a historian write well on a broad subject without researching specialized materials?

A January 1983 Justice Department memorandum on fee waivers suggests that the imposition of fees and the denial of waivers became a way of discouraging FOIA requests and thereby our historical research. The memorandum interprets "public interest" this way: "No matter how interesting or vital the subject matter of a request, the public is benefitted only if the information released meaningfully contributes to the public development or understanding of the subjects." Are we to leave to government censors the definition of what is "meaningful"?

A twist on this issue came in 1984–1985 when a doctoral student at the University of Virginia requested from the Department of State some documents relating to United States policy toward the People's Republic of China in the 1960s. The student asked for a fee waiver. Back came the reply that his request "did not adequately demonstrate that a significant potential benefit will accrue to the general public as a result of a fee waiver." A dissertation, the State Department claimed, did not meet the "public interest" criterion. This constitutes a curious understanding of how knowledge and ideas are advanced. Doctoral dissertations often reflect new thinking; they often bring new documentation to familiar topics; they study some subjects for the very first time. Doctoral dissertations in many ways represent the thinking of the nation's next generation of educators, diplomats, and other leaders. Yet the State Department has been saying that this rich resource does not serve the public interest. Public debate will surely be poorer because of such a narrow view.

In the Fall of 1986 Congress amended the Freedom of Information Act to make more precise the language on fee waivers. The new wording waived search and review fees for requests that come from "educational or noncommercial scientific" institutions "whose purpose is scholarly or scientific research." In a report to their colleagues, two House members explained that this provision meant that "a request made by a professor or other member of the professional staff of an educational or scientific institution should be presumed to have been made by the institution." They noted that this change was necessary to "remove from further debate or consideration the erroneous standards" in the Justice Department's guidelines. As to the "public interest" criterion, the legislators reported that a fee waiver was in order even if the subject matter was not of interest to the public at large. "Public understanding is enhanced when information is disclosed to the subset of the public most interested, concerned, or affected by a particular action or matter." As of this writing, it is not clear how the new legislation will be implemented. Congressman Glenn English of Oklahoma feared, however, that government agencies may "dream up new procedural devices to discourage disclosures." If they do, English promised that they "will be invited to explain their creativity to my subcommittee."

Besides long delays, heavy deletions, and fees, another threat to the FOIA came from the CIA. The agency asked Congress to exempt the agency's operational files from the act. Congress obliged in 1984. The law represents a serious obstacle to historical research: it permits the CIA to determine what to release or what to review; and the CIA will be tempted to define "operational" broadly so as to deny scholars documents. The late CIA director, William Casey, said that "historians would have to trust us." Since the CIA is openly hostile to the Freedom of Information Act and has even refused to cooperate with the Office of the Historian of the Department of State, he must have been kidding.

66   The terrible state of the declassification process in the State Department has also commanded our attention, bogged down as it is in the environment of thought control. President Reagan's 1982 executive order abandoned the systematic declassification process established by previous orders (Richard Nixon's order provided for the release of all documents thirty years old and Jimmy Carter's order reduced the figure to twenty years). One provision of Reagan's order permitted the reclassification of material. It continued to exempt from declassification documents that contain information from a foreign government (such as a memorandum of a conversation with a foreign diplomat). Policy followed the guideline that, when in doubt, do not declassify. In fiscal year 1983, showing a decline over 1982, the State Department granted in full only 47 percent of the requests for declassification under the mandatory review procedures that apply to documents which have been deposited in the National Archives and Records Service, including the presidential libraries. The figure for the CIA was 28 percent; for the National Security Council, 47 percent; and for the Department of Defense, 62 percent. In 1983, moreover, only 46 percent of mandatory review requests were even processed, creating a large backlog of unanswered queries from scholars. Of FOIA requests processed in 1984, the Department of State granted in full only 29 percent. Secrecy has been winning; openness has been losing. The issue, of course, is not quantity, but quality—what are we getting for documents and what kind of history is going to be written from such an incomplete record?

The Classification/Declassification Center (CDC) of the Department of State works under Executive Order 12356. Created in 1979 and staffed by some 150 former foreign service officers, the CDC follows country-by-country guidelines that are in themselves classified. The CDC has stood as a major obstacle to good scholarship in diplomatic history. Documents for the 1950s have been released very slowly; it appears that documents for the years 1955 to 1960 will not be opened to research for a long time. Worse still, the CDC has been engaged in reclassification. Some foreign service post records stored at the federal depository in Suitland, Maryland, for example, have been called back for rereview by State Department classifiers. These materials once had been open to scholars. There is a huge backlog in the joint National Archives/Department of State declassification project. State Department lawyers are extremely cautious about releasing documents containing controversial topics. Large deletions and long delays await any scholar who seeks the declassification of a specific document. And there are the ridiculous cases. For my research on Cuban–United States relations, for example, I applied for the declassification of many documents held at the Dwight D. Eisenhower Library. After a two- to four-year wait, some documents I have received show a four-letter word to have been deleted. It required no detective skills whatsoever to determine that the letters were "C-u-b-a." Who in the bureaucracy spent so much time doing that sort of useless task?

The much-valued *Foreign Relations of the United States* series published by the Department of State has suffered under the stricter declassification rules, and the Office of the Historian has found its work on volumes that cover the 1960s hindered. There have been shortages of staff, but as the Advisory Committee on Historical Diplomatic Documentation stated in its 1983 report: "The revised declassification procedures have been largely responsible for the delay." The CDC has even pulled back volumes ready for the presses to rereview them. Volumes prepared at least five years ago have not yet been printed because clearance has been held up. Some of the volumes being published are disappointing because they are incomplete. Take, for example, the Indochina volume for 1952–1954 (published in 1982). Its "List of Sources" does not include the CIA. And the Preface and Introduction do not tell us if CIA files were researched or if the CIA, as has happened in the past, denied State Department requests for relevant materials. The Preface reads: "The publication of *Foreign Relations of the United States* constitutes the official record of the foreign policy of the United States. The volumes in this series include, subject to necessary security considerations, all documents needed to give a comprehensive record of the major foreign policy decisions of the United States." This surely claims too much. The wording—"official," "all," and "comprehensive" —suggests thoroughness, when in fact the volume appears incomplete.

The American Republics volume for 1952–1954 (compiled from 1974 to 1977 but not published until 1983) is another disappointment. Even though the 1954 intervention in Guatemala was a CIA operation, as excellent recent books have explained, the CIA denied the State Department editors of the *Foreign Relations* series permission to publish documents on the covert role of the agency. The volume covering Iran and the CIA-engineered coup of 1953 has been held up because of similar declassification snarls, no doubt because of fears that a public accounting of past United States relations with the Shah's Iran would further inflame today's hostile relations with revolutionary Teheran. And what about the volumes that cover Saudi Arabia? Will they also be gutted because many documents that mention the royal family will remain classified? Will we have more cases like the 1950 volume on Korea, which includes no minutes of National Security Council meetings, because NSC would not permit the Office of the Historian to print them? The series is in danger of taking on the character of an official White Paper, losing its reputation as a respected scholarly tool.

The message of this disconcerting story is that in so many ways our history has been managed for us in recent years. The piecemeal, document-by-document, incomplete declassification of documents permits the State De-

68   partment, the CIA, and other agencies to control our writing of history, to manage the questions we ask, to set the terms of historical inquiry and research. For example, we would not be carefully discussing the questions of lost opportunities for negotiations with Mao Zedong's China in 1949, and we would not have several excellent recent books on Sino-American relations in the 1940s, had the *Foreign Relations* volume, published in 1977, not printed Zhou Enlai's démarche. What if the Office of the Historian had lost the debate and the document had not been published? As it was, the volume was held up for some time before the go-ahead decision was made. What kind of history will we be getting in the future if similar cases arise? Not only does this management of information—this thought control—determine in part what questions we can answer, it also leaves the field to the memoirists—self-serving, incomplete, and suspect. How long must we rely on the autobiographies of Richard M. Nixon and Henry A. Kissinger for the history of 1970s diplomacy?

Professor Anna K. Nelson of American University, who has for years thoughtfully spoken to these questions, has suggested, with others, that we as historians should concentrate on the long run—on preparing a statutory law governing declassification of national security materials after twenty, twenty-five, or like Australia and Britain, thirty years. The American Historical Association Council, at its December 27, 1983, meeting passed a resolution with a recommendation to amend the Federal Records Act to provide for "basic criteria for all forms of security classification systems in all agencies of the United States Government," including a twenty-year rule. Until we abandon the current system of item-by-item review, we cannot with much confidence write the history of the recent past. Until we achieve a statutory basis for declassification, we remain at the mercy of leaks or "public disclosures" and individual presidents who can issue their obstructionist executive orders when they please. It produces little but frustration to challenge the technical language of the latest order, guideline, or directive. We need a permanent system that presidents will leave alone. But a better declassification system alone will not yield better history. The many instances of thought control discussed here and in other chapters in this book reveal that government officials believe it necessary and proper to control information, to keep the public ignorant, to prevent historians from writing about the recent past. Vigilant public oversight, including protest essays like this one, and close congressional scrutiny—holding officials accountable—thus become essential to historical scholarship and to the flourishing of a free society.

[Diana M. T. K. Autin]

4

THE REAGAN ADMINISTRATION AND

THE FREEDOM OF INFORMATION ACT

INTRODUCTION

The essence of democracy is decision-making by an informed public. As James Madison said, "Knowledge will forever govern ignorance, and a people who mean to be their own government must arm themselves with the power that knowledge brings."

No government ever shares all its information with its citizens, but a government must be fundamentally open if it is to have any legitimate claim to democracy in this, the "information age."

For 190 years the American people had no right of access to the information compiled and held by their government. It was not until the passage of the Freedom of Information Act (FOIA) in 1966 that the American public's "right to know" was established.

The FOIA, strengthened in 1974 as a direct result of the Watergate revelations of the consequences of secret, unaccountable government, is the single most important tool in uncovering the plans and activities of our government. It has been invaluable in obtaining information concerning the environment and nuclear power, health and safety, unsafe products and drugs, discrimination, intelligence agency abuses, and foreign policy.

INFORMATION RESTRICTIONS

Despite the value of the Freedom of Information Act, the Reagan administration has consistently attempted to cripple it through legislative and executive

70   initiatives. At the same time it has moved to increase the government's power
to monitor and influence citizen activities. In order to understand the administration's motives, it is vital to examine the context in which these attempts
to increase secrecy occur, with regard to both foreign and domestic policy
issues—an examination that will leave little doubt that secrecy and control of
information are hallmarks of the Reagan administration.

FOREIGN POLICY

James Madison observed, "Perhaps it is a universal truth that the loss of liberty at home is to be charged to provisions of danger, real or pretended,
from abroad." The administration's rationales for increased secrecy often center around the professed needs of "national security," despite its inability to
present concrete evidence that a need for increased secrecy exists.

With regard to foreign policy and international affairs, President Reagan
moved quickly to eliminate public interference with his policy-making and its
implementation.

The administration proposed and lobbied strongly for S. 1730, a full-scale
attack on the FOIA. This bill was promoted by the Senate Subcommittee
on the Constitution, chaired by Senator Orrin Hatch, (R-Utah). It would
have given the attorney general the power to declare entire categories of
records exempt from disclosure under the FOIA, including all files relating
to "counterintelligence," "terrorism," and "organized crime." Although this
bill was decisively defeated, a compromise bill, S. 774, has been unanimously
approved by the entire Senate Judiciary Committee. Under S. 774, law enforcement records would receive a broader exemption and Secret Service
and "organized crime" information would be completely exempt. Use of
the FOIA would be restricted to citizens or permanent legal residents, and
requesters would be charged for agency time spent censoring documents.

What the president has not been able to accomplish directly, he has attempted to accomplish through "backdoor" amendments to the FOIA and by
executive orders. Backdoor amendments are possible because of the (b) (3) exemption to the FOIA, which allows agencies to withhold information that is
made secret by other federal law. (B) (3) amendments have the same force as
direct amendments to the act, but do not go through the usual FOIA oversight
committees. Instead, they originate in committees with little background in
the FOIA and who are often sympathetic to agencies proposing new restrictions. Notices in the *Congressional Record* do not indicate that a new secrecy
law is under consideration; no public hearings are held on them. They are

often attached to authorization or funding bills and thus slip through without discussion of their merits.

Two important foreign policy backdoor amendments have been passed in the last several years.

The Department of Energy (DOE) is rewriting regulations for a backdoor amendment designed to block public access to even *unclassified* information concerning all facets of nuclear power, from production, storage, and transportation of nuclear materials and weapons to the disposal of nuclear waste. The first set of proposed regulations was met with intense opposition by labor unions, universities, antinuclear activists, and six state governors. (Penalties for violation of this amendment include twenty years in jail and up to a $100,000 fine).

The Department of Energy has already issued a regulation limiting the dissemination of information that cannot be classified under present laws but is deemed "sensitive." The new category is "Unclassified with Deletion," and it joins Confidential, Secret, Top Secret, Restricted Data, Formerly Restricted Data, and National Security Information as possible grounds for withholding DOE documents.

At the same time, the Reagan administration has implemented a new policy concerning public announcement of underground nuclear testing. Since 1975, the government policy had been to announce all such tests. Now, however, only those tests designated as "large" will be announced. Because the trend has been toward smaller explosions in American nuclear testing, the policy will work to keep a growing number of such tests secret.

The Defense Department solicited comments on a proposal to implement legislation exempting from the FOIA *unclassified* technical data with possible military or space application. It is insisting on the power to censor the findings of nonclassified university research prior to publication.

Even the Export Administration Act, enacted to regulate the export of technical *devices,* is being interpreted to forbid the export of technical *ideas*.

These measures prohibiting the release of unclassified information are all the more troubling when viewed in the context of Reagan's executive order on national security information, governing the classification of government documents. For the first time in forty years, a president has issued a classification order providing less access to information, and more classification, than his predecessors. (Classified documents are not accessible under the FOIA).

Executive Order 12356 removed the need to show "identifiable damage" to national security through release of information, and eliminated the Carter order's test requiring the balancing of the public's interest in disclosure against the potential harm to national security through release. It lengthened the duration of classification, and eliminated the automatic declassification of docu-

72   ments after twenty or thirty years and empowered agencies to *reclassify* and recall previously declassified documents. Finally, it gave new agencies, such as the Environmental Protection Agency, the power to wield the classification stamp.

RUSH TO RECLASSIFY

The administration was so eager to take advantage of the new order's provision that it attempted to reclassify embarrassing or otherwise revealing information already in the public domain even before the order became effective.

On March 11, 1983, Reagan issued an "addendum" to his classification order. National Security Directive 84 (NSDD 84), "safeguarding national security information," imposed prior lifetime censorship, secrecy pledges, and lie detector tests on *any* government employee with access to classified information. Because NSDD 84 was issued as an "addendum" to an existing executive order, it did not have to be published in the *Federal Register* for public and congressional review and comment. There was an immediate dissemination of "contracts" by various agencies covered by the directive, containing clauses regarding lie-detector tests and lifetime prepublication review, and many government employees were forced to sign such agreements.

After widespread public outcry, Congress voted to temporarily block its implementation. However, it was not until October 20, 1983—seven months after its implementation—that the Senate voted 56–34 against lifetime censorship for government officials. In February of 1984, eleven months after the directive was issued, President Reagan advised Congress that he would suspend the two paragraphs of the directive regarding lifetime prior censorship and use of lie-detector tests. Although he said that those provisions "would be held in abeyance," he did not withdraw them entirely.

Immediately thereafter, agencies began disseminating an earlier 1981 version of a nondisclosure agreement, Form 4193. A General Accounting Office (GAO) study in 1984 found that 120,000 government employees, *excluding* employees of the CIA and the National Security Agency (NSA), had already signed lifetime censorship contracts on Form 4193.

Further, Steven Garfinkle, director of the Information Security Oversight Office, has been quoted as saying that the government will be able to obtain the same results in court, that is, lifetime prepublication review, against employees who have signed agreements even if those agreements do not expressly contain such provisions.

As of early 1987, Form 4193 was still in use. Thus, contrary to the stated will of Congress, and the requirements of the Constitution, government em- ployees continue to be forced to sign lifetime censorship agreements.

The administration was successful in lobbying the Agents Identities Protection Act ("Names of Agents Bill") through Congress. This law prohibits the disclosure of information that *could* lead to the identification of an intelligence agent, regardless of the public nature of the source of the information or the illegal or unauthorized nature of the agent's activities.

More recently, the CIA succeeded in obtaining a new exemption from the FOIA, allowing it to shield its "operational files" from public scrutiny. Operational files are those files that contain information on how the CIA organizes and carries out its covert action and intelligence-gathering activities.

These moves have resulted in a dramatic decrease in information released under the FOIA concerning the intelligence agencies and foreign and military policy.

Our right to know about other countries and peoples, and the impact of our foreign policy, have been curtailed by other government actions. The U.S. Supreme Court upheld the administration's ban on travel to Cuba. The State Department has repeatedly invoked the McCarran-Walter Act to deny visas to progressives from around the world. The administration has also confiscated publications, notes, and other materials from reporters and others returning from Cuba, Nicaragua, and Iran.

These restrictions on public access to information concerning foreign policy have been accompanied by a dramatic military buildup, increased military and covert intervention in the affairs of other nations, the unleashing of the intelligence agencies through executive order and attorney general fiat, and an unprecedented government assertion of unlimited powers in the name of national security.

The U.S. invasion of Grenada is one example of the government's approach. It was accompanied by secrecy unprecedented in modern U.S. history. Congress was not consulted during preparations for the invasion. Rather, it was "informed" just hours before the invasion took place, long after the marines were on their way.

No reporters were allowed on Grenada until days after the invasion began. Thus, the only available information came from U.S. government sources. During the first crucial days of the invasion the administration was able to win the battle of public opinion by controlling what information the public would have on which to base its opinions.

It was weeks before the assertions of the administration were challenged with facts gathered from independent sources, facts that directly contradicted the story told to the American people.

Reagan also issued an executive order on intelligence activities (E.O. 12333),

74   which authorizes domestic surveillance by the CIA and infiltration of domestic groups, and could be interpreted to authorize warrantless wiretaps if the attorney general finds probable cause to believe that such wiretaps are directed by a foreign power or the agent of a foreign power.

The executive order legitimizes the worst abuses of the intelligence agencies. Although the order prohibits direct assassination by the CIA, it does not prohibit the furnishing of weapons to such assassins, thus allowing the intelligence agencies to sidestep the EO's prohibitions against assassination. The order also does not prohibit torture, weather modification, the overthrow of governments, or the poisoning of wells and livestock. Given what we have learned about the past practices of the intelligence agencies, it is probable that they will read prohibitions on their activities narrowly and the lack of specific prohibitions broadly.

The order gives the intelligence community the right to

- conduct warrantless searches and seizures, including unconsented physical searches, mail and physical surveillance, theft, and in the case of the attorney general's determination that wiretaps are directed against a foreign power or its agent, electronic surveillance;
- launch operations against anyone associated with a "foreign" person or organization, for example, foreign friends, the United Nations, international peace and solidarity groups, churches, relief societies, and travelers;
- infiltrate and influence the activities of law-abiding organizations in the United States, without any need to suspect or allege illegal activities;
- use journalists, missionaries, academics, businesspeople, students, and others as undercover agents; and
- conduct secret campus research, if authorized by unspecified "appropriate officials."

Some have claimed that most of the activities permitted by Reagan's order are identical to activities permitted by the Carter and Ford executive orders on intelligence. However, there are major differences between Carter's order and Reagan's. For example, the new order reverses Carter administration policy by allowing the FBI to monitor and infiltrate press and academic groups on the "belief" that it is "necessary for national security."

It is important to note that the infiltration and influence of law-abiding organizations allowed by the order is predicated on a foreign intelligence/foreign counterintelligence rationale and a perception that a target organization is acting as the agent of a foreign power. But that restriction is not as limiting as it sounds. This administration has loudly proclaimed its belief that the Committee in Solidarity with the People of El Salvador (CISPES) and other solidarity groups, the church Sanctuary movement, and the antinuclear movement, are all national security threats and heavily influenced by foreign elements, and recent headlines have proven that the intelligence agencies have acted on this **75** belief in numerous instances.

Some critics of the Reagan administration have denied that the order authorizes warrantless wiretaps, although they have found many provisions of the order odious. A close reading of the order reveals that its language is vague enough to be interpreted to allow such wiretaps. The order appears to put the attorney general's determination of probable cause to believe that surveillance techniques are directed against a foreign power or its agent on a par with the Foreign Intelligence Surveillance Act (FISA) by authorizing the attorney general to approve the use of *any* surveillance technique under those circumstances. The order does not specifically require that the government request authorization to use such techniques from the secret court empaneled pursuant to FISA if the attorney general has made his determination. Wiretapping is undoubtedly a covered surveillance technique, and if the attorney general can authorize wiretaps without a court order or permission from the FISA court, based solely on his determination of probable cause, the order authorizes warrantless wiretaps.

The signing of this order was followed by renewed intelligence operations including wiretaps (which increased by over 30 percent in one year of the Reagan administration), infiltration, and other illegal activities by law enforcement agencies. (Such activities may be "illegal" regardless of any executive order or legislation purporting to permit them. The Constitution and the Bill of Rights bind the executive branch, and a violation of the rights of the people protected by the Bill of Rights is clearly illegal).

Organizations such as the Fund for Open Information and Accountability (FOIA, Inc.) and the Center for Constitutional Rights were immediately besieged by groups following the implementation of the order, requesting help in filing FOIA requests to try to determine whether or not they were under surveillance or had been infiltrated. These organizations were experiencing problems similar to those faced by groups targeted for disruption in the 1960s —mail-tampering, phone problems, loss of membership lists, and disruptive influences at meetings.

The center filed a lawsuit against the order on behalf of a number of organizations, including church groups. The court case was dismissed by the judge, who said that the plaintiffs had to find a "smoking gun" in order to bring the case. The center established a special monitoring project to document the numerous instances of disruptive activity directed against progressive organizations since the EO's implementation.

More recent headlines provide documentary support for the intelligence agencies' renewed efforts. For example, the government's indictment of eleven defendants accused of conspiring to illegally transport Central American refugees into the United States was based largely on information gathered by paid government informants through infiltration of church meetings and Bible study groups and secret tape recordings of conversations with clergy and church workers. Another example is the 1984 intelligence agency infiltration of Washington, D.C., meetings of CISPES to obtain intelligence on planned sit-ins at a congressional office.

As for evidence regarding an increase in wiretaps, the following may be indicative: in 1981, before the order was implemented, there were 106 "legal" wiretaps (i.e., authorized by judges); in 1982, that number jumped to 130; in 1983, to 208; and by 1984, to 289 (a 38.9 percent increase from 1983 to 1984!). The new order was not the only reason for this increase. The Reagan administration's expanded definition of foreign intelligence was the basis for increased applications for wiretaps under the Foreign Intelligence Surveillance Act, which contributed to the dramatic increase. (These figures do not, of course, reflect the number of wiretaps that the administration may be conducting *without* court order.)

It is important to note that under the Carter administration, wiretaps decreased his first year from 137 (last year of Ford) to 77, and the number throughout his presidency remained fairly constant in the mid-80's range.

Not satisfied with the wide-ranging powers granted the FBI in this executive order, Attorney General William French Smith revoked the Levi guidelines in March of 1983. The Levi guidelines, instituted during the Carter administration, provided some degree of protection against FBI abuses.

The guidelines introduced under Reagan authorize investigations of political groups based on the mere advocacy of ideas, as well as the use of such highly intrusive techniques as informers or infiltrators during the preliminary stages of an investigation. They also allow the FBI to collect "publicly available information" from periodicals and similar sources concerning legal political activities of individuals and groups not even suspected of a crime.

When testifying in Senate hearings on the revised guidelines, FBI Director Webster and other administration officials, who were the only witnesses, could not name one concrete reason for the change.

The Reagan administration also revised the government's position in *National Lawyers Guild* versus *Attorney General*, FBI, *et al.* This suit forced the release of over 300,000 pages of FBI files documenting a campaign of harassment directed against civil rights and civil liberties attorneys.

These documents have revealed the FBI's definition of an "investigation": breaking and entering; warrantless, unauthorized wiretapping; physical surveillance; interference with public election campaigns; vigilante violence; defamation of character; trash-can searches; active participation in the work and decision-making of target organizations; the widespread use of informants; and identifying activists for "detention" in private concentration camps in time of undefined "national emergency."

In motions filed in 1984, the government argued that it is immune from suit for any actions committed in the name of national security, even if those actions are illegal or unconstitutional, and that courts have no jurisdiction to hear cases involving national security matters.

Further, the administration has claimed the absolute right to

- infiltrate organizations with informants;
- spy on anyone it claims is a potential national security threat, even if there is no evidence to support that claim;
- convince banks, landlords, health insurance carriers, janitors, and others to divulge confidential information to the FBI; and
- spy on citizens who maintain contact with foreign governments or individuals, or travel to countries of which it disapproves.

After seven years of pretrial discovery, the administration moved to dismiss the suit, arguing that, because decisions to disrupt and destroy the National Lawyers Guild were made by high government officials acting in the name of national security, they are immune from liability and outside the jurisdiction of the courts. If this argument is successful, citizens will be left with no legal redress against government violations of constitutional rights whenever the government claims national security motives.

The following quotation from the government's Memorandum in Support of United States' Motion for Partial Summary Judgment, pp. 88–90, is illustrative of the government's position:

> Decisions relating to this investigation were made by high-level officials of the Government balancing competing policy considerations. These decisions included Congress and the President's determinations to charge the FBI with investigating and gathering intelligence relating to national security, regardless of *whether a criminal prosecution would result;* the explicit Presidential authorizations, implemented by Attorneys General for decades, of *warrantless electronic surveillance* in national security investigations; implicit Presidential authorization to the FBI similarly to employ *warrantless entries* in such investigations; the decision of the Director of the FBI to infiltrate organizations subject to national security investigations with informants; and the decision of the Director of the FBI, known to and acquiesced in by Attorneys General, the President, and Congress, to disrupt organizations believed to be subversive by means of dissemination of information about the organization or its members. *Whether each of these decisions was wise, or even constitutionally valid, is not the point.* They were not ad hoc decisions arrived at negligently. They were deliberative

decisions, undertaken for a public purpose that required consideration of public policy. The United States cannot be held liable in damages for such policies" [emphasis added].

Not only does the government argue in these papers that it is immune from liability for damages for such policies, it further argues that the federal courts cannot even consider issuing equitable relief in this case because it *involves* national security (even though all the government's investigations never came up with any evidence to support its contention that the guild was a national security threat). The government argues that there are not questions of law for the courts to determine or enforce through injunctions in the national security arena—there are only questions of policy for Congress and the executive to resolve.

The fact that the government is defending its actions in this case despite the fact that at least twice during the course of its "investigations" the Department of Justice admitted that it could not document its contention that the guild was "subversive" is clear evidence that it believes that it should be able to take such actions without any evidence to support its claims.

The case has not been dismissed despite the government's motions, but it also has not yet gone to trial. As of early 1987, the case is still pending.

The FBI is also attempting to strengthen its ability to keep track of and limit lawful dissent, through a proposal to broaden the categories for inclusion on its national crime computer. Currently only those charged with or convicted of a crime may be entered on the computer. The FBI's plan would add the names of those considered to be "threats" to the president or to national security. The dangers of this plan are heightened by this administration's belief that activists and solidarity groups are foreign-controlled national security threats.

In April 1984 the president sent four bills to Congress, purportedly designed to slow the rapid growth of "terrorism." The administration unsuccessfully asked Congress for broad authority to prosecute U.S. citizens who aid any foreign government or group that the Secretary of State determines is involved in terrorism.

One proposed bill would have imposed prison terms and fines for people who provide training, "support services," and other assistance to any groups named by the Secretary of State. The terms of the bill were so broad that peaceful international solidarity work by churches in El Salvador, Nicaragua, and South Africa could be prosecuted.

Reagan's National Security Directive 138 allows U.S. military forces and intelligence agents to use preemptive strikes and reprisal raids against anyone thought to be planning operations against U.S. targets at home and abroad.

The public's right of access to information on domestic policies has also been drastically curtailed. In 1982, the Chamber of Commerce's major lobbying focus was the gutting of the FOIA. To accommodate them, the administration introduced S. 1730, which would have given businesses a virtual veto power over the disclosure of information relating to health and safety conditions in the workplace, industrial pollution, consumer fraud, and product safety. The compromise bill, S. 774, eliminates some of these proposals, but would require federal agencies to notify corporations when a request was made to see data they had submitted to the government. This provision could be used by corporations to delay or prevent the release of vital health and safety and other information under the guise of protecting "trade secrets."

In November 1986, the FOIA was amended by language tacked onto the Anti-Drug Abuse Act. The new legislation allows agencies to treat certain law enforcement records as not subject to the FOIA by "neither confirming nor denying" their existence. The records covered by this exemption include records of criminal investigations or proceedings; informant records of law enforcement agencies; and FBI records pertaining to foreign intelligence, counterintelligence, and international terrorism.

The legislation does not specify the language that agencies are authorized to use in response to requests for these records. However, agencies will undoubtedly interpret the new section as allowing them to respond untruthfully, that is, to lie about the existence of records.

The (b) (7) exemption for law enforcement records was also broadened. Confidential information supplied in a criminal or intelligence investigation may be withheld even if the confidential source is not the sole source of that information. Subsection (D) now specifically enumerates state, local, or foreign authorities and private institutions as potential "confidential sources."

The most significant amendment to this section is found in the threshold language. Formerly, the introduction to the (b) (7) exemption allowed agencies to withhold "*investigatory* records compiled for law enforcement purposes"; now *all* records compiled for such purposes are exempt from disclosure. That exemption was also previously limited to records that "*would* (A) interfere with law enforcement proceedings, . . . (C) constitute an unwarranted invasion of personal privacy, (D) disclose the identity of a confidential source . . . or (F) endanger the life or physical safety of law enforcement personnel." Now those records can be withheld if their disclosure "*could reasonably be expected to*" do so.

Despite the protestations to the contrary of Congressman Kindness, Senator Leahy, and the American Civil Liberties Union, the new language has already

80   had a negative impact on the availability of information under the FOIA. In
the first court decision interpreting the amendments, the federal District Court
for the District of Columbia allowed the CIA to withhold documents on the
Kennedy assassination originally provided to the House Select Committee on
Assassinations. In his decision, Judge Thomas Flannery wrote, "The amended
language of exemption (7) (C) creates a broader protection than had originally
existed under the old language of the statute."

A new fee waiver structure was implemented, granting automatic waiver of
all search fees for the media and organizations who can qualify as "educational
or scientific." The general public will be provided as a matter of right two
free hours of agency search time and one hundred free pages of copying. Any
additional fees can only be waived if the requester can show that the release
of the information is in the public interest and not primarily in their commercial interest. It is unclear what impact this new fee waiver language will
have on the restrictive fee waiver policy announced by the administration in
1983.

Agencies are also now prohibited from demanding advance payment for
records unless the fee is over $250 or the requester has previously neglected to
pay for released documents. They may not charge for indirect costs, for example, for time spent settling policy questions raised by requests. The Office of
Management and the Budget has been directed to establish guidelines for all
agencies to use in setting a uniform schedule of fees, which shall be "reasonable."

Although there are positive features to the new fee waiver language, the
amendment package represents a significant net loss for public access to information.

The (b) (3) amendment to the FOIA has been used extensively by opponents of the FOIA to sneak in backdoor attacks on public access to domestic
policy information. The Consumer Product Safety Commission was given
an exemption that prohibits the disclosure of most information submitted by
manufacturers concerning hazardous products if the businesses object to its release. The information may become available only if the commission enforces
the law and issues a complaint or remedial action order.

Legislation has not been the administration's only means of preventing release of domestic information under the FOIA. One of the first acts of Attorney General Smith was to revoke the Bell guidelines issued under former President Carter. These guidelines ordered federal agencies to release information
requested under the FOIA unless it clearly fell within one of the nine exemptions to the act.

The new guidelines offered Justice Department legal support to agencies
refusing to release information unless the requester clearly had a right to the

information, shifting the burden of proof to the requester, who often does not
have access to the information needed to justify release.

In January 1983 the Justice Department issued a memorandum on fee waivers under the FOIA. The act provides for free release of information that would benefit the public interest, but the new policy lays out five criteria not contained in the act which substantially reduce the possibility of obtaining fee waivers for most requesters.

The five criteria are

- the material sought must already be the subject of "genuine public interest";
- it must "meaningfully contribute to the public development or understanding of the subject";
- the requester must have the qualifications to understand and evaluate the materials and the ability to interpret and disseminate the information to the public;
- the agency must make "an assessment, based upon information provided by the requester, as well as information independently available to the agency, of any personal interest of the requester"; and
- if the requested information is already "in the public domain," such as in the agency's reading room in Washington, D.C., there will be no fee waiver granted.

This fee waiver policy had an immediate detrimental impact on the granting of fee waivers by government agencies. It appears that the policy is being used to deny legitimate requests for information, or to make it so difficult or expensive to obtain information that requesters are discouraged from attempting to obtain information in the first place.

The administration has made other attempts to restrict public access to domestic information. The Environmental Protection Agency (EPA) eliminated 86 out of their 104 publications in 1981, saying they were "out of date." Other government publications on occupational safety, alternative energy, and the dangers of lead shot, among others, have been withdrawn from circulation and in some cases destroyed.

In August of 1982, the thirst for secrecy motivated a top EPA official to circulate a memo titled "How and When to Purge Divisional Case Files of Material Which Could Prove Embarrassing if Released Under an FOIA or Congressional Request." At the same time, then-EPA Director Ann Gorsuch Burford refused to turn over subpoenaed information to Congress, and the attorney general invented a new category of classification, "enforcement sensitive," to justify her refusal. Unknown numbers of EPA documents were shredded in order to avoid their contents coming to light. Other agencies also refused to submit information requested by Congress, perhaps fearing that the requested documents would reveal conflicts of interest and dereliction of duty.

82   Former Secretary of the Interior James Watt was cited for contempt for refusing to turn over documents on the government's complicity in the destruction of public lands for the benefit of corporate interests. Several federal agencies, including the Justice Department, have consistently refused to submit to the U.S. Civil Rights Commission information on their equal employment opportunity compliance. The attorney general refused to give the House Post Office and Civil Service committees information they requested on the president's Private Sector Survey on Cost Control.

Laws and regulations regarding workplace health and safety, consumer product safety, and equal employment were established after public outcry about countless episodes of tainted food, dangerous drugs, dangerous workplaces, polluted air and water, and employment discrimination. A government that was working to combat those problems would want the public to know about its efforts. A government that was not fulfilling its regulatory obligations might understandably oppose the release of information that could document its failures.

The regulatory agencies under Reagan have not only failed to regulate, they have actively conspired with corporations to allow and cover up toxic waste dumping, falsification of test data on drugs and toxic chemicals, the production and distribution of unsafe products, and the weakening of civil rights enforcement.

To prevent conscientious government employees from alerting the public, the administration has restricted their First Amendment rights and attacked them for upholding their civic responsibility.

Because the president's executive order on classification increased classification and gave additional agencies the classification stamp, thousands of additional government employees are now subject to prior censorship. The Department of Energy (b) (3) amendment restricting the release of information on nuclear energy contains a provision directed at government employees providing for penalties of up to twenty years in jail and up to a $100,000 fine if they are courageous enough to warn the public about nuclear dangers.

The Agriculture Department has instituted political loyalty tests on university scientists who provide expert advice on the quality of grant applications. The Department of Education conducted security investigations on more than six hundred employees in their civil rights division until two employees won a court case banning those investigations two years after they were initiated. Middle-level employees are being subjected to polygraph tests whenever a "leak" of information is discovered.

The Supreme Court held recently that the Constitution does not necessarily protect public employees from discharge for complaining about mismanagement of the agencies for which they work. This was good news to an administration that has made a habit of eliminating even career officials for not toeing the secrecy line.

LACK OF GOVERNMENT
ACCOUNTABILITY

An examination of the information the administration has tried to keep secret reveals the true purpose of this secrecy—to hide from the public the evidence of their lack of accountability. Three examples serve to illustrate this assertion.

(1) Women Employed, a Chicago-based nonprofit organization, was forced to sue the Equal Employment Opportunity Commission (EEOC) and the Office of Federal Contract Compliance Programs (OFCCP) for information on their relaxed enforcement of equal employment laws, although they had routinely been granted such information under the Carter administration.

When they reviewed the performance statistics and internal reports they obtained through their suit, they were able to document the Reagan administration's dismantling of federal enforcement of equal employment opportunity laws. Their study, "Damage Report: The Decline of Equal Employment Opportunity Under Reagan," reveals startling and damning statistics:

- the average benefit to victims of discrimination is at its lowest level since 1976, reflecting a one-year decline of over 43 percent;
- the length of time for processing individual charges is nearly double the amount of time cases took in the last year of the Carter administration;
- the number of equal employment cases filed in court by the EEOC has declined by more than 70 percent;
- the OFCCP, the agency responsible for ensuring that federal contractors do not discriminate, has decreased its compliance review activity. In 1982, it completed only 56 percent of its projected reviews, a substantial decrease from the previous year. The number of administrative complaints and conciliation agreements has also decreased.

(2) After a four-year battle and a successful court suit, Common Cause obtained copies of the audits of ten major defense contractors' Washington offices. Although significant portions of the audits were deleted, the documents clearly show a pattern of defense contractors charging their lobbying costs against government contracts, thus forcing taxpayers to foot the bill for corporate lobbying for expensive weapons systems, and even entertainment for corporate executives and their friends.

(3) Probably the best example of the use of secrecy to hide unaccountability

84   can be found in the Occupational Safety and Health Administration (OSHA). Two recent studies, using data pried from OSHA under the FOIA, document the dangerous approach to workers' and community health and safety adopted by the Reagan administration.

Poisons on the Job, by the Sierra Club, outlines the government's program of (1) weakening existing health standards, (2) failing to enforce other standards, as evidenced by a 55 percent drop in response-to-complaint inspections, an 86 percent decline in follow-up inspections, and a 77 percent decrease in penalties, (3) delaying new regulations, such as those recently implemented by court order protecting the health of farm workers, and (4) covering up its inaction.

Reagan in the Workplace: Unraveling the Health and Safety Net, a study released by the Center for the Study of Responsive Law, reveals that the number of workers covered by OSHA inspections has gone down by 41 percent since Reagan took office. The study documents the implementation of a "cooperative" relationship between business and government that has resulted in a policy of responding promptly only to complaints that are likely to cause immediate death or injury. Funds for worker education programs have been slashed, whereas millions of dollars have been spent on "voluntary compliance" programs.

Other documents released through the FOIA have revealed that the former head of OSHA, Robert Rowland, who presided over this dismantling of the OSHA program and personally intervened in several major cases, had a personal financial interest in doing so. He owns stock in eight corporations affected by OSHA regulations of formaldehyde, ethylene oxide, and benzene—all toxic chemicals for which strengthened regulations were delayed by OSHA.

CONCLUSION

It seems clear that this administration would prefer to shroud its foreign and domestic plans and actions in secrecy rather than to submit to the public scrutiny and debate that should be the identifying features of a democracy. This is particularly puzzling given the "mandate" of the last election, where the president posted a lopsided victory. It may be that the administration is not certain that the public supports its restriction on the rights of workers and the public and expansion of the rights of corporations and the government. Perhaps President Reagan is familiar with the words of Thomas Jefferson:

"Whenever the people are well-informed, they can be trusted with their government, for whenever things go so far wrong to attract their notice, they can be relied on to set things right."

Depending on what each and every one of us does in the coming years, the story of this decade can either be another chapter in the book of government atrocities and threats to our lives and liberties *or* the story of our attempts—and successes—to set things right.

[Janet Raloff]

5

COMING: THE BIG CHILL?

For years, the Reagan administration has been stepping up its campaign to counter foreign espionage. These efforts have tended to focus on increased surveillance and prosecution of suspected spies and on a strengthening of national security controls affecting the "export" of technologies believed to be militarily critical. But several measures launched quietly over the past year go beyond these. In the view of some, they threaten to overstep the statutory powers of the United States' national security agencies.

Among the measures in question are the following:

- The recent visits to commercial data-base vendors by teams of national security officials. The stated intent of the visits—which were widely viewed by the recipients as "intimidating"—was to suggest that these private businesses begin voluntarily restricting the unclassified data (including newspaper articles, publicly released government reports, and congressional-hearings transcripts) they sell to foreign subscribers.
- A new Department of Energy (DOE) program aimed at discouraging scientists at national laboratories from sharing unclassified research data.
- The recent revelation that NASA has compiled what it calls a "No-No List" aimed at preventing people involved in foreign technology-exchange programs, including U.S. academics, from subscribing to an unclassified federal publication. Although the list may not be new to this administration, it came to light only in the past few months and is a reflection of current administration policy.

One thing these programs share is the potential to impose a "chilling effect" on the free flow of nonclassified scientific information, says Robert L. Park, executive director of the public affairs office of the American Physical Society. Park is a leading critic of government controls on nonclassified data. Not only does he question the utility of such controls in keeping new technologies out of the hands of the Warsaw Pact, but he also sees them threatening "to hold back our own [U.S.] research program."

"To a very large extent," says Park, "the work force we'll be keeping ignorant will be our own."

One of the new programs to slow the flow of U.S. technical data to the Soviets is known as SAFE—Security Awareness for Employees. Launched at Lawrence Livermore National Laboratory (LLNL) in Livermore, California, last year by the Department of Energy, it is the prototype for a program that is expected ultimately to be implemented throughout the rest of DOE's laboratories and contractors. SAFE not only aims to acquaint laboratory scientists with the notion that they may inadvertently become the targets of potential recruitment by Soviet agents, but it also teaches them how foreign spies operate, what they want, and how they can be foiled.

To bring home the message, the program provides video presentations, such as "The KGB and You," and talks by such guest speakers as a Soviet defector and the director of intelligence and counterintelligence for the National Security Council.

According to a staff announcement on the program circulated among laboratory managers last year, "The insider threat is defined as something an employee may do, either wittingly or unwittingly, to jeopardize the laboratory and national security. This threat runs the gamut from deliberately selling or giving away classified information to innocently providing unclassified information which may complete a part of a classified puzzle." (Livermore officials refused to discuss the program with *Science News*.)

There is also another goal, one not stated in the official handouts. As explained to *Science News* by Edward V. Badolato, then assistant secretary for security affairs at DOE and one of the designers of the SAFE program, "We want to put the fear of God in them [DOE scientists]." Talking informally after a Heritage Foundation seminar in Washington, D.C., on the use of Soviet scientists for information gathering, Badolato voiced concern about what he sees as the dangerous naïveté of U.S. scientists in dealing with Eastern Bloc colleagues.

Many DOE scientists, he says, don't seem to know whether their unclassified work is subject to export controls, and so they might accidentally reveal too much to a foreign colleague during casual conversation. With DOE's stepped-up security awareness program, he says, scientists would be informed that such ignorance would not protect them against felony prosecution if they were caught. This knowledge should make them think before they talk, and

88   should curtail discussion of many of the research details they might otherwise openly share with friend and foe alike, Badolato says.

If the scientists encouraged to participate in this program were only those whose work is classified, or unclassified but subject to export controls (SN: 1/24/87, p. 55), then DOE's SAFE program might prove both educational and beneficial, says Park. But, he charges, if the SAFE program includes laboratory personnel whose work is not subject to censoring controls, then it risks "imposing on them a chilling effect" with regard to the normal free flow of scientific information. One national security official at DOE told *Science News* that this program is widely directed to all DOE laboratory personnel.

Even among scientists whose work is subject to export controls, Park says, it behooves DOE to alert them to that fact and to tell them why their work is controlled. The agency does not do this.

But Sidney Stembridge, who coordinated LLNL's SAFE program until his retirement last March, has justified the program, saying, "We do know that [LLNL] has been 'targeted' by certain foreign intelligence agencies. We do know that a number of employees and contract workers have been approached. And the DOE assumes, for planning purposes, that each DOE facility has at least one insider [internal spy]." Stembridge's remarks were printed in *Management News Notes*, an internal LLNL publication. He declined to be interviewed by *Science News* on the SAFE program. DOE also has declined to offer additional information about the extent of spying at its facilities, including LLNL, or to furnish the names of any employees approached by foreign agents.

The SAFE program is not very visible outside LLNL. But some who have heard of it are concerned about its potential for encouraging more self-censorship than national security laws require. In fact, Park maintains, "I think they [DOE] have used uncertainty all along as a kind of weapon"—to pose not only the implied threat of possible legal action, but also the implied threat that a scientist's research contracts through the agency might not be renewed. For this reason, he sees DOE's SAFE program as potentially ripe for abuse by the administration's national security apparatus. Regarding Park's comments, an official of DOE's defense programs office—which oversees the SAFE program—told *Science News*, "It's not appropriate for us to give you a comment."

Another recent administration initiative responsible for sending shivers through much of the commercial data industry came to light as national security officials began visiting private business leaders to propose new restrictions on the commercial packaging and sale of nonclassified information.

Jack W. Simpson, president of Mead Data Central, which is based in Dayton, Ohio, learned of the proposal last year through "suggestions" made to him during four visits by members of the Department of Defense, Federal Bureau of Investigation, Central Intelligence Agency, and National Security Agency.

At an information Industry Association meeting last November, he described these "friendly" meetings as "involving only suggestions and questions. But their ultimate intent," he said, "is absolutely chilling."

The discussions involved how best these agencies might implement new measures consistent with National Security Decision Directive 145, or the National Policy on Telecommunications and Automated Information Systems Security. Portions of the ten-page directive, issued in September 1984, deal with how to safeguard nonclassified data in private data bases. For example, it says, when doing so would benefit national security, "the private sector shall be encouraged and advised, and where appropriate assisted," by the federal government in adopting new data-security measures.

What kinds of data were envisioned as falling under this directive? Potentially the kind Simpson's company now sells—the texts of unclassified government reports, newspaper articles, wire-service stories, or other documents typical of what might be found at a public library.

The directive says that "such information, even if unclassified in isolation, often can reveal highly classified and other sensitive information when taken in aggregate." To protect this, NSDD 145 proposed a new category of controllable data: "sensitive but unclassified government or government-derived information, the loss of which could adversely affect the national security interest." According to the White House directive, this information "shall be protected in proportion to the threat of exploitation and the associated potential damage to the national security."

The commercial information industry had few clues as to whether or how the federal government intended to implement NSDD 145 until high-level national security officials began making the rounds and talking to owners of some of the nation's biggest commercial data bases last year.

Simpson says those officials asked whether he might consider restricting the sale of any sensitive but unclassified data he might have to Eastern Bloc customers. They asked whether, alternatively, he would consider instituting on-line monitoring of various customers' requests so that subscribers interested in potentially sensitive subjects might be surreptitiously identified.

Their concern, Simpson recalls, was that even though a newspaper article might contain only a piece of a puzzle, if that article is sold along with the texts of related items, such as government reports, speeches, or congressional hearings transcripts, the sum might turn out to be more dangerous—and therefore more in need of controls—than the individual pieces.

This decades-old concept is known as the "mosaic or compilation theory," explains Steve Garfinkel of the General Services Administrations' Information Security Oversight Office. His department seeks to prevent abuse of the federal classification system. In the past, Garfinkel says, mosaic theory has been

90   used to justify only the *classification* of data—not restrictions on the publication of *unclassified* material.

But an October 29, 1986, policy statement on data-base security by John Poindexter, the recently resigned White House national security adviser, suggests that evolving administration policy indeed intended to extend mosaic theory. Specifically, it says that the "disclosure" of "sensitive, but unclassified information . . . could adversely affect national security or other federal government interests." To protect those interests, the statement requires the director of the CIA to identify such information and to establish "the protection required for such information." It also calls for the development, funding, and applications of new security measures or systems "as appropriate, to satisfy [these] security or protection requirements."

Garfinkel says that if mosaic theory were used to justify controls on material the government concedes is unclassified, it would constitute a major broadening of this concept's administration, and one he says he has always assumed would be legally unenforceable.

But not necessarily unthinkable. He notes that in the past few years several government agencies "have taken [this theory] a little bit farther than it's ever been taken before." And in at least one or two of those cases, he told *Science News*, "they've taken it too far," necessitating behind-the-scenes moves by his office to redress the situation.

The American Civil Liberties Union (ACLU) believes the administration also anticipated that its expansion of mosaic theory would be legally unenforceable, and therefore resorted to merely "suggesting" that commercial data vendors like Mead Data Central voluntarily control their data. Voluntary enactment of such measures, says Jerry Berman, chief legislative counsel in the ACLU's Washington, D.C., office, would get around the need to test their legality.

But Simpson had no intention of offering Mead Data Central's voluntary compliance. Nor did the Information Industry Association (IIA), a Washington, D.C.–based association of 460 private companies that specialize in disseminating computer data. In a Dec. 17, 1986, letter to Defense Secretary Caspar Weinberger, IIA president Paul G. Zurkowski charged that "certain persons within the U.S. defense establishment—in a manner that is inconsistent with democratic principles and law—are attempting to restrict or monitor citizen access to unclassified information now available to the public. Such restrictions on the flow of unclassified information could severely limit the information available to citizens, have a chilling effect on those who wish to acquire information, restrict our nation's technological development, and hinder the ability of U.S. companies to do business."

A January 9 response by Donald C. Latham, chairman of the Defense

Department's National Telecommunications and Information Systems Security Committee, said "the scope, purpose and applicability of the policy is being misunderstood." But the letter did not assuage IIA's concerns nor the ACLU's.

IIA pointed out, for example, that Latham's letter not only contradicted previous statements he had made before Congress on the intended scope of new NSDD 145–based controls, but also ignored IIA's concern about controversial recommendations contained in a new, classified air force study. Simpson says the national security officials who visited data-base vendors last year mentioned that their suggestions for new controls had been spurred at least in part by recommendations in this study.

David Y. Peyton, director of government relations for IIA in Washington, D.C., says he has "been told by people who have read the air force study" that it makes twenty-seven recommendations for protecting sensitive information stored in electronic-data-retrieval systems—including commercial ones. Among the most troubling, according to IIA, is a recommendation that commercial data vendors restrict their foreign sales of unclassified data to licensed customers. Currently, they can sell these data freely to all.

On March 17, apparently responding to pressure from the IIA and others, Frank C. Carlucci III, newly appointed as the administration's national security adviser, delivered a letter to the House Subcommittee on Legislation and National Security of Congressman Jack Brooks (D-Texas). It said that the administration was not only withdrawing Poindexter's October 29 policy statement, but also reconsidering the need for NSDD 145 and its new category of "sensitive but unclassified information."

Though IIA and the ACLU's Berman view this as a triumph of the concerted public campaigning they launched over the issue, neither is satisfied with the gesture. Peyton of IIA says the problem of which restrictions might be imposed on commercial, nonclassified data "isn't solved by any means." He notes that a nonclassified summary of the air force report still is not available, FBI counterintelligence agents are still making intimidating visits to IIA member companies, and NSDD 145 and "its shadowy definition of sensitive information remain in effect."

Finally, there is the case of Michael Radnor, director of Northwestern University's Center for the Interdisciplinary Study of Science and Technology (CISST), in Evanston, Illinois. Late last year he learned that NASA had included his name on its little-known "No-No List," an informal compilation of individuals and companies that would not be allowed to subscribe to *NASA Tech Briefs*. The ten-times-yearly magazine, available free to some 150,000 U.S. scientists, engineers, and businesses, offers nonclassified descriptions of new technologies resulting from NASA research.

92   The existence of the list was revealed late last year by IIA in an announcement to its members and to the public. IIA provided *Science News* with the list and an accompanying cover letter, signed by Walter M. Heiland, manager of NASA's Technology Utilization Office, describing the listed parties as having ties with foreign countries, firms, or agencies. Radnor's offense, according to the list, was that CISST ran a technology-transfer program with Japan. Funded by the state of Illinois, this program seeks out foreign technologies of possible use to Illinois businesses.

Radnor notes that while Heiland initially denied the existence of a "No-No List," he later promised to take Radnor's name off it once he learned CISST was sharing Japanese data, not U.S. technologies. When Heiland was questioned by *Science News* about the list, he responded, "There isn't really such a thing." But he then acknowledged that a list does exist, that Radnor's name "got on the list through a misunderstanding" and that the list "reflects NASA policy . . . that documents and services available through the [NASA] Technology Utilization Program are not available to requesters outside the United States or their in-country representatives." Heiland added that such lists have existed for twenty years, but that their distribution has always been "internal."

This has not placated Radnor. He says he considers the listing carelessly prepared (since its compilers never checked with Radnor's group to discern which country's technology was getting transferred), "extralegal" (because it attempts to place controls on unclassified, nonsensitive data), and "immoral" (by impugning Radnor's character—as a potential foreign agent—to any recipients of the list). Even if the listing were legal, Radnor says, it is "stupid," since anyone prevented from subscribing to *NASA Tech Briefs* can get the magazine at their local library.

After initially asking Heiland to send a retraction to all original recipients of the list, and getting no response, Radnor is now having the university's lawyers petition their senators to investigate this matter.

Berman, who directs the ACLU's Project on Information Technology and Civil Liberties, says the three programs described here are not isolated instances, but part of a "broad, stepped-up attack by the Reagan administration to control scientific and technical information in the name of national security."

He is also concerned, he says, about the recent participation of CIA and National Security Agency officials in visits to data-base vendors. Their "suggestions" about voluntary monitoring of who gets access to unclassified data indicate an interest in domestic intelligence surveillance—perhaps, he says, with an eye toward extending that surveillance beyond what is now permitted by law.

"These are very troubling times," says Mead Data's Simpson. It is the classic battle of national security versus freedom of speech, he says, and security is winning. Berman agrees, adding that "in the face of government pressure and in the current legal environment, the scientific community has read the writing on the wall and has moved increasingly toward self-censorship."

Simpson would look to the Congress for relief. Berman would look to a political consortium of the affected parties. But Stephen Gould, project director of the American Association for the Advancement of Science's program on scientific communications and national security, would throw the responsibility for motivating change back into the lap of the research community. "It is the unwanted responsibility of the research community to document the costs of regulation," says Gould, "and seek relief if serious disruptions in the advancement of science and technology can be proven."

[Stephen H. Unger]

6

A PROPOSAL TO LIMIT

GOVERNMENT-IMPOSED SECRECY

INTRODUCTION
A Pseudo-conflict

It has been argued (for instance, by Admiral Inman[1]) that the question of determining the extent to which scientific and engineering knowledge should be kept secret must be determined by balancing the rights of scientists and engineers against the needs of national security. This formulation of the problem is seriously misleading. There is actually no significant conflict between national security and the rights of those who develop and apply scientific and engineering ideas. On the contrary, both of these interests are best served by the openness that characterizes basic American traditions and the scientific process. Secrecy, with few exceptions, undermines the national security by impeding progress in the development of the technology that is one of its important pillars.

The free exchange of knowledge among scientists and engineers is a key factor in promoting progress. An integral part of the scientific process is the publication and wide dissemination of new ideas, discoveries, and experimental results. By this means, critics may detect errors or faulty reasoning, point out possible improvements, or confirm the validity of what was done. Colleagues (often complete strangers) may suggest solutions or alternative approaches to

Reprinted from *IEEE Technology and Society Magazine* 2 (December 1983), pp. 3–6, by permission of the author and the publishers. Copyright 1983 by IEEE.

problems raised. They may find applications other than those that the author had in mind—sometimes in entirely different fields. The mention in a technical paper of unsuccessful approaches to a problem helps others avoid wasting effort in exploring blind alleys. Publication of successful solutions to problems makes it unnecessary for others to expend time and energy in solving them again, although it is common for a solution to inspire others to find better, often simpler, solutions to the same problems. They may also generalize published solutions to cover broader classes of problems.

Both those who publish results and those who read about them profit. Science is a vast cooperative enterprise in which the free communication of ideas is a crucial element. The wider the community to which ideas are exposed, the more effective is the process. One may also use the analogy of a free market of ideas in which the good ones tend to prosper and the defective ones are discarded (or mended).

But why should we permit the fruits of American research and development efforts to be used to improve the quality of the Soviet military establishment? Don't they benefit greatly by using technology originated by us? Wouldn't we be more likely to retain our technological superiority in weaponry if we curtailed the dissemination of information in areas of technology most relevant to military systems?

First, there is no doubt that a great deal of technology originating in the United States has been utilized for military purposes by the Soviet Union. This follows from the fact that we have been in the forefront of scientific and engineering progress since World War II, particularly in the related areas of electronics and computers. It is not possible to build any advanced military system without utilizing concepts developed by Americans.

It therefore follows that, if we could somehow shut off, or even significantly attenuate, the flow of technological knowledge between the United States and the USSR, weapons (as well as general industrial) development in the USSR would be slowed. But this does not necessarily mean that we would thereby increase our lead in technology. There is no way to block the flow of information to the Soviets without also seriously restricting the flow of information within the American technological community. The probable result would be that the damage at home to the scientific process outlined above would slow our own progress more than it would slow theirs. A significant factor here is that a large portion of material published in the journals of the technological leaders is on topics that are of little interest to those lagging behind, simply because the latter haven't yet reached the point where they could utilize the results discussed.

Another secondary harm that would result is that when certain topics are judged to be of sufficient importance to the national security as to justify being

96 subjected to censorship, those researchers in this country who have the freedom to choose the problems that they work on would tend to avoid those areas so as to escape the onerous burden of operating under a veil of secrecy. A rather different consideration is that the United States by no means has a monopoly on high technology. Unless Japan, Canada, and most West European nations followed the same restrictive policies, their effect would be severely limited. Efforts to pressure them into doing so, or to include them in the forbidden area could have serious detrimental effects on our international relations.

It is important not to overstate the importance of pieces of paper in conveying technological know-how. Those who have been involved in efforts to transfer technology to people in other organizations, within the same corporation, in other companies, or in other countries, agree that the job can seldom be accomplished by simply sending along documents. Hands-on training of personnel and personal visits to the receiving organization's facilities by the teaching organization's experts are generally necessary to get things going. This is the case even where hardware is conveyed along with documentation. Hence the idea that American know-how is being passed on to its rivals in the form of published papers is not a realistic one.

Is There Really Cause for Alarm?

Despite the fact that there have been no governmental efforts (until recently) to impede the publication of ideas in computers and electronics, the Soviet Union has lagged far behind in these fields, and there is little evidence that they are making significant progress in closing the gap. Interesting support for this assertion is contained in a 1982 CIA report.[2] It mentions that the Soviet Union was, at that time, beginning to get into full-scale production of LSI (large-scale integrated) circuits. Fully ten years previously, Hewlett-Packard began marketing sophisticated hand-held calculators utilizing LSI technology. The United States, Japan, and several West European nations have, for at least five years, been commercially producing chips containing many times the number of active elements incorporated in LSI chips; I refer here to VLSI (very large scale integration) technology. It is clear from this same report that, from a practical point of view, the most advanced Soviet use of Western ideas in electronics is in the form of imported equipment used in the production of integrated circuits.

Why are the Soviets so far behind, despite the fact that their educational system has, for a generation, been producing many more scientists and engineers than has ours? It is not because that system is of low quality; on the contrary,

scientists and engineers who have emigrated here from the Soviet Union, in- **97**
cluding recent graduates and students, appear to be reasonably well educated
by American standards. A factor generally accepted as an important part of
the explanation (though by no means the complete explanation) is the deeply
rooted and pervasive practice of secrecy. Within the Soviet Union, a compul-
sive concern with secrecy has severely hampered the cooperative aspect of the
scientific endeavor.

There is little reason to believe that the Soviets are threatening our lead in
high technology, and ample reason to have confidence that openness is likely
to continue to prevail over secrecy.

SCIENCE, SECRECY, AND PUBLIC POLICY

It has been argued above that impeding the flow of technological knowledge
is a counterproductive approach to a nonexistent problem. If the public-policy
implications of secrecy are examined, it becomes evident that the damage
wrought to the day-to-day working of the scientific process is reflected on
another level by similar damage to the democratic decision-making process.

A great many issues of national importance involve significant technological aspects. If information about the technology involved is made secret, then
a meaningful debate becomes impossible, and those who control the flow of
information can dominate the decision-making process. Their decisions will
be made without benefit of the same sort of critical exchanges that were described above in connection with the scientific process. There is ample historical evidence that a closed decision-making process is prone to all manner of
dangerous blunders. It is of course a basic premise of our own system that an
open, democratic process is the best way we know for minimizing harmful
error.

Should the present trend to clamp down on the flow of technological information continue, consider the effects on debates involving such critical matters
as the MX missile; acid rain; waste in Department of Defense procurement
practices; the use of satellite-based lasers for defense against ICBMs; the ability
to monitor arms control agreements; disposal of nuclear waste products.

It is clearly central to the concept of government envisioned by the authors
of the First Amendment that the information necessary for intelligent discussion of issues such as these be freely available.

Reference has been made to governmental efforts over the last several years to enlarge the realm of secrecy to encompass information developed outside the areas usually regarded as subject to secrecy, such as Department of Defense facilities or classified projects undertaken by DoD contractors. Only a few examples will be presented here; others can be found in the literature.[3]

In 1980 the Rohm and Haas Chemical Corporation filed a patent application for an improved storage battery that they had developed in their own laboratories with company funds. The response from the Patent Office was a secrecy order, issued at the request of the U.S. Army under the authority of the Invention Secrets Act. It took the company about six months to get the order rescinded, during which time all work on the battery was halted.[4]

In 1982, three papers based on work done at the Texas Instruments Corporation under an unclassified air force contract were submitted for presentation at an IEEE conference on reliability. They became the subject of a furor over secrecy.[5] Although the papers were on an unclassified subject, dealt with no military related matters, and had been approved for publication by the contract monitors, a different set of air force officials decided about a week before the conference (and after the conference proceedings, including the three papers, had already been printed) that the papers should not have been cleared. Strenuous last-minute arguments led to a withdrawal of the objections to presentation.

Perhaps one of the more absurd episodes occurred in 1976, when the distinguished Soviet physicist L. I. Rudakov delivered a series of lectures at a number of American research laboratories on his work in electron-beam fusion. One can only speculate as to why Energy Research and Development Agency (ERDA) officials chose to notify those at each host laboratory that the subject matter of Rudakov's lectures was classified so that the ideas he presented should not be disseminated.[6]

PROPOSED REMEDIES
Basic Principles

I suggest that the following basic principles be used as guides in formulating solutions to the problems discussed above.

1. Secrecy should be restricted to specific details of direct military significance that would, if released, be helpful to a potential enemy in replicating or

countering a useful American military weapon or system. For example, it **99** would be appropriate to classify the details of specific decoys to be associated with some class of ICBMs.

2. The need for secrecy should be balanced in each case against the value of releasing the information.
3. The burden of proof should be on the advocate of secrecy in each case.
4. In each instance where an item is declared secret, a time interval should be specified after which the case for secrecy must be made again or the item automatically becomes declassified.
5. There should be an appeal procedure, independent of the agency doing the classifying.
6. In order to facilitate accountability, and to discourage casual acts of censorship, written records should be kept justifying the case for secrecy in each instance.
7. Mechanisms should be established to deter the overzealous use of secrecy.
8. Provision should be made for congressional oversight of secrecy regulations.
9. No attempt should be made to restrict basic scientific and engineering knowledge or information important in assessing the efficacy or cost of a military system.

It would be a happy situation if those in the executive branch of government acted in a manner consistent with the above principles. Unfortunately, more than forty years of history make all too clear the fact that both military and civil administrators are unable to resist abusing the power to withhold information. (The disappointing lack of a positive response by the present administration to the very conciliatory approach taken by the Corson Committee[7] serves to underscore this point.) There is thus a pressing need for legislation to reverse a trend that, if left unchecked, threatens to stifle our scientific and engineering efforts under a veil of secrecy. What follows are two specific proposals aimed at restoring a balanced view of the role of secrecy in promoting the national security. The first deals with regulations such as the ITAR that derive from existing legislation, and the second concerns regulations derived from executive orders.

Clarifying Existing Laws

A few years ago, DoD official Larry Sumney said that "the ITAR, if enforced to the letter, would cover virtually everything done in the United States." He was referring to a combination of clauses and footnotes that, in combination, would require prior government clearance for publication of material on any

100   topic that was remotely relevant to a wide range of military applications. In the 1977 IEEE cryptology episode, an attempt was made to use just such provisions of the ITAR to coerce the IEEE into canceling the presentation of certain papers.[8] Although Sumney added that they have never been so applied, the fact remains that such regulations depending on the good sense of bureaucrats to avoid serious abuses have no place in our system. Even if not actually enforced, they may cause people to refrain from communicating information out of fear that some official may suddenly decide to apply them strictly.

It would clear the air if Congress were to pass a law explicitly stating that no provisions of the Arms Export Control Act, the Export Administration Act, the Invention Secrecy Act, The Atomic Energy Act, or any other legislation should be interpreted as authorizing restrictions on the dissemination of scientific or engineering information not derived from classified projects. In particular, the "born secret" concept should be stricken from all laws and regulations. (Rather than passing a single law, it may be necessary or desirable to amend each existing relevant piece of legislation to attain the same end.)

The result of such action would be to prevent further attempts by government officials to interfere with the dissemination of knowledge generated by people working outside areas clearly marked for security reasons as classified. Next, it is necessary to ensure that this restricted area not be made unduly large.

Controlling the Classifiers

The system under which information is declared classified grew up in a rather haphazard manner over a period spanning the administrations of perhaps nine presidents. Congress played essentially no role in its development. Now that it is evident that this system has profound effects on our nation's course as well as on the lives of its citizens, it would be highly appropriate for the Congress to remedy what is evidently an encroachment by the executive branch on its lawmaking powers as spelled out in the Constitution. I propose that legislation be enacted either to replace or to restrict executive orders pertaining to the classification of information. (I am addressing myself specifically to scientific and engineering information, although it may be desirable to cover the subject more broadly at one stroke.) In conformity with the aforementioned list of basic principles, the following points should be incorporated in any procedures for classifying scientific or engineering information:

1. Specific harm anticipated by release of the information to be classified must be described.
2. Specific harm considered if the information is *not* released must be described.

3. A clear case must be made for the proposition that more harm is likely to result from the release of the information than from its suppression.
4. Doubtful cases must be resolved in favor of openness.
5. The proposal for classification must include a time limit after which the information must be declassified or the case for classification made anew.
6. Classification must be applied to specific pieces of information—not to entire documents that may also deal with other matters that do not merit classification.
7. An appeal procedure should be set up outside the agency doing the classifying, for timely hearings of complaints about improper decisions to classify information.
8. The workings of the appeal process should be subjected to congressional oversight by means of periodic reviews, by a congressional committee, of randomly selected cases. Particular attention should be paid to principle 9—that is, that certain classes of information not be subject to classification. To facilitate this accountability process, each application of the procedures outlined above should be fully documented.
9. Those found responsible for repeatedly overclassifying information must be deprived of classification authority.

It should be evident that, if the above ideas are implemented, classifying technical information would entail considerable thought and effort. It would be done only where significant matters were involved, and abuses would be much easier to detect and correct. The result would be a great reduction in the amount of information classified. This is precisely what is intended.

CONCLUSIONS

The proposals made here depend on the premise that the harm done by secrecy is of a far-reaching and pervasive nature, and that it significantly outweighs the damage that might be wrought by an occasional instance where a particular piece of information proves to be of value to a real or potential enemy. No doubt one could cite real or hypothetical instances where the suggested procedures would fail to protect some piece of information to the detriment of the nation's security. But it must be understood that human institutions are inherently imperfect; no system can be expected to operate flawlessly. In particular, any system that attempts to prevent all instances in which useful information passes across an unfriendly border will inevitably wreak havoc within our own borders that will be far greater than the damage that it seeks to avoid.

An important contention in this article, and one widely accepted within the scientific and engineering community, is that all but the narrowest appli-

102 cations of secrecy are counterproductive to the national security, even if it is defined strictly in terms of military power. It would, however, be unfortunate if arguments against secrecy such as the present one were to lend credence to that definition. First, it would be understood that our national security involves important elements other than military strength: for example, our economic well-being and the health of our democratic institutions, factors that are also adversely affected by secrecy. Furthermore, given the enormous power wielded by the military establishments of the superpowers, it is highly unlikely that marginal improvements in the military technology of either would have any practical consequences.

The concept of openness, both in society in general and in the realm of science and technology, is not a fragile luxury to be enjoyed in tranquil times and abandoned when the going gets rough. On the contrary, it is a robust mechanism for coping with difficult matters, and its value is greatest in situations of maximum stress. It would indeed be tragic if a loss of nerve brought about perhaps by a distorted view of reality should cause our country to abandon what has been one of its principal sources of strength.

NOTES

1. B. R. Inman, "One View of National Security and Technical Information," *Technology and Society* 1 (September 1982), pp. 19–21.

2. "Soviet Acquisition of Western Technology," CIA report, April 1982.

3. Stephen H. Unger, "The Growing Threat of Government Secrecy," *Technology Review* 85, 2 (February/March, 1982), pp. 31–39, 84–85.

4. Lois R. Ember, "Secrecy in Science: A Contradiction in Terms?" *Chemical and Engineering News* (April 5, 1982), pp. 10–17.

5. Ellis Rubinstein, "Air Force Bids to Block Papers; IEEE Officers Stirred," *The Institute* 7, 1 (January 1983), pp. 1, 7.

6. William D. Metz, "Thermonuclear Fusion: U.S. Puts Wraps on Latest Soviet Work," *Science* (Oct. 8, 1976), p. 166.

7. Dale R. Corson (ch), "Scientific Communication and National Security," report by a panel under the auspices of the National Academy of Sciences, National Academy Press, Washington, D.C., 1982.

8. Gina Bari Kolata, "Cryptography: A New Clash Between Academic Freedom and National Security," *Science* (May 1, 1980), pp. 523–526.

[Donna A. Demac]

7

OFFICE OF MANAGEMENT AND

BUDGET: THE HIDDEN POWER

"To put across goals of a military build-up, tax cuts and a balanced budget," former OMB director David Stockman recounted in his memoirs, "called for trench-style political warfare." Reagan administration officials viewed themselves as warriors on the battlefield of Washington, ready to tear down the old and implement a new approach to governance.

At the center of this operation was the Office of Management and Budget. This agency within the White House became one of the leading power centers in Washington, the ultimate authority for programs of great importance to all sectors of society. Of lasting importance, OMB, by directing its efforts to essentially political ends, demonstrated that the relations between the federal government and many groups could swiftly be altered by the decisions of one agency with authority over budgets and government-wide information policy.

HISTORY

The OMB started out in 1921 as the Bureau of the Budget, the agency responsible for assembling and coordinating the funding requirements of the federal government. Under Franklin Roosevelt, it was moved from the Treasury Department to the office of the president. The Federal Reports Act of 1942 then put it in charge of clearing reports. Agencies were required to submit proposals for collecting data and were limited to activities that were not vetoed by the

104 bureau. Not long after this, in 1950, the bureau's responsibilities were again enlarged to include the coordination of federal statistical operations.

In the 1960s and 1970s, the government grew to include new nationwide social and economic programs, moved into important areas of occupational and environmental regulation, and became more involved in scientific research. Often overlooked is the fact that, on account of these changes, political issues were more and more raised through regulatory channels and the budget process at least as much as they were pursued through electoral politics.

During this period, officials in the executive branch perceived a need for some kind of central agency that would oversee the rapidly growing activities of government. In 1970, following extensive examination of this issue, Congress renamed the Bureau of the Budget and it became the Office of Management and Budget. Less than a decade later, the agency's role was again enlarged, as President Jimmy Carter sought to give the OMB an advisory role in decision-making by federal agencies.

Carter's plan was still in rough form when Congress designated the OMB as the coordinator of a legislative initiative to stem the growth of federal paperwork and improve the quality of the information collected by government. The Paperwork Reduction Act of 1980 was a turning point in OMB's evolution. The act created a new Office of Information and Regulatory Affairs (OIRA) within the OMB. This was given primary responsibility for achieving the act's objectives. Its duties included improving management of information resources within the government, oversight of federal statistical programs, enforcement of privacy protections, the introduction of computer technologies, and paperwork reduction.

In addition, the scope of the report-clearance function that had been assigned to the OMB's predecessor agency in 1942 was expanded. Under the Paperwork Reduction Act, all agency efforts to collect information from ten or more persons had to be approved by the OMB.

OMB IN THE 1980S

By the time Ronald Reagan was inaugurated in 1981, the OMB already had grown from its original role as federal budget accountant into a manager of information. But the Reagan administration had still wider ambitions for it; the OMB was called upon to play a central role in the administration's plan to drastically limit the scope of federal activities and to transfer numerous programs to the private sector.

Only two months into his first term, the president issued Executive Order 12291, which empowered the OMB to mold and supervise all the operations of the executive branch agencies. This order required agencies to clear proposed regulations with the OMB before publishing them in the *Federal Register* and to prepare regulatory impact analyses for most plans for new regulations, justifying any proposal in terms of the potential benefits versus the cost of the proposed regulation. Most important, it provided OMB with an opportunity to comment on, require revisions in, and, as often occurred, delay agency action.

In late 1984, OMB's hold on the regulatory process was again strengthened by a second executive order, #12498, which mandated the creation of a unified regulatory plan for the entire executive branch and gave the OMB director authority to review every regulatory activity "planned or under way," including the development of any documents that could lead to rule-making proceedings at a later date.

The purpose of these two executive orders was to allow the president's aides to intervene at the earliest possible moment in significant agency activities. Under the new procedures, federal agencies were required to advise OMB in February of each year of all plans for regulatory action for the forthcoming year. If OMB decided that an agency initiative would not be consistent with White House objectives, the agency plan was halted, unless it appealed successfully to the president.

By now, OMB was firmly astride three of the administration's priorities: a balanced budget, deregulation, and reduction of paperwork. At the hub of the wheel was OIRA, which soon became an Orwellian ministry of information. Desk officers at OIRA, assigned to review programs at specific agencies, vetoed forms, statistical studies, budget proposals and plans for new regulations. As in Orwell's novel *1984*, the bland, faceless nature of OIRA guaranteed machinelike efficiency and little public scrutiny.

OMB AND THE REGULATORY AGENCIES

Susan and Martin Tolchin, in their book *Dismantling America*, described how OMB intervention "created a new regulatory landscape, a still life actually, with the presidential agencies fearful of issuing new regulations." An example of this occurred in January 1986 when OMB vetoed plans by the Environmental Protection Agency to conduct a survey of the impact on public health of certain chemicals in drinking water. Nongovernmental studies had suggested

106 that there was a link between the ingestion of chlorine—which is often found in drinking water—and organ toxicity or cardiovascular disease. In disapproving this study, OMB indicated that deregulation was paramount: "What is the practical utility of the information? What will EPA do with either a positive confirmation or negative confirmation of a relationship in humans?"

In another instance, OMB disapproved a study proposed by the National Institute for Mental Health to assess the effects of federal budget cuts on certain patients' use of available health services and the actual link between outpatient and inpatient care. This study would have gone beyond standard evaluations obtained upon patient discharge from hospitals by tracking a sample of individuals over a year.

In rejecting this study, an OIRA desk officer wrote: "Disapproved. NIMH has not made a convincing case of the federal need for the data that would be produced from this study. This is particularly true in view of the absence of an administration position to expand mental health services reimbursement under the federal government health care financing programs. In addition, the NIMH proposal is not designed to 'minimize costs to the federal government' as prescribed in (the Paperwork Reduction Act)."[1]

As OMB pursued the administration's priorities, it often came into conflict with congressional objectives. A report of the Congressional Research Service concluded that the executive orders expanding OMB's authority effectively undermined congressional statutes and "are redolent with possibilities for secret, undisclosed, and unreviewable communications and contacts by parties interested in influencing the substance of agency action."[2]

During congressional hearings on the toxic waste program of the EPA, for example, OMB was accused of withholding essential information and of meeting secretly with industry representatives. The OMB resisted Congress's requests for information until this inquiry threatened to become a major national scandal. There were numerous other such instances involving OMB's efforts to delay or block agency action.

The central issue that regularly surfaced in heated exchanges between OMB and congressional oversight committees but was never fully resolved concerned the basis of OMB's authority. Congress had delegated a great deal of responsibility to OMB in the Paperwork Reduction Act, the Privacy Act, and other laws. Yet it did not give the OMB authority to supplant agency decisions. Nonetheless, as time went by it became virtually impossible to establish the limits of authority for an agency which, like an octopus, had arms extending from the highest level of government into virtually every sphere of life affected by federal policies and expenditures.

The budget process is an elaborate series of overlapping negotiations renewed each year when the president announces his blueprint for the allocation of the nation's resources. From start of finish, the president's priorities are being tested, even as valuable information is being provided in regard to his views on foreign policy, taxation, the military, and many other important issues.

After the Reagan administration took office, the OMB was given a mandate to make sweeping budget cuts, leaving no agency unscathed. In *The Triumph of Politics*, Stockman states that their plans called for a "frontal assault on the American welfare state . . . risky and mortal political combat with all the mass constituencies of Washington's largesse—Social Security recipients, veterans, farmers, educators, state and local officials, the housing industry, and many more."[3]

Large annual increases for the military and significant tax reductions early in Reagan's first term created a deficit that would make shrinking the operations of federal agencies, as well as large cuts in domestic spending programs, difficult to circumvent. The link between budget planning and deregulation was thus established for the long term.

The budget was also used to implement cutbacks in many research and information-dissemination programs that were an integral part of federal programs. Testifying before Congress in 1985, OMB Director James Miller highlighted as a major accomplishment of the administration the elimination of 3,800 government publications, or one quarter of all federal publications that existed in 1981. Many of these were publications which were no longer being published or were new pamphlets and reports that had been planned but then dropped. Their content ranged from consumer and health information to annual reports of agencies such as the Department of Housing and Urban Development.

In addition, several agency research budgets were subjected to large cuts each year. The Environmental Protection Agency was one of those that suffered most. For example, between 1980 and 1984, as environmental problems in most areas deepened, EPA's funding for research on air quality declined $25 million; for research on water quality, $60 million; for research on toxic substances, $15 million.

108 THE INFORMATION COLLECTION
BUDGET

Backing up the fiscal budget as a tool for implementing the Reagan administration's priorities was OMB's annual Information Collection Budget, yet another facet of OMB's multifaceted control. Each year, running parallel to the regular budget, but one year later to take account of regulatory changes, agencies submitted reports of their record-keeping requirements estimated in terms of "burden hours." OMB then designated "burden hour" allowances for each agency and assembled the comprehensive Information Collection Budget. This budget was reported to Congress as part of OMB's report on the Paperwork Reduction Act, though veto power on agency requirements lay solely with the OMB. In this way, the agencies' information activities could be trimmed, nearly always without public discussion or attention from Congress.

The OMB found the Information Collection Budget an effective management tool. Its main purpose was to limit the amount of time, measured in burden hours, that businesses and other organizations were required to spend filling out government forms. Indeed, the ICB was the primary source for the president's periodic announcements concerning the elimination of hundreds of millions of hours of government-required paperwork.[4]

Yet the significance of paperwork reduction needed to be weighed in terms of content as well as volume. In many cases, it was a signal that deregulation was creating information gaps in important areas of public policy.

For example, in 1983, both the Highway Traffic Accident Report and Accident Investigation Reporting forms were eliminated. The OMB calculated that each of these actions saved 18 million burden hours. Left unsaid was the fact that the elimination of these forms reflected a declining commitment to transit safety.

More generally, 56 percent of federal paperwork was associated with people obtaining federal benefits, including Social Security, Medicare, and disability payments. Here paperwork reduction touched upon tangible and immediate human need. The elimination of forms used to gather information could have serious negative effects. But the administration's boasts about eliminating paperwork typically failed to indicate who was expected to benefit from this and ignored the possibility that the agency involved might now be without information needed to carry out its legislated mandate.

THE PRIVATIZATION OF
GOVERNMENT INFORMATION

As the government's central manager of information, OMB was at the center of a historic debate concerning the transfer of information functions from the federal government to the private sector. Unknown to many people, during this century the government had become the primary provider of information about hundreds of subjects, including marketing trends, health care, housing, employment, agriculture, and more. However, in the 1970s, new technologies that processed information into new components and products had greatly increased its profit potential.

Many small and large corporations now saw great promise in moving government information functions into the private sector. On the other side were groups that maintained that the government had an obligation to provide certain types of information to the American public, especially about its own activities, and were concerned that privatization would mean that the price attached to large quantities of information would be prohibitive.

Reagan's policies aimed at eliminating numerous federal programs guaranteed that the trend toward privatization would be accelerated. OMB pressed this objective through general budget reductions that necessitated cutbacks in agency research, collection and analysis and through its own policy circulars.

In 1982, the president's budget blueprint for the next six years, "Reform 88," included plans for continuing big reductions in agency publications that had begun during Reagan's first months in office and stepping up efforts to transfer government information functions to the private sector. Soon hundreds of government publications were picked up by private firms. These included the *Morbidity and Mortality Weekly Report* of the Department of Health and Human Services, *The Car Book*, a widely read book on automobile safety, and the *Federal Statistical Directory*, as well as the regulatory notices and decisions of several federal agencies.

OMB'S CIRCULAR A-130
CODIFIES NEW RULES

Yet the administration's boldest move toward privatization took place at the end of 1985 when OMB issued a policy circular establishing sweeping new ground rules for government information policy, limiting agency information

110   functions to those that the private sector was unlikely to adopt.[5] At the time it was released, an editorial in *The Washington Post* observed that the new policy "would likely reduce the number of printed government publications available free to libraries or at low cost and increase the already widespread practice of private outfits interfacing with government computers and providing printouts for users at hefty fees."

In the circular, OMB recognized the importance to society of government information. The free flow of information from the government to its citizens and vice versa was said to be essential to a democratic society. Yet more emphasis was placed on the notion that government information is a commodity with economic value in the marketplace, and it was the administration's policy not to compete with the private sector in the provision of information.

In many respects, the circular only formalized what had been going on for five years. However, similar to the way in which the executive orders for the regulatory agencies had tied them to the OMB through procedural requirements, the information circular included numerous conditions that agencies had to meet before they would be allowed to collect or disseminate information.

Among these, agencies henceforth were to try to satisfy many new information needs through commercial sources before collecting or creating new information. They were also expected to show that the public and private benefits derived from government information would exceed the public and private costs of the new information program. The inclusion of such a cost/ benefit ratio greatly enhanced OMB's veto authority and suggested that it was creating a wall that agencies would find nearly impossible to scale.

The main problem with this circular was that it made sweeping changes while complicated issues were still being researched and discussed. Privatization of information originally paid for with tax dollars requires that decisions be made about how much business should be asked to pay for information received and whether conditions should be attached to private firms assuming responsibility to provide certain types of information to the public. Of greatest significance is the value of certain categories of information for public evaluation of government policies. Assessments must also be made of the value of hundreds of different categories of information that are central to the economy, to education, and to the nation's foreign policy. Finally, long-term projections are needed of the ways in which various sectors of society will gain access to information in the future.

Given its preoccupation with limiting the scope of government, the OMB was not the optimal agency to establish guidelines for government information policy in the new era of electronically generated information. As the agency established new rules and saw to their implementation, few people

were in a position to comprehend the ways in which OMB's new information-
management policy could be used to further the Reagan administration's vision
of a much narrower federal structure and the orientation of the government
away from service to the public. Such far-ranging changes were what Stockman referred to in his book as "frontal assault on the American welfare state"
and posed a lasting problem for those concerned about the preservation of
popular government in the Information Age.

MAGIC ASTERISKS AND STATISTICS

The gathering of statistics on many facets of American life has long been accepted as a primary responsibility of the government. Americans live in a
quantitative society. Numerical estimates are used to chart literacy rates, unemployment, poverty, and economic deficits. Today, more than ninety federal
departments are involved in the preparation of data that are used for economic
planning, housing programs, law enforcement, and many other purposes.

The importance of statistical activity was underscored by two high-level
studies produced in the late 1970s which recommended a strengthening of such
programs.[6] A major concern of these reports was that high-level policymakers
did not understand the extraordinary significance of statistical analysis. According to economist James T. Bonnen, director of a report on statistics for
the Carter administration, statistical programs "all too frequently flit rapidly
from one ideological goal, media or market event after another."[7]

This aptly describes the attitude of many Reagan officials. As Stockman's
memoirs attest, the Reagan administration typically viewed numbers as a plus
or minus for the president's image. As the deficit projections grew, devices
such as "budget plugs," "magic asterisks," and the "rosy scenario" were invented, as the following passage from *The Triumph of Politics*, describing Stockman's meetings with the president and others, indicates.

> "I had already casually moved the target date for a balanced budget
> from 1983, which Reagan promised during the campaign, to 1984. There
> hadn't been so much as a "what's *that* again?" from anyone in the White
> House. But then everyone's nose was so deep in paper they simply hadn't
> noticed.
>
> "But that was merely a straw in the wind compared to what would
> come next. I soon became a veritable incubator of shortcuts, schemes,
> and devices to overcome the truth now upon us—that the budget gap
> couldn't be closed except by a dictator.

"The more I flopped and staggered around, however, the more they went along. I could have been wearing a sandwich board saying: *Stop me, I'm dangerous!* Even then they might not have done so. . . . Bookkeeping invention thus began its wondrous works. We invented the "magic asterisk." If we couldn't find the savings in time—and we couldn't—we would issue an I O U. We would call it "Future savings to be identified." It was marvelously creative. A magic asterisk would cost *negative* $30 billion . . . 40 billion . . . whatever it took to get to a balanced budget in 1984 after we toted up all the individual budget cuts we'd approved."[8]

In describing such budget ploys, Stockman at various points stopped to say mea culpa, yet the action says all. The administration cared little for accuracy, even about something as vitally important as national expenditures.

Moreover, as part of its deregulatory objectives, the Reagan administration moved to confine federal data collection and analysis strictly to the needs of the federal government, abandoning numerous programs that indirectly benefited local governments and major institutions nationwide.

Under the Paperwork Reduction Act, OIRA was given responsibility for providing overall direction in the development and implementation of federal statistical activities. However, OIRA's response was to gradually downgrade its statistical branch, until it was abolished in 1982. For the first time in nearly fifty years, the federal government was without a central statistical unit.

A 1982 congressional report gave examples of nearly sixty statistical programs that had been eliminated or reduced under OIRA's supervision.[9] Three years later, a study of the Congressional Research Service confirmed that under OIRA's direction statistical programs, budgets, and personnel levels had all been cut back significantly.[10]

This decline in quality had become all too clear to organizations that used federal statistics. As Katherine K. Wallman, director of the Council of Professional Associations on Federal Statistics, said, "Those who have worked within the government's statistical system . . . have long stressed the irony of the inverse relationship between the growth in the scope and importance of our federal statistical programs and the decline in resources allocated for planning, evaluating and improving the products of the federal statistical agencies. Within the past two years, this anomaly has moved from the realm of chronic weaknesses to the domain of acute problems."[11]

The OMB's response to criticism in this area revealed an important disagreement over the importance in maintaining the federal government's central role as a provider of statistical information, a role that had expanded steadily over the last half century but which the OMB was seeking to confine. OMB officials subordinated statistical operations to deregulation and paperwork re-

duction. In addition, agency data collection was now supposed to serve the **113**
needs of federal agencies alone, not of states, local governments, or private
entities.

This approach was often challenged by leaders of industry and major institutions who argued that the federal government was the only reliable source of
data about national economic and social trends. Donald Woolley, chief economist of Bankers Trust Company, provided examples of the private sector's
need for federal statistics in his 1982 testimony before Congress. He said,

> We work with almost all of the banking and financial data compiled
> by the Federal Reserve System and the federal budget data provided by
> the Office of Management and Budget and the Treasury Department.
> But we also use regularly the Commerce Department's national income
> data and its data on retail trade, homebuilding, nonresidential construc-
> tion activity, manufacturing and trade inventories, business fixed invest-
> ment, and the U.S. foreign trade and balance of international payments
> data, much of which is compiled by the Census Bureau.[12]

Woolley's argument about the essential importance of government data was
also made by dozens of experienced statisticians and policymakers. Courtenay
Slater, former chief economist of the Department of Commerce, stated:

> Only the federal government can produce statistical series which are
> uniform and consistent for the nation as a whole and which are of un-
> questioned honesty and objectivity. The federal government also has
> a responsibility to produce statistical information for which there is a
> national need even if there is not a direct federal government need. State
> governments need information, uniformly presented, about other states.
> Private individuals and businesses need uniformly presented informa-
> tion on a wide variety of economic and demographic matters. The free
> market is a marvelous mechanism, but one of the preconditions for its
> effectiveness is the availability of information to participate.[13]

The changes in statistical programs carried out in the Reagan administration were of long-term significance. Data series need continual fine-tuning in
order to remain of high quality. Gaps in data collection and disruptions in the
recruitment and training of personnel could take years to reverse. Even over
the short term, the impact of major changes in government policy was harder
to assess without reliable data. At a time when major responsibilities were
being transferred to the state and local level, statistical information was more
essential than ever.

114 OMB'S NEGLECT OF PRIVACY PROTECTION

The Privacy Act of 1974 put the OMB in charge of monitoring the compliance of federal agencies with federal privacy laws and promoted individual privacy protection through rules of nondisclosure as well as procedures enabling individuals to seek correction of inaccurate information. A few years later, reflecting a perceived need for stronger protection, the Paperwork Reduction Act of 1980 included among the numerous tasks of the new Office of Information and Regulatory Affairs the issuance of updated guidelines for government-wide privacy protection and oversight of agency compliance with the Privacy Act.

Yet OIRA devoted little attention to this important area. Few new privacy regulations were issued and no additional personnel were assigned to this area. Furthermore, the OMB actively supported Reagan administration initiatives that posed serious threats to individual privacy.

One of these involved the sharing of computerized information collected by different government agencies and private companies. This practice, which had begun on a small scale before Reagan took office, was expanded significantly after OMB withdrew related restrictions in 1981.

Before long, the names of welfare recipients were matched against federal payrolls. In addition, the Social Security Administration gave what was supposed to be confidential information on the whereabouts of thousands of people to the Selective Service, which was trying to locate young men who had not registered for the draft. And in 1984, several agencies were authorized to trade information with the bigger national credit agencies.

The administration's indifference to individual privacy could be seen in other areas as well. Polygraph testing, which had been limited almost exclusively to the military and intelligence agencies, was vastly expanded to include many more agencies and individuals, as part of the administration's efforts to tightly control the disclosure of information about its own activities. Indeed, in 1985 alone, 100,000 government employees were subjected to polygraph examinations!

In another area, wiretaps installed by the Reagan administration in criminal cases reached an all-time high in 1985. The highest level of wiretaps by U.S. attorneys before this, 285 wiretaps, had occurred in 1971, just before the Watergate revelations. After that, the number of wiretaps requested by the Justice Department dropped to around 100 a year and then increased sharply, beginning in 1983.[14]

While the OMB often was not the direct source of such privacy incursions, it was responsible for setting standards and for advising agencies on what policies to adopt. Thus, such practices as computer-matching and polygraph-testing were in fact encouraged by the OMB through its indifference to privacy rights and by policies that favored efficiency and control far more than they tended toward the protection of constitutional freedoms.

CONCLUSION

In 1981, the OMB took the power it had received from Congress to oversee the budget, paperwork reduction, statistics, privacy, and the complex web of regulatory information and carried it much further. It frequently overrode agency decisions and thwarted congressional objectives by subordinating regulation to the interests of industry. In other areas, including privacy, OMB ignored its legislated responsibilities.

Moreover, as more knowledgeable people were studying the complicated issues related to privatizing public sector information, OMB acted independently to accelerate this process, thereby endangering the existence and quality of many government programs as well as the public's access to information about the operations of government.

Yet perhaps most detrimental of all was the way in which this agency devalued the objective of open government in the name of efficiency and deregulation. Indifferent to the need for widespread dissemination of information about government, fond of meeting behind closed doors, and concerned almost exclusively with the interests of business, the OMB used its vast powers to seal the government off from many sectors of society that had only recently come to view the procedures and programs of the regulatory agencies as effective, and perhaps the only, means of trying to ensure that important issues were addressed.

Congress had not anticipated these results, but also did not act quickly enough to control the OMB's endeavors. One year into Reagan's second term, this superagency continued to exploit the authority conferred upon it by the Paperwork Reduction Act of 1980, albeit compelled from time to time to do more lobbying to assure continued authorization.

The day that separate assessments are made and standards are set to guide the enforcement of government information policy, the privatization of government information programs, individual privacy protection, and the many regulatory programs written into legislation, that will be the day the OMB is once again brought to heel as merely a subsidiary agency of the executive branch. Until then, the powers of the OMB are almost certain to work in favor of the tendency of the modern bureaucratic state to coalesce power unto itself.

1. A detailed record of OMB's involvement in agency rule-making proceedings can be found in the monthly reports of the Washington, D.C.–based organization OMB Watch, entitled "Eye on Paperwork: OMB Control of Government Information."

2. Congressional Research Service, *Presidential Control of Agency Rulemaking: An Analysis of Constitutional Issues That May Be Raised by Executive Order 12291*, 15 June 1981. For a longer discussion of conflicts that have arisen between the OMB and Congress, see Donna Demac, *Keeping America Uninformed* (New York: Pilgrim Press, 1984), Ch. 4, "Oversight Undermined."

3. David Stockman, *The Triumph of Politics: Why the Reagan Revolution Failed* (New York, Harper & Row, 1986), p. 8.

4. For example, State of the Union Message, January 25, 1984.

5. OMB Circular A-130, "Management of Federal Information Resources," December 12, 1985.

6. J. T. Bonnen *et al.*, "Improving the Federal Statistical Systems: Report of the President's Reorganization Project for the Federal Statistical System," *Statistical Reporter* 80–82 (May 1980): 197–212; J. W. Duncan and W. C. Shelton, *Revolution in United States Government Statistics, 1926–1976* (Washington, D.C.: Department of Commerce, Office of Federal Statistical Policy and Standards, 1978).

7. House Committee on Post Office and Civil Service, Subcommittee on Census and Population, *Impact of Budget Cuts on Federal Statistical Programs*, Hearing I, testimony of James T. Bonnen, March 16, 1982.

8. Stockman, *Triumph of Politics*, pp. 123–124.

9. House Committee on Post Office and Civil Service, *Impact of Budget Cuts* (report on hearings).

10. Congressional Research Service, *Recent Changes in the Coordinating of Federal Statistical Data Collection*, Washington, D.C.: Government Printing Office, April 8, 1982.

11. Senate Committee on Governmental Affairs, Subcommittee on Information Management and Regulatory Affairs, hearings, May 6, 1983, p. 99.

12. House Committee on Post Office and Civil Service, *Impact of Budget Cuts*, hearings, p. 43.

13. "Report of the President's Reorganization Project for the Federal Statistical System," Washington, D.C., p. 1.

14. *Privacy Journal* vol. XI, no. 8 (June 1985), published by Robert Ellis Smith.

[Steven Burkholder]

8

THE MORISON CASE:

THE LEAKER AS "SPY"

A lover of ships, Samuel Loring Morison may be imprisoned for the way he handled some secret photographs of one. He has been convicted of espionage, but he is no spy.

In late July 1984, Morison, the namesake grandson of the famed maritime historian Samuel Eliot Morison, sent to the British publication *Jane's Defence Weekly* three classified photos of the Soviet Union's first nuclear-powered aircraft carrier. The secret snapshots were taken by a U.S. spy satellite that flew over the Black Sea shipyard where the ship was being built. Morison, who was the American editor of *Jane's Fighting Ships*, a sister publication of the *Weekly*, had taken them from a desk at the Naval Intelligence Support Center in Suitland, Maryland, where he worked as a Soviet ship analyst. His $5,000-a-year job with *Jane's* was a moonlighting arrangement known to the navy.

That August, the military weekly published the photos with an article reporting that work on the 75,000-ton carrier had been speeded up. The photos were distributed by the Associated Press and on August 8, 1984, the *Washington Post* ran one. The next day, FBI and navy counterintelligence agents began tracing the leak. On October 1, authorities arrested Morison at Dulles International Airport as he was about to board a plane for what friends said was a long-planned vacation in England, as the *Post* reported.[1]

Morison was tried and found guilty of spying on October 17, 1985, by a federal court jury in Baltimore. He is the first person to be convicted under the U.S. espionage laws for leaking information to the press. He had "willfully" communicated and retained information that "could be used to the injury of the United States or to the advantage of any foreign nation," as the seventy-

118   year-old law reads. For those crimes and for theft of government property, Morison, forty at the time, was sentenced to two years in prison, a good portion of which he will have to serve if his pending appeal fails. However, as civil libertarians assert, much more is at stake than simply the fate of one man.

Since Morison's arrest and conviction, editors and columnists have condemned the government's action as a dangerously inappropriate application of the country's key anti-spying statutes, which date back to 1917. With one exception—the aborted prosecution of the "Pentagon Papers" leakers Daniel Ellsberg and Anthony Russo in 1971—government attorneys had never before attempted to use the espionage laws to prosecute government employees or others who provide classified information to the press.

Beyond that, critics of the prosecution writing in publications as diverse as *Publishers Weekly*, the *New York Times*, and the *Progressive* say that the action represents a fresh attempt to curtail public dialogue and debate in the name of national security. The conviction probably offered encouragement to Reagan administration officials long frustrated by what they see as a profusion of unauthorized leaks. Justice Department attorneys, in effect, had persuaded a court to legislate what Congress had refused to legislate for seventy years: a law approaching Great Britain's Official Secrets Act, which can lead to imprisonment of not only those who leak official government information but also journalists, authors, and publishers who print or broadcast that information. Finally, if the case goes to the Supreme Court, it may lead to the first constitutional test of the espionage laws in a case involving an unauthorized disclosure to the media.

At Morison's trial and in statements and documents relating to the case, defense attorneys and supporters of Morison described him as a patriotic American, a navy veteran of Vietnam concerned about growing Soviet naval strength. The government's prosecutor, on the other hand, portrayed him as a less-than-well-motivated government employee who called the naval intelligence center a "pit" and wanted nothing more than to win a full-time job at *Jane's*. The prosecution sent a message to jurors that Morison is a man who would compromise his country in selling secret information to a magazine in order to impress the magazine's editors.

Whatever Morison's motive—whether it was commercial or altruistic, or a mixture of the two—"the Government's broad legal theory would indiscriminately catch idealistic whistle-blowers, officials caught up in public-policy debates and the writers who rely upon them to illuminate public affairs," the *New York Times* stated in an editorial.[2] The *New Republic* castigated Morison for acting on his "unscrupulous ambitions" that led to the "reckless disclosure." But the magazine and others said his actions likely did not aid the Soviets, who already had significant information on the operation of the spy satellite and its capabilities. (The manual for the KH-11, the reconnaissance satellite that took **119** the photos purloined by Morison, had been sold by a CIA agent to the KGB in 1978.)[3]

Apart from First Amendment considerations, the government's case "goes against the letter of the law," the *New Republic* argued. Moreover, they wrote, the government, in prosecuting Morison, was "circumventing Congress in an attempt to write new laws through the courts."[4] As others have noted, the Reagan administration has denounced judges for carrying out such invention of law.

Martin Garbus, a New York attorney who specializes in publishing cases, pointed out a darker prospect. Writing in the December 20, 1985, issue of *Publishers Weekly*, Garbus, a former American Civil Liberties Union attorney, argued that publishers of books on arms control, defense spending, "Star Wars," or the Strategic Defense Initiative, and nearly every area of foreign policy should be worried by the Morison conviction. "Any time they publish information not based on officially approved sources, they now face the threat of prosecution," he wrote. "The future publishers of books like Strobe Talbot's *Deadly Gambit*, William Shawcross's *Sideshow*, even Jimmy Carter's *Keeping Faith*, could face prosecution. So, too, could the bookstores that sell the books, the printers that print them, as well as those involved in the distribution process."

To gauge the reaction of publishers, *Publishers Weekly* spoke to several publishing executives and editors, at least one of whom was not aware of the issues in the case. All registered alarm. "The conviction of Samuel Morison, if sustained, may be the single most crippling blow by government to First Amendment speech and press freedom in the recent history of our country," said Random House president and chief executive officer Robert Bernstein. Alice Mayhew, who was William Shawcross's editor at Simon & Schuster, recalled that Shawcross wrote in *Sideshow*, which deals with Nixon administration policy in Cambodia, that a book like his could not have been published in his native Britain because of the Official Secrets Act. "Shawcross would be surprised to know that as a result of the Morison case his books, and books like it, might not be able to be published in the U.S.," Mayhew said.

It is difficult to determine how likely it is that would-be government censors and prosecutors would go after journalists, authors, and publishers if the Morison conviction is upheld. But there is some evidence of such an eventuality. The evidence lies in statements given to newspapers by anonymous administration officials. Those officials keep in mind Justice White's contention in *New York Times* v. *United States*—the Pentagon Papers case—that the Congress in 1917 wanted to bar prior restraints but permit prosecutions of newspapers after publication. Finally, Justice Department and executive branch reports and memoranda focusing on concerted long-term efforts to stop the leaks provide some insight into official thinking on the potential for prosecution.

Those documents on unauthorized disclosures of classified information—obtained through the federal Freedom of Information Act—deserve a careful look. That in turn leads to a detailed discussion of the Morison case and the legal arguments. Logically, that requires at least a long glance at the legal underpinning of the Morison case, the Espionage Act of 1917.

While Morison was being prosecuted, a Justice Department official confided anonymously to the *Washington Post* that "neither the Government officials who do the leaking, nor the news publications at the receiving end [of leaked information] . . . should consider themselves immune from prosecution under the Espionage Act."[5]

Indeed, a leading Justice Department attorney and officials in the executive branch said as much, on the record, in a revealing report issued in 1982.

On February 4 of that year, William French Smith, the attorney general at the time, announced the formation of an "Inter-agency Group on Unauthorized Disclosure of Classified Information." William P. Clark, the president's national security adviser, had requested that the group get together to hash out a strategy to combat the epidemic of leaks. A deputy assistant attorney general named Richard K. Willard was designated chairman of the seven-member group, which was composed of representatives from the Departments of State, Treasury, Defense, and Energy and the Central Intelligence Agency.

About seven weeks later, the group issued a lengthy paper that became known as "the Willard report." The report led directly to President Reagan's issuing on March 11, 1983, of National Security Decision Directive 84 (NSDD 84), which seeks to safeguard national security information.

The Willard report explains the need for tightening the government's systems of controlling information by stating that the "unauthorized disclosure of classified information is a longstanding problem that has increased in severity over the past decade. . . . The continuing large number of unauthorized disclosures has damaged the national security interests of the United States and has raised serious questions about the government's ability to protect its most sensitive secrets from disclosure in the media."[6]

The "theft and publication" of the Pentagon Papers ushered in a "new era of heightened media interest in the exposure of classified information," according to the report.[7]

The document reserves harsh words for some reporters and writers. It criticizes those "journalists who seem to believe that quoting from 'highly classified' documents is an appropriate means of entertaining as well as informing the public."[8] In the thinking of such reporters, the Willard report continues, "leaks are part of a game in which the government tries to keep information secret and the media tries to find it out. Some journalists are unwilling to assume responsibility for damage to the national security in situations where they win this 'game.'" The report asserts that "the person who solicits and receives classified information may be no less responsible for an unauthorized disclosure . . . than the government employee who transmits it."[9]

To stop the flow of illicitly disclosed information, the government seems willing, if not ready, to move legally against journalists who receive such information, even as the cautious officials acknowledge the First and Fourth Amendment concerns of, first, finding the journalists who get the goods and, second, prosecuting them.

The report refers to the espionage laws, and specifically to 18 U.S. Code 793 (d) and (e), in citing legal authority.

> These provisions have not been used in the past to prosecute unauthorized disclosures of classified information. However, the Department of Justice has taken the position that these statutes would be violated by an unauthorized disclosure to a member of the media of classified documents or information relating to the national defense, although intent to injure the United States or benefit a foreign nation would have to be present where the disclosure is of "information" rather than documents or other tangible materials. *These laws could also be used to prosecute a journalist who knowingly receives and publishes classified documents or information*" [emphasis added].[10]

Of course, the above quote was rendered out of date by the Morison prosecution, for the government depended heavily on Subsections 793(d) and (e) to gain conviction of the naval analyst.* The Nixon administration had tried to use the same provisions against Ellsberg and Russo twelve years before, but the judge dismissed that case because of government misconduct, which

---

* Morison also was convicted of theft of government property—both the satellite-generated photos and the excerpts of NISC intelligence reports known as Weekly Wires—under provisions of 18 U.S.C. 641. The Weekly Wire reports in question concerned a 1984 explosion at a Soviet naval base. Testimony showed that Morison used the documents and other information to prepare a memorandum sent to *Jane's* in the summer of 1984. Thus, in regard to the photographs, Morison was convicted of one count of illegal disclosure of national defense documents [18 U.S.C. 793 (d)] and one count of theft of government property (18 U.S.C. 641). In regard to the Weekly Wires, he was convicted of one count of illegal retention of defense information that had not been in his authorized possession [18 U.S.C. 793 (e)] and of one count of theft of government property (18 U.S.C. 641).

There were strenuous debates between Morison's attorneys and the government on the applicability of section 641, but the prosecution tools of more interest because of their First Amendment implications are the espionage statutes. They are the focus here.

122   included the burglary of the office of Ellsberg's psychiatrist by overzealous investigators.

Briefly, Subsection 793(d) bars an authorized bearer of national defense information—the disclosure of which the bearer "has reason to believe" could bring injury to the United States or given advantage to "any foreign nation" —from "willfully" communicating or transmitting such information "to any person not entitled to receive it." The other key subsection, 793(e), makes it a crime for any person having "unauthorized" possession or access to such information to pass it to others "not entitled to receive it" or to "willfully" retain it.

In *United States* v. *Morison,* defense and prosecuting attorneys were not only at loggerheads over the specific legal arguments and the reading of the relevant case law. They also, as might be expected, disputed the very complexity or facility of the issues in the case. The four attorneys for Morison cited the "complex legal questions involved." They sought to demonstrate what they see as the misapplication and inadequacy of the two provisions of the espionage acts as they related to leaks. To do that, they cited the legislative history and the apparent doubt other government officials—including some in the Reagan administration—have felt regarding the statutes' use.

For his part, Michael Schatzow, the assistant U.S. attorney who waged the government's case, argued that virtually every issue of constitutionality of 793 (d) and (e) raised by Morison "has been resolved favorably to the government" by a federal appeals court in 1978. That case, *United States* v. *Dedeyan,* involved a Maryland man accused by the government of violating another subsection of the espionage acts. Schatzow, in discounting the issues raised by Morison's attorneys, argued on the question of an intent requirement, for example, that Morison's effort to read a "subversive intent" element into 793 (d) and (e) "ignores the plain language of the statute."

In their counterargument, Morison's attorneys decried "the government's facile attempt to convince the court that all the issues" raised by Morison's initial legal arguments "have been settled in the government's favor." The defense attorneys continued: "[T]his case confronts the Court with numerous unresolved issues of statutory construction and constitutional law that go to the heart of the delicate problem of protecting both free speech and national security in our democratic society." The fundamental arguments of Morison's attorneys include the following: Subsections 793(d) and (e) are misapplied because they were intended to stop espionage, or spying; there was no "fair notice" that Morison might have been committing a crime because of the statutes' long history of disuse and the doubt over the laws' applicability to press leaks; the laws' term "willfully" requires proof that Morison "acted with an evil purpose"; and the laws, in their use of such terms as "relating to the national defense" and "not entitled to receive," are unconstitutionally vague and overbroad.

The prosecution disagreed with all those propositions, of course. Schatzow called "ridiculous" the argument that the phrase "not entitled to receive" is unconstitutionally vague. From his training and briefings, Morison knew of his responsibilities to safeguard classified information, the prosecutor argued. On the issue of the alleged vagueness of "relating to the national defense," Schatzow said the concept is broad, but not unconstitutionally vague. Schatzow argued also that the federal appeals court in California had rejected a First Amendment attack on Section 793 of the espionage acts on the grounds of unconstitutional vagueness in *United States* v. *Boyce,* the so-called "Falcon and Snowman" case.

It is worth noting, however, that *Boyce* and other cases mentioned by Schatzow as proof of constitutional muster involved spying or "classic espionage," and not unauthorized disclosures to the media. The distinction is important.

Other issues beside those that required mention of case law arose in the Morison trial. And the contentions at the trial centering on such issues proved startling.

Motive was one of those issues. Thus, the federal investigators who found Morison did not believe that he was passing the photos and information to an agent of another country. One official from the Naval Investigative Service testified that he suggested to Morison that he believed the naval analyst passed the items to *Jane's* to alert the American public to a Soviet naval buildup. "You hit it," Morison replied.[11]

Responding to such arguments on motive, Schatzow said in a government brief that Morison and his attorneys were confusing motive and intent. If a defendant such as Morison intentionally turns over photographs relating to national defense to someone who is not entitled to receive them, he has violated the espionage laws, "no matter how laudable his motives," the prosecutor argued in a response to Morison's motion for dismissal.

> Thus, if Morison had been inspired to violate his oath and disclose the photographs due to a desire to expose obvious wrongdoing in high official circles, he would be just as guilty as if he were acting, as he was here, on considerably baser motives concerning career advancement.

Judge Joseph H. Young, in whose court the Morison case was tried, agreed with the government in denying the admissibility of testimony on the patriotism of Morison on the grounds that it was irrelevant to the prosecution. But civil libertarians bridle at such a position. First Amendment advocates such as Jack Landau, onetime director of the Reporters Committee for Freedom of the

124 Press, point out that it represents an attitude that would allow government to prevent publication of such articles as those on the Pentagon Papers, the My Lai massacre, and CIA and FBI domestic spying—publication of which did not lead to a proved harm to the national security but to enhance public debate and, inconveniently to some people, the diminished stature of officials in the public eye.

On the issue of Morison's motives, University of Texas law professor Scot Powe, concludes, "If Morison's motives were not the highest, they were hardly the lowest. No one accuses him of betraying his country. He neither gave nor sold information to foreign agents. Morison did not intend to harm the United States, nor did he have reason to believe he had done so."[12]

Morison's attorneys also argued that their client was selectively prosecuted in a "test case" that indicates the government seeks a broad antileak law or at least wanted to counter, with a courtroom victory, a decade of official frustration caused by unauthorized disclosures. The defense attorneys quoted (without naming the source) testimony on Capitol Hill by the CIA's onetime general counsel, Anthony A. Lapham. The intelligence agency's chief lawyer expressed his "confusion" about the meaning of the Espionage Acts of 1917, what they define obscurely as criminal behavior and against whom they ought to be applied. Lapham, speaking before a subcommittee of the House Intelligence Committee in 1979, voiced doubt about a Justice Department view that, under the espionage laws, leaks to the press are prosecutable offenses.

> If [that] view is correct, then what must be realized is that we have had in this country for the last 60 years an absolutely unprecedented crime wave because surely there have been thousands upon thousands of unauthorized disclosures of classified information, all criminal acts in the [Justice] Department's view, as I understand it, and yet none, none has ever been prosecuted.[13]

In fact, with the Morison case, there was such a prosecution. However, the substance of Lapham's message remains valid, and, perhaps the Justice Department saw a challenge in such a statement. Lapham and others have noted the years-long conflict over leaks between the Justice Department and the CIA. By the early 1980s and the advent of the Reagan administration, the Justice Department view—aided by the attitudes of Director of Central Intelligence William Casey—had gained the upper hand. At any rate, demands for a successful court case involving leaks likely came into play. At the same time, frustration over obtaining legislation to stop the leaks might have led to a kind of last-ditch effort to use the untested espionage laws to obtain a conviction in such a case.

Government attorneys and other high-ranking officials writing in the Willard report and elsewhere have noted the difficulty in waging a successful leak investigation. One factor is the sheer number of people who have access to a single piece of classified information. In a ten-page Justice Department memorandum dated September 21, 1982, an analyst working on what became known in the department as "the leaks project" found that in twenty-nine cases of leaks referred to the FBI for investigation, "the average number of persons found to have had access to the information [in question] was 260." The Willard report, which concluded that past experience with leak investigations had been "totally unsatisfactory," also noted that even if a leaker is identified, there are "numerous practical barriers to criminal prosecution." [14] One barrier is the requirement that the government, to prove that the disclosure in question was damaging to the national security, may have to further disclose classified information—which in turn could lead to a defendant resorting to "graymail." An agency also might not want to prosecute a case to bolster its denials of the accuracy of the disclosed information.

In light of those factors, Morison made an easy target. His relationship with *Jane's* was well known to his navy employers and the subject of some dispute. He left fingerprints on the photographs. And his typewriter ribbon, when taken as evidence, revealed that letters had been written to the editor of the *Defence Weekly*. In addition, there was little fear of unwanted disclosures of classified information in court, although the government fought against public access to more sensitive information. Again, the manual for the KH-11 satellite describing the secret intelligence methods used to take the photos was already in Soviet hands.★ Moreover, the photographs were already in the public domain. Clearly the deterrent aspect of the prosecution—sending a message to

---

★ As is made clear in its brief on appeal filed in 1987, the government, however, was concerned about the damage it said was inflicted (or likely was done) by the publication of the satellite-generated photographs. The government argued that "an analyst using unclassified techniques" in examining the photos "can determine various capabilities of the satellite, including ground sample distance and resolution." The government also argued that the publication of the photos "revealed that the KH-11 was still operational [in July 1984], allowing a comparison of current capabilities with previous estimates, thus permitting informed counter-measures." Defense witnesses countered that the potential damage from the photos' publication in *Jane's*—in light of the Kampiles sale to the Soviets, Iranian students printing KH-11-generated "imagery" recovered after the aborted 1980 hostage rescue mission, and the publication of another KH-11 photo by *Aviation Week and Space Technology* in its Dec. 14, 1981 issue—was "zero," as retired CIA official Roland Inlow testified. In rebuttal, two government witnesses testified that the photos offered current, graphic confirmation of the spy satellite's capabilities and thus could cause the Soviets to take active countermeasures and modify "a denial program," as Army and CIA intelligence expert General Rutledge Hazzard put it.

126 leakers, present and future—combined with the lack of risk, lent some attraction to the idea of arresting and trying Morison.

The government's attorney disagreed with the defense's contention that "it is plain that the defendant has been selected for prosecution from a vast number of potential targets." To prove selective prosecution had occurred, Schatzow argued, Morison would have to show that the government had not pursued other cases involving the same specific characteristics as found in the Morison case: the top secret clearance; the deliberate disclosure of the same "most secret and crucial" information to someone for "the base motive of hoping to find employment;" and lying when confronted.

Schatzow went on to argue: "The defendant makes broad statements about alleged violations of this statute over a long period of time. The defendant makes no claims that the government has had sufficient evidence for prosecution in those cases." He described the problem officials have in pinning leaks to specific employees when many people have access to classified information. But, he adds, "The defendant, by the egregious nature of his conduct, eliminated that difficulty for the government in this case." Finally, as if offering an afterthought, the assistant U.S. attorney argued that in the same court, Judge Young had noted in a civil case that "inconsistent application of a provision does not rise to a constitutional violation."

All in all, although it is still open to question whether the government's action against Morison amounted to selective prosecution, it seems likely that it was viewed within the government as a test case. Other unauthorized leaks had been traced to single employees, as the Willard report attests, but charges were not filed for a variety of reasons. Why was a dormant law—dormant, at least, in this particular application—brought out in this case? Government attorneys clearly thought they had a good case, at least one that was better than others before it. Argument in their confident briefs indicated as much. However, a more in-depth look at the law, how it has been viewed by other attorneys and officials, and finally the legislative history would lead to some doubt.

Former Director of Central Intelligence William E. Colby, who has had occasion to be concerned about leaks, maintained that concern when he testified in 1979 before a panel of the House Intelligence Committee on the subject of espionage laws and leaks. At that time, he expressed some caution in the description of his and the Congress's views on the issue.

> The constitutional rights of our press and our tradition of a free society are, of course, factors in this exposure [of intelligence agents and methods], but they are principles which I, for one, would not change. On a

number of occasions during this century, the Congress has considered proposals to establish an official secrets act on the British model and has turned them down. It has drawn a line between espionage and simple disclosure of defense secrets, and decided that the latter problems are an acceptable cost of the kind of society we prefer.[15]

Colby then called for charter legislation providing criminal penalties for the unauthorized disclosure of secret intelligence sources and techniques by government officials who have agreed to protect the secrecy of such information.

However, Colby added, such a statute would have to be narrowly drawn and "would run only against officials with authorized access to the information, not against the recipients of the information disclosed, such as journalists. The latter should be protected not only against conspiracy charges, but also against being required to reveal the name of the official from whom they obtained the information if they repeated it in the course of exercising first amendment rights."[16]

Colby infers that the laws currently on the books, despite the existence of those statutes protecting certain classes of information such as cryptographic methods, are flawed or inadequate. That view was confirmed by the chief counsel of Colby's agency at the time, Anthony Lapham.★ Testifying before the House Intelligence Committee one week before Colby, Lapham said frankly that he believed Sections 793 and 794, the core of the espionage acts, "are so vague and opaque as to be virtually worthless." Lapham's views are worth an extended quote.

> I would like to be able to say to you that the meaning and scope of these statutes are reasonably definite. Unhappily, I can give you no such assurance. Even in relation to the kind of conduct that typifies the classical espionage case, involving clandestine dealings with foreign agents, the statutes are not altogether clear on their face, although most of the uncertainties in this regard have been sorted out in the course of related prosecutions and through a process of judicial interpretation. What has never been sorted out is whether these statutes can be applied, and would be constitutional if applied, to the compromise of national security information that occurs as a result of anonymous leaks to the press or attributed publications. *I cannot tell you with any confidence what these laws mean in these contexts. I cannot tell you, for example, whether the leak of classified information to the press is a criminal act, or whether the publication of*

★ Lapham has since left the CIA and is in private practice in Washington, D.C.

that information by a newspaper is a criminal act, or whether this conduct be-
comes criminal if committed with a provable intent to injure the United States,
but remains noncriminal if committed without such intent[17] [emphasis added].

Lapham, in the testimony, goes on to describe his own confusion over the statutes. His words give support to the position of leakers such as Morison on the question of "fair notice" that they might be breaking a law. "On the one hand," Lapham testified, "the laws stand idle and are not enforced at least in part because their meaning is so obscure, and on the other hand, it is likely that the very obscurity of those laws serves to deter perfectly legitimate expression and debate by persons who must be as unsure of their liabilities as I am unsure of their obligations."[18]

Lapham disagreed with the view, put forward by a Justice Department attorney that day, that the espionage laws make criminal the unauthorized disclosure to the press of national security information and the publishing of such information. He said the legislative history of the laws does not support such a view. However, Lapham deferred to two scholars whom he termed far more expert than he on the evolution of the laws.

Harold Edgar and Benno C. Schmidt, Jr., were both professors of law at Columbia University when they testified before the Legislation Subcommittee of the House Intelligence Committee in 1979.* Six years before, in the wake of the Pentagon Papers case, *Columbia Law Review* published their 158-page article that is widely considered the definitive study of the espionage statutes and issues surrounding laws pertaining to the publication of defense information.

The basic point of the article by Edgar and Schmidt is that the espionage statutes are so fraught with confusion that meaning can only be extracted from the legislative history. An examination of that history, however, does not yield much more understanding of the meaning and applicability of the laws, they argued. The wording of the laws in many cases runs counter to the legislators' apparent intent as extracted from the recorded congressional debates, Edgar and Schmidt wrote. Concerns about censorship were raised in the debate during World War I and proposals for more far-reaching laws were rejected. But Congress then accepted legislative language that negates or contradicts the reason for other language (or for the rejection of some clauses), the authors wrote.

"The basic espionage statutes are totally inadequate," wrote Edgar and Schmidt. "Even in their treatment of outright spying they are poorly conceived and clumsily drafted."

Edgar and Schmidt reserved even unkinder words—if it is possible—for

---

*At the time of this writing, Edgar remains a professor at Columbia. Schmidt, however, became the president of Yale University in 1986.

Subsections 793(d) and (e), the laws by which Morison was convicted. "These
two statutes are undoubtedly the most confusing and complex of all the federal
espionage statutes," they wrote. "Unfortunately, they are also the statutes that
pose the greatest threat to the acquisition and publication of defense information by reporters and newspapers. The legislative drafting is at its scattergun
worst precisely where greatest caution should have been exercised."[19]

The legal scholars resort to such phrases as "formulated with hopeless im-
precision" when they describe the key elements of the provisions. They say the
final drafts of the statutes are proof of "congressional confusion about the ends
sought to be achieved."[20]

To shed light on the meaning of the laws, their legislative history—however
muddled—should be examined carefully, the law professors wrote. The Espionage Acts of 1917, which form the core of the current espionage laws, had
their genesis in the Civil War. Union leaders damned their fate of having to
read about their military plans in newspapers before the plans were carried out
on the battlefield. By the same token, the Congress in 1917 was acutely aware
of the implications for the First Amendment that the laws, if carelessly drafted,
could carry. President Wilson had planned to censor "or punish after the fact
[exactly which, was never resolved] the publication of defense information in
violation of presidential regulations," wrote Edgar and Schmidt.[21]

"In response to these proposals Congress engaged in its most important
and extensive debate on freedom of speech and the press since the Alien and
Sedition Acts. The preoccupation was not academic. Congressmen feared that
President Wilson or his subordinates would impede, or even suppress, informed criticism of his administration's war effort and foreign policy under the
guise of protecting military secrets." Proposals with express publication controls not conditioned on a narrow intent requirement were defeated by narrow
margins.[22]

In light of the denial of broad powers of censorship, therefore, the sweeping
language of Subsections 793(d) and (e) seems incredible, argue Edgar and
Schmidt. No special requirement of culpability restricts the provisions' reach.
For example, narrow interpretations of the term "willfully" are common where
laws affect freedom of speech and other "boundaries of constitutional power."
But neither the language nor the legislative intent of the statute gives the term
"willfully" such a narrow meaning. In the same way, any "communicating"
of defense material or information to anyone "not entitled" or authorized to
receive it is regarded as a serious criminal offense. Even keeping such material
presumably is illegal for those people who lack official sanction.

"If these statutes mean what they say and are constitutional, public speech
in this country since World War II has been rife with criminality," Edgar and
Schmidt wrote. "The source who leaks defense information to the press com-

130   mits an offense; the reporter who holds onto defense material commits an offense; and the retired official who used defense material in his memoirs commits an offense."[23]

It is difficult to do justice to the analysis of Edgar and Schmidt as it is laid out in their very detailed study. Anyone seriously interested in the past and future of the espionage laws should read the article. Here it is useful, however, to extract a few points from the authors' thinking on the legislative history of the two provisions, 793(d) and (e), the "broad literal meaning" of which "is almost certainly unconstitutionally vague and overbroad."

Besides interpretative problems with such undefined terms as "not entitled to receive it" and the issues of culpability and of what materials and information are covered under the two provisions, someone struggling to understand the laws must tackle the problem of what Congress said, on the one hand, and what it wrote into law and maintained as law in subsequent years. Subsections 793(d) and (e) are framed in sweeping language, Edgar and Schmidt write. How is that language reconciled "with the clear message of the 1917 and 1950 legislative histories that publication of defense information for the purpose of selling newspapers or engaging in public debate is not a criminal act"?★

Taken together, the messages of the 1917 and 1950 congresses are relatively strong on the issue of censorship. Despite a direct appeal by President Wilson, Congress deleted a provision that would have given the president broad controls on all information having to do with military plans and policy. The president would have power to restrict the divulgence of government secrets, public access to defense sites, and public discussion and reporting of issues relating to war.

An absence of an intent requirement drew the most criticism, according to Edgar and Schmidt. Senator Cummins, for example, attacked the proposed provision as "absolute suppression of free speech" and "an absolute overthrow of a free press." Running strongly throughout the 1917 debate was not only an apparent fear of an abridgement of First Amendment rights, but also an unwillingness to cede broad authority to the executive.

In 1950, during debate on amendments to the 1917 acts, Congress again attempted to clarify its purpose in the earlier laws. It had little success. A look at the 1950 legislative record shows that Congress still "had virtually no understanding and effect of 793(d) and (e)," Edgar and Schmidt wrote.[24] The lawmakers added an anticensorship provision that asserts, "Nothing in this

---

★ In 1950, Congress amended the Espionage Acts and split Section 1(d) of the 1917 act into two parts, the current 793 (d) and (e). The latter subsection was a new one that covered people not connected with the government. The amended statutes were part of the Internal Security Act of 1950 [64 Stat. 1003 (1950)].

Act shall be construed to authorize, require, or establish military censorship or civilian censorship or in any way to limit or infringe upon freedom of the press or speech as guaranteed by the Constitution of the United States and no regulation shall be promulgated hereunder having that effect."

The U.S. attorney general and the Legislative Reference Service (today, the Congressional Research Service of the Library of Congress) gave assurances that the new Subsections 793(d) and (e) would not infringe on free speech or a free press, but they offered no plausible interpretations of the law's language in light of the promises, according to Edgar and Schmidt. Senator McCarran and other key sponsors suggested no basis for a narrow reading of the law, so the legislative history leaves open the question of how the law can be reconciled with legislative intent, the scholars concluded.

In the 1985 trial of Morison, defense attorneys cited the analysis of Edgar and Schmidt, along with another law review article. In light of the dearth of case law on the espionage statutes in instances involving the press or so-called nonclassic espionage, the attorneys also included the congressional testimony of Colby and Lapham. For his part, the government's attorney criticized the defense's reliance on the law-review articles and called the articles "biased." Schatzow also wrote that Colby and Lapham—and, by extension, the inter-agency Willard report—did not represent official government thinking. He, as an attorney for the Justice Department, did, he wrote.

Schatzow, in prosecuting the Morison case, uses language more cutting and direct than the normal legal lexicon when he seeks to diminish the positions of Edgar and Schmidt, the former CIA officials, and Melville B. Nimmer, a UCLA law professor who wrote the second law-review article cited by Morison's attorney.* Referring to the articles by the law professors, the assistant U.S. attorney writes, "Each is by admission of its own authors, biased," and is written "more in the nature of a brief rather than a disinterested analysis." The article by Edgar and Schmidt was written in the aftermath of the Pentagon Papers case and "the original conception of the authors was to demonstrate the unconstitutionality of the espionage statutes," Schatzow writes. He adds, however, that the bulk of the article is an objective discussion of the legislative history of those laws. He goes on to argue that the law professors' conclusions in the *Columbia Law Review* article, that the application of 793(d) and (e) should be confined to traditional espionage, have been rejected by subsequent court decisions. Finally, Schatzow's condemnation of the other article begins with the words, "Worse yet is Nimmer, . . ." and concludes that his arguments also have been rejected by the courts.

---

* Nimmer's article is "National Security Secrets v. Free Speech: The Issues Left Undecided in the Ellsberg Case," for the 1974 volume of the *Stanford Law Review*, pp. 311–333.

Schatzow makes a point in identifying the fact that Morison's attorneys
fail to mention in their initial brief that Nimmer appeared as an attorney for
the American Civil Liberties Union, as friend of the court, in the Ellsberg
defense. Most of the ideas in his article had germinated in the briefs for the
case, Nimmer wrote.

Schatzow is on less firm ground, however, when he faults the article by
Edgar and Schmidt for alleged bias. Again, the CIA's chief counsel, Anthony
Lapham, when testifying at the House Intelligence Committee's subcommittee
hearing, praised the professors. He deferred discussion of the espionage statutes
to them. At the same hearing, Congressman Robert McClory, the ranking Republican on the subcommittee, was effusive in his praise of the impartiality of
Edgar and Schmidt and offered testimony that reiterated the points contained
in their article. "I think you have given some very astute and informed views
to the committee. . . . As I analyze it, it seems to me entirely objective," said
McClory. In other congressional publications, the work by Edgar and Schmidt
is mentioned as authoritative writing on the espionage statutes. In light of that,
one can understand that Morison's attorneys might use it in their arguments.

It is not so easy to understand, however, Schatzow's discounting of the
Willard report—unless, of course, it is realized that the report's official sizing
up of the spying statutes weakens their efficacy in reaching the prosecution's
ends. "These provisions [793 (d) and (e)] have not been used in the past to
prosecute unauthorized disclosures of classified information, *and their application to such cases is not entirely clear*," the Willard report acknowledges, although
inaccurately and in obsolete language. "*However, the Department of Justice has
taken the position that these statutes would be violated by the unauthorized disclosure
to a member of the media of classified documents or information relating to the national
defense*" [emphasis added]. The report also states that Section 641, which out-
laws the theft of government property and is the other statute under which
Morison was convicted, is considered by the Justice Department to be another
prosecutorial tool in cases of leaks of classified information. It notes that there
has been no definitive court test of such a proposition.

Schatzow discounted the Willard report, despite its administration imprimatur—as well as the opinions of the CIA officials, Colby and Lapham, in
their testimony before Congress.

> Whatever comfort the defendant finds in legislative efforts over the years
> by previous sponsors of legislation, and in testimony of government em-
> ployees and the conclusions of interagency reports, those conclusions are
> not the conclusions of the Justice Department, which speaks for the gov-
> ernment on legal matters. One need not be a genius nor [*sic*] a cynic to

recognize that the hidden agendas of those introducing legislation, testifying before Congress and writing reports may be far more less [*sic*] apparent and worthy of attention than the opinions, conclusions, and holdings of the courts of the United States which have actually interpreted the statutes involved.[25]

Various observers have pointed out that some executive agencies and congressional sponsors have, over the years, sought new laws to stop unauthorized leaks of certain protected information on military and foreign affairs. Congress as a whole, however, has either balked at legislation to create something akin to an official secrets act or has approved laws to counter leaks only when their language is narrowly drawn, as when it pertains to specific classes of information such as government codes, or to certain persons.

The strong inference is, as Lapham and others say, that the espionage acts have not been adequate in dealing with the problem of leaks. If they were, and 793(d) and (e) applied to leaks, these and other statutes would have been unnecessary. Edgar and Schmidt reach similar conclusions.

Finally, it is difficult to avoid the conclusion that the system of classification —or of overclassification, as some would call it—has something to do with the epidemic of leaks. "When in doubt, classify" is a philosophy that many inside and outside government ascribe to the guardians of official secrets. In a 1978 Senate committee report on national security secrets and the justice system, Senator Malcolm Wallop, a Wyoming Republican, said that there is information so important that its disclosure would harm the country. But, he asserted, "it is useful to start from the fact that officials of the executive branch who classify information often do it erroneously and sometimes maliciously. . . . Civil libertarians are correct in stating that information is often improperly and sometimes maliciously classified, and that those who bring it into the public domain deserve praise."[26]

The Reporters Committee for Freedom of the Press is straightforward in its view of the classification system and how it contributes to the problem of leaks. The committee's editorial board stated in 1985: "If everything is 'top secret,' classification becomes meaningless, and the risk of leaks of truly sensitive information escalates. One way to deal with the problem is to revamp government classification procedures."[27]

The Willard report and various government officials have recommended passage of a law that would criminalize all unauthorized disclosures of classified information by government employees. But, as the *New Republic* said that the Morison case demonstrates, the espionage acts allow the attorney general to choose which leaks are permissible and which are to be prosecuted.

That leaves far too much power in the hands of the government to curb free debate on military issues. . . . The mere fact that information has been classified should not be enough to warrant prosecution. If every leak to the press of classified military information led to prosecution for espionage, the entire defense establishment from [Secretary of Defense Caspar] Weinberger on down would probably have been indicted by now.[28]

Similar outcomes would accompany a broad antileak law that would apply to government employees. The potential for arbitrary or selective prosecution would be disturbing.

The Willard report, in recommending a new law to make it a crime for government employees to leak classified information, would not treat such disclosures as espionage any longer. The report also suggests that a companion provision would be helpful in setting up a procedure to ensure that the information in question was properly classified. More specifically, the Willard report lays out a prototype for the law, something "simple and general in order to cover all situations":

Whoever, being an officer or employee of the United States or a person with authorized access to classified information, willfully discloses, or attempts to disclose, any classified information to a person who is not an officer or employee of the United States and who is not authorized to receive it shall be fined not more than $10,000, or imprisoned not more than three years, or both.[29]

The report suggests more specific language than that found in the espionage laws. But what safeguards will such a statute provide to prevent arbitrary enforcement, given the daily practice of leaking, and to allay First Amendment concerns?

Perhaps more disturbing is a Willard report conclusion that civil statutes and regulations providing disciplinary action for leaks by officials are adequate, "except that they apply only to persons who disclose classified information, *not to those who receive it*"[30] [emphasis added].

A person who solicits and receives classified information may be no less responsible for an unauthorized disclosure of such information than the government employee who transmits it, but his conduct is not prohibited by a civil statute.[31]

The report asserts, in effect, that independent citizens and journalists have the same responsibilities in serving government policy as officials who sign agreements to abide by certain regulations to keep secret certain information. With such a view, the larger goals of rectifying what might be seen as injudicious policy are foreclosed. At any rate, the Willard report pulls back from urging adoption of a civil statute to get at those who receive leaked information. "Although we make no recommendation with respect to introduction of legislation providing for civil penalties or other remedies against persons who receive classified information, we believe the subject merits further study as an effective, *though probably controversial* [emphasis added], method of deterring unauthorized disclosures," the 1982 report states.[32]

Other observers express other views on what to do to clarify the laws on leaks. Harold Edgar, in testifying before Congress in 1979, cautioned against making it a crime to disclose any classified information. The New York *Times* and the *New Republic* agree with Admiral Stansfield Turner, former chief of the CIA, in suggesting that it is more appropriate for government agencies to reprimand or fire an employee who mishandles classified information than to resort to the anti-spying statutes.

At the same time, Edgar and Schmidt warn of the dangers of allowing the executive branch to enforce secrecy by seeking court injunctions for breach of employee contracts, as in the Marchetti and Snepp cases, which involved the writings of former CIA employees. Schmidt testified that he saw a number of problems with those CIA contracts, which enforce secrecy of information acquired as an employee and require prepublication review of manuscripts by the agency. Those problems identified by Schmidt include the contracts' non-negotiable nature and their all-inclusiveness. "I believe that those contracts are a result of the CIA's appreciation of the inadequacy and the confusion of the current espionage statutes," Schmidt said in his testimony.[33]

To recover from such inadequacies and to protect what they see as national defense secrets worth keeping without infringing on First Amendment rights, Edgar and Schmidt suggest starting from scratch and not simply building on already flawed laws. First, they say, Congress must view three groups independently: "Spies, government employees and ex-employees, and the newspapers and the rest of us."[34] There should be a law against the unauthorized or clandestine transfer of any classified information to agents of a foreign power. However, a law governing revelation of information by current and former government employees should contain a narrower definition of information than that which is protected against espionage.[35]

Edgar and Schmidt would allow the opportunity for an official to use a justification defense "no matter what information is protected." Such a defense would allow a jury to either balance the information's national security importance against its significance in public debate, or to consider that the employee's superiors were derelict in their duties. "To do otherwise [not make possible a justification defense] would not recognize that the employee serves both the government and the public," they write.[36]

Finally, there is the sensitive problem of publication of defense information and the discussion of public affairs among family and friends. In the past, when Congress was faced with weighing the social value of public dialogue against the adverse consequences of leaks of information, it came down firmly on the side of public debate. Edgar and Schmidt conclude that that must continue. "We think that only very narrowly drawn categories of defense and intelligence information, categories of great security or intelligence significance, and in most cases of little import for public debate, only these categories ought to be prohibited from public disclosure by the press and by the rest of us," the legal scholars told Congress.[37] But even in those cases, a justification defense should be available to officials and the press, and Congress should recognize that there may arise situations where even information that is most worthy of protection should be revealed in the national interest, according to Edgar and Schmidt.[38]

The Morison case has raised the paramount issue of the clash of national security with the First Amendment protections of free speech and a free press —and, beyond that, as Edgar put it to a congressional subcommittee in 1979, "the right of the rest of us to hear." The Pentagon Papers case raised the same issues in 1971. However, because the Morison conviction's risks to a free press were less apparent than in the historic Vietnam war–era legal battle, much of the press was slow to realize the significance of the Morison case for itself and for the public as a whole. Thus, The Reporters Committee for Freedom of the Press concluded at the time of Morison's conviction: "We don't really have a formal reaction to his conviction because we've never really seen this as a First Amendment case. He was a Government employee and he was subject to the rules and regulations of his employer."[39]

In much the same way, and perhaps out of its general attitude of accommodation to government, the mainstream media was slow to respond to the constitutional threat posed in *U.S.* v. *The Progressive,* the "H-bomb secret" case that had the government using censorship provisions of the Atomic Energy Act against the iconoclastic magazine published in Wisconsin.

The media came around, however, and in 1986 joined Morison's appeal filed in the U.S. Court of Appeals for the Fourth Circuit, in Richmond. More than thirty newspapers, broadcasting companies and media, and publishing groups joined in a friend-of-court brief recommending that the conviction be reversed. Among those signing as *amici curiae* were the *Washington Post*, the *New York Times*, the three major television networks, AP (but not UPI), the

American Society of Newspaper Editors, the American Booksellers Associa- **137**
tion, and The Reporters Committee for Freedom of the Press.

"Whatever one might think of government officials who release confidential
or secret information to the press, it seems clear that leaking is not the same
as espionage, and it is not the same as theft," the media representatives argue.
"Unlike the betrayal of one's country to a foreign power, and unlike the theft of
the government's property, the leaking of government information to the press
can proceed from honorable motives. More importantly, press leaks can and
do benefit the public—by exposing incompetence, illegality or abuse of power,
or simply by keeping the public informed about the affairs of government."

The brief traced the history of Congress's refusal to make criminal the disclosure of classified or defense-related information. If upheld, the Morison
conviction not only would "restrict an important source of public information" about government, "it will expose journalists and government officials
alike to the threat of criminal prosecution for activity which, no matter how
offensive to those in power, has never before been viewed as criminal," the
media group concluded. The laws, although confused, are on the books.

In 1917, Senator Hiram Johnson, one of the key actors in the congressional
debates over what became known as the Espionage Acts, said, "The first casualty when war comes is truth." If a wartime anti-spying statute is allowed to
put a person behind bars when no spying has taken place, truth may be a
casualty in peacetime as well.

UPDATE

On Oct. 8, 1987, attorneys for Samuel L. Morison and for the government
argued Morison's appeal before the U.S. Court of Appeals for the Fourth Circuit in Richmond. Debate before a three-judge panel was vigorous. Each attorney was peppered with questions from Judges James D. Phillips Jr., Donald S.
Russell and J. Harvie Wilkinson III.

Mark H. Lynch, the Washington attorney who argued Morison's case, reiterated the points made in two appeals briefs. Foremost, he said, the laws
were misapplied in the case; the case is not one of espionage. Citing "a very
impressive history of the statutes' confusion," he called sections 793(d) and
(e) of the espionage laws unconstitutionally vague and overbroad as applied
to leaks. Lynch warned that if Morison's conviction is upheld, the government will have obtained an official secrets act without having gone through
Congress and the legislative process. "If you rule in our favor, you will not

138 leave the government undefended, as the government argues," Lynch said. If the court upholds the conviction, "the government will have succeeded in getting a broad anti-leak statute that it's not succeeded at getting in the last four decades."

Breckinridge L. Willcox, the U.S. attorney for Maryland, argued, "This is not a leak case. . . . We are not dealing here with a well-intentioned government employee." The case does not involve First Amendment issues, he said. "It is not a prosecution of a news organization. It is not a prior restraint." Willcox argued that the law's plain, not overbroad language bars such actions as Morison's, whose motives he called in a brief "purely base and venal." Significantly, Willcox acknowledged that the law could be used against the press, but added, "The government would be loathe, very loathe" to apply it in that way.

On April 4, 1988, the U.S. Court of Appeals for the Fourth Circuit ruled unanimously to uphold the conviction of Samuel Loring Morison. Lynch said that the ruling would be appealed.

NOTES

1. *Washington Post*, Oct. 8, 1985.
2. *New York Times*, March 4, 1985.
3. *New Republic*, Nov. 18, 1985.
4. *Ibid.*
5. *Washington Post* story quoted by Nat Hentoff, in the *Progressive*, February 1986.
6. Willard Report—hereinafter "Willard"—March 31, 1982, p. A-1.
7. Willard, p. B-1.
8. Willard, p. B-1.
9. Willard, pp. B-3 and C-16.
10. Willard, p. C-5.
11. *New York Times*, Oct. 10, 1985, and the joint appendix to both sides' appeals briefs, pp. 511–513.
12. Powe, *Bulletin of the Atomic Scientists*, June/July 1986, p. 8.
13. "Espionage Laws and Leaks," House Intelligence Committee hearings, 1979, p. 22.
14. Willard, p. C-7.
15. "Espionage Laws and Leaks," p. 146.
16. *Ibid.*, p. 146.
17. *Ibid.*, p. 13.
18. *Ibid.*, p. 22.

19. *Columbia Law Review* 73 (May 1973): 998.
20. *Ibid.*, p. 999.
21. *Ibid.*, p. 940.
22. *Ibid.*, p. 941.
23. *Ibid.*, p. 1000.
24. *Ibid.*, p. 1022.
25. Willard, p. C-5 and "Government's Response to Defendant's Motion for Dismissal," Trial Transcript, U.S. District Court, Baltimore, Md., 1985, p. 8.
26. "National Security Secrets . . . ," Senate Intelligence Committee report, 1978, p. 35.
27. *News Media & The Law*, Fall/Winter 1985, p. 1.
28. "Do Loose Lips Sink Ships?" The *New Republic*, Nov. 18, 1985.
29. Willard, p. C-14.
30. *Ibid.*, p. C-15.
31. *Ibid.*, pp. C-15–C-16.
32. *Ibid.*, p. C-16.
33. "Espionage Laws and Leaks," hearings, p. 120.
34. *Columbia Law Review* 73 (May 1973): 1083.
35. *Ibid.*, pp. 1084–1086.
36. *Ibid.*, p. 1085.
37. "Espionage Laws and Leaks," hearings, p. 119.
38. *Ibid.*, pp. 118–119.
39. *New York Times*, Oct. 18, 1985.

[Judith Schenck Koffler]

9

THE NEW SEDITIOUS LIBEL

Seditious libel is the crime of criticizing the government. It transforms dissent, which the First Amendment has traditionally been thought to protect, into heresy. Fundamentally antidemocratic, the distinguishing feature of seditious libel is, as its nomenclature suggests, injury to the reputation of government or its functionaries. Those who impugn authority's good image are diabolized and their criticisms punished as blasphemy. In this way, the doctrine lends a juristic mask to political repression.

Although we like to think that such attitudes have gone the way of the Megalosaurus, seditious libel is alive and well despite attempts of judges and scholars to knock it on the head once and for all. It is difficult to recognize, however, for it wears the mantle of official secrecy and waves the banner of national security. It creeps into legislative chambers, inspiring measures to silence those who accuse the Central Intelligence Agency of treachery and deceit. It captures the mind of a president who admonishes that those who exercise First Amendment rights have "the responsibility to be right." More insidiously, it has infiltrated the courts, where it threatens to sabotage the core of the First Amendment.

What matters most about the doctrine is its life in the courts, for only the judiciary can deliver the *coup de grâce* to a force that corrodes freedoms of speech and press. Legislators may revive the crime of seditious libel, and presidents may deploy it to persecute their rivals, but as long as courts have believed that the fundamental purpose of the First Amendment is to protect the right of political dissent, seditious libel has been beaten back. Whenever courts have become frightened, confused, or forgetful, seditious libel has reemerged to do its mischief.

In these days of nuclear weapons, one of the most awesome roles of established authority is that of guardian of national security—the current idiom for what was once the king's peace. National security, whatever else it may mean, has lately been invoked to silence public discussion of information deemed by the authorities to be secret or "classified." Yet some dissidents have questioned the fitness of established authority to be the guardian of national security. Several former government officials and even a curious journalist or two, not content with the paternal "you've just got to trust us," have sought, despite attacks on their loyalty, to test whether the shield of secrecy is a veil for incompetence, corruption, or even deceit.

Surely the government is entitled to some secrets in these days of potential instant annihilation. The point is whether the government is entitled to those secrets simply because secrecy is necessary to enhance its reputation. To penetrate this secrecy state for the purpose of public discussion would seem, on democratic principles, a duty of the highest order. How else will citizens be certain that those to whom they have entrusted so much power—megatons of destructive force in the case of the hydrogen bomb or the worldwide network of espionage and "intelligence" activities in the case of the CIA—have not become intoxicated by it? Yet the assault on official secrecy has lately been treated as a kind of lèse-majesté, as an examination of three court decisions will reveal. Two cases decided by the Supreme Court arose out of whistle-blowing by former C.I.A. agents, Frank Snepp and Philip Agee. The third and most alarming decision never got to the Supreme Court in form, but its substance nevertheless dominates the Court's mind. That case is the *Progressive's* censored article on the hydrogen bomb. Some historical discussion is necessary to frame the perspective from which to judge the Court's new stance on seditious libel.

SEDITIOUS LIBEL IN HISTORICAL PERSPECTIVE
English Roots

"All silencing of discussion," wrote John Stuart Mill, "is an assumption of infallibility." If Mill is correct, debates about freedom of speech ultimately are debates about power and its legitimacy—in short, about authority. Historically, the power to silence unorthodox political expression has required an autocratic regime with a license to suppress dissent.

The crime of seditious libel did not take hold until the early seventeenth century. As Frederick Siebert explains, the treason laws, designed to combat armed rebellion, "were too cumbersome to be used to suppress the fleabites of political or religious pamphleteers." Consequently, the Stuarts turned to the criminal doctrine of seditious libel, which prohibited the publishing of scandalous or discordant opinions about the crown, its policies, or its officers, to combat these pamphleteers. Yet the idea underlying the law of seditious libel was the very same notion of royal infallibility that underlay Queen Elizabeth's use of the treason laws against dissenters. As the historian Sir James Stephen explained: "If the ruler is regarded as the superior of the subject, as being by the nature of his position presumably wise and good . . . it must necessarily follow that it is wrong to censure him openly." Accordingly, the doctrine of seditious libel prohibited any person from casting blame upon the ruler or taking any action that might diminish his authority even when the ruler was in error. To question authority was not allowed, not simply because the crown prohibited it, but because authority existed for the people's own good and because only the crown had the capacity to judge what was right and wrong in matters of state and religion.

Political discourse under the Tudor-Stuart view of sovereignty, then, was thought to consist of an official monologue of power, expressed through rigid licensing of the press and enforced by harsh penal laws. The idea of a political dialogue, in which the subjects could participate in formulating the ideas of statecraft and in judging the aims and policies of the government, lay centuries dormant, buried in the dust of democratic Athens. That is hardly surprising, however, for given the Tudor-Stuart notion of the people as politically puerile, permitting them to participate in a political dialogue would be as silly as allowing children to sit in Parliament.

Writing in 1768, Sir William Blackstone, who had celebrated the abolition of censorship by licensing, made no objection to the crime of seditious libel. Blackstone thought that, although in theory any person might lay whatever sentiments he wished before the public, the government could subsequently punish any such utterance that proved to be of a seditious nature. Blackstone's definition of the liberty of the press—the absence of previous restraints upon publication—reveals a generous acceptance of the idea that government may silence criticism. Licensing was evil, he believed, because it subjected all freedom of sentiment to the arbitrary and infallible authority of the licensor. Although Blackstone's rationale against prior restraint is widely accepted, it is difficult to understand why subsequent punishment for the same utterance is not just as civil as a prior restraint, particularly when the decision to punish originates with another practically infallible and not demonstrably less arbitrary authority, the judge. Blackstone failed to address this question. He simply asserted that the malicious defamation of a magistrate for the purpose of exposing him to public hatred, contempt, and ridicule threatened a breach of the public peace "by stirring up the objects . . . to revenge, and perhaps to bloodshed."

THE MODERN TRADITION
OF SEDITIOUS LIBEL

Dark Shadows

The history of the First Amendment has been the history of intolerance of political dissent, a story of dark shadows of fear and orthodoxy illumined periodically by brilliant rays of enlightenment. The Sedition Act of 1798 and Lincoln's Civil War repression helped to forge a hidden link between the Tudor authoritarian tradition and a more irrational modern tradition—the use of seditious libel to persecute dissenters in the twentieth century.

Two eras in First Amendment jurisprudence demonstrate that the Supreme Court is not immune to epidemics of fear and orthodoxy. First was the "Red Menace" era, arising in the aftermath of World War I, when the right to freedom of speech not only underwent severe legislative assaults but also suffered its worst Supreme Court beatings. The second was the McCarthy era, when the Communist witch-hunt mentality infected judicial decision-making.

Red Menace

The Supreme Court's earliest and most enduring efforts to pronounce a stable First Amendment doctrine reveal the Court at its weakest, vulnerable to periodic inflamed public hysteria against dissenters despite the outward appearance of detached, dispassionate adjudication. It is all the more remarkable that these monumental decisions flowed from the pen of Justice Oliver Wendell Holmes, Jr., a jurist who could display his political detachment with artistlike aplomb, posturing as one standing far from the madding crowd, aloof and nonchalant.

The trilogy of Red Menace cases, all decided in 1919, involved the antiwar protests of Charles Schenck, Jacob Frohwerk, and Eugene Debs. In none of these cases did the defendants threaten force or physical violence. Schenck, a Socialist, helped to print a leaflet deploring the draft; Frohwerk's newspaper accused the government of murder for sending American troops to France; Debs's speech deplored the war and prophesied a sane Socialist society. Applying the "clear and present danger" test, under which sufficiently "dangerous" speech could be outlawed, the Court upheld the convictions of all three pursuant to the Espionage Act of 1917, finding that their verbal attacks on the government had obstructed the draft.

The presumption of innocence is absent from the Red Menace trilogy. Read with a skeptical eye, each decision reveals the apprehended "clear and present danger" to have been speech typically associated with seditious libel. Schenck,

144 Frohwerk, and Debs had, by written or spoken word, defamed the government. Holding the administration up to hatred, contempt, and ridicule, they had, like CIA whistle-blowers Frank Snepp and Philip Agee some sixty years later, attacked official judgment as corrupt and mercenary; they had accused the government of deception; and they had, like Howard Morland in the *Progressive,* aimed to reveal to the public the real state of events obscured by official orthodoxy. Although none had set foot on the bailiwick of the recruiting office, each had set foot within the conscience of his hearers, and each had trespassed upon the hawklike public mentality that authority required to be kept clear of intruders. Justice Holmes's assertion in Frohwerk that "[w]e do not lose our right to condemn either measures or men because the Country is at war," rings hollow in light of the Court's judgments sustaining the convictions in all three cases.

The McCarthy Era

Through the groundwork laid by Holmes, seditious libel became firmly but invisibly embedded in the foundations of the First Amendment. Paradoxically, however, it was Holmes's own dissents that later erected the temple to freedom upon those foundations. As the hysteria of the Red Menace period subsided, Brandeis's and Holmes's dissents became blueprints for tolerance. The Court developed respect for the First Amendment rights of agitators and constructed the principle that the First Amendment protects expression of even the most execrable ideologies, short of incitement to insurrection. When the witch-hunts of the McCarthy era began, however, the temple collapsed.

A prominent instrument in this collapse was the *Dennis* case, in which the Court sustained the convictions of twelve Communist party members for conspiracy to violate the Smith Act. This statute made it a crime to help organize any group of persons "who teach, advocate, or encourage the overthrow or destruction of any government in the United States by force or violence," and also proscribed the advocacy of these doctrines. The *Dennis* decision witnessed the Court's return to and strengthening of the invisible tradition of seditious libel. One of the most influential decisions of the postwar period, *Dennis* has never been overruled. Indeed, it has been cited as a precedent in the Court's boldest tributes to the First Amendment.

The evidence in *Dennis* showed only that the defendants had organized people to teach "doctrines of Marxism-Leninism" as set forth in such standard works as *The Communist Manifesto.* There was not a shred of evidence indicating that any of them had advocated any immediate or specific acts of violence. The indictment charged that the defendants had transformed a peaceful

Communist group into one that worked toward the overthrow of the government by force and violence. The group had formed "a highly organized conspiracy, with rigidly disciplined members subject to call when the leaders, these petitioners, felt that the time had come for action." The Court portrayed the Communist party not as an ordinary political party but as the equivalent of a satanic conspiracy possessing the uncanny power to turn human beings into automatons: "[T]he Communist Party is a highly disciplined organization, adept at infiltration into strategic positions, use of aliases, and double-meaning language. . . . [It] is rigidly controlled; . . . Communists, unlike other political parties, tolerate no dissension from the policy laid down by the guiding forces."

Although a survey of the decision from *Schenck* through the more recent liberal freedom-of-speech opinions demonstrated to Justice Vinson that the Holmes-Brandeis dissents had won the day, Vinson was convinced that the times and the impending threat of communism demanded an exceptional response. Holmes and Brandeis had faced only isolated and limited threats, and thus had given no thought to more serious threats to the national security. By contrast, Justice Vinson faced what he perceived to be an "apparatus designed and dedicated to the overthrow of the Government" in an environment of "world crisis after crisis."

"Speech is not an absolute," wrote Vinson, and the proof of his declaration resided in yet another sententious maxim: "Nothing is more certain in modern society than the principle that there are no absolutes." For Vinson, the liberalized clear and present danger test, which protected nonviolent dissent, had to give way to the felt necessities of the day. "To those who would paralyze our Government in the face of impending threat by encasing it in a semantic straitjacket we must reply that all concepts are relative."

What connection does the *Dennis* case bear to the doctrine of seditious libel? Advocacy of communism does not defame the government or its officials in the way that ordinary scandalmongering does. But it certainly does make statements "likely or designed to diminish" government's authority. As Frederick Siebert reminds us, "During the entire period [of the late seventeenth century] any reflection on the government in written or printed form was a seditious libel." Marxist doctrine was a threat because it suggested that the prevailing system did not have a monopoly on ideas of freedom and human liberation. As a practicable theory, Marxism had demonstrated international appeal not only for authoritarian terror, but also for the struggles of the oppressed. In short, Marxism made the establishment tremble in its boots.

The *Dennis* decision was not entirely devoid of principle. Justice Vinson did make a valiant effort through use of logic to justify saving the government —"our Government"—from "paralysis." He began, as would *The Progressive*

146   court later, with a self-evident proposition designed to appeal to fear: The government must have the power to protect itself from armed internal attack, for otherwise "no subordinate value" could be protected. From this proposition the Court reasoned that the government could put down any "clear and present danger" of violent overthrow. Applying this logic to the issue in *Dennis,* Vinson concluded that Marxist ideologues teaching their doctrine posed a clear and present danger and hence could be outlawed. The most striking aspect of his reasoning, however, is the question-begging manner in which he equated authority with freedom and dissent with sedition—reasoning harking back to the law of seditious libel in the age of autocracy. Established government, in Vinson's rhetoric, as in that of the Tudors and Stuarts, took on the aspect of divinity in the combat between the forces of darkness and light.

The party leaders' supposedly diabolical nature may help to explain why Justice Vinson was undeterred by the gaping absence of evidence of any plans or conduct of armed revolt on the part of the defendants. As he conceded, no specific threat could be perceived; it sufficed that "the revolutionists would strike when they thought the time was ripe."

The *Dennis* Court seemed untroubled by the long-standing principle that mere preparation for a crime is not an accepted ground for punishment. In response to the defendants' argument that a conspiracy to advocate, as distinct from advocacy itself, comprised only the preparation and thus was not punishable, Justice Vinson was again categorical. The conspiracy itself, he asserted, created the requisite danger even though no overtly violent act occurred. The Court substituted for the overt act "the inflammable nature of world conditions, similar uprisings in other countries, and the touch-and-go nature of our relations with countries with whom petitioners were in the very least ideologically attuned." The unverbalized apprehensions that domestic Communists were invisibly connected with violent Communist activities abroad helped supply the missing proof of "danger."

SEDITIOUS LIBEL IN THE SECRECY STATE: SNEPP, AGEE, AND THE PROGRESSIVE

Against the background we have traced, it is not surprising that seditious libel should reemerge given our present national mentality. Just as the government during the Red Menace and McCarthy eras invoked national defense to defend the indefensible, so today does the secrecy state invoke national security to disguise fear and authoritarianism. In our present national state of insecurity, the mere labeling of dissenters and critics as menaces and the government as **147** infallible protector suffices to set in motion the judicial engines of repression.

The *Snepp, Agee,* and *Progressive* cases reveal the dark tradition to be in the ascendancy. The courts in those cases inflicted unprecedented penalties upon governmental critics who had exposed secrecy as a sham and security as an illusion. Under the reasoning employed in these cases, the ideology of dissent no longer matters; criticism is libel *per se.* If secrecy is the cost of the nuclear age, as other signals from the administration suggest, then seditious libel threatens permanently to dislodge freedom of speech.

Snepp v. United States

In *Snepp* v. *United States,* decided in 1980, the Supreme Court purported to resolve an apparently simple question of contract law: whether an agreement by a former CIA official "not . . . [to] publish . . . any information or material relating to the Agency, its activities or intelligence activities generally, either during or after the term of [his] employment . . . without specific prior approval by the Agency" is enforceable.

Frank Snepp had signed such an agreement when he began working for the CIA in 1968. After leaving his post as a CIA officer in Vietnam, he published *Decent Interval,* a narrative exposing incidents of malfeasance, dishonesty, and corruption he had witnessed in the CIA, particularly in its role in the U.S. withdrawal from Vietnam. Snepp claimed that his book revealed no classified information. The agency did not challenge his claim, but it sued him for violating the secrecy agreement. According to the government's theory, the book's defamatory content did not matter. Snepp's wrong was his failure to clear his manuscript with the agency's censors. The reality of the case, however, is otherwise. Persuading the trial court that the book had caused the government "irreparable harm and loss," the CIA scored an unprecedented victory when the court imposed a constructive trust on Snepp's profits. In addition, the agency won an injunction prohibiting Snepp from speaking or writing about the CIA without the agency's permission for the rest of his life. The appellate court agreed but set aside the constructive trust as an unwarranted restriction of Snepp's First Amendment right to publish unclassified information.

The reasons for the Court's not basing its decision exclusively on the contractual claim of the government are only partly explained by its condemnation of ill-gotten gains. First, there is a serious question whether the document Snepp signed when he joined the CIA was enforceable even under contract principles. Second, even assuming that the agreement was a valid contract, attempted enforcement through censorship implicates the First Amendment.

148   Third, resolving this case solely on the contractual grounds would make all the government's subsequent claims to secrecy dependent upon whether the official insider had signed the relevant document. Finally, the CIA's unwillingness to enforce similar agreements against other governmental officials, such as Henry Kissinger, who have published secrets without permission, strongly suggests that the real motive underlying the Snepp prosecution was the CIA's desire to silence arbitrarily a hostile critic.

Of these points, the last indicates most clearly the trend toward seditious libel. Although dozens of former CIA employees had published books about the CIA without first having submitted their manuscripts to the censors, the CIA elected to prosecute only Frank Snepp and Victor Marchetti, both strident critics of the agency. The CIA subsequently admitted in congressional hearings that it had selectively enforced the prepublication review requirement solely to silence critics. Nonetheless, the Court ignored the selective enforcement argument when Snepp attempted to raise it as a defense to the CIA's suit against him.

The importance of the Snepp decision to the discussion of seditious libel lies in the nature of the harm the book was said to have caused. The trial judge found that a former intelligence agent's disclosures "can be detrimental to vital national interests even if the published information is unclassified." Ignoring the speculative nature of the word "can," the Supreme Court recounted the evidence, concluding that it established "irreparable harm and loss."

The "undisputed evidence" consisted of testimony by CIA director Admiral Stansfield Turner who "testified without contradiction" that Snepp's book and "others like it" had caused the CIA to lose face abroad.

If actual loss of confidential information had been the standard for relief, the government would have had no case because Snepp disclosed no classified information. Indeed, under that theory, Snepp's strict guarding of classified secrets may well have enhanced the reputation of the CIA, by conveying an image of continuing faithfulness on the part of a former CIA agent despite his violent disagreement with the agency's operations. From this perspective, Snepp was not a radical seeking to destroy the CIA, but rather a reformer who recognized the importance of the CIA's function in American government and refused to exploit and sensationalize classified information.

The most telling part of the opinion lies in the Court's vast silence about freedom of speech. Snepp had claimed that the CIA could not enforce its claims of censorship over him because publication of *unclassified* information was protected by the First Amendment. Snepp's claim was reasonable in light of the ruling in the *Marchetti* litigation in 1972. In *Marchetti,* a federal appeals court explicitly refused to enforce a secrecy oath on the ground that the First Amendment protected the disclosure of unclassified information. Why, then,

did the Court treat Snepp as a willful, deliberate, and surreptitious oath viola- **149**
tor with no First Amendment rights?

Applying a psychopathology of footnotes, some expert might give us an analysis of the Court's enigmatic footnote Number 3. In that marginalium the Court casually disposed of Snepp's First Amendment claim by noting that he had not signed the agreement under duress. The government, the Court asserted, had a "compelling interest in protecting . . . the appearance of confidentiality so essential to the effective operation of our foreign intelligence service." Commentators have detailed the grotesqueness of the Court's arguments and its bizarre use of precedent in that footnote. A logician might tell us that the Court's response to Snepp's argument was a classic case of *ignoratio elenchi,* an exemplary begging of the question. As the Court well knows, it is a cardinal rule of argument that one does not assert what needs to be proved.

By its silence, the Court denied that Snepp had a right to speak against governmental policy; by its soft-pedaling of Snepp's First Amendment argument in the margin on the page, it denigrated the right of dissent to marginal status. Such question-begging of constitutional claims fortunately is infrequent. But when it occurs, it often signals that the Court has answered the question begged in a monumentally important way. Would that the Court had been so explicit about its premises in Snepp. A more honest opinion, for example, might have asserted that the First Amendment does not operate in the area of national security, and that, like obscenity, certain sensitive political matters are beyond the pale of its protection. At least when the Court makes explicit such premises, they can be examined, evaluated, and exposed as congenial to seditious libel. When, however, the Court refuses to confront the issue and turns its back on a constitutional claim of the right to criticize the government, it has smoothed the path for orthodoxy and facilitated the reemergence of seditious libel in a disguised form.

The Court's true perception of the issue as one of seditious libel seems evident in its footnote remark: "The problem is to ensure in advance, and by proper procedures, that information detrimental to national interest is not published." Thus, it is not danger to the national security nor loss of sensitive secrets but adverse reflections on government that constitute the forbidden evil. By sanctioning the idea that authority can outlaw injury to its reputation and punish those who bring it into public contempt, scorn, or disrepute, the Snepp decision delivers a discouraging blow to the First Amendment. This new seditious libel is not the more enlightened doctrine whereby the truth of the criticisms and honest motives would exonerate the defendant. Indeed, the very truth of the criticisms would seem to magnify the offense of the libeler.

150 *Haig* v. *Agee*

The case of Philip Agee, a CIA agent who quit his job with the CIA and embarked on an international campaign to discredit the agency as "the Gestapo and S.S. of our time" presented a more dramatic case of seditious libel. Unlike Snepp, Agee was neither temperate nor cautious in his attacks on the CIA. He conceived of the CIA not as an institution for gathering intelligence against hostile nations but as a "sinister secret police force" committing crimes abroad in the name of the American people. These "crimes" included infiltrating government, the military, the police, and trade unions of foreign nations, propping up friends and beating down enemies, particularly the enemies of American multinational companies. His repeated exposures of the identities of CIA operatives abroad were deliberate attempts to embarrass, defame, and ultimately destroy the network of secrecy cloaking the CIA in worldwide "military coups, torture chambers, and terrorism." Deeming the CIA's existence a threat to national and world peace, Agee made good use of his training in undercover operations to reveal in detail to an international public the nature and size of "the enemy" among them.

Like Snepp, Agee had signed a secrecy oath. Unlike Snepp, he divulged classified information. He initially thwarted the CIA censors by traveling and publishing abroad. There were indications, however, that the CIA intended to strike back. In West Germany, after having been deported from Britain, France, and Holland, Agee received word that the secretary of state had revoked his passport on the ground that Agee's activities were "causing or [were] likely to cause serious damage to the national security or the foreign policy of the United States."

Agee immediately brought suit against the secretary of state, arguing that the passport revocation violated his right to travel and his First Amendment right to criticize the government. Both the trial and appellate courts, deciding the case on statutory rather than constitutional grounds, agreed that the executive's action was unauthorized and ordered the secretary of state to reinstate Agee's passport.

Chief Justice Burger, writing for the majority, reversed the judgment of the lower courts on the statutory issue and dismissed the constitutional claims. In the opinion, Burger strained to legitimize the executive's exercise of power in the face of strong precedent to the contrary. To that end, he described in detail the extensive efforts of Agee and his collaborators to expose the identities of CIA employees abroad. Agee's First Amendment claim received little more than a "*Snepp* footnote" treatment in the concluding part of the opinion. My analysis does not aim to level counterarguments against the Supreme Court's rationale in upholding the revocation of Agee's passport. Rather, I aim to explore the significance of the Court's marginal statements on the First Amendment issue and to probe the reasons for its silences about Agee's status as dissenter. As in *Snepp*, it is in the Court's footnotes, ellipses, and lacunae that seditious libel emerges.

Justice Burger opened his opinion with an exordium that accused Agee of soliciting murder through his campaign to expose the atrocities of the CIA abroad. In the familiar idiom of seditious libel, he portrayed Agee as a diabolic international sneak, a contract breaker, and an accomplice to murder, all the while stressing that Agee's "identifications . . . have been followed by episodes of violence against the persons and organizations identified." This statement was graphically amplified in a footnote with examples of murder and machine-gun fire directed at CIA personnel abroad.

Despite a complete lack of evidence indicating a casual link between Agee's activities and this violence, the Court denounced Agee's revelations as "thinly-veiled invitations to violence." One CIA official asserted that these revelations "markedly increased the likelihood of individuals so identified being the victims of violence, [and] could, in [then current] circumstances, [have] result[ed] in someone's death." In a manner reminiscent of Holmes's metaphysics of socialist "obstruction," the Court conjured up a conspiratorial web linking criticism of the CIA with physical attacks on CIA personnel.

One possible explanation for the exceptional dismissal of Agee's First Amendment claim lies in the Court's alternative ground for holding that Agee's criticism of the government falls outside the protection of the First Amendment. Justice Burger, echoing the Court's pronouncements in the Red Menace era, asserted that Agee's disclosures were "clearly not protected by the Constitution" because they had the declared purpose of "obstructing intelligence operations and the recruiting of intelligence personnel." In the Court's view, Agee's discrediting of the CIA was merely a punishable form of obstruction that was adventitiously related to protected criticism of the government. His denunciations and exposures were categorically declared to be "conduct" and were divested of any privileged status they may have had as "ideas." The Court wryly observed, however, that he remained free to criticize the government.

In a manner representative of the Holmes trilogy, the Court obfuscated the contour between speech and conduct. Despite its assertion that Agee's disclosures were conduct rather than speech, the Court did not attempt to connect those disclosures to any concrete harm such as physical violence or assault. Instead, the court relied on the ambiguous term "obstruct," again reminiscent of the Holmes trilogy, to bridge the gap between speech and conduct. One has but to recall Eugene Debs's conviction for "obstructing" the draft—a conviction based solely on his speech on socialism—to fully appreciate how the Court could transform expression into criminal action.

152 *United States* v. *The Progressive, Inc.*

In *Snepp* and *Agee*, the Court made no overtures toward any First Amendment formula, disregarding even the "clear and present danger" test of the Red Menace and McCarthy era cases. Instead, the Court was content to dispatch freedom of speech arguments with the litany of "national security" and the "explosive" nature of foreign relations. Although these terms resist decoding within the individual context of each opinion, taken together they suggest a looming, omnipresent fear of sudden destruction.

The concrete form of that fear took on precise definition in the case of *United States* v. *The Progressive, Inc.*, which involved the threatened exposure of the secrecy state's most awesome secret: the hydrogen bomb. The *Progressive* court upheld the censorship of an article that attempted to discredit the government's classification and control of information by showing that secrecy over the bomb was a sham. Following the Supreme Court's lead in *Agee*, the district court compared the *Progressive*'s exposé to the publication of troop movements in wartime. The opinion not only turned settled principles on their head but ingenuously disclosed the defining symbols of national security. With its concrete images of destruction and its historic defense of censorship, *The Progressive* case supplies the missing link in the Supreme Court's revival of seditious libel.

The offending article, "The H-Bomb Secret: How We Got It; Why We're Telling It," was written by Howard Morland, a free-lance journalist and recent autodidact on the subject of nuclear weapons. Morland's intent was to stimulate public discussion of a forbidden but vitally important topic: the nature, composition, and reaction processes of the hydrogen bomb. This technical information, he argued, was essential for public understanding and debate over the merits of the nuclear weapons industry, "the vast industrial complex that turns out three new nuclear weapons a day." According to Morland, the information in his article was taken exclusively from public sources, such as the *Encyclopedia Americana,* in which Dr. Edward Teller's article on the hydrogen bomb had appeared over a decade earlier.

Morland launched his investigation upon learning of an incident in which a congressman had requested the Department of Energy to explain its reasons for a projected shortage of plutonium in the nuclear weapons program. The congressman had inquired whether the neutron bomb, then scheduled for production, would consume more plutonium than did standard nuclear weapons, and he also sought information about new multiple-warhead missiles and particular production plants. The Department of Energy, replying that it would not provide an unclassified response to the questions, insisted that *the questions themselves* should be classified because they contained "secret restrictive data." In short, Morland observed, not only could energy officials withhold answers, they could also "confiscate the questions."

Thus, Morland's objective in publishing the article was political, not scientific; he wanted to discredit the official shroud of secrecy surrounding the hydrogen bomb as a pernicious illusion: "Secrecy itself, especially the power . . . to declare some topics off limits, contributes to a political climate in which the nuclear establishment can conduct business as usual, protecting and perpetuating the production of these horror weapons." Arguing that the price of secrecy was to stifle healthy debate about nuclear policy, Morland set out to disabuse the public of the "secret" nature of nuclear weapons and to generate public discussion about their continued production. Before the article went to press, however, the government obtained a temporary restraining order enjoining its publication in the *Progressive*. The prosecution claimed that the Atomic Energy Act authorized an injunction against the disclosure of "restricted data," including information relating to the design, manufacture, or utilization of nuclear weapons.

The district court, without holding an evidentiary hearing, decided the matter amid a snowstorm of contending affidavits. The publication of the article, concluded Judge Warren, was "analogous to publication of troop movements or locations in time of war" and, therefore, posed a grave danger to the national security. That danger, in Judge Warren's words, was that the technical information set forth in Morland's article "could accelerate the membership of a candidate nation in the thermonuclear club." The "club" metaphor, ingenious enough, gave way to a more emotional image when Judge Warren commented from the bench, "I want to think a long, hard time before I'd give a hydrogen bomb to Idi Amin." The words "could accelerate" also reveal the speculative and subjective nature of Judge Warren's conclusions. Indeed, no facts were advanced to show how the publication of Morland's article would even remotely pose the danger fantasized by Judge Warren.

While the case was on appeal, however, the First Amendment issue became moot. An enterprising reporter, after spending a week in local public libraries, had written and published essentially the same information in the Milwaukee *Sentinel*. When comparable information began to appear in other publications, the government abandoned the case. As in the *Pentagon Papers* case, the government claimed that the republic would virtually crumble unless publication was enjoined. In *The Progressive*, just as in the *Pentagon Papers*, eventual publication made the government lose face. Morland's article not only fulfilled its political aim of discrediting secrecy and promoting public debate, but it also dramatized embarrassing facts. If two scientifically unsophisticated journalists

154 could discover dangerous "secrets" about the bomb with a little research and thought, it is difficult to imagine how the government can keep smaller fringe nations or groups out of the "thermonuclear club."

What bearing does *The Progressive* have on the resurgence of seditious libel? Prior to the Supreme Court's decisions in *Snepp* and *Agee*, *The Progressive* stood as the one federal decision in which the *Near* exception was transformed into the rule for cases involving "national security." *The Progressive* suggests that whenever the administration can bring forth a claim sufficiently threatening to a frightened judiciary, publication of even readily available data may be censored. The case also suggests that the judiciary will not scrutinize the alleged threat but will silence the dissenter upon a showing of embarrassment to the government. The case was such an aberration that one is tempted to dismiss one's own fears as hysterical or alarmist. Because it was unprecedented and never affirmed by an appellate court, *The Progressive* decision would not ordinarily be thought to have disturbed the constitutional order. Inasmuch as it foreshadowed *Snepp* and *Agee,* however, we owe *The Progressive* decision some attention. Judge Warren's unmediated prose contains elements of seditious libel that lie concealed in the more sophisticated language of the Supreme Court in *Snepp* and *Agee:* a rhetoric of fear and hysteria, a portrait of the governmental critic as a public menace, a suspension of the rules of logic and evidence, and a bow to the infallible authority of the secrecy state. The fact that political criticism was at the core of the censored article, when coupled with the lack of demonstrable harm to anything other than the illusion of secrecy, squarely lodges *The Progressive* in the tradition of seditious libel.

SEDITIOUS LIBEL IN THE SUN

The dark origins and modern shadows of the First Amendment are not, fortunately, the entire story. Into this tradition of gloom the Supreme Court has, on occasion, cast brilliant rays of enlightenment, repudiating seditious libel, protecting dissent, and occasionally celebrating the primacy of its role in a democracy. This section traces that contrasting tradition and considers how *Snepp, Agee,* and *The Progressive* might have been decided in the light.

Pencils of Light: Subversive Dissents

Although Justice Holmes never repudiated the Red Menace trilogy, he announced just a few months later in his great *Abrams* dissent that seditious libel was dead. What distinguished *Abrams*'s case from *Schenck, Debs,* and *Frohwerk* was an amendment to the Espionage Act of 1917 that made it a crime to urge curtailment of munitions production. Abrams received a twenty-year jail sentence for printing and distributing a leaflet urging a strike. Taking issue with the majority opinion—and, indeed, with the very approach he had employed only months earlier in *Schenck, Debs,* and *Frohwerk*—Holmes insisted that the statute should be strictly construed, that Abrams could be punished only on a showing of specific intent, and that no one could contend that the distribution of a "silly leaflet by an unknown man" could pose any threat to the government's war effort. It was clear to Holmes that Abrams's only crime was criticism of the war and that this criticism was privileged under the First Amendment. Holmes's *Abrams* dissent boldly declared that the First Amendment outlawed seditious libel and that the Sedition Act of 1798 had been a travesty. He formulated a liberal rule for the protection of dissent based on the theory of a "free trade in ideas." This reformulation of the First Amendment owed much of its appeal to Holmes's engaging metaphor of the marketplace of ideas—a metaphor that replaced the hysterical rhetoric and fiery imagery and proffered instead a vision of ideas as commodities. Such a vision was particularly congenial to the American mentality so solidly ensconced on free enterprise and the workings of the marketplace.

The consequences of this metaphoric displacement soon became apparent. In 1925, Holmes penned another dissenting opinion in *Gitlow v. New York* that repudiated the rhetoric of seditious libel. "Every idea is an incitement," he asserted, rebuffing the majority's finding that a left-wing leaflet was written in "the language of direct incitement." He tempered this fiery imagery with a sobering, indeed shocking, statement of his theory of the right of dissent: "Eloquence may set fire to reason. . . . If in the long run the beliefs expressed in proletarian dictatorships are destined to be accepted by the dominant forces of the community, the only meaning of free speech is that they should be given their chance and have their way."

The virtue of this free-market metaphor is that it insulates even the most execrable forms of dissent from suppression and thus acts as a shield against the doctrine of seditious libel. The Court has never pursued to its limits the Holmesean version of speech as commodity.

Even more celebrated than Holmes's dissents was Brandeis's concurring opinion in *Whitney v. California,* which has come to be regarded as the definitive statement on freedom of speech. Brandeis, in developing an eloquent defense of the right of dissent, delivered a tribute to the Founding Fathers and the ideals of the Enlightenment that he believed they wanted to secure in the First Amendment:

Those who won our independence believed that the final end of the State was to make men free to develop their faculties; and that in its government the deliberative forces should prevail over the arbitrary. . . . They believed liberty to be the secret of happiness and courage to be the secret of liberty. They believed that freedom to think as you will and to speak as you think are means indispensable to the discovery and spread of political truth; that without free speech and assembly discussion would be futile; that with them, discussion affords ordinarily adequate protection against the dissemination of noxious doctrine.

In Brandeis's view, more speech, not enforced silence, was the proper remedy to expose falsehoods. Suppression of speech was like burning witches, irrational per se. According to Brandeis, even advocacy of lawbreaking could not justify denial of free speech so long as the advocacy fell short of incitement.

The Holmes dissents and Brandeis concurrence have a brilliance unmatched in any majority opinion, a liberating, ebullient antiauthoritarian style. Seen as part of a struggle against authoritarianism, the opinions of Holmes and Brandeis help us to view some other celebrated cases in the perspective of seditious libel.

Shafts of Sunlight on Seditious Libel

The First Amendment case of *Near* v. *Minnesota* has already figured in our discussion of *Agee* and *The Progressive,* although less for its luminous rays than for the black spot that courts have recently discovered in it. Celebrated for its rule against prior restraint, *Near* deserves equal accolades for its place in the enlightened tradition against seditious libel.

In *Near,* the Court considered the validity of a Minnesota statute that criminalized publication of "malicious, scandalous, and defamatory newspapers" on the grounds that such newspapers tended to disturb the peace of the community and to provoke assaults and the commission of crime. The Court did not challenge the validity of the state's proffered rationale; indeed, it casually observed that one of the original defendants was apparently shot by gangsters after publication of the first issue. Further, the Court acknowledged that a newspaper charging public officers with corruption, malfeasance, or neglect of duty naturally creates a public scandal. Conceding the power of authority to enforce "the primary requirements of decency" against obscene publications, the Court categorically separated the criticism of public officials from the realm of "indecencies" subject to the censor. The Court concluded that even though

charges of official malfeasance "unquestionably create a public scandal," cen- **157**
sorship would create an even more serious public evil.

More important than its vaunted rule against prior restraint is the Court's
elaboration of the reasons for protecting criticism of public officers even when
such criticism inspires violent reaction. Recognition that accusations of official corruption may create "resentment and the disposition to resort to violent
means of redress" did not, in the *Near* Court's view, warrant curtailment of the
press. In words that the *Agee* Court would have done well to heed, the Court
boldly warned that if the danger of violent reaction could justify governmental
interference with the freedom of initial publication, "the constitutional protection would be reduced to a mere form of words." The threat of a hostile
and defiant organization resorting to violence did not diminish this protection. Thus, although *Near* specifically addressed the constitutionality of prior
restraints, the court's elaborate defense of press freedoms argues compellingly
against the doctrine of seditious libel.

What the *Near* decision was to seditious libel in the form of injunction, *New
York Times Co.* v. *Sullivan* was to seditious libel in the form of damages. This
historic case gave the Court its first opportunity to repudiate the law of seditious libel. *Sullivan* involved an advertisement in the *New York Times* soliciting
contributions for the civil rights campaign of Dr. Martin Luther King, Jr. The
advertisement complained of police brutality toward civil rights protesters and
contained factual inaccuracies. Under Alabama's libel statute, a publication was
"libelous per se" if it tended to injure a person's reputation or to bring him into
public contempt. Finding that the advertisement had implied public misconduct, or at least a lack of official integrity, on the part of Sullivan, the police
commissioner in Montgomery, the jury returned a half-million-dollar damage
award against the *Times* company.

In striking down the award, the Court declared:

> [W]e consider this case against the background of a profound national
> commitment to the principle that debate on public issues should be un-
> inhibited, robust, and wide open, and that it may well include vehement,
> caustic, and sometimes unpleasantly sharp attacks on government and
> public officials. . . . Criticism of . . . official conduct does not lose
> its constitutional protection merely because it is effective criticism and
> hence diminishes . . . official reputations.

Harry Kalven celebrated this historic decision in an article in which he suggested that *Sullivan* had revolutionized First Amendment theory. He suggested
that in *Sullivan* the Court, by emphasizing the doctrine of seditious libel as
the key to the meaning of the First Amendment, had at last understood how

158 seditious libel strikes at the very heart of democracy. "Political freedom," he asserted, "ends when government can use its powers and its courts to silence its critics":

> My point is not the tepid one that there should be leeway for criticism of the government. It is rather that defamation of the government is an impossible notion for a democracy. In brief, I suggest that the presence or absence in the law of the concept of seditious libel defines the society. A society may or may not treat obscenity or contempt by publication as legal offenses without altering its basic nature. If, however, it makes seditious libel an offense, it is not a free society no matter what its other characteristics.

In Kalven's view, the *Sullivan* decision set right side up for the first time the theory of the freedom-of-speech clause: The Court had finally discovered in the controversy over seditious libel that the clue to the "central meaning" was unusually apt, he wrote, in view of the Court's finding that the amendment protected a core of speech essential to the working of a democracy. After *Sullivan*, Kalven predicted, the "analysis of free speech issues should hereafter begin with the significant issue of seditious libel and defamation of government by its critics rather than with the sterile [Holmesian] example of a man falsely yelling fire in a crowded theater."

Despite Kalven's prognostication, however, neither the courts nor other commentators responded to his call. Finally, in 1971, Kalven had cause to celebrate the apparent fulfillment of his prophecy when the court received another opportunity in *The Pentagon Papers* case to reassess the central role of seditious libel. The Court's *per curiam* opinion upheld the right of the *Washington Post* and the *New York Times* to publish classified documents that detailed the U.S. involvement in the Vietnam War and were embarrassing to the government. The *per curiam* opinion rested its holding on *Near's* presumption against prior restraints. In his concurring opinion, however, Justice Douglas, citing *Sullivan*, resumed the discussion of seditious libel. The dominant purpose of the First Amendment, he explained, was to stamp out the use of seditious libel to punish utterances that were "embarrassing to the powers-that-be." This historic purpose underscored the relevance of *Sullivan's* protection of "robust, uninhibited discussion" to the problem of government secrecy: "Secrecy in government is fundamentally antidemocratic, perpetuating bureaucratic errors. Open debate and discussion of public issues are vital to our national health." Justice Black, in his concurring opinion, agreed that the historic aim of the First Amendment was to protect the press "so that it could bare the secrets of government and inform the people."

The glaring fact that the administration's reputation had been damaged may

have clarified for at least some members of the Court the relation between **159**
the government's theory of the case and the doctrine of seditious libel. Justice White, for example, was convinced that the newspapers' previous disclosures had indeed damaged public interest, but he concurred nevertheless. On
a generous reading, if the Court acknowledged that public confidence in the
government would be shattered by the disclosures, then the implication of the
Pentagon Papers decision may well be that the First Amendment invites such a
shattering.

In summary, the Court's modern tradition of seditious libel consists of
two distinct and fundamentally irreconcilable traditions. The dark tradition, in
which government critics were throttled, began with the Holmes Red Menace
trilogy and was carried forward in *Dennis*. The enlightened tradition is one
of tolerance for those who defy the prevailing orthodoxies of the day. *Near,
Sullivan,* and *The Pentagon Papers* carry forward the bold tributes to freedom
of expression and the right to criticize the government that Holmes and Brandeis had formulated as defiant dissenters on the Court. Although the *Sullivan*
decision had apparently finally ousted seditious libel from our system of government, the courts in *Agee, Snepp,* and *The Progressive* have restored life to
that doctrine in the guise of protecting the national security. The question that
remains, as darkness once again overtakes enlightenment, is the same troublesome question raised by the Sedition Act of 1798: How far may authority go
to suppress the free and full expression of disapproval of the government?

CONCLUSION

The ideal that was grafted onto the Constitution in the First Amendment
did not originate with the framers. The Greeks recognized that freedom of
speech is integral to democracy and equality. For the ancient Athenians, the
greatest political freedom, that which was the very essence of the democratic
form of government, was *isegoria*—the equal right of speech in public assembly. At the core of this great freedom lay dialectic, a method that presupposes
the confrontation of opposing opinions freely expressed and thus, it has been
argued, sharpens the mind for philosophy and critical thought. With its emphasis on multivocality, on the confrontation of a multiplicity of equal voices
with discordant ideas, dialectic parallels the democratic ideal that authority
dwells in dialogue, that it resists a finalizing determinacy. Both the philosophical method of dialectic and the political right of dialogue ultimately rest upon
the view that each individual participant has the capacity to form opinions and
make judgments on matters of common concern. In Athens, because power

160   was in the hands of the citizenry, it was expected that each citizen would be interested in the affairs of the state; if he lacked such interest, he was considered useless. Euripides cogently conveyed this attitude in dramatic dialogue:

> This is true Liberty when free born men
> Having to advise the public may speak free,
> Which he who can, and will, deserves high praise,
> Who neither can nor will, may hold his peace;
> What can be juster in a State than this?

Centuries later, Milton, declaring his legacy, quoted Euripides' dramatic speech in the title page of his attack on the licensing of the press. In his defense of political pluralism in the *Areopagitica,* Milton carried forward the Athenian idea that truth is not revealed through divine inspiration but arises from the clash of opinions. Addressing the Long Parliament, Milton railed against the parliamentary suppression of dissenting opinion. Censorship, he asserted, reduces humans to brutes and elevates censors to tyrants:

> Ye cannot make us now less capable, less knowing, less eagerly pursuing of the truth, unless ye first make yourselves, that made us so, less the lovers, less the founders of our true liberty. We can grow ignorant again, brutish, formal and slavish . . . ; but you then must first become that which ye cannot be, oppressive, arbitrary and tyrannous, as they were from whom ye have freed us.

More eloquent than Milton's frequently quoted paean to truth, this passage illumines the organic connections between the suppression of dissent and despotism, and it suggests how the confinement of political discourse to official monologue stunts the body politic. To Milton, the multivocality of voices promoted—indeed, was essential to—truth. And although those lively, vigorous things called books might, like the fabled dragon's teeth, chance to "spring up armed men," insisted:

> Since . . . the knowledge and survey of vice is in this world so necessary to the constituting of human virtue, and the scanning of error to the confirmation of truth, how can we more safely, and with less danger, scout into the regions of sin and falsity than by reading all manner of tractates, and hearing all manner of reason? And this is the benefit which may be had of books promiscuously read.

The idea that the road to truth is through error, by going astray, was not original with Milton. Socrates had discovered the secret meaning of truth in the etymology of *aletheia,* the Greek word for truth: *aletheia,* a "divine wan- **161** dering." To both Milton and Socrates, "wandering" and "going astray" were positive terms; they signal the vitality of a mind that turns from the trodden path to the unknown. To speak, to think, and to read "promiscuously" means to deviate and to celebrate one's deviation, mixing all manner of thought and opinion while defying conventions and propriety. Through a process of intellectual promiscuity, the mind begets offspring and claims them as her own. The ravishing censors would, however, use her to bear only those ideas that reproduced their patriarchal authority.

We capture the spirit of Socrates, the polemic of Milton, and the prophecies of Brandeis and Kalven in a passage in Dostoevsky's *Crime and Punishment* where Razumikhin declares:

> I like people to talk nonsense. It is man's unique privilege, among all other organisms. By pursuing falsehood you will arrive at the truth! The fact that I am in error shows that I am human. You will not attain to one single truth until you have produced at least fourteen false theories, and perhaps a hundred and fourteen. . . . It is almost better to tell your own lies than somebody else's truth; in the first case you are a man, in the second you are no better than a parrot!

The one theme uniting the voices of Pericles, Milton, and Dostoevsky is dialogue, the idea of the polyphony of voices contending for truth. Political dialogue, disengaging the mind from orthodoxy, opposes the official monologue of power, which can triumph only by silencing other voices, as by censorship and seditious libel. The notion that human beings should be silenced rather than free to pursue their own consciences; licensed rather than free to write something that rattles the catechism of the day; bound up by paternalistic laws rather than free to investigate everything under the sun—such a notion reduces human beings to a brutish condition. It was just this "mutilation of the thinking process" that Alexander Meiklejohn, the leading First Amendment theorist of our time, insisted that the Constitution outlawed.

The theme that freedom of speech rests upon a dialogic dynamic in which many equal consciousnesses participate is implicit in the enlightened tradition against seditious libel. In repudiating the idea that government may punish persons for their discord with the official truth, the Court's enlightened tradition has captured this theme and claimed it for the forces of democracy. It has been our aim to suggest that this theme has recently been taken hostage in the camp of darkness and that official monologue has supplanted political dialogue. The task that remains is for the Court, exposed to its conflicting traditions of democracy and seditious libel, to choose which shall prevail.

[Mark Schapiro]

10

THE EXCLUDABLES

Dario Fo, the Italian author of more than forty satirical plays, seems an unlikely threat to the security of the United States. One of Fo's plays, *Accidental Death of an Anarchist*, debuted on Broadway in 1984, but the author was not allowed to supervise rehearsals. After Fo was invited by the producers, the U.S. State Department denied him a visa, deciding that his membership in a prisoners' rights organization known as Soccorso Rosso branded him a "terrorist sympathizer." After the American Civil Liberties Union and a dozen other civil liberties and theatrical groups launched a public campaign in Fo's behalf, the State Department reversed itself and gave the playwright a visa just before his play's premiere. The novel approach taken by the play's producers may have been the key to the State Department's about-face: they claimed that denying Fo a visa infringed on their ability to earn a living as investors in the play.

In 1983 Hortensia Allende, the widow of Salvador Allende and a resident of Mexico, was invited by several universities in the United States to speak about the role of women in the opposition to the Chilean dictatorship. But the U.S. embassy in Mexico denied her a visa; it cites Mrs. Allende's ties to the World Peace Council, which the State Department claims is a Soviet front. The rejection of Mrs. Allende's request for a visa came at a time when the Reagan administration was considering the resumption of arms sales to Chile. The denial had a particularly ironic denouement: Soon afterward, Hortensia Allende's "successor," Mrs. Augusto Pinochet, was Nancy Reagan's guest for tea at the White House.

In the 1960s Nino Pasti was Italy's representative to the NATO Military Committee, stationed at the Pentagon. Later he served as NATO's vice-supreme allied commander in Europe for nuclear affairs and, after retiring

Reprinted from *Mother Jones* 11 (January 1986), pp. 29–32 by permission of the publishers.

from the military, served two terms in the Italian senate. But Pasti's sentiments have changed since his days as a four-star general. Now more than
seventy years old, he claims to have American military documents that dispute NATO's assertion of Soviet military superiority in Europe. After Pasti
was invited by peace groups to speak against the cruise and Pershing II missile
deployments, his request for a visa was denied in the fall of 1983. His entry
into the United States, said the State Department, would be "prejudicial to the
public interest."

Fo, Allende, and Pasti are three among thousands of foreign intellectuals,
authors, and political figures who have been denied U.S. visas because of their
political beliefs. The case of Farley Mowat, the renowned Canadian writer,
provides another recent example.

Last April, Mowat was snared by the U.S. Immigration and Naturalization Service at Toronto's Pearson International Airport before his flight to Los
Angeles to kick off a publicity tour for his book *Sea of Slaughter*. The INS performed a routine check of airline passengers against its visa lookout book of
"excludable" aliens and discovered that Mowat was included. The Canadian–
U.S. border is supposedly open, and Mowat did not legally require a visa.

The INS refused to explain why it excluded Mowat, as it does with all
foreign citizens denied entry. An anonymous source later issued a partial explanation: Mowat, the author of over a dozen naturalist books, was put on
the INS "hot" list after being quoted in a 1968 newspaper article saying that
he was ready to defy American B-52 bombers with a .22 rifle during their
low-level training runs over Newfoundland. "My threat still holds," Mowat
explained during an interview after the airport incident. Soon after, the immigration service made what it considered a conciliatory gesture, offering Mowat
a one-shot waiver to complete his publicity tour. In a now-celebrated declaration of Canadian nationalism, Mowat retorted to the immigration service,
"Stuff it." (He subsequently indicated that he would accept the offer only if it
were accompanied by an apology from President Reagan and if he were flown
into the country on Air Force One.) "It was a scurrilous, scatological offer,"
explained Mowat, who has since written a book on the border controversy,
My Discovery of America.

As Mowat's case illustrates, some of the State Department's "excludables"
are issued visas with highly restricted travel rights, limited to particular cities
or special public appearances. Some are denied once, then admitted after
another try. The practice makes the United States the only Western democracy
to exclude foreign citizens on ideological grounds.

The Bureau of Consular Affairs' excludable list includes some of the world's
most distinguished authors and artists, all of whom have experienced visa
difficulties with the United States at one time or another: Nobel laureates

164 Gabriel García Márquez, Pablo Neruda, and Czeslaw Milosz; Mexican writer Carlos Fuentes, English novelist Graham Greene, South African dissident poet Dennis Brutus, and Spanish filmmaker Luis Buñuel.

Every administration since Eisenhower's has abused the ideological exclusion provision of U.S. immigration law. The Reagan administration, however, has gone a step farther to limit public debate—most notably concerning its Central American policies.

Eloquent spokespersons opposing the administration's policies have been repeatedly denied visas, preventing them from keeping speaking engagements, appearing at congressional hearings, or attending meetings with activists, business organizations, or university officials. For example, prior to last year's congressional vote on funding the Nicaraguan contras, Efraín Mondragon, a Contra defector, was prevented from traveling to Washington, D.C., to tell his inside story about Contra connections to the CIA. In 1983 Nicaraguan Interior Minister Tomás Borge was denied a visa, thus preventing him from making a speaking tour of the United States, although other members of Nicaragua's junta have been granted extremely limited travel rights. Opposition leaders from El Salvador such as Rubén Zamora and even right-wing politico Roberto d'Aubuisson (after falling out of favor with the State Department) have been denied visas during the past three years—as were four Salvadoran women who received the Robert F. Kennedy Human Rights Award for their work on behalf of families searching for their "disappeared" relatives.

After Borge was barred from entering the United States, Elliot Abrams, assistant secretary for human rights and humanitarian affairs, bluntly expressed the Reagan administration's position: "We're not keeping anybody's views out. . . . We are keeping out certain officials for certain policy reasons."

In October 1985 Margaret Randall, the American-born feminist writer and critic of U.S. policy in Latin America, was denied permanent residency status by the Immigration and Naturalization Service. The State Department says that Randall, who has recently taken a teaching position at the University of New Mexico, renounced her U.S. citizenship eighteen years ago to live in Mexico. In supporting its decision, the INS cited a series of passages from Randall's books—many of which are available in U.S. public libraries—that express support for the governments of Nicaragua and Cuba. The Center for Constitutional Rights is suing Attorney General Edwin Meese III and immigration officials. The center is representing a group of plaintiffs including Norman Mailer, Alice Walker, Kurt Vonnegut, Grace Paley, Arthur Miller, Toni Morrison, and William Styron. They allege that their constitutional rights to associate with and receive information from Randall are being violated.

Representative Barney Frank (D-Massachusetts) has challenged the administration with a bill that would revamp American visa policies and prevent the

State Department from considering its own foreign policy interest in deciding who is allowed to enter the United States. "Getting into the United States should not be seen as some mark of approval," says Frank.

The American Civil Liberties Union is challenging several of the visa denials in court. Representing some of the people who invited Hortensia Allende, the ACLU is suing the State Department for violating their right to hear her speak. The ACLU also claims that the latest rash of exclusions is contrary to congressional intent, which was aimed at barring the entry of espionage agents, saboteurs, and active revolutionaries, not those with controversial political views.

Gay rights groups have unsuccessfully challenged the ban on homosexuals, who are excludable under immigration law as sexual deviants. Even the State Department now supports repealing this provision of the immigration law relating to homosexuals—one of the few areas of agreement between Barney Frank and the administration.

Hodding Carter III, who was assistant secretary of state for public affairs during the administration of Jimmy Carter, sees the issue as one of the more absurd contradictions of U.S. human rights policy. "If you're in Moscow," he comments, "the Russians have made it hard for Nobel laureates to get out of the Soviet Union. We have made it hard for Nobel laureates to get into the United States." Carter describes the policies of the Reagan administration as "creating its [the administration's] own form of electronic curtain."

The law keeping America pure is the 1952 McCarran-Walter Act, which forms the basis for current U.S. immigration law; it is described by playwright Arthur Miller as "one of the pieces of garbage left behind by the sinking of the great scow of McCarthyism." Miller suffered his own travel problems in reverse when Joe McCarthy's Senate committee succeeded in getting his passport revoked in the 1950s, thereby preventing Miller from legally leaving the United States. President Truman excoriated Congress after it passed the law over his veto: "Seldom has a bill exhibited the distrust evidenced here for citizens and aliens alike."

The McCarran-Walter Act sets out thirty-three reasons for excluding individuals from the United States, combining prostitutes, paupers, and the insane with ideological undesirables and homosexuals. Of the two political sections in the act, one permits the exclusion of individuals associated with the Communist party or affiliated organizations. The other section can be used to exclude individuals considered a danger to the "welfare, safety, or security of the United States," or whose entry is deemed "prejudicial to the public interest." Both Nino Pasti and Hortensia Allende were denied visas on this basis. "Under section 27," says Charles Gordon, former general counsel to the Immigration and Naturalization Service and author of an eight-volume text on

166   immigration law, "you don't even need to call someone a Communist. You don't like Mrs. Allende, you don't give her a visa."

The State Department has repeatedly refused to publicly explain its support of the Act's political provisions, but at least one staunch supporter of the government's visa restrictions remained eager to defend them: the late Roy Cohn, chief architect of McCarthy's frenzied search for Communists in the 1950's. Thirty years later, Cohn's zeal for corking the flow of unfriendly ideas remained unabated. "There's no basic constitutional right to enter our shores," he said. "Many times these people are not what they look like. I don't think we have the compulsion to put the Statue of Liberty at their feet."

Yet even Cohn was critical of the State Department for excluding authors like Dario Fo and others. "Who cares about a playwright, a poet, or a ninety-year-old actress?" asked an exasperated Cohn. "Let them come and then fall of their own weight."*

Cohn's legacy lives on in more ways than one. The State Department maintains what is probably the world's largest blacklist, a global computer network known as the Automated Visa Lookout System (AVLOS).

There are about a million names in AVLOS, according to the Legislative and Intergovernmental Affairs Office of the State Department. The list includes all people considered offenders under the provisions of the McCarran-Walter Act. An estimated 40,000 to 50,000 individuals have been judged excludable for ideological reasons. A classified list of "proscribed organizations" is in the *Foreign Service Manual* issued to diplomatic staff in American embassies and missions overseas.

According to Charles Gordon, the list of individuals and organizations is compiled from a number of confidential intelligence sources, including the Central Intelligence Agency, local informants, and a host country's police services. The Royal Canadian Mounted Police, for example, provided the information on Farley Mowat that formed the basis for his exclusion.

When people apply for visas at their local U.S. consulate or at border checkpoints (as is the case for Canadians), their names are automatically checked against the AVLOS memory bank. Membership in any proscribed organization is reason enough for getting on the list.

Most excludable aliens are ultimately "waived" in and issued visas. But once a name is added to AVLOS, it is nearly impossible to have it erased, as Mowat and others have discovered. The only guaranteed method is to prove that one's association with a proscribed organization was involuntary, or to engage in a ritual of repentance by demonstrating five years of active opposition to the principles of communism. Aficionados of this escape clause refer to it as the

---

* Cohn died shortly after the publication of this article. [Ed.]

"Koestler Amendment," named after Hungarian author Arthur Koestler, who **167** defected, renounced his ties to the Communist party, and wrote about his negative experiences in the Soviet bloc for the next forty years.

The most haunting aspect of the Automated Visa Lookout System is that an individual may never know what activity qualifies him or her for exclusion. Like poor Josef K. in Franz Kafka's *Trial*, an alien is never informed of the specific cause of a denial. The case of Angel Rama, a distinguished Uruguayan author and literary critic, provides a case in point. Rama left Uruguay after a military coup in 1972 and became a Venezuelan citizen. Though technically excludable, he was granted waivers for periodic visits to the United States through the 1970s. But when he applied for permanent residency in 1981, after being offered a professorship at the University of Maryland, his request was denied, and his saga through a bureaucratic hallway of mirrors began.

Having accused Rama of "publishing, writing, or causing to be circulated writings which advocate the doctrines of international communism," the State Department refused to reveal its evidence of these activities. Rama, who was never a Communist and professed admiration for the social-democratic movements of Sweden and Austria, fought unsuccessfully for two years to have this evidence revealed to him.

He found himself in a surreal conundrum. As Michael Maggio, an immigration attorney who represented Rama for the Center for Constitutional Rights, explains, "We were not notified [as to] what he did, where he did it, or how he did it; but if we could prove that he didn't do what they wouldn't tell us he did, he could get his permit." Rama did not live long enough to resolve his catch-22, as he was killed in a Madrid plane crash in November 1983.

Critics charge that U.S. visa policies violate the human rights provisions of the 1975 Helsinki accords, which guarantee the free flow of ideas between nations. Helsinki Watch, the Fund for Free Expression, the Association of American Publishers' International Freedom to Publish Committee, and more than thirty civil liberties, political, and cultural groups have organized the Coalition for Free Trade in Ideas to repeal the ideological exclusion sections of the McCarran-Walter Act. PEN, the international writers' group, held its forty-eighth congress in New York in January, 1986 and a score of excludable writers were invited as a test of the law.*

Satirist Dario Fo offers comfort to the excluded. Unable to cross the American frontier last year to address a Free Trade in Ideas conference, he spoke via satellite from a Toronto television studio. Appearing on a screen in a Washington meeting hall, Fo told the conference: "The fact that the State Department

---

*In this particular instance, the State Department chose to avoid a confrontation with PEN and approved the visas. [Ed.]

168   denied . . . the visa is something which makes me very proud. I took a look
       at the list of people denied visas to the United States, and then I realized that I
       am in beautiful company."
          Carlos Fuentes, who has faced the fitful experience of applying and reapply-
       ing for waivers to enter this country since he was first denied a visa in 1961,
       also spoke out at the conference. In his talk, Fuentes captured the absurdity
       of U.S. policy. "It is hard to imagine," Fuentes declared, "that the institutions
       of this great republic, its democratic edifice, its vast economic and military
       power, can in any way be endangered by the physical presence of Graham
       Greene, Gabriel García Márquez, Dario Fo, or Mrs. Salvador Allende. On the
       contrary: Experience has taught us all that it is the application of the exclusion-
       ary clause that endangers the republic, mocks democracy, demoralizes the true
       friends of the United States, and offers undeserved aces to the Soviet Union.
       . . . This is a clause that belongs to the realm of sadomasochism, not to the
       legal ledgers of a self-respecting, powerful democracy." *

---

* See page 10 for a brief discussion of the temporary suspension by Congress of the ideological
exclusion provisions of the McCarren-Walter Act and the decision by the INS to drop deportation
proceedings against Margaret Randall. [Ed.]

[Margaret Randall]

II

WHEN THE IMAGINATION

OF THE WRITER IS CONFRONTED

BY THE IMAGINATION

OF THE STATE

Her writings go far beyond mere dissent, disagreement with, or criticism of the United States or its policies . . .

Your pending application for adjustment of status is hereby DENIED.
> —Decision on Application for Status as Permanent Resident,
> Immigration and Naturalization Service,
> El Paso, Texas, October 2, 1985

With these words, a representative of the State (the INS regional director in El Paso, Texas) ended his seven-page decision and my seventeen-month wait. He wielded his discretion to use the ideological exclusion clause of the McCarran-Walter Immigration, Naturalization, and Nationality Act. He exercised his

---

This essay was originally published under the title "The State's Imagination—And Mine" in *Against the Current* 1 (September/October 1986), pp. 7–10. Reprinted by permission of the author.

170 "imagination" as well as his authority when he handed down a negative response to my petition to reside in the land of my birth.

An artist, a writer, I was being excluded *on the basis of my written opinions.* In books published more than a decade ago, I had criticized U.S. government policy in Southeast Asia; more recently I had criticized U.S. policy in Central America. In the sixties I had upon occasion spelled America with a "K"; in the seventies, I called the Attica prisoners in revolt "my brothers" and the police attacking them, "pigs." Moreover, I had written enthusiastically about many aspects of Cuba's socialist experiment and the innovative pluralist experiment in Nicaragua.

Perhaps most dangerous of all, many of my books have given voice to those who were previously silenced, or ignored. For more than fifteen years I have done oral history with the ordinary people of countries about which the U.S. public is fed information geared to produce an image of childlike incapacity, racial inferiority, and uniform yearning for the American Way of Life —all packaged in a context devoid of any real historical continuity. By searching out, translating, and transcribing the words of a granddaughter of slaves in Cuba's western tobacco fields, a teenage peasant antiaircraft gunner from a coastal fishing village in Vietnam, a Puerto Rican patriot whose two children died of hunger, a Cuban farmer who writes peasant theatre in verse, nuns and priests who took an active part in the Nicaraguan struggle, and ordinary and extraordinary women in Cuba, Nicaragua, Vietnam, Peru, and Chile, I participated in a developing literary genre which seems particularly threatening to the current interpreters and enforcers of immigration law in this country.

This is nothing new. Socrates was put to death in a terminal exercise in thought control. Shelley, in his time, cried out in defense of the writer's imagination. The "witches" of Salem and countless other women who throughout history followed their deepest needs to speak or write the truth as they knew it, have paid with their lives. Julius Fucek was hanged by the Nazis. Persecution of writers and artists during China's "cultural revolution" or under the more rigorously Stalinist periods in some of the eastern bloc countries is well known. Classism, racism, sexism, heterosexism, ageism, and able-bodyism are constant challenges to the writer's imagination.

Many, perhaps, would say that persecution of the freedom to think and express oneself does not take place in the United States.

They would be wrong.

The McCarran-Walter Immigration, Naturalization, and Nationality Act is less studied by most Americans than the Constitution or Bill of Rights (this latter judged "subversive" some years back by more than 80 percent in a street poll held in the nation's capital). The McCarran-Walter Act was passed by a McCarthy-inspired Congress over President Truman's veto in 1952. Truman, in his veto message, said the act would place constraints on citizens and aliens **171** alike. Yet this law, with its vague clauses, clear First Amendment infringement, and the broad discretionary powers it gives INS employees, would still —more than thirty years later—keep out literary giants of the stature of Nobel Prize winners Pablo Neruda and Gabriel García Márquez, or an American-born writer like myself whose American family lives in this country.

The list of writers excluded by this legislation is a long one. It includes the English novelist Graham Greene. Farley Mowat, the Canadian environmentalist and author of such best-sellers as *Never Cry Wolf*, describes an experience interestingly similar (in its essential points) to my own. *My Discovery of America*[1] is his recently published and lively account of being stopped by INS at the border when he attempted to comply with an invitation to give a lecture at Chico State College in California. Mexico's Carlos Fuentes and Uruguay's Angel Rama have been denied visas. And many who are not writers but who certainly provide important points of view to which the American people have a right—personalities like Chile's Hortensia Bussi de Allende or Italy's Nino Pasti (the NATO General who speaks against the arms race)—have also been judged excludable.

Angel Rama's case is the one that bears most similarities to my own. Rama was not seeking a temporary visa in order to give a lecture, teach one term at a university, or promote a book. Like me, he had applied for permanent residency status. He did not have family ties in this country, but he had been invited to teach at an American university and he wanted to live here. Angel Rama's political philosophy was iconoclastic, to say the least. He had virulently criticized the Cuban Revolution, although INS officials proclaimed him a Communist! He was not kindly looked upon by a number of Socialist governments, which considered him a conservative! The case against him came down to a denial of his right to express his views, and he was not even told what the government claimed those views were! He was fighting the decision against him, when an airplane accident over Madrid tragically put an end to his life.

Why, some may ask, does a U.S.-born writer need to apply for residency in her own country? How can that residency be denied in the context of immigration law—the essential premise of which is supposed to be family reunification —when the person in question's husband, mother, father, brother, sister, and oldest son are all American citizens? Again and again I have been asked how I lost my original citizenship, if marriage to an American does not "automatically" qualify one for residency, why I find myself in this situation. Briefly, I'll give some of the history.

In the late fifties I was living in New York City, trying to become a writer. In 1960 I had my first child. As a single mother, in the New York of those

172 years, there wasn't much of a support system; child care was almost nonexistent, women had not yet come together in the organizations we were later to develop in order to meet our needs. I moved to Mexico with my son in 1961, hoping to find a way of life that would enable me to write, and to spend more time with him—as I supported us both.

The sixties saw a tremendous renaissance in what would be known as the "little" publishing phenomenon: little magazines, small presses, groups of poets and writers whose work was avant-garde in any one of the ways in which every generation produces its cultural nonconformists. *El Corno Emplumado (The Plumed Horn)* was the bilingual quarterly I cofounded and edited from Mexico City during the next eight years. In its pages, important American poets and writers like William Carlos Williams, Ezra Pound, Charles Olsen, Robert Creeley, Allen Ginsberg, Lawrence Ferlinghetti, Denise Levertov, Diane Wakoski, and others were introduced for the first time to a Latin American public. Readers north of the Rio Grande had access to the work of Ernesto Cardenal, Violeta Parra, Roberto Fernandez Retamar, Roque Dalton, Nancy Morejon, Octavio Paz—and even those classics whose names we knew but whose work we had never read: Vallejo, Neruda, Rulfo, Cortazar.

The imagination of the writer and the imagination of the State were matters deeply explored in the thirty-two issues of *El Corno Emplumado*. Some States—such as Cuba—imagined the writer as important, providing a context for creativity even in the midst of a survival struggle that demanded constant vigilance and produced, from time to time, no small degree of defensiveness. States like Somoza's Nicaragua felt threatened by the imaginations of vastly differing writers: to have one's name on the list of authors whose books were not allowed past that country's censors in the sixties and early seventies was the sad pride of many.

Consequently, in many places, the writers' imagination was forced into opposition with the death-dealing imagination of the State.

Poets felt and expressed the struggles and dreams of their people. Some of the most outstanding died participating in the armed struggles that ensued. Javier Heraud, Otto-Rene Castillo, Leonel Rugama, Monica Ertl, Rodolfo Walsh, Paco Urondo, Nestor Paz, Haroldo Conti, Roque Dalton, Alaide Foppa, and Lil Milagros Gonzales come to mind.* In the developing, dependent countries of the so-called Third World, the writer's imagination has

---

*Javier Heraud was Peruvian; Otto-Rene Castillo and Alaide Foppa, Guatemalan; Leonel Rugama, Nicaraguan; Monica Ertl and Nestor Paz, Bolivian; Rodolfo Walsh, Paco Urondo, and Haroldo Conti, from Argentina; and Roque Dalton and Lil Milagros Gonzalez, from El Salvador. They are simply a few of the important poets and writers killed over the past two decades by the repressive forces in their countries.

traditionally been more closely engaged with the daily forces of life and death. **173**
The best of Latin American letters has bridged the fabricated gap between
magic realism and social testimony. Precisely the same McCarthy era madness
that produced legislation like the McCarran-Walter Act cast a slow-thawing
chill on such engagement in this country.

To be sure, the danger of State-imposed conformity and rhetoric also exists
in the world of art. Witness the weight of a misunderstood social realism, or
the tragic disregard for cultural continuity seen during the Chinese cultural
revolution.

Open discussion about these issues is a part of every really profound period
of social change, and nations bring their own particular cultural history to
bear on these discussions. In the pages of *El Corno Emplumado* I first experienced the individual artist or small group of unaffiliated artists dealing with
this phenomenon. Later, in Cuba, I would live through a period of collective
exploration of the same, and in Nicaragua witness quite a remarkable example
of one revolution's creative handling of the problem.

As a result of my involvement, through the magazine, with the vanguard of
young writers and artists during those years, I myself moved from a position
of "art beyond politics" to one in which a more humanistic approach to artistic
expression included a much broader approach to life—very much including
the political.

Oral history, especially with women, became a necessity. The *voice,* the
voice of the ordinary woman and man, became central to my work. It found
its way into my poetry as well as becoming the backbone for books of essays
and interviews. In Cuba and in Nicaragua I would come to understand how
testimonio—or oral history—grew as a new literary genre within the context of
a people's revolution.

But I'm getting beyond myself in this story. In the mid-sixties, living in
Mexico, married to a Mexican poet, and with three small children to support,
I took out Mexican citizenship as a way of enlarging my job possibilities in
a time of economic need. I was told by my lawyer that I must inform the
American embassy of my acquisition of Mexican nationality. When I did so,
and without adequate information as to other options, I allowed myself to be
placed in a position where I simply signed my American citizenship away.
Less than two years later, in 1969, I realized my error and attempted to regain
my original status. Although taking out Mexican citizenship was an economic
move, and not a political statement (as some have tried to claim), I now consider it a mistake—not one, however, for which I believe I should be penalized
forever.

My personal story is important only in that it is part of a larger one. The
imagination of the state exists only insofar as it is the sum of the best and

174   most lasting elements created by the imaginations of the people of that State. And imagination is, perhaps, the element that most successfully moves beyond State-imposed boundaries, to link all peoples in the uniquely priceless parts of a common vision.

The celebration of our differences as well as of our commonalities is what makes it possible for those of us in vastly differing cultural milieus to thrill to works as varied as those produced by the classic Greek dramatists, Sappho, Shakespeare, the Russian novelists, the Latin American magic realists, the passion of a Ginsberg, the insight of an Alice Walker, or the deep knowledge of an Adrienne Rich.

These are writers' imaginations, each in its time and space, which both challenge and change the imagination of the State, pushing it to new limits of life and power. It is not the traditionally assumed State power of "law and order," "authority and force," but the power of ideas, of evocations and of dreams, alive in all that lasts from what we make and do.

It is within the context of this view of the relationship between the writer's imagination and the imagination of the State that a number of prominent American writers have joined me as plaintiffs in a civil action filed in Washington's federal district court in October of 1985. Norman Mailer, Arthur Miller, Toni Morrison, Grace Paley, Rose Styron, William Styron, Kurt Vonnegut, Alice Walker, and PEN's American Center—among others—have joined in the filing of this complaint against the U. S. attorney general, the commissioner of immigration and the INS regional director who signed the denial, both to attempt to get a reversal of the decision in my case, and to legally challenge the constitutionality of the ideological exclusion clause of the McCarran-Walter Act. The National Writers Union, the Writers Guild, and other organizations are supporting our action in an amicus brief.

In part, the complaint reads: "Defendants denied Randall's application because of her political views, as reflected in the contents of her writings. . . . Defendants' activities have cast and will continue to cast a chill over Randall's First Amendment freedoms. These actions convey to her the message that she will be separated from her home, her family, her friends, her colleagues, and her job to the extent that her writings are subjectively viewed as 'beyond mere dissent, disagreement with or criticism of the United States or its policies.' "

It goes on to state that "defendants' actions have caused and continue to threaten irreparable damage to plaintiffs' First Amendment rights as citizens and voters to meet, converse, and inform themselves about some of the most critical issues facing Americans today, and to associate and exchange ideas face-to-face with Randall respecting their mutual aesthetic and literary interests."

In my writer's imagination, I have believed and continue to believe that a critical view is consistent with love, not hate; that the principles from which

I criticize U.S. policy are not "subversive" but in fact those upon which the **175** greatest traditions of any democracy rest; that the imagination of the State is informed and enriched most meaningfully by the imagination of her writers and artists; and that only in a climate of absolute artistic freedom can the imagination flourish and grow.

People ask me how I *feel*, forced into the role of protagonist in a case like this. It would be a lie to evade the uncentering nature of the situation. Engaging my imagination and the greatest output of my physical energies in this new way has disrupted my creative life as well as my work life, my family life —at times, even my sanity. But I deeply believe the issues at stake are larger than my personal situation.

I feel I am engaged in a struggle for many besides myself—for writers and others who do not have the good fortune to be represented by the Center for Constitutional Rights, who do not enjoy the support of PEN, the Writers Union, the Guild, or other writers of stature and conscience. If I win, we all win. And if I lose I only lose in a very personal sense; we will still have provided a forum through which hundreds of thousands are reexamining our personal and collective freedoms, and working to create a world society more just for all its members.

I would like to close with two poems, both written in the context of these past two years of reentry, bringing together the multiple threads of two quarter-centuries of experience—one in Latin America, the other here where I grew up. Both parts of my life, in one way or another, inform the struggle to become, the struggle to come home. I offer these poems as pieces of a writer's memory, a writer's imagination, a writer's reality:

THE GLOVES

for Rhoda Waller

Yes we did "march around somewhere" and yes it was cold,
we shared our gloves because we had a pair between us
and a New York City cop also shared his big gloves
with me—strange,
he was there to keep our order
and he could do that
and I could take that
back then.
We were marching for the Santa Maria, Rhoda,
a Portuguese ship whose crew had mutinied.
they demanded asylum in Goulart's Brazil
and we marched in support of that demand,

in winter, in New York City,
back and forth before the Portuguese consulate,
Rockefeller Center, 1961.
I gauge the date by my first child
—Gregory was born late in 1960—as I gauge
so many dates by the first, the second, the third, the fourth,
and I feel his body now, again, close to my breast,
held against cold to our strong steps of dignity.
That was my first public protest, Rhoda,
strange you should retrieve it now
in a letter out of this love of ours
alive these many years.
How many protests since that one, how many
marches and rallies
for greater causes, larger wars, deeper wounds
cleansed or untouched by our rage.
Today a cop would hardly unbuckle his gloves
and press them around my blue-red hands.
Today a baby held to breast
would be a child of my child, a generation removed.
The world is older and I in it
am older,
burning, slower, with the same passions.
The passions are older and so I am also younger
for knowing them more deeply and moving in them
pregnant with fear and fighting.
The gloves are still there, in the cold,
passing from hand to hand.

That was written in March of last year. In October, already cognizant of the need to shore up for a long struggle, I wrote:

IMMIGRATION LAW

When I ask the experts
how much time do I have?
I do not want an answer in years
or arguments.

I must know if there are hours enough
to mend this relationship,
see a book all the way to its birthing,

stand beside my father
on his journey.

I want to know how many seasons of chamisa
will be yellow, then grey-green
and yellow
/light/
again,
how many red cactus flowers
will bloom beside my door.

I do not want to follow language
like a dog with its tail between its legs.

I need time equated with music,
hours rising in bread,
years deep from connections.

The present always holds a tremor of the past.

Give me a handful of future
to rub against my lips.

NOTE

1. Farley Mowat, *My Discovery of America* (Atlantic Monthly Press, 1985).

[Richard O. Curry]

12

PARANOIA—REAGAN

STYLE:

ENCOUNTERS WITH

THE USIA

Between late May and early September 1981, I taught two courses on nineteenth-century American history at the University of Waikato in Hamilton, New Zealand, and lectured at several other New Zealand universities on a Fulbright award. I also spent ten days in Australia under International Communication Agency (ICA) auspices lecturing primarily to college and university audiences in Canberra, Melbourne, Launceston, and Hobart. My experiences as a Fulbrighter in New Zealand were pleasant and relaxed; but

---

This essay is a revised and integrated version of two previously published pieces, "An American Scholar Abroad" and "The USIA Revisited," which appeared in the Organization of American Historians *Newsletter* (August 1982): 10–11, and (November 1983): 15–18. These essays were also published in the *Congressional Record,* the first by former Congressman Toby Moffett under the title, "Paranoia—Reagan Style," September 23, 1982, E 4384-85, and the second, by Congressman Sam Gejdenson, January 31, 1984, E 223-25. To avoid confusion, the terms ICA and USIA are used interchangeably. The agency's name was not changed from USICA to USIA until the Fall of 1982.

contacts with ICA officials in Canberra and elsewhere in Australia can only be described as Orwellian.

Politically, I am not aligned with the left, and my areas of scholarly specialization focus on nineteenth-century American history, which have no direct bearing on contemporary American politics and foreign policy. Therefore, I was not only angered but also somewhat bewildered at the time on being subjected to blatant attempts at intimidation by ICA officials who were fearful that I might criticize President Reagan's foreign and domestic policies. Later I compared notes with two colleagues who had lectured for ICA in Scandinavia and Eastern Europe during the summer of 1981. Since neither had experiences comparable to my own, I was somewhat inclined to dismiss my encounters with ICA in Australia as exceptional. Fred Warner Neal's article, however, "Reaganizing Scholars" (*New York Times*, February 26, 1982), made it clear that harassment and intimidation were no longer the name of the game. It was far worse. Neal was denied funds by ICA to attend a scholarly conference in Belgrade, Yugoslavia, because his views on Reagan's foreign policy appeared problematic. Neal's experience, combined with the argument by Charles Wick, head of ICA in Washington, that scholarly activities overseas ought to be an extension of President Reagan's foreign policy, reflect a calculated effort to eliminate criticism abroad whenever and wherever the current administration has the power to do so (*New York Times*, March 9, 1982). Attempts to cut back the Fulbright program in 1981 on grounds of fiscal necessity can now reasonably be viewed as a major part of that policy. Such a policy is shortsighted, counterproductive, and self-defeating.

My first direct contact with the Australian branch of ICA began with a long-distance call in New Zealand from the head of the agency in Canberra. "Dr. Curry," a voice rasped, "let's clear the air." Somewhat startled, I responded that I wasn't aware the air needed clearing. The voice continued, "I am under intense pressure by Australian academics to bring you over. Precisely what is it that you do that fits into the Australian 'game plan' of ICA which is the 'propaganda agency' of the United States government?" My contact, a man called Merton Bland, went on to say that ICA in Wellington had informed him that I didn't have any topics. "Topics?" I said, taken aback. "Topics? I have several invitations to lecture at Australian universiti——"

"I know all that," he interrupted, "will you please listen?" Bland proceeded to explain that ICA didn't often use the services of Fulbrighters. Ordinarily ICA brought over its own "handpicked" speakers who lectured on topics related to its "game plan" which, in 1981, included global defense strategies, energy questions, and social and political processes. "Precisely where do you fit in?" he continued. I pointed out that my primary scholarly interests focused on nineteenth-century American political and intellectual history, especially

180 slavery, abolitionism, the Civil War and Reconstruction, and the omnipresence of conspiracy fears and conspiracy rhetoric throughout American history. All these topics, I suggested, provided historical background for understanding contemporary "social and political processes." "Don't be so technical," he snapped. "What I want from you is a cable which not only lists your topics but includes the point of view you intend to express." At that point I mentioned the name of the high-ranking ICA official who had offered to write a letter recommending me, and which I had declined because I did not think it was necessary at the time. In retrospect, mentioning his name seems to be a more critical factor in being invited to Australia than the "intense pressure" exerted by Australian academics and the relatively noncontroversial nature of the topics (in geopolitical terms) that I proposed on nineteenth-century political and intellectual history.

Arriving in Canberra I noticed that my itinerary had been revised to include media interviews, as well as lectures at various Australian university centers. Because of the hostile and suspicious nature of my original phone conversation, I could not resist the temptation to comment in private to a junior ICA official that one of my colleagues at the University of Connecticut had jokingly cautioned against creating an international incident, but added that if I did, to make it a "big one." Were I so inclined, I said, the media interviews provided a great opportunity. I really didn't expect the ICA official to break down in laughter. But neither did I expect to strike such a raw nerve. "If you do," he warned, "you'll never get another Fulbright!" Taken aback, I explained that while I had no intention of provoking political controversy, I did expect to speak freely and constructively about American political, social, and economic problems. After all, wasn't that what scholarly and cultural exchange programs were supposed to be about? And besides, most of the Australian academics with whom I was acquainted either personally or by reputation were educated in the United Kingdom or the United States and were as sophisticated in their approaches to international politics in general and American society in particular as I was. Individuals who attempted to peddle a "party line" would not only forfeit their own personal credibility but would generate even more anti-American sentiment than already existed. The willingness and ability of American scholars to speak freely was, from my point of view, the best publicity that American society could get in academic circles. Privately this particular official agreed with most of what I had to say; however, he still cautioned me to be discreet. Democratic administrations, he stated, had rarely attempted to muzzle American intellectuals overseas; but Republican presidents, especially Nixon and the incumbent, were extremely sensitive to views that could be construed as criticism of administration policies.

By mid-1981 new signals, evidenced by Mr. Wick's own argument about scholarly activities abroad, were clearly being sent by Washington to overseas offices. But in my particular case, I think the fear and suspicion I encountered also stemmed from the fact that the title of a book I coedited, *Conspiracy: The Fear of Subversion in American History* (1972) had triggered an alarm bell at ICA headquarters in Australia. This I was told by a New Zealand historian who had been in Canberra earlier in the year and who was asked by Merton Bland what he knew about my political opinions in general and the contents of this book in particular. In fact, I was also informed by one ICA official that before inviting me to Australia they had received cables about me from "all over the world." I was totally astonished by this comment. In the first place, I said, I didn't know people all over the world. My foreign travels had been confined primarily to the Philippines, Australia, and New Zealand. In 1978, I said in a sarcastic vein, I had lectured under ICA auspices in the Philippines, and that so far as I knew no violent upheavals had taken place as a result.

Before leaving Canberra, my wife and I were asked to stop by ICA head-quarters where I was handed a two-inch-thick sheaf of speeches on American foreign policy by President Reagan, former Secretary Haig, former National Security Adviser Richard Allen, and the American ambassador to Australia. I found this material informative. What I resented was ICA's parting suggestion that I read the speeches before reaching Melbourne and that I pay particular attention to the points of view expressed. Allen's speech dealt with the concept of human rights—a fact that I found amusing in a grim sort of way since, in my view, mine were being violated by U.S. government officials.

The climate of opinion at the U.S. consulate in Melbourne, in contrast to the embassy in Canberra, was comparatively relaxed and friendly. In fact, I could hardly believe that we were dealing with officials of the same government on the same planet during the same century. But any fleeting doubts I may have entertained in Melbourne about the official policies of the Reagan administration disappeared in Tasmania.

After lecturing at the College of Advanced Education in Launceston on the idea of mission in American history—a critical concept having enormous implications for understanding modern American foreign policy (a lecture scheduled, or should I say permitted, by ICA officials in Melbourne, *not Canberra*)— a friendly and knowledgeable individual took me aside. "They tried to intimidate you in Canberra, didn't they?" "Yes, they did," I said. "Well," he chuckled, "they didn't succeed, did they?" "No, they didn't," I answered. I was then informed that Peter Wolcott, an ICA official in Melbourne, who had incurred the ambassador's wrath for exercising "poor judgment," would not, in all probability, return to Australia after taking home leave. The "poor judgment," I was told, consisted of Wolcott's opposition to politicizing ICA. I was later informed that Wolcott, on returning to the United States for home leave, was to be reassigned before his normal tour of duty in Australia was over. As a result, Wolcott resigned from the USIA and accepted an offer from the State of Victoria to work in Melbourne.

In Hobart, Tasmania, our contact person (who was not an ICA employee) struck me on first impression as being an exceedingly nervous, eccentric, and lonely individual—an American expatriate in his fifties whose only visible means of support was some sort of tenuous connection as a "research fellow" in the political science department at the University of Tasmania. I found it somewhat amusing but sad that this person was rumored to be the local CIA agent because of his habit of taking notes on anything and everything anyone said.

On one occasion, when asked to present my views on President Reagan's economic policies to Apex, a local civic group, the ICA contact brought along a tape recorder. I quietly protested its use without prior consultation and permission. He assured me, however, that there was nothing to worry about. He simply wanted a record of the "evening's entertainment" and wouldn't I like to have a copy for my own files? He would mail one to me in New Zealand, he said. He never did, despite two subsequent requests that he do so. At the time I could have pressed the issue or could simply have pulled the plug; but I had nothing to hide and the idea of having a copy for personal reference appealed to me.

At first, I didn't take seriously the idea that this person could be an intelligence agent. He didn't measure up to any of the stereotypical notions formed by reading spy novels. In retrospect, however, I haven't the vaguest idea who this particular individual was since he was not an ICA employee. Nor do I know why this particular talk—but no other—was signaled out for preservation in this man's or any one else's files. It is possible that this particular incident was innocuous; but the overt and heavy-handed attempts at intimidation by ICA officials in Canberra most assuredly were not. Surely, informed Americans willing to "paint the warts as well as the dimples" (as Oliver Cromwell once instructed his portrait artist) can do more to establish credibility overseas than all the canned "party-line" media hype ICA can manufacture or orchestrate. But then, such a view requires not only common sense, but confidence in the principles on which this nation was founded.

This brief account of my own personal encounters with USIA officials in Australia produced a number of responses and reactions: in the media, from academics in New Zealand, Australia, and the United States, from USIA officials in Washington (including its director, Charles Z. Wick), and from several members of Congress.

First of all, the article received quite a bit of media attention in the northeast: radio interviews, talk-show appearances, an Associated Press wire story

(August 12, 1983), a feature article in the *Hartford Courant* (August 29, 1982), **183** and an extremely critical *Courant* editorial entitled "American Propaganda Machine" (September 21, 1982). "Richard O. Curry's unhappy experience with the U.S. International Communications Agency," the editorial began,

> was not unique either for this or previous administrations. Any effort by the government to stifle free speech does this nation far more damage than could any criticism by an American scholar. This administration, in particular, has been blatant in trying to impose its mindset on others.

> The Voice of America (VOA), a semi-autonomous unit of ICA, has been in turmoil for the past year amid charges it is turning from objective news and information to provide a good-guys-versus-bad-guys view of the world.

> The effectiveness of American cultural and academic exchange programs is compromised to the extent that they are viewed by foreigners as mere instruments of national propaganda.

It is also a matter of public record that the Reagan administration made a serious effort in Congress to undermine the Fulbright program. As Congressman Toby Moffett phrased it: "Last year, proponents of cultural exchange were successful in blocking a proposal *to reduce Fulbright funds by 66 percent* [italics mine]. If the bipartisan coalition remains strong, we can continue this cultural initiative" (letter to the author, March 30, 1982).

At the same time, however, the Reagan administration called for substantial increases in USIA's total budget. Why? In part, USIA wanted to modernize its equipment—for example, to improve the transmission capabilities of the Voice of America. However, it is also clear that the Reagan administration wanted total control of all exchange programs. The Fulbright program, although administered by USIA, has a number of safeguards built into the selection process. Fulbright awards are based upon bilateral agreements with 120 foreign countries. Nearly a third of these nations have their own Fulbright commissions, which play important roles in selecting Fulbrighters. Moreover, CIES (Council for the International Exchange of Scholars), which is funded by USIA, but which administers the Fulbright program, has traditionally had a great deal of independence in screening and nominating Fulbright recipients. The best way to control its activities, therefore, was simply to reduce CIES to virtual impotence by eliminating most of its funding. On the other hand, all participants in USIA's AMPARTS Program (American Participation), which provides speakers for overseas audiences, are handpicked by agency

184 officials. Little wonder, then, that USIA officials wanted to increase funding for AMPARTS while drastically reducing the scope and influence of the
Fulbright program.*

The most amazing aspect of USIA's politicization was the candor of Director Charles Wick and other agency officials in declaring publicly that the
agency's primary function was to serve as an arm of the Reagan administration's foreign policy rather than presenting a balanced account of American
life and society required by its charter. Mr. Wick took this position in his response to Fred Warner Neal's "Reaganizing Scholars" (*New York Times*, March
9, 1983), as did other agency officials in response to my own criticisms.

For example, Rosemary Keogh, a *Hartford Courant* staff writer, did a feature
based on "An American Scholar Abroad" entitled "Professor Claims Intimidation by U.S. Overseas" (August 29, 1982). In the process, she elicited some
revealing comments from USIA official Leslie Lisle. According to Keogh:

> An ICA spokesman acknowledged this week that the agency tries to se-
> lect speakers who know and support the administration's foreign policy.

> "If they're going to talk about the current foreign policy of this ad-
> ministration, we insist they be informed and that they not go out and talk
> against it. . . . We want them to make a clear and convincing statement;
> otherwise it destroys our credibility."

> Lisle said the policy does impinge upon the speakers' right to freedom
> of speech "to a certain extent," but added, "they are being sent out as
> current foreign policy spokesmen."

> Former administrations have had similar policies, he said, but it has
> never been stated "quite so clearly."

---

*Ronald L. Trowbridge, former director of USIA's bureau of educational and cultural affairs,
informed me on October 14, 1985, that Mr. Wick was not an enemy of the Fulbright program.
His recommendation for drastic cuts in the Fulbright program in 1981 resulted, Trowbridge
said, from OMB director David Stockman's demand that all federal agencies cut their budgets
by 15 percent. Trowbridge went on to say that Wick knew that the Fulbright program was a
"sacred cow," and that his proposed cuts would later be restored by Congress. But this "best case"
scenario does not mesh with the irrefutable evidence that USIA, under Wick's leadership, views
the world in a rigid, ideological, and counterproductive way. In fairness to Wick, however, it is
an issue that future writers ought to investigate.

Still another USIA functionary, Phyllis Kaminsky, director of USIA's
Public Liaison Office, in identical letters to the *Hartford Courant* (September
28, 1982) and the OAH *Newsletter* (November 1982), reaffirmed that political considerations played a major role in selecting speakers sent out to discuss "current administration foreign policy." Kaminsky implied, however, that
since I was not a foreign policy "expert," USIA was not concerned about my
political views. Kaminsky neatly dodged the issue I raised by stating: "We are
unable to verify Mr. Curry's account of his conversations with our diplomats
in Australia." If for "the sake of discussion we accept his version," Kaminsky
declared, it was clear that I had misunderstood "the import" of my briefings.

It was rather difficult, however, to mistake "the import" of a warning by an
ICA official in Canberra that sharp criticism of Reagan administration policies
could have only one result: "You'll never get another Fulbright!" (My detailed
response to Kaminsky appeared in the OAH *Newsletter,* February 1983).

Foreign policy "expert" or not, the fact that I was prepared to lecture on
the concepts of Manifest Destiny and Mission in American history and on the
prevalence of conspiracy fears and conspiracy rhetoric in American politics—
subjects which have important contemporary overtones—had not been overlooked by the head of USIA in Australia.

As evidenced by Fred Neal's encounter with USIA, and indeed those of
Professors John Seiler and Harold M. Hyman, among others, it is clear that my
own experiences were not atypical. Seiler's treatment by USIA in 1981 was
the worst example of partisan political abuse that came to light prior to the
dramatic revelation in late January 1984, of the existence of an official USIA
blacklist. Seiler's experiences, however, did not receive the media attention
they deserved. Seiler, who, at the time, was teaching at Dutchess County
Community College in Poughkeepsie, New York, wrote to Congressman
Sam Gejdenson on May 1, 1983:

> In my case the Agency planned a lecture tour of six African countries; an
> overall itinerary was developed, specific appointments made for me in
> each of these countries, and flights booked from New York City to leave
> in November 1981. Eight days before the planned departure date, the
> Agency phoned to tell me of the cancellation, because (as the Agency told
> first me and then Congressional callers) my published views were not
> considered sufficiently supportive of U.S. policy toward South Africa.
> I subsequently sued the Agency and Mr. Wick in the Federal District
> Court in the District of Columbia. On 23 December 1982, Mr. Wick
> offered a settlement, just one day before depositions were to be taken
> from his and other Agency officials involved in the case. Although I
> promised not to make public the terms of that settlement, I can say that

I sued for $285,000 and that, of course, I remain free constitutionally to testify in writing and orally or otherwise to write about the decision-making process in which I was involved.

Gejdenson (responding to letters from Seiler, Hyman, and several from me that included copies of letters received from correspondents in Australia, New Zealand, and the United States regarding USIA abuse) wrote a very pointed letter to Director Wick on June 6, 1983, asking for a detailed explanation of alleged malfeasance on USIA's part.

Wick's reply to Gejdenson on June 20, 1983, was truly astonishing. It was, in fact, a repudiation of policy positions that Wick and other agency officials had taken publicly only a few months earlier. "First," Wick declared, "I would like to reiterate this Agency's commitment to the integrity of the Fulbright Program" (quite a contrast to the Reagan administration's earlier attempts to cut funding by two-thirds). Equally important, Wick also *denied* that the political views of individuals sent abroad under USIA auspices were taken into consideration in their selection process. Keep in mind that Wick did not state that the agency had changed or repudiated its earlier publicly stated policy positions. Rather, he declared: "When a lecturer speaks on a topic which bears on current administration policy, we expect him to be able to explain what this policy is. *He is not, however,* required to defend it" [italics mine].

Moreover, Wick—in contrast to Phyllis Kaminsky, who questioned the accuracy of my account in the OAH *Newsletter*—admitted that the charges had some substance. It was not, however, the result of agency policy. "Dr. Curry's topics were historical in nature," Wick said, "and did not therefore require an exposition of American policy." But Wick admitted nevertheless: "This does not deny Dr. Curry's perception of tactlessness by a USIA officer."

For a time, I was puzzled by Wick's reply to Gejdenson. How, I wondered, could Wick possibly deny to a member of the House Foreign Affairs Committee that political considerations were not a factor in choosing individuals to participate in USIA's Speakers' Program since he and several other agency bureaucrats had earlier admitted in public that this was precisely their policy?

The answer was not long in coming. In late June, Gejdenson sent to me a copy of the House Foreign Affairs Committee Report on the State Department Authorization Bill (Report No. 98-130). "In this report," Gejdenson wrote, "the committee expresses its concern about claims that USIA has violated its charter in a number of ways. . . . This is an important warning to USIA officials that Congress will not tolerate these types of actions."

In part, the committee report was a bombshell. It was not covered in the national media and deserves quotation. "Over the past 2 years," the report stated,

USIA has arguably violated the letter and spirit of its charter by (a) **187**
attempting unsuccessfully, virtually to eliminate the funding for the educational and cultural affairs programs which have stood the test of time
and proved their worth; (b) reflecting partisan political ideology in its
choice of USIA grantees; (c) providing funds to friends of USIA officials without regard to the USIA charter, or proper grant guidelines and
procedures; (d) attempting to influence the activities and comments of
USIA grantees so that they reflected executive branch policy positions;
(e) withholding or delaying the granting of USIA funds to grantees due
to partisan political considerations; and (f) placing in career Foreign Service and civil service positions, political appointees who reflect partisan
political views, or who are friends and relations of current Government
political appointees, without regard to the requirements of specific positions, or the effect on the career services (pp. 64–65).

Having expended a great deal of time and effort publicizing these issues,
reading these conclusions was quite satisfying. My exuberance lessened considerably, however, as the report concluded:

When these matters were brought to the attention of USIA Director
Charles Z. Wick, he took immediate steps to make the necessary ad-
justments and corrections to restore the integrity of these programs, and
to restore the confidence of the grantees, the Congress, and the public.
He is to be commended for his prompt, sincere and effective efforts to
remedy the situation (p. 65).

Thus, an extremely critical report by the House Foreign Affairs Committee
concluded by giving Mr. Wick and USIA high marks for cleaning up his/its
act.

For several months, Mr. Wick continued to occupy the high ground. In a
profile by Bernard Weinraub, (*New York Times,* August 11, 1983), Wick stated:

At the beginning there was this concern that we'd have a conservative,
hardline bent. . . . My defense was that this is preposterous. The VOA
charter says we must tell about America in a balanced way. To do what
was alleged and feared would be illegal.

The fact that this statement contradicts earlier USIA policy positions and
ignores the House Foreign Affairs Committee report about past USIA improprieties and illegalities *may* not be as important as Wick's awareness that his
agency was now being carefully monitored by Congress.

188   In the Weinraub interview Wick also stated that "after two troubled and dismaying years as the organization's leader, he had not only buoyed it [USIA] but also begun to quell criticisms of his personal style." Even so, Wick admitted: "The criticisms are hard for me to deal with and, frankly, there are a lot of moles in this place." USIA's mission "had been consistent," Wick declared. "We want to explain the policies of our Government and the values and character of its people to other countries and other people." According to Weinraub, Wick stated that his effectiveness:

> was best measured by the Soviet reactions to his efforts. "There's this vituperativeness against me personally. . . . Sometimes it's a bit frightening, intimidating. They said I made millions of dollars in brothels, they call me a right-wing ideologue." He shrugged, and said he sometimes wondered if the K.G.B., the Soviet secret police, was "going to be after you."

At this point John W. Shirley, a career diplomat who then served as Mr. Wick's deputy, intervened. "The Soviets squawk when they're getting hurt," he said. "And they've been squawking a great deal more recently than any time in memory."

Whatever the validity of Wick's and Shirley's perceptions about the effects that USIA activities have had on the Russians, it cannot be too strongly emphasized that past USIA improprieties have created a credibility gap with friends and allies overseas (as well as many academics at home)—a fact that Wick and his associates conveniently overlooked or failed to recognize.

For example, Harold M. Hyman, one of our most distinguished constitutional historians, was not sent overseas by USIA in 1982 despite numerous requests for lectures by scholars in the United Kingdom and Western European countries. Hyman was told that USIA's failure to send him abroad was the result of "bureaucratic inefficiency." "Your agency," Hyman wrote to W. Scott Thompson (USIA's associate director for programs) on April 4, 1983,

> certainly created no respect for itself or for the United States as represented by your agency, among the several eminent professors of American Studies in the UK and in European countries, who wished to have me lecture there. I enclose copies of some letters of this import. Some academics abroad did request me through the U.S. Embassy in their nations . . . and so that technical point seems not to exonerate USIA.

> Other American scholars have, as you perhaps know, expressed their displeasure and concerns recently about ICA/USIA operations.

I understand their positions better now. Can USIA really afford the accumulation of such dour estimates of your value and values?

Another American academic wrote that a visiting lecturer at his institution from the State Department "indicated that the Reagan administration had gone farther than any other in recent memory to employ ideologues in the ICA. Further, as a career diplomat, he went on to conclude that most of our international friends see through this transparent effort at propaganda." Still another American declared that in West Germany the only people connected with USIA who really understood American ideals were German employees of long standing.

Numerous letters received from Australian and New Zealand academics reflect almost identical attitudes. One Australian wrote:

> I am most grateful for your offprint of the OAH *Newsletter* item. Its content would be appalling were one not reasonably aware of ICA's general tendencies toward secretiveness & control. We—I—*always* suspect it, but your experience & the overt pressures are evidence which is both confirming and disturbing.

This individual went on to say that contacts with the Australian USIA constituted "an intellectual humiliation." In another letter the same person expressed the opinion that "often, the problem (believe it or not) is as much ignorance on their part as bad-intentions/evil. I *am* amazed that State cannot recruit better people." The letter concludes: "Like the d—— foreign policy: they're both stupid and dangerous."

"I was really horrified," a New Zealand academic wrote,

> to read about your experiences in Australia. . . . I think you have done a great service to the academic community here and in America by extracting this for publication. The actions in the Australian I.C.A. have set us back 15 years. . . . How stupid can they be?

Another New Zealander confided: "To be honest, I have always felt a little compromised in my relationships with the office." "Here in New Zealand," another Kiwi wrote,

> the I.C.A. people have been very cautious in comment although amusingly, and possibly because of "the Curry incident" they have been very anxious that we have our share (and more) of Fulbrights for 1983 and 1984. . . . I may be putting two and two together and coming up with

22 but our relations with I.C.A. seem to have cooled and warmed at the same time—treating us more cautiously but eager to help! However, am glad that you have put a spoke in the Reagan wheel!

Still other examples of reactions from scholars in the Antiptodes could be cited; but the central points have been made with one major exception—the determination of Australians and New Zealanders to resist any attempt to politicize the Fulbright program. As one individual phrased it:

I have no fears for the Fulbright Programme in N.Z. Any attempt by the U.S. Government to politicize it will be strongly resisted by the N.Z. members of the Foundation's Board of Directors. In your case our mistake was letting you go to Australia under the sponsorship of USICA. In future any of our Fulbrighters who wish to go to Australia will do so under the sponsorship of the Fulbright Program.

These letters provide a sad commentary on the low esteem in which USIA is currently held abroad. In some cases, contempt would not be too strong a word.

If controversy has surrounded Mr. Wick and the USIA from the very beginning of the Reagan era, it was not until the end of January 1984 that the politicization of USIA's AMPARTS program became a national scandal. Howard Kurtz, a reporter for the *Washington Post* obtained a copy of an official USIA blacklist, covering the period from August 1981 to January 1984. The blacklist contained eighty-four names, including those of Walter Cronkite, Ralph Nader, Coretta Scott King, Senator Gary Hart, David Brinkley, John Kenneth Galbraith, Admiral Stansfield Turner, Tom Wicker, and Congressman Jack Brooks, D-Texas, chairman of the Government Operations Committee.

Agency officials also admitted that about 720 documents were destroyed that "contained their handwritten notations indicating why the names of certain people were stricken from the list of candidates for overseas speaking engagements." (*New York Times*, February 27, 1984).

Mr. Wick, who was out of the country when news of the blacklist came to light, later admitted to a House subcommittee that politics was involved in selecting AMPARTS speakers, but insisted that the blacklist was "a lot less onerous than has been implied." Wick, however, went on to say: "I personally would not sanction a blacklist. It is un-American." ★

★On October 14, 1985, I happened to be seated at dinner next to Ronald L. Trowbridge, former director of USIA's Bureau of Educational and Cultural Affairs. "Professor Curry," he

Leslie Lenkowsky, then acting deputy director of USIA, "told several reporters that top-level officials had no knowledge of the blacklist, whose existence he then blamed on 'mindless gnomes' in the agency," by which he meant career officials (*National Journal*, June 9, 1984, p. 1138). Lenkowsky also stated that on learning of the blacklist's existence he ordered a halt to its use. To discriminate against individuals "for political and ideological reasons," he declared, "was wrong" (*New York Times,* Feb. 27, 1984).

The blacklist continued to make headlines throughout the winter and spring of 1984—not only in the media but in hearings held by the Subcommittee on International Operations of the House Foreign Affairs Committee, and in the Senate where, on May 15, 1984, Lenkowsky was denied confirmation as deputy director of USIA by a vote of 11 to 6. Lenkowsky's testimony, in which he denied complicity, was challenged by both colleagues and subordinates, including career officials, who resented what they termed Lenkowsky's attempt to use them as scapegoats. Senator Charles Mathias, Jr., R-Maryland, summed up Lenkowsky's fate: "Clearly, Mr. Lenkowsky is not responsible for the politicization process. But he is part of it and he has arrived on the scene at a time when all evidence suggests that we must put a stop to it." (*National Journal*, June 9, 1984).

Director Charles Wick, a close personal friend of the president, escaped the hearings without penalty if not criticism. During the past three years, however, Wick has granted no interviews to the press; and relatively little new information on USIA activities that would further damage the agency's credibility has come to light. But, as we have argued, the existence of an official blacklist is only one among many issues and incidents that bear upon the politicization of USIA activities and programs. Whatever its current policies, USIA's integrity has been compromised, and the image it has projected abroad will not soon be dispelled.

---

said, "I want you to know that even Mr. Wick didn't approve of the way you were treated in Australia." "Is that an admission and an apology?" I replied. "No," he said. "But it's the closest thing to it that you're ever going to get."

[Richard O. Curry]

13

CHOICES: INTERNATIONAL

EDUCATION, CIVIL LIBERTIES,

AND DOMESTIC POLITICS

DURING THE 1980s

The Fulbright program originated in 1946, when Senator J. William Fulbright proposed using foreign war debts to finance international exchanges so that people, in Fulbright's words, "might develop a capacity for empathy, a distaste for killing other men, and an inclination for peace." More recently, the senator phrased it somewhat differently. "Education," he said, "is a slow moving but powerful force. It may not be fast enough or strong enough to save us from catastrophe, but it is the strongest force available."

The Fulbright program was a product of imaginative and innovative thinking; and it has been one of the most long-lived programs in modern American

This paper was delivered at the eighth annual meetings of the Fulbright Alumni Association at the University of Arkansas, October 12, 1985, which commemorated the fortieth anniversary of the Fulbright program; at Marshall University on April 26, 1986; and at the annual meetings of the Society for Historians of American Foreign Relations (SHAFR) held at Georgetown University, June 28, 1986.

history. It reached its height during the mid-1960s, but then suffered a decline of nearly two-thirds in terms of constant dollars by the early 1980s.

Then, in 1981, the Reagan administration called for a 15 percent across-the-board cut for all government agencies. Mr. Charles Z. Wick, head of the United States Information Agency, responded to the OMB's demands by recommending that cultural and educational exchange programs bear the brunt of the budget cuts. The agency not only proposed that Fulbright funds be cut by 56 percent, which would have ended the program in sixty-one countries—primarily in Third World nations; it also recommended the elimination of the critically important Hubert H. Humphrey Fellowship program and cutting by half the funding for the equally important International Visitors Program.

These shortsighted—and potentially disastrous—recommendations were rejected by a bipartisan coalition in Congress. And in 1982, Congress adopted the Pell amendment, which called upon the USIA to double the amount then being spent for educational and cultural exchange programs. As a result, the Fulbright program once again is progressing. Congress has appropriated approximately $128 million for fiscal year 1986 and nearly $142 million for fiscal year 1987 for Fulbright exchanges and additional funds for the International Visitors Program, Humphrey fellowships, and other programs.

This action will not only provide money for increasing the number of Fulbright awards; but it will, I hope, result in increasing the size of stipends as well. In the past, many Fulbrighters have accepted appointments at considerable financial sacrifice; and some of our best senior scholars are unable to accept a Fulbright award unless it is combined with a sabbatic leave. But this arrangement is not always feasible for a variety of reasons.

If the Fulbright program is currently being restored to financial health, the Reagan administration has continued its attack on other aspects of international education in general and the Fulbright program in particular. Each year since 1981 the administration has asked Congress to eliminate all funding under Title VI of the Higher Education Act. Had this recommendation been adopted, funding for some ninety-one international education and foreign language research centers and seventy-two undergraduate international studies programs in the United States would have been eliminated. In addition, some $5 million designated for Fulbright graduate student research fellowships would also have been eliminated. The total amount involved was relatively modest—approximately $33 million; but the Congress has restored these funds each year.

Conversely, the Reagan administration, reacting to a recommendation of the Kissinger Commission Report, has called for the implementation of a fellowship program that would bring approximately ten thousand undergraduate students from Central America over the course of the next five years at a cost

194 of about $380 million. Congress has authorized funding in fiscal years 1986 and 1987 for this program but not at the levels requested by the administration.

These contradictory initiatives raise several important questions. Hugh M. Hamill, Jr., pointedly asked last year in an article published in the Latin American Studies Association *Forum:* "Why does the Reagan Administration try to weaken U.S. international education?" "Perhaps the President," Hamill continued,

> hopes that the Salvadorans, Hondurans and Guatemalans who study here will be so impressed by their experiences that they will return home to eschew possible revolutionary solutions to their problems and to inculcate North American values and institutions in place of Hispanic ones.
>
> We, on the other hand, apparently should not learn or teach about other societies. The administration may have recognized that many educators and students who do learn about Latin America and other areas of the world are articulate and effective critics of Reagan's policies there.

Senator Fulbright, in a major foreign policy address, "The Two Americas," delivered at the University of Connecticut in 1966, stated (in terms still relevant today):

> The Latin American policies of the United States have been distorted by a tendency to identify reform with revolution and revolution with communism. It is assumed, because they have something to do with each other, as indeed they do, that they are one and the same thing, which indeed they are not. The pervading suspicion of social revolutionary movements on the part of United States policy makers is most unfortunate, because there is a strong possibility of more explosions in Latin America, and insofar as the United States makes itself the enemy of revolutionary movements, communism is able to make itself their friend. The anti-revolutionary bias in United States policy, which is rooted in the fear of communism, can only have the effect of strengthening communism.

"We must choose between the two Americas," Fulbright concluded, "the one imperious in its wealth and power, the other a civilized example for the world."

What I have said (and quoted) thus far suggests not only that the attitude of the current administration is shortsighted (and clearly, it has no monopoly on that score), but is the most stridently ideological administration to hold office in the United States in decades. Its domestic and foreign policy implications are enormous. This includes attacks on civil liberties and academic freedom at home as well as the politicization of international educational and exchange programs.

Some of the evidence supporting this view is provided by the administration of the United States Information Agency's (USIA) AMPARTS program, which sends some five hundred to six hundred speakers overseas each year. It would be unrealistic to suggest that other presidential administrations have not used the AMPARTS program to send some speakers overseas to explain or lobby for support of their policies. However, there is irrefutable evidence that the AMPARTS program under the Reagan administration has gone to extremes in applying ideological litmus tests in selecting speakers, whether their topics deal with foreign policy or domestic issues.

In May 1983, the House Foreign Affairs Committee (HFAC) Report on the State Department and the USIA *et al* Authorization Bill (Report 98-130) provided a scathing critique of USIA policies. "Over the past two years," the report stated,

> USIA has arguably violated the letter and spirit of its charter by (a) attempting, unsuccessfully, virtually to eliminate the funding for the educational and cultural affairs programs which have stood the test of time and proved their worth; (b) reflecting partisan political ideology in its choice of USIA grantees; (c) providing funds to friends of USIA officials without regard to the USIA charter, or proper grant guidelines and procedures; (d) attempting to influence the comments of USIA grantees so that they reflected executive branch policy positions; (e) withholding or delaying the granting of USIA funds to grantees due to partisan political considerations; and (f) placing in career Foreign Service and civil service positions, political appointees who reflect partisan political views, or who are friends and relations of current political appointees, without regard to the requirements of specific positions, or the effect on the career services.

My own encounters with USIA officials in Australia in 1981 as an AMPARTS speaker provide personal testimony corroborating the accuracy of the HFAC report.

On one occasion, I was asked by the Cultural Affairs officer (CAO) in Canberra: "Dr. Curry, what is it that you do that fits into the 'game plan' of the International Communications Agency [now called the U.S.I.A.] which is the propaganda agency of the United States government?" He then asked for a list of topics on which I had been asked to speak by Australian academics. I was instructed to include a summary of the points of view I intended to express. On another occasion, I was informed point blank by another USIA official

196 that if I said anything too critical about the Reagan administration: "You'll never get another Fulbright!"[1]

But the politicization of USIA's AMPARTS program has other dimensions besides attempts at intimidation or screening processes based on ideology rather than qualifications.

One unexpected result of my articles on the USIA was an unsolicited letter received from a history professor in Western Europe.

"I read your pieces with great interest for two reasons," the professor began:

> One, they helped me to better understand the change in reaction and attitude on the part of USIA officials. . . . Before 1981, support of the scholarly activities of our [national] association has been generous and liberal without ever any attempt being made of interfering with our activities. . . . Subtle changes, however, occurred after 1981. The lump sum approach was abandoned in favour of an itemized approach regarding financial support for our activities, with the effect that every individual item—conferences, symposia, publications, etc.—are now being 'discussed' as to their 'relevance' and suggestions are being made as to content as well as . . . financial support. . . . Up to this point, we have not yet actually been denied anything which we have been granted in the past. It may, however, happen any time and we are under subtle and constant pressure to consider whether we are doing the 'right things.' . . .
> I should add, however, that American Embassy/USIA officials appear to be . . . embarrassed about this change in the official line. At least the American officials convey the impression that they are being forced to act the way they do act and that they, personally, do not like it.
>
> As regards the Fulbright program more specifically I should add that . . . [it] is being partially financed, as far as I know even the greater part of it, by . . . [our] side so there is the chance at least of neutralizing non-scholarly influences. And from my knowledge of people on this side I am convinced they would act more freely the (liberal, open) American way than some of the American officials you describe.

This letter, candid and disturbing, was written (it should be emphasized) shortly before the *Washington Post*'s dramatic revelation on January 31, 1984, of the existence of an official USIA blacklist and adds an alarming new dimension to our knowledge of USIA's "covert" activities even in friendly nations. The blacklist itself was characterized by USIA officials in congressional testimony in May 1984 not as a blacklist per se, but as an error in the screening process for selecting AMPARTS speakers which has now been corrected.

I must observe, however, that in 1983, a year before the existence of a black-list became public, the HFAC report that condemned the politicization of USIA programs ended by commending Mr. Wick "for his prompt, sincere, and effective efforts to remedy the situation."

I do not question Mr. Wick's sincerity. I am aware that he is a controversial public figure; but I have no evidence proving that grounds exist for laying *all* blame for USIA's past improprieties and illegalities at his doorstep. More-over, in recent congressional testimony, Mr. Wick stated that he recognizes the need to separate the short-term functions from the longer-range goals of USIA's programs.

It is a matter of public record, however, that less than a year after the HFAC report gave Mr. Wick a personal vote of confidence, Mr. Les Lenkow-sky, then deputy director–designate of USIA, was denied confirmation by the U.S. Senate because of conflicting testimony by agency officials (including Mr. Lenkowsky's) regarding responsibility for the blacklist and the shredding of documents by agency officials. Furthermore, the pressures exerted by USIA/American embassy officials, which were described by my correspondent in Western Europe, occurred both before and after Mr. Wick, in a letter dated May 4, 1983, assured Congressman Dante B. Fascell, then chairman of the Subcommittee on International Operations of the HFAC, that the USIA had put its house in order.

What the future holds in store remains to be seen. Past performance by the USIA, however, does not offer much ground for optimism.

The Fulbright program was administered until 1977 in the State Depart-ment by the assistant secretary for educational and cultural affairs. In that year, that post was abolished, and the responsibility for administering the Fulbright program was transferred to the USIA. Many thoughtful observers—includ-ing Senator Fulbright—opposed this change. In a letter addressed to me earlier this year (April 11, 1985), Senator Fulbright wrote: "When the merger of the program with U.S.I.A. was proposed by President Carter in 1977, I testified against it in the Committee because of concern that it would be politicized and subjected to short term political objectives. It is clearly a danger and must be opposed."

Former U.S. ambassador to Italy (1977–1981) Richard N. Gardner, in a *New York Times Magazine* article, "Selling America in the Marketplace of Ideas" (March 20, 1983), takes the same position, arguing that the "time has come to separate these functions again" by returning the administration of educational and cultural affairs to the State Department. But this "will work," Gardner warns, "only if the Secretary of State is prepared to appoint a non-political personality of superior quality from the private sector to the re-created post of Assistant Secretary for Educational and Cultural Affairs, with the necessary

198   independence to assure the integrity of these essential programs." If this cannot be accomplished, Gardner, among others, advocates the creation of a hybrid public-private foundation to administer our educational and cultural exchange programs.

Dr. Rose Lee Hayden, a former high ranking USIA official, who is now president of the National Council on Foreign Language and International Studies in New York, has a similar, but somewhat different idea. Hayden recommends the creation of an independent National Trust financed by "flow-back" funds received by the U.S. treasury each year. Since these flow-back funds amount to some $4 or 5 billion annually, the allocation of only 3 percent a year would provide an additional $100 million a year for financing innovative programs in international education.

Initiatives such as those recommended by Ambassador Gardner, Dr. Hayden, and others deserve not only serious discussion but implementation in some form that will ensure the integrity of international educational and cultural exchange programs regardless of which administration, Democratic or Republican, is in power at a given time.

Support for innovative changes in terms of both ideas and reorganization needs to be generated in Congress; and, if I am not mistaken, that process is already underway. To use President Lincoln's phrase: "The signs of the times are changing."

The House/Senate Conference Report on the Foreign Relations Authorization Act, Fiscal Years 1986 and 1987 (Report 99-240) makes several important recommendations and observations. First of all, the conference report states that past educational and cultural exchange programs have neglected vast regions of the world vital to U.S. national security interests. Moreover, past programs have been too elitist in nature. Students "from families of limited financial means," the report declares, "have, in the past, largely not had the opportunity to study in the United States, and scholarship programs sponsored by the United States have made no provision for identifying, preparing, or supporting such students in the United States."

The conference report further observes that Soviet-bloc countries offer twelve times the number of scholarships to students in developing countries than does the United States government. And "this disparity entails the serious long-run cost of having so many potential future leaders of the developing world educated in Soviet-bloc countries." This does not necessarily mean that these leaders will become pro-Russian as a result; but clearly they won't know anything firsthand about us.

The conference report also deplores the failure of American students in particular and the citizenry in general to have what someone called "international competence"—that is, knowledge and understanding of the "languages, cultures and socioeconomic composition" of developing countries "as these areas assume an ever larger role in the world community." Only one in twenty U.S. college graduates can communicate effectively in a foreign language.

Although the report doesn't say so directly, implicit in its conclusions is the idea that not our lack of weapons of awesome destructive power but our political and cultural isolation in a constantly shrinking, increasingly interdependent world is our real "window of vulnerability."

Thus, the report not only calls upon the president of the United States to take the necessary steps to bring increasing numbers of promising Third World students to the United States, but authorizes him to take whatever action is necessary "to expand opportunities for Americans *from all economic classes* [italics mine] to study in developing countries." The report fully recognizes that its recommendations will require as much intensive preparation on the part of American undergraduate students in the languages, history, and culture of developing countries as it will in providing advance training overseas in the English language for nonelitist students in participating developing nations.

Finally, the conference report calls upon the Agency for International Development (AID) and USIA to establish programs for graduate study by students of limited means and the establishment of ongoing orientation and counseling programs to counter the problem of "culture shock" for all American and foreign students involved.

The conference managers, who wrote the report, also call for private sector contributions in promoting these new programs. During the 1960s, for example, the Ford Foundation provided as much as $27 million a year for international education. In recent years its contribution has declined to from $3 to $4 million per annum.

Although the conference report does not recommend any specific dollar amounts, it does state that not less than 25 percent of funds allocated for educational exchanges with developing countries should be spent in the Caribbean and Latin America.

Whether or not the Reagan administration will respond in a major way to these congressional recommendations remains to be seen; but bipartisan support for such initiatives clearly does exist; and further action must be encouraged by the Fulbright Alumni Association and other organizations committed to expanding our exchange programs in neglected areas such as southern Europe, Africa, Asia, the Middle East, the Caribbean basin, and Latin America.

We must heed warnings, however, such as those made recently by one of my European correspondents. "I might remind you," he wrote, not you, of course, but your audience—that if there is any substance to the charge of anti-Americanism in Europe . . . this phenomenon in most cases grew out of a disappointed love affair with America. Educational/cultural exchanges and international education are indispensable in a "survival community" (to paraphrase Karl W. Deutsch). But if . . . agents [of the U.S. government] view cultural exchanges as a short-range political instrument—they should forget about [them]. . . .

If responsible policy-makers in the U.S. care at all for this country—even if only for prudential reasons—and if they care for the reaction of the academic community, if not per se then for its influence on a future generation of political, economic, cultural leaders, etc., they should take the long view. Any visible short-range effort to tie the Agency [USIA] and its activities to the purposes of American politics and [Administration] policies will be destructive of a potential for friendly even if sometimes critical cooperation.

Earlier on, I quoted Senator Fulbright's ironic statement: "The anti-revolutionary bias in United States policy, which is rooted in the fear of communism, can only have the effect of strengthening communism." An important corrolary is this: Many of the domestic policies adopted by the current administration *in the name of national security* can only have the long-range effect of *weakening national security itself.* In sum, if American ideals are to be a force in the world, we must also practice them at home.

But the point is that, at the present time, we are not practicing them at home. The Reagan administration's attack on international educational and cultural exchange programs is but one aspect of a much larger scenario in which neo-McCarthyism has reemerged in American society with a vengeance.

The government has used the term *national security* to justify secrecy, censorship, surveillance, and repression—in an effort not only to keep the American public uninformed or misinformed, but to eliminate criticism of many of its policies.

In the brief space allotted here a few examples will have to suffice. How, may I ask, is *national security* (to reiterate that magical phrase) going to be improved by requiring 290,000 federal employees to sign lifetime pledges to submit all speeches, articles, and books to federal censors before they can be published or delivered? In 1983 alone, 28,364 books, articles, speeches, and other writings were reviewed by government censors. As historian Thomas G. Paterson phrased it: "When we speak of thought control we're not talking about the burning of books, but rather the prevention of books. . . . Is a modern-day George Kennan to be muzzled for life?" John Shattuck, vice president for government, community and public affairs at Harvard, points to other "disastrous effects of government censorship." "From now on," he wrote, "there will be no inducement for academics to serve in government; and, as a result, the government will be deprived of much needed expertise and advice." How is that going to improve *national security*?

Moreover, how is *national security* going to be protected by denying visas to foreigners under the terms of the ill-advised McCarran-Walter Act? What do we have to fear by allowing people such as Hortensia Allende, Nobel laureate Gabriel García Márquez, and Canadian conservationist Farley Mowatt to speak to American audiences?

And why, may I ask, has the Reagan administration attempted to limit or destroy the effectiveness of the Freedom of Information Act (FOIA)? The FOIA (enacted by Congress in 1966) and strengthened after the Watergate revelations has been an invaluable tool in obtaining information on such issues as the environment, toxic wastes, discrimination, intelligence agency abuses, foreign policy, unsafe products, and the inadequate design of some nuclear plants. If, in a democratic society, the people are ill-informed or misinformed about the vital issues of our day, how can we expect to have intelligent public-policy debates and hold public officials strictly accountable for their actions? President Reagan's Executive Order 12356 contains extremely regressive procedures for the classification of government documents; and indeed it has re-classified some documents released to the public by previous administrations. Executive Order 12356 not only deals a crippling blow to the FOIA, but contains other provisions that attack academic freedom by asserting the right to classify basic scientific research whether or not it was sponsored and paid for by the government and whether or not it is even remotely related to *national security* interests.

Add to this cauldron of censorship and secrecy and paranoia another prime ingredient: Executive Order 12333, which permits the resumption of unrestrained surveillance and harassment of U.S. citizens by the FBI, the CIA, and other intelligence agencies—and this despite the excesses and abuses brought to light by Watergate.

What I am suggesting, of course, is the existence of a darker side in American history, as indeed there is in every nation that has ever existed. If the United States has often served as a beacon light for oppressed peoples, and if the United States, in relative terms, has been the most open society the world has ever known, we have too often taken counsel from our fears rather than from our hopes and ideals. Today, not only are the Bill of Rights and other constitutional safeguards under attack, but our sense of mission once again has fallen victim to a Manichean view of the world.

If, over the long haul, the United States falls victim to the mindless repres-

202 sion of neo-McCarthyism, international educational and exchange programs
won't amount to a tinker's damn for the simple reason that no one with good
sense will want to listen to anything we have to say.

Today we are faced with perils at home and abroad, but we still have
choices. Are we to pursue the ideals embodied in the Declaration of Independence and the Bill of Rights, or are we to become a barracks state which at
best will lead to that "symbolic year, 1984," and at worst the silence of nuclear
winter? As Senator Fulbright has phrased it: "We must choose between the
two Americas, the one imperious in its wealth and power, the other a civilized
example for the world."

NOTE

1. See my prepared statement in the Addendum of hearings held on May 10
and 15, 1984, by the Subcommittee on International Operations of the HFAC
on the USIA blacklist ("Addendum to Oversight of the U.S. Information
Agency Hearings.") Washington, D.C.: Government Printing Office, 1985),
pp. 1–7.

[William Preston, Jr., and Ellen Ray]

14

DISINFORMATION AND MASS

DECEPTION: DEMOCRACY AS A

COVER STORY

During World War I, the atrocity story came into its own as an instrument of foreign policy. In those simpler days, governments could turn public opinion against the enemy with tales of individual brutality: the rape of a nun, the bayoneting of a baby, or the execution of a Red Cross nurse. Such propaganda externalized the issues and focused national attention on an appropriate scapegoat. Doubters or dissenters were swept aside in the patriotic fallout, in an emotional downpour that insisted, "Once at war, to reason is treason."

This crude propaganda, however, had a temporary, war-related quality that often foundered on its own exaggerations. The idea of truth in those days had not yet been obliterated by the continuous covert manipulation of information in peacetime just as in war; nor had deception, secrecy, and lying come to be so much a part of the national menu as to be swallowed whole like the junk food that satiates the public appetite. Today there is no better example of the corrupted circumstances that now confront the consumer of news than the undercover campaign of official disinformation about Cuba and Nicaragua.

This essay is an updated version of an article first published in *Our Right to Know* (Spring 1983). Reprinted with permission of the authors and the publishers. Copyright 1983 by the Fund for Open Information and Accountability, Inc.

204   Having failed to restore its hegemony over Cuba in the Bay of Pigs invasion or in the long, secret war waged under the code name "Operation Mongoose," the United States Central Intelligence Agency recently stepped up its twenty-year psychological warfare operations to discredit and destroy the Cuban government and any other Latin American or Caribbean government that stands in ideological unity with it. Propaganda aimed at that small, struggling country intentionally manipulates emotions of horror, revulsion, and fear in the uninformed citizen of the Yankee Colossus. Cuba is falsely pictured by the United States as embracing in its foreign policy the contemporary apocalyptic trio: drugs, criminality, and terrorism—a far more terrible spectre than the individual bloodletting of the World War I propaganda. Images of corrupted American youth, gangsterism, and revolutionary violence sent from Cuba throughout Latin America are daily media fare for the American public.

A similar, covert campaign has been waged against the Sandinista government of Nicaragua, adding massive disinformation to the proxy war that the United States, through the CIA and the NSC, has waged for more than five years against the people of Nicaragua.

Cuba and Nicaragua as scapegoats and Fidel Castro and Daniel Ortega as the implacable enemy of world national security interests have become easy answers for the complex realities of hemispheric change. And the sophisticated techniques with which official information about Cuba and Nicaragua is concealed, denied, created, regulated, shaped, and planted seem to have heightened public acceptance of the Big Lie.

Though a shoot-out at credibility gap might not rescue the truth from the hands of its abductors, a historical perspective of official U.S. deception operations against its own people might at least innoculate some against further ravages of this advancing affliction.

THE OVERT ERA OF INFORMATION
ABUSE, 1898–1945

No one with any knowledge of governments would ever insist there was a utopian past. Governments have always monitored dissent to impose their version of events on the public consciousness, to control the circulation of hostile opinion, and to manage the news. Secrecy always had a place, as had executive privilege. But the First Amendment guarantees, as well as the separation and checking of powers, seemed designed to limit the U.S. government's inherent tendency to manipulate information for its own interest. As we shall see, this is not the case.

During and after the Civil War, though not engaging in deliberate deception, the government nevertheless insisted on "codes of press behavior" (the same for which we criticize UNESCO and Third World nations, for daring to put forth in the New World Information and Communication Order) and could classify information as too poisonous to circulate if judged "incendiary," "seditious," "treasonable," "immoral," "indecent," or "obscene."

The buildup of the North American Empire, then, added a new dimension of danger for information. During the Spanish-American War, the brutal military mop-up against the "rebels" in the Philippines, Puerto Rico, and Cuba involved secret planning, undercover operations, and premeditated cover-ups in the face of public and congressional opposition.

It was the first World War, however, that led the United States to move beyond censorship and overt suppression into the heady realm of disinformation itself. In April 1917, President Woodrow Wilson authorized the Committee on Public Information, headed by George Creel, to take an active part in disseminating and propagandizing an official point of view. To unite public opinion behind the war, Creel's CPI conducted "a fight for the mind of mankind." Fake intelligence suggesting that German spies were everywhere generated waves of hatred and hysteria against the "barbaric Huns." In disinformation coups reminiscent of today, the State Department used selective information to "prove" Germany was funding American pacifist organizations.

The capacity for covert conduct also gained ground as U.S. military intelligence expanded its role in domestic surveillance, laying plans in 1920 for a secret, domestic, counterinsurgency program aimed at radicals—an authentic progenitor of the COINTELPRO operations of the later Hoover years. Anticipating the CIA mania for cover, U.S. intelligence also dispatched agents to Europe as members of the International Red Cross.

By the end of the war, the country had acquired an institutionalized intelligence system, initiated the classification of sensitive information, and bitten into the apple of deception. The Committee for Public Information left a legacy of experience for later generations of disinformationists to apply, if not to duplicate.

PUBLIC RELATIONS IS BORN
AS DISINFORMATION

During two subsequent decades of peace in which the trauma of an economic collapse followed the delirium of a perilous prosperity, a subtle yet significant development shaped the future of information: the rise of public relations and its professional advocates.

206   Exemplified by Edward Bernays, a man who began his career as consultant to the U.S. delegation to the Versailles Peace Conference that terminated World War I and ended it as a hired hand for United Fruit Company in Latin America, public relations and its covert marketing strategies quickly seeped into the very core of American life. As Bernays cynically stated in a PR manual in 1928, "The conscious and intelligent manipulation of the organized habits and opinions of the masses is an important element in democratic society. Those who manipulate this unseen mechanism of society constitute an invisible government which is the true ruling power of our country. . . . It is the intelligent minorities which need to make use of propaganda continuously and systematically."

The New Deal thirties witnessed further assaults on the integrity of information. In the United States, the realities of the depression inspired a militant labor union campaign for recognition and power, one in which the Communists participated as allies. The conservative reaction to this movement was vicious, projecting an image of it as the secret "red" subversion of U.S. society —a mindless image that haunts the public consciousness even today. Imagined threats from front organizations and fifth columns brought further waves of tainted information. Thus the stage was set for the massive escalation of mistrust in any information not certified "pure" by the U.S. government. Since it could have the field to itself, all competitors were labeled un-American.

What the government would do with this power was not yet clear, but its existence and potential for abuse could not be denied—an incredible opportunity for any proponent of the Bernays school of manipulation.

Other trends in the years immediately preceding Pearl Harbor accelerated the information counterrevolution. The growth of classification expanded the domain of U.S. secrecy and the ability of government officials to conceal or selectively leak information on behalf of their own political agendas. Loyalty oaths and security checks came into being, designed to eliminate disclosure of this same material.

"Subversive activities" and espionage, meanwhile, became top priorities for the U.S. government, justifying generalized surveillance of a population considered suspect. Covert intelligence activity would soon come to serve the information management of successive U.S. administrations.

WORLD WAR II AND THE NEW
DISINFORMATION

On the eve of its second crusade to save the world, the United States was also poised on the brink of a new information era. How secret its policies would become, to what extent it would adopt the techniques of deception, and how each of these would affect democratic decision-making began to emerge as the war progressed. These questions were illuminated in the dramatic struggle for power that occurred between the Office of War Information (OWI), essentially a civilian organization charged with the mission of promoting an understanding of the war to the world at large, and the Office of Strategic Services (OSS), the wartime predecessor of today's CIA. These two agencies had irreconcilable differences over the nature and purpose of propaganda. The OSS victory in this struggle would foreshadow the growth of an Orwellian ministry of truth to be used as a covert instrument of Cold War policies against a new enemy—the Soviet Union. But all that came later.

Elmer Davis, OWI director and ex-newsman, began World War II believing his agency should deal in facts, not opinion, disseminating truths to friend and enemy alike—something the BBC's wartime broadcasts were attempting to accomplish. But neither President Roosevelt nor the Army, Navy, and State departments believed that the public had a right to know what was really going on. (Documents recently obtained under the Freedom of Information Act even suggest U.S. foreknowledge of Pearl Harbor.) In any case, the war-related bureaucracy remained adamant about sharing information with the OWI, seriously undermining its mission.

Colonel William J. Donovan, head of the OSS, on the other hand, had an adventurer's enthusiasm for secret operations, dirty tricks, and disinformation of the crudest sort. Psychological warfare dominated the OSS approach to the war, though neither its costs nor its benefits to the American people were evaluated. Nor was truth considered a weapon of any potential.

Psychological warfare thus sold itself to the high command, and the OWI was forced to adopt the methods of its competitor, subordinating all information projects to the expedient of winning the war. Interestingly, it was hardly this capitulation that influenced the course of the war, since the same methods of manipulation were carried to the extreme by the enemy—the Goebbels approach to information.

By the time hostilities ended, the OWI had become a converted exponent of American power, its liberal one-world ideology long since subordinated to the commitment of U.S. involvement in every region of the world. Nowhere, their propaganda now claimed, could the United States "renounce its moral and ideological interests . . . as a powerful and righteous nation."

In the OSS, similar readjustments of priorities took place. Where once psychological warfare had at least been balanced by careful intelligence analysis to secure and interpret information, covert operations with their deceptive components of subverting and transforming facts became the new intelligence obsession.

In sum, a watershed had been reached. Information thereafter became

208   Bernays's reality—an "unseen mechanism" by which "intelligent minorities" shaped the opinions of the masses by deceiving them.

THE INTELLIGENCE ERA:
INFORMATION GOES UNDERGROUND

During the controversy surrounding publication of the Pentagon Papers in 1971, Leslie Gelb, in charge of producing that voluminous and revealing report for the *New York Times*, commented on the continuing Cold War dedication to the philosophy of Bernays. "Most of our elected and appointed leaders in the national security establishment," he confirmed, "felt they had the right—and beyond that the obligation—to manipulate the American public in the national interest as they defined it." The same notion in abbreviated form slipped out in an exchange between Defense Secretary McNamara's press spokesman and a group of reporters in 1962: "It's inherent in the government's right, if necessary, to lie to save itself," the aide argued.

The right to manipulate and the right to lie have had other postwar companions: the right to plausibly deny; the right to a cover story; the right to conceal; and the need to know, a standard of classification that created another right, that of privileged access, with its stepchild, the right to selectively leak.

In analyzing the period since the atom bombs leveled the Japanese will to resist, it is as if the intelligence agencies had not yet heard that the war was over, and are still hiding in caves on some Washington atoll. Yet the patterns that have unfolded are a logical outcome of the wartime experience, beginning with the failure to reorganize, control, or totally dismantle the secret coercive machinery which was created for that war. Quite the contrary. Stopping international communism provided the rationale for the even broader mandate for worldwide conquest—the neocolonialism and imperialism of the new empire. And to help in those operations, the U.S. intelligence agencies had no qualms about enlisting the support of their former enemies—the Gehlen intelligence network of Nazi Germany.

Documents of some of the early proposals to set up the central intelligence unit—the present CIA—give a flavor of the crisis atmosphere with which they viewed the future struggle against the Soviet Union: "the task of detecting . . . any developments which threaten the security of the *world*"; "to create a system in which every U.S. citizen who travels abroad . . . is a source of political intelligence"; "maintaining a constant check on foreign intelligence and propaganda, including propagandized U.S. citizens"; and "keep . . . informed on political trends inside the U.S. . . . because state legislatures are peculiarly vulnerable to outside influences and would be a logical objective of foreign intelligence services." It is small wonder that the CIA's fears became self-fulfilling prophesies.

Early CIA postwar victories over communism, such as the Italian elections of 1948, bought and paid for unwittingly by the American people, brought about unholy alliances as distasteful as those the intelligence agencies had made with the war criminals, dealings with the Mafia and the attendant corruption that comes with sharing a dirty secret with thugs.

Later, the Korean War produced an equally important impact on the spy operatives' own psychological outlook. Korea revived the atmosphere of total war, and created an "anything goes" philosophy directed against the "enemy." It meant, as General Maxwell Taylor argued in 1961 with reference to Fidel Castro, there would be a policy of "no long-term living with . . . dangerously effective exponents of communism and anti-Americanism." Iran (1953), Guatemala (1954), Vietnam (1954–1973), Brazil (1962), Indonesia (1965), and Chile (1973) were among the targets of covert operations encouraged by this philosophy.

But the strangest outcome of all in this web of deceit and disinformation was its coming home to roost. The intelligence establishment actually began to eat its own vomit. False propaganda fed into foreign outlets came to be reported back to the United States, and the government began to make policy decisions based on its own lies.

U.S. DISINFORMATION TODAY

In spite of the long history of U.S. government propaganda, disinformation, and lying, each succeeding administration insists it is clean, inventing alternative sources on whom to place the blame for the corruption of communications and dialogue. None of them wants the public to find the pea under the shell in this age-old con game. President Reagan has naturally accused the Soviets of introducing the practice. The State Department has fostered the myth that disinformation is a Russian word. *Dezinformatsiya*, according to one of their busy little defectors, Ladislav Bittman, is the province of "Directorate A" of the KGB. Bittman, a Czech who left his country well over ten years ago, only recently began making these widely reported pronouncements about disinformation. The *au courant* darling of the right-wing press, he conveniently confirms their suspicions about Soviet global intentions, while Reagan warns television audiences about Soviet-style runways and Cuban-style army barracks. The danger is that through incessant repetition of the word, disinforma-

210   tion has become synonymous in the minds of the American public with Soviet intelligence operations.

Historical facts, however, point to quite another conclusion, as the preceding sections have indicated. Disinformation has clearly been part of the U.S. intelligence, military, and Cold War offensive waged in peacetime since the end of World War II, an integral part of national security which has no clear relationship to truth or the beliefs of its practitioners. And as the activists of U.S. foreign policy, the CIA is its chief author.

EXPOSING MEDIA OPERATIONS

In 1975, the Senate Select Committee on Intelligence (the Church Committee), in an investigation of CIA wrongdoing, revealed just a tiny portion of the extent of CIA penetration of world media. It was patently obvious to the investigators that only U.S. intelligence agencies could practice the art of disinformation on such a grand scale, given the extraordinary expense of manipulating, influencing, and outright purchasing of news throughout the world. The number of organizations and persons who must be paid off to place fictitious stories across the globe is staggering. More than ten years ago the Church Committee said it had found evidence of more than two hundred wire services, newspapers, magazines, and book publishing complexes owned outright by the CIA. A 1977 *New York Times* exposé uncovered another fifty media outlets run by the CIA, inside and outside the United States, with more than twelve publishing houses responsible for over 1000 books, some 250 of them in English. Beyond the wholly owned proprietaries there were countless agents and friendly insiders working in media operations around the world. These exposures are, of course, only the tip of the iceberg. The mind reels at what remained hidden from Congress and the *New York Times* and continues so to the present.

Estimates of the portion of the U.S. intelligence budget—kept secret from the American people and Congress—devoted to propaganda range from a few to many billions of dollars a year. An extremely conservative guess in the December 1981 *Defense Electronics* put the overall U.S. intelligence budget for that year at $70 billion, of which about $10 billion, they said, went to the CIA. Media specialists have estimated that at least one third of the CIA's budget is devoted each year to the spread of disinformation, conservatively placing CIA covert media manipulation alone for that year at almost three and a half billion dollars. None of this takes into account the myriad of income-generating proprietaries owned by the CIA, firms that make a profit which is then poured back into more covert operations: CIA banks, holding companies, airlines, investment firms, and the like.

Anyone who has even a casual knowledge of the world hard-currency situation knows that the Soviet Union does not have the kind of foreign exchange that billion-dollar operations entail. Only the secret U.S. intelligence budget —taken from unwitting American taxpayers—can pay for inventing news on such a mammoth scale. And invent they do, as we shall see below in an examination of a few of their hysterical scenarios.

THE LEVELS OF DISINFORMATION

Spreading disinformation involves four levels of activity, a complex architecture that suggests how devious, costly, and important this activity has become. It currently runs from overt propaganda of the more traditional sort through covert operators and various public, nongovernmental disinformation peddlers to the deliberate scapegoating of the enemy as the source of documents and events that have been manufactured domestically.

The most well-known overt propaganda outlet for foreign consumption available to the United States is the Voice of America (VOA) and other projects of the United States Information Agency (USIA). Radio Free Europe (RFE) and Radio Liberty (RL), propaganda operations directed against Eastern Europe and the Soviet Union, were originally covert U.S. intelligence operations. But when it became an open secret that they were financed by the CIA, they were taken out of the closet for direct congressional funding in 1971. Though the government claims they are "private corporations," their employees must still go through extensive security clearances. Recent revelations about ex-Nazis who were absorbed into RFE/RL after World War II should invite closer scrutiny of these propaganda tools.

Inflammatory broadcasts by RFE in the 1950s misled a small number of Hungarian people to rebel in 1956, believing the United States was ready to intervene on their behalf. The ensuing uproar forced RFE to modify its broadcasting methods, though its recent diatribes against Poland are reminiscent of the Hungarian fare—but on a more sophisticated plane. Similarly, broadcast propaganda by the CIA's Radio Swan played a part in inducing the Bay of Pigs invaders of Cuba in 1961 to believe, quite incorrectly, that the Cuban population would support them. And, as the United States seldom learns from its mistakes, the energy the Reagan administration has spent establishing Radio Marti against Cuba will surely backfire again.

In addition to its broadcasts, RFE/RL openly operate the largest "private"

212   research facility in the West. It concentrates on information gathering—or spying—on Soviet and Eastern European nations, and on Communist and Socialist affairs.

But perhaps the most chilling "overt" propaganda project of the U.S. government to date is "Project Democracy," unveiled by President Reagan (as the Democracy Institute) in a 1982 speech to the British Parliament, established by executive orders and acts of Congress over the next two years.

This $85 million-a-year panorama of intelligence collection, recruitment, and training complete with a covert operations section, rivals the CIA's most ambitious media plans. This plan is discussed more fully below.

The second level of media activities of the U.S. government is the covert operations in the traditional sense. In theory, these deception operations are directed at influencing foreign, not domestic, opinion. Prior to December 1981, domestic activities were theoretically forbidden by the CIA's charter and by the executive orders governing CIA behavior. For all practical purposes, however, the charter was systematically violated. But now under President Reagan's Executive Order 12333, the CIA can operate within the United States so long as what it does is not "intended" to influence public opinion domestically. Who or what determines CIA "intentions" is not specified, leaving a wide-open field for more blatant manipulation of U.S. public opinion.

Even operations conducted entirely abroad are likely to cause "blowback," the situation wherein the U.S. media picks up reports from overseas, disseminating them at home, without realizing (or caring) that the reports are false and emanate from U.S. intelligence in the first place. Blowback is very dangerous; in Vietnam there was so much CIA disinformation being spread that U.S. military intelligence reports were often unwittingly based on complete fabrications that had been produced at CIA headquarters. In other cases, the CIA itself performed as an anti-intelligence agency in which the covert operators had to supply the information that the policymakers wanted. Government thus became the victim of its own disinformation line, compounding the original damage and leading officials to be twice removed from reality. (Numerous examples of this are documented in *Deadly Deceits: My 25 Years in the CIA*, by Ralph W. McGehee [New York: Sheridan Square Publications, 1983].

One of the most graphic examples of an intentional blowback operation was cited by former CIA officer John Stockwell in his book about Angola, *In Search of Enemies*. In order to discredit the Cuban troops who were aiding the Movimento Popular de Libertação de Angola (MPLA) government forces in that country's war with South Africa, CIA propagandists in Kinshasa, Zaire, came up with a story about Cuban soldiers raping Angolan women. Using an agent/stringer for a wire service, the agency had the story passed into the world media. Subsequently it was embellished by further spurious reports of **213** the capture of some of the Cubans by the women they had raped, of their trial, and of their execution by their own weapons. The entire series, spread out in the U.S. press over a period of several months, was a complete CIA fabrication.

Some covert media operations have been run on a very grand scale. One of the largest was Forum World Features, ostensibly a global feature-news service based in London, but in fact a CIA operation from the beginning. When its cover was blown it was forced to suspend operations. Similarly, the CIA owned outright, among other papers, the *Rome Daily American*, for decades the only English language paper in Italy.

In the third instance of press manipulation, the United States disguises its handiwork by engaging in the double whammy—accusing the Soviet Union of disseminating the phoney documents it has itself produced. Given the widespread coverage these charges receive, the "proof" is astonishingly contradictory. In 1982, for example, a supposedly bogus letter from President Reagan to King Juan Carlos of Spain was publicly denounced by the State Department as a Soviet forgery because it had errors in language and, as one officer noted, "it fits the pattern of known Soviet behavior." The previous year, another document was called a Soviet forgery because it was "so good" it had to be a Soviet product. In 1984, a letter purportedly from the Ku Klux Klan to various African Olympic committees warning them not to attend the Los Angeles Olympic Games was also denounced as a KGB forgery, although there was, once again, no evidence that some KKK group had written it.

Periodically the government will call forth one of their stable of "defectors" to confirm that something is a forgery, and the U.S. media buy it without much question. Several short-lived triumphs of the intelligence establishment show, however, that sometimes the people are not fooled, causing the press to reexamine their proffered themes. The State Department "White Paper" on Cuban aid to El Salvador, and the incredible Libyan "hit squad" saga are two examples. The White Paper, an unsuccessful attempt to recreate a Gulf of Tonkin situation, was shown by the *Wall Street Journal*, and *Washington Post*, and Philip Agee to have been based on government forgeries and mistranslations. The hit squad rumors that made headlines in 1981 disappeared—from the country and from the news—when Jack Anderson finally admitted he had been duped by his "intelligence sources." In fact, the major source of this disinformation was Manucher Ghorbanifar, an Iranian arms dealer later deeply implicated in the Irangate scandal. By at least as early as 1983, the CIA knew that the charges were false and that Ghorbanifar was the source, but it was not until January 31, 1987, that this information appeared, in the *Washington Post*.

Finally there are the disinformation peddlers—people who may or may not at a given moment be in the direct employ of the CIA or other intelligence agencies, but who can be counted on to repeat, embellish, or pass on whatever their disinformation masters in Washington decree. Here ideology is often as important as salary. Organizations like the Heritage Foundation and Accuracy in Media can be counted on to run with whatever balderdash the government wants spread, when they are not inventing it themselves.

The greatest assistance in disinformation—especially during the current administration—is always forthcoming from the *Reader's Digest*. In 1977 the *New York Times* series exposed *Digest* editor John Barron as having worked hand in glove with the CIA on a book about the KGB. Other fraudulent journalists like Robert Moss, Arnaud de Borchgrave, Daniel James, Claire Sterling, and Michael Ledeen, among others, seem to pick up disinformation themes almost automatically. In fact, coordination among the development of propaganda and disinformation themes by the covert media assets, the overt propaganda machine, and the bevy of puppet journalists is quite calculated. A theme floated on one level—a feature item on VOA about Cuba, for example—will appear within record time as a lead article in *Reader's Digest*, or a feature in a Heritage Foundation report, or a series of "exposés" by Moss and de Borchgrave or Daniel James in some reactionary tabloid like *Human Events* or the *Washington Times* or *Inquirer*. Then they would be called to testify by Senator Denton's Subcommittee on Security and Terrorism, repeating one another's allegations as "expert witnesses."

After that they are given credibility by the "respectable" Cold War publications like the *National Review*, *Commentary*, and the *New Republic*. And finally, since they have repeated the theme so many times that it must be true, they are given the opportunity to write Op-Ed pieces for the *New York Times* or the *Washington Post*. Paul Henze, the former CIA chief of station in Turkey, then wrote the first book on the Bulgarian Connection; Sterling, the second.

These interconnections are by no means fortuitous. There is practically a revolving-door policy from organization to organization, from the government, the CIA, to the "private" media, or the reversal of that process. The director of VOA, Kenneth Tomlinson, for example, was formerly a *Reader's Digest* editor who hosted at black-tie parties given by his old friend, the late McCarthyite Roy Cohn. Arnaud de Borchgrave, who works actively with several government security services, has a difficult time keeping his "journalism" and his spying separate. One of the reasons the current editor in chief of Reverend Moon's *Washington Times* was fired from *Newsweek* magazine was that he kept dossiers on the co-workers whom he suspected of being KGB dupes. Robert Moss has also had a longtime relationship with the CIA, which **215** financed his book on Chile. He too was "let go" from his job as editor of the London *Economist's Foreign Report* because his intelligence connections gave his columns a taint that could not be ignored. *The Spike*, a badly written novel by these two unsavory characters, de Borchgrave and Moss, presaged the disinformation era with all its ramifications.

THE PLOT AGAINST THE POPE

In 1982, USIA Director Charles Z. Wick commented that the United States is "waging a war of ideas with our adversaries," whereupon he begged for more funds for VOA broadcasts. In testimony before the Senate Foreign Relations Committee, Wick said, "we are refuting the massive Soviet campaign of disinformation and misinformation about us and our intentions in the world." In particular, according to Wick, the Soviets are guilty of spreading "rumors and lies" such as the contention that the United States was involved in the attempted assassination of Pope John Paul II. While no documentation was presented to Congress, it is now apparent that Wick and the Reagan government believe in the adage that the best defense is a good offense. At the same time he was testifying, the VOA had already prepared a major campaign to assert the contrary, that the KGB through its Bulgarian "surrogates" was behind the plot to kill the pope.

All the disinformationists joined in. Claire Sterling wrote the first major article espousing this argument, replete with "confirmations" from unidentified "confidential" sources. (Sterling's disinformation efforts go back to postwar Italy, when she worked with William Colby to ensure the defeat of the Italian Communist party, spreading propaganda in the *Rome Daily American*, a CIA proprietary.)

Reader's Digest ran the Sterling piece on the pope, and variations on the theme soon appeared throughout the right-wing press. Then the TV networks picked it up, particularly Marvin Kalb of NBC, who narrated a "documentary" following the Sterling thesis, though Kalb was forced to admit (rather unprecedented in a prime time "documentary") that there was no proof whatsoever for the claim that was being advanced at that time. No matter; "proof" would soon be forthcoming.

The situation became even more complicated when, in the absence of any resounding denouement to the hysteria, conservative legislators, led by New York Senator Alfonse D'Amato, blamed the CIA for hampering efforts to prove the KGB guilty. The logic of this argument is missing. Nevertheless,

Wick took to the air in February 1983 to say that the VOA believed the CIA was not hampering the investigation. This "news" was apparently based on assurances from Vice President Bush, a former director of the CIA.

Given the absurdity of the original charge, and the total absence of evidence, it was a very clever ploy of the right wing to assert a cover-up, keeping the whole story playing in the news.

However, when the case for Bulgarian involvement collapsed at the Rome trial of the would-be assassin—who asserted that he was Jesus Christ and offered to raise the dead in the courtroom—the disinformationists blamed "détente" for the subsequent acquittal of all the Bulgarians. They have since been completely silent on the subject, as was predicted by Edward S. Herman and Frank Brodhead in their exhaustive analysis of the disinformation campaign, *The Rise and Fall of the Bulgarian Connection* (New York: Sheridan Square Publications, 1986).

THE NUCLEAR FREEZE PLOT

Nearly all the cast of characters discussed above are involved actively in pursuing another major theme that strains credulity: that the nuclear freeze movement in part, and the disarmament movement in general, are also KGB plots, and their proponents, Soviet dupes or "agents of influence." The litany for this sermon was, once again, an article in *Reader's Digest*, cited by no less avid a reader than President Reagan. The president, however, was not eager to give his source. Having referred to "proof positive" at a press conference, he left it to his aides later to reveal that his "intelligence source" was, in fact, *Reader's Digest.*

Some of the covert media experts who have pushed the nuclear freeze plot include self-described police agents and informants such as John Rees, a fanatical right-wing activist who spent much of the 1960s and 1970s infiltrating first the antiwar movement and then the antinuclear movement. He is now a writer for the John Birch Society's *Review of the News*, editor of a police intelligence report on the left called *Information Digest*, and he was the editor of *Western Goals Reports*, a far-right organization connected with the late congressman, Larry McDonald. Rees is the author of a book entitled *The War Called Peace*, which advances the theory that Soviet disarmament proposals are in reality warmongering that must be countered with massive weapons buildups in the name of peace. This is the level of logic surrounding the entire anti-freeze movement, adopted even by the lunatic fringe of rightists, Lyndon LaRouche and his "National Democratic Policy Committee."

Another major disinformation campaign was the allegation that Vietnam (and the Soviet Union) were carrying on chemical warfare, using the so-called yellow rain, in Laos and Kampuchea. In September 1981, the then secretary of state, Alexander Haig, announced that there was definite proof that lethal toxins were being deliberately used. However, subsequent scientific investigation has confirmed that the toxins are naturally produced, in bee feces, and are endemic to the region. Nevertheless, the administration periodically rages about the perfidious use of chemical warfare by Vietnam and the Soviet Union. (Another example of "irrefutable" proof that was nonexistent was the president's assurance that the Libyans were responsible for the Berlin disco bombing, which was used as the excuse to launch a military attack on Libya. As the investigating police, and most European journalists, knew well before the U.S. attack, there was *no* evidence linking Libya to the disco bombing.)

CUBA AND THE DRUG TRADE

One of the most insidious of the continually unfolding disinformation themes currently propagated by the U.S. government is the attempt to implicate high Cuban government officials—including the commander of the Cuban armed forces, Raul Castro—in international drug-trafficking. This campaign involved the blatant covert manipulation of the U.S. judicial system on a scale hardly seen since the Rosenberg-Sobell proceedings.

The creation of this theme can be traced to the highest levels of the Reagan administration: from a VOA campaign orchestrated by President Reagan's good friend, USIA Director Charles Z. Wick, to a trial in Miami sponsored by the Justice Department. The criminal charges—at least those purporting to show Cuban government involvement—were so ludicrous that at first only the *Miami Herald* (with deep ties to the Cuban exile community) saw fit to play them up. But in 1983, Senator Alfonse D'Amato held "hearings" in New York and got big play in the *New York Times* and on national TV with his informant testifying behind a screen.

The VOA campaign began in early 1982 with a series of reports in February and March suggesting Cuba's involvement in drug traffic to the U.S. Some reports said that the purpose was to get drug smugglers to run guns to the FMLN (Farabanda Movimiento Liberación Nacional) in El Salvador or to the M-19 (a radical left-wing guerilla group) in Colombia; some said it was to raise money for those guns; and some said it was to drug the American people into a stupor, presumably to facilitate a takeover. None of the reports seemed concerned that one reason was inconsistent with another.

The VOA then broadcast an interview with the foreign minister of Colombia, who repeated the charges and speculated that the Cubans were working with the Mafia. This was rather ironic, considering that for more than twenty years the Mafia has worked hand in glove with the CIA trying to assassinate Fidel Castro, out of bitterness for having lost their drug, gambling, and prostitution empires in Cuba as a result of the revolution. The VOA also gave extensive coverage to similar stories from a Colombian newspaper, suggesting that Cuba and the Mafia were cooperating in the drug business. These reports came from the same Colombian news outlets which had spread the scurrilous story that Celia Sanchez, one of the heroines of the Cuban revolution who had long been suffering with cancer, had been killed in a shoot-out between Raul and Fidel Castro.

In March, Deputy Secretary of State Thomas Enders was broadcast by VOA throughout Latin America repeating almost verbatim the Colombian news reports about drugs and Cuba.

While this disinformation was being spread in the hemisphere, a similar campaign was being waged within the United States. But before analyzing that propaganda that was geared to domestic consumption, it is well to understand the significance of the campaign abroad. The goal, as with most propaganda directed against Cuba, is to isolate Cuba from the rest of Latin America, to make it appear a foreign—that is, a Soviet—entity, divorced from other Latin American or Caribbean countries. It is only by so isolating Cuba that the United States can encourage active measures against it—like the breaking of diplomatic relations—without creating contradictions in its own Monroe Doctrine pronouncements. Moreover, traditionally, both politically and culturally, Cuba has been in the mainstream of Latin American and, more recently, Caribbean thought, with an influence the United States has taken great pains to lessen.

During the middle of 1982, the campaign against Cuba was less intensive because of the hemisphere's preoccupation with the Malvinas crisis. American disregard for Latin American opinion in aiding the United Kingdom in that war underscored the hypocrisy of the U.S. position. But the VOA's loss was the *New York Post*'s gain. In June, the *Post*, Rupert Murdoch's gutter paper, ran a three-part series entitled "Castro's Secret War," by Arnaud de Borchgrave and Robert Moss. The articles by these sleazy fabricators not only repeated the basic charge of Cuban involvement in the drug trade, but also gave minute details—names and dates and alleged meetings. Not sourced, the "facts" presented were that several middle-level drug smugglers had had meetings with Raul Castro and Nicaraguan leader Daniel Ortega. They hinted that this information might have come from a Colombian smuggler named Jaime Guillot.

Indeed, Guillot starred in the next chapter of the saga, when, in July, *Reader's Digest* ran a five-page article by a Nathan M. Adams based on unnamed "law-enforcement and intelligence sources." This "exposé," even more detailed than the Moss/de Borchgrave tripe, alleged that Guillot met with René Rodriguez, a member of the Central Committee of Cuba and the president of the Cuban Friendship Institute, and that Rodriguez "was in charge of coordinating the smuggling." It further claimed that Guillot traveled from Colombia to Cuba to Nicaragua, meeting with Raul Castro and receiving huge sums of money; that he was given $700,000 in Mexico for a flight to France, but that he was arrested by the Mexicans, whereupon he began "talking his head off," providing all the details for the article. What happened to the money—rather a large sum for a trip to France—and why Guillot was never extradited to the United States are not explained. Later reports suggest that Guillot was released by the Mexicans and went to Europe.

In August the drug story gained further dubious currency as the *Washington Times*, Reverend Moon's paper, reprinted the original *Post* series. By November, VOA was picking up the theme again, and just before the U.S. congressional elections Vice President Bush made a Republican campaign speech in Miami in which he reiterated the charges. Hot on his heels, on November 5, 1982, a Miami federal grand jury issued an indictment against Guillot, nine other drug smugglers, mostly Cuban exiles, and—in an unprecedented move—four Cuban officials: Rodriguez, an admiral of the Cuban Navy, and two former officials of the Cuban embassy in Bogotá, one of them the ambassador.

Eight of the nine smugglers were arrested in Miami, and one of them, David Lorenzo Perez, testified against the others. His statements, similar to those attributed to Guillot in the earlier articles, and those of another unindicted dealer, a self-described reformed Cuban spy, Mario Estevez Gonzalez, were the only evidence against the Cuban officials.

In fact, no drugs were actually introduced at the subsequent trial. It was said the drugs were all thrown overboard when the smugglers panicked. The Estevez confession, according to his own testimony, was given in exchange for "an unspecified amount of money and a short jail sentence" in another drug case.

The payment is extraordinary, almost unheard of. Four Cuban officials were indicted on the statement of a man who was paid to make the statement! What, if anything, happened to Guillot is not known; but it was reported that his drug-dealing partner, who also "cooperated" with the U.S. Justice Department, got a twenty-five-year jail sentence, *all* of which was suspended.

Although the indictment describes in great detail the movements and travels of the exiled drug dealer, the references to the four Cuban officials are extremely vague. It alleges that they agreed to let Cuba be used as a "loading station and source of supplies for ships" transporting drugs. The indictment,

220 eight counts and nineteen pages, says nothing else about the Cuban officials. It does not say when this "agreement" was made, where it was made, who met with whom, nor who said what to whom.

In the February 1983 trial, five of the seven hapless defendants were found guilty, on the testimony of the alleged former spy and the indicted smuggler who turned state's evidence. The two told similar tales, of backslapping jovial meetings with the Cuban officials who, they claimed, said things like "Now we are going to fill Miami with drugs" and "It is important to fill the United States with drugs." (As if Miami were not already filled with drugs.) The "spy" said that he replied, "Well, if it has to be filled, let's do it."

Evidently this B-movie dialogue was sufficient to convict five of the defendants, who presumably were involved in some kind of drug trafficking.

The use of this trial by the U.S. government was blatant; there was no concern about Miami's drug problem, only about Cuba. When Lorenzo Perez agreed to plead guilty and testify against the others, the spokesman for the Drug Enforcement Administration announced that "when you have people pleading guilty, it just disproves" the denials of the Cuban government. And when the five were convicted, the assistant U.S. attorney said that the outcome "demonstrates" the involvement of Cuba.

The Cuban government indignantly denied the charges, pointing out in government statements and broadcasts and in an editorial in *Granma* the idiocy of the charges. The Cubans also stressed a point that had been virtually ignored in the U.S. press—that for more than ten years, despite all sorts of ideological disputes, Cuban authorities had been cooperating with U.S. officials in tracking and capturing drug smugglers in the Caribbean. At least thirty-six ships and twenty-one planes had been taken in this endeavor and more than 230 drug smugglers prosecuted. Because of the insulting and specious indictment the Cuban government announced that it was discontinuing its cooperation with the U.S. Coast Guard.

Even Michael Ledeen, another disinformationist, pretended to be puzzled in his rehash of the Guillot story in the February 28, 1983, *New Republic*. He conceded that "Fidel Castro used to boast of his hatred of drug traffickers; he even cooperated with the United States by arresting some smugglers and turning them over to American authorities." But, consistent with this season's disinformation theme, Ledeen refers to the current situation as a "turnabout," designed to provide hard currency for the Soviet Union.

There are countless other indications that it is the United States that is more interested in propaganda than in actually stopping drug traffic. During the aftermath of the pope's shooting it was learned that Bulgaria had been cooperating with U.S. narcotics-control officials for twelve years, but that the program had been terminated by President Reagan shortly after he took office.

As if the allegations against Cuba were not enough, the administration has waged a similar campaign against Nicaragua, complete with fuzzy photographs purporting to be of high Nicaragua officials loading cocaine onto an airplane. The pilot of the plane, however, and the sole source of the allegations against the Sandinistas, Adler Berryman ("Barry") Seal, was a drug dealer turned U.S. government informant, and the cocaine was his own. He received an almost incredible reduction of his pending long jail sentence to parole for spreading the story against Nicaragua. In February 1986, Seal was shot to death in Baton Rouge, Louisiana, by what was described as a Colombian cocaine mafia hit squad.

"PROJECT DEMOCRACY" AND PUBLIC DIPLOMACY

On June 8, 1982, in an address to the British Parliament, President Reagan announced a new ideological offensive to turn the tide against communism in the battle for the mind of the world's population. Designed to "foster the infrastructure of democracy" in a dozen ways, it clearly enlisted information as its top recruit. Charles Wick said there would be "a new assertive propagandistic role" to "win the war of ideas."

In November 1983, Congress established what has been called the "public arm" of Project Democracy, the National Endowment for Democracy. Simultaneously, a secret arm developed. During the Tower Commission investigation of Irangate, it was disclosed that the National Security Council used "Project Democracy" to refer to "everything Ollie [Lt. Col. Oliver North] was doing in Central America."

As the democracy project unfolded, there were references to information as "a vital part of the strategic and tactical arsenal of the United States." Wick again pictured ideas as the only useful weapons that could be shot at an enemy in the absence of hostilities—such as the Radio Marti venture aimed at Cuba. Other government officials elevated public diplomacy to the status of diplomatic and military policy in serving the needs of national security. But all spokesmen insisted that the United States at all times "must speak the truth, clearly, vigorously, and persuasively."

Since truth is the first casualty in war, whether total, limited, or ideological, as Woodrow Wilson put it, how is the Reagan administration planning to pull off this miracle? They are *not* planning to, in all probability. What they *are* doing is building a new Trojan Horse so that the covert programs of deception, fake propaganda, slanted information, and disinformation can move forward without being under the suspect auspices of the CIA, DIA (Defense Intelligence Agency), and others of that ilk. "Project Democracy" and public diplomacy are clearly a rehabilitation process for government propaganda, an attempt to restore information manipulation under new sponsorship. Will it work? Will you believe it? Or are you ready to be fooled?

First of all, the proposal was born with original sin. Conceived in secrecy as a *classified* executive order, Project Democracy can hardly live up to its claim of democratic openness. A CIA covert feature initially existed in the plan, but was withdrawn, or so we and the Congress are told. Still, National Security Council Decision Directive 77 placed the program under the National Security assistant's control where it is "to support U.S. policies and interests." Those chairing the top four committees come from agencies with longtime commitments to secrecy and the protective cover of classification. But there are more serious problems with this deformed Reagan progeny besides the wartime psychology that gave it birth and the secrecy with which it was raised.

On its face the idea is implausible because American foreign policies and CIA operations have not evidenced any connection with an infrastructure of democratic principles, except as they are manipulated to suit the purposes of the United States. Democracies have had empires before, from Athens on. Whatever the United States may call its overseas political, economic, and cultural mission, its support of client regimes, its overthrow of leftist democratic governments, its active support of "moderately authoritarian" right-wing allies, its backing of powerful multinational corporations—none of that has ever been analyzed internally for its democratic fallout. The credibility of any government information must inevitably be tested against the deeds as well as the rhetoric of a nation.

What chance does Project Democracy have to gain access to the truth it insists it will disseminate? How will it know it is not part of the cover story, the way Adlai Stevenson was used at the United Nations during the Bay of Pigs? The very administration that is increasing classification, unleashing the spy agencies, and restricting freedom of information now says it will spread the truth to the world to enhance democratic values out there. Tell that to the people of Chile.

Since the National Endowment for Democracy calls for a heavy reliance on nongovernmental institutions, it is interesting to examine what has already been funded. One grant helped "media officials" from right-wing governments—including El Salvador—to learn how to handle the U.S. press. Ian MacKenzie, a slick ideologue who was a registered agent for Anastasio Somoza, is directing the program, at a cost of $170,000 to the taxpayers. (See Covert Action Information Bulletin Number 12). Another grant gave Ernest Lefever's Ethics and Public Policy Center almost $200,000 to run four seminars pushing the "ethics of nuclear arms." It has also given funds to the right-wing Force Ouvrière in France, and to a U.S. group called Prodemca, which in turn gives financial support to the Nicaraguan contras.

As these "democratic" projects went up to Congress, many of them smacked of the CIA's old bag of dirty tricks finally getting laundered: a worldwide book-publishing venture, a center for free enterprise (is business a democratic institution?), a foundation and organizations to promote Latin American "democracy," and academic programs at two foreign universities. The announced objectives such as "leadership training" sound like recruitment for covert futures, as the CIA does routinely with foreign students on American campuses. Project Democracy is the soft-core version of hard-core deception.

CONCLUSION

It is time the American people took a good dose of their own history to begin to understand what ails this society. One benefit might be a revival of old-fashioned American skepticism toward authoritative pronouncements. History has rebutted the argument of disinformation's origin as a KGB plot and traced its twentieth-century development as a hidden partner of the imperial process and national-security apparatus. We have learned that propaganda intruded itself into the democratic process long ago.

The most important lesson of history's warnings, however, would be an understanding of what went wrong with information in the past to help people resist the inroads of further deception. The next time the government floats a story, demand in each instance to know why it is propagating this information, whose interests it is serving, and what is being concealed. Then perhaps this country can abandon the process of government by the misinformed.

[Richard Delgado]

15

THE LANGUAGE OF THE ARMS

RACE: SHOULD THE PEOPLE

LIMIT GOVERNMENT SPEECH?

In the typical free speech case, a private individual or group challenges the government's suppression of private speech. At issue is whether the First Amendment prohibits the type of suppression that has occurred. In recent years, the growing scale of the government's persuasion apparatus has prompted a number of scholars to question whether the First Amendment has a reverse side—an implied prohibition on the government that may be invoked when the people wish to silence the government or when one part of government seeks to silence another. A prominent theme in this "government speech" debate is that the government's powerful voice can easily overwhelm weaker private voices, creating a monopoly of ideas and inhibiting the dialectic on which we rely to reach decisions.

This debate is still unresolved. The Supreme Court has yet to decide whether certain forms of government speech themselves abridge the freedom of speech guaranteed by the First Amendment. Nor has the Court determined whether or to what extent government speech is protected by the First Amendment. Congress also has declined to act on the scholars' invitation by enacting

Reprinted without footnotes from the *Boston University Law Review* 64 (November 1984): 961–1001 by permission of the author.

comprehensive legislation regulating the content or the manner of government speech.

This article examines the case for limiting government speech in an area where the case for regulation seems particularly strong: nuclear armaments and strategy. My thesis is that the executive branch of the government engages in systematic dissembling in this area, and that the one-sided views that the government propagates are unlikely to be corrected in the marketplace of ideas because of widely shared human response mechanisms and official secrecy. This situation has profound implications for democratic decision theory and suggests that various remedies may be in order.

PROLOGUE: THE CURRENT NUCLEAR SITUATION

As everyone knows, the United States and Soviet Union are engaged in a nuclear arms race. Despite their importance and frequency throughout history, not much is known about arms races—how they start or what sustains them. Scholars have even questioned whether the current race between the Soviet Union and the United States is about anything at all. Whatever the reason for it, the current arms race has produced a world bristling with nuclear weaponry. The Soviet Union and the United States currently possess, between them, about fifty thousand warheads and are each building an additional four to five per day. About nine thousand of the warheads of the United States are "strategic," capable of being launched from American soil and reaching the Soviet Union. The remainder are located in Europe or other areas close to the Soviet Union, or are based on submarines. Most strategic warheads have an explosive force in the megaton range, that is, equivalent to one million tons of TNT. Large American and Soviet cities are probably targeted with tens of such weapons.

In an all-out thermonuclear war, 100 to 150 million Americans would die from the "prompt" effects of the explosions: blast, heat, and radiation. Others would die of injuries, fallout, starvation, and breakdowns in sanitation and medical care. Comparable numbers would die in Europe and the Soviet Union. The World Health Organization has estimated that a major war would kill approximately 1.1 billion persons worldwide from prompt effects, and a similar number from injuries inflicted in the exchanges. Recent attention has focused on the long-range environmental effects of nuclear warfare, including planetary temperature changes and damage to the earth's ozone layer. A number of investigators have warned that these changes could render the planet uninhabitable to human life.

Whether these grim scenarios will materialize is, of course, disputed. Some believe that mutual deterrence will work and that the danger of an accidental launch is low. Others believe that a major war between the superpowers is likely before the end of the century. These disputes aside, the nuclear arms race itself is alleged to exact a psychological toll, particularly on children and young adults. Investigators have found that many young children suffer from fears and nightmares about the destruction of the world. Older children may show skepticism about the future and a tendency to plan in hypothetical terms such as "If I finish high school . . ." Even if predictions of nuclear disaster prove to be alarmist, therefore, the arms race exacts a significant cost in current anxiety.

THE LANGUAGE OF THE ARMS RACE: LINGUISTIC DEVICES AND PSYCHOLOGICAL RESPONSE MECHANISMS

The nuclear reality just reviewed is, if nothing else, unsettling. Left to its own devices, the citizenry thus might well press for measures to reduce the magnitude of the threat, measures such as reduction in the number of existing warheads and enactment of international agreements limiting deployment of new weapons systems. Government communication on nuclear arms, however, has included a number of psycholinguistic devices whose practical effect is to check the flow of information and silence effective dissent. A review of those devices follows below. Response mechanisms that give the devices unusual power and effect are examined farther along in the article.

Linguistic Devices

Euphemism and Metaphor

As author George Orwell and others have pointed out, governments often use euphemisms—words that put a positive gloss on a frightening object or event —to justify their actions and rally the citizenry. When successful, euphemisms cause the reader to respond to a word's innocent or positive connotations, rather than to the threatening reality it conceals. Euphemisms heighten and facilitate a psychological mechanism, *denial,* discussed in the next section.

Metaphors and similes serve similar functions—they borrow meanings and attitudes from one context and apply them to another. Like euphemisms, meta- phors and similes may reinforce the audience's unconscious response mecha- nisms that block out the threat. Some euphemisms and metaphors may be coined unconsciously, as a means for the speaker to avoid confronting a ter- rible reality. Other euphemisms seem to have been designed deliberately to mislead the public. For example, in the early days of nuclear power, publi- cists urged that reports be "word-engineered" to reassure the public. Units of radiation became "sunshine units." Publicists and government officials spoke of presenting the "sunny side" of the atom.

Euphemism proliferates in times of war. Thus, in Vietnam, bombers gave "close air support" and carried out "protective reaction strikes" or "reconnais- sance by fire." Regions were "pacified," targets were "taken out," and our side sustained "casualties." The recent American invasion of Grenada was called a "rescue mission." The Soviets also use euphemism—their 100,000-troop force that invaded Afganistan was described as a "limited contingent."

Nuclear strategy and weaponry are also prime breeding grounds for eu- phemism. Apocalyptic weapons promote "deterrence" (the ability to react to an enemy nation's political or military initiatives with nuclear force), are used as "bargaining chips," or help avoid a "window of vulnerability." Potentially cataclysmic nuclear attacks are "surgical strikes" aimed at "counterforce" tar- gets and inflicting "collateral damage." Cities are to be "interdicted," not "de- stroyed." "Tactical" weapons are devised for "theater" wars. A huge, deadly missile was initially named "Peacemaker." The Pentagon called the neutron bomb a "radiation enhancement weapon," a designation that won the agency an award from the Committee on Public Doublespeak. Nuclear bombs are simple "devices." Nuclear attacks are "exchanges" (like Christmas presents) or "flexible responses." New weapons are members of a "nuclear family."

Metaphors and similes also figure prominently in the nuclear lexicon. Mili- tary talk is often couched in the language of sports: the Pentagon develops a "game plan," making plans to "take out" enemy cities and installations. As in sports, mistakes are admitted "in hindsight." Historical and physical analogies are also common. The government compares the Soviets to past enemies and urges the people to avoid repeating the error of appeasement. Our strategic aim is to preserve "equilibrium" and avoid a "power vacuum." These analo- gies convey the idea that the events they describe are regular and predictable, even lawlike. The disaster that may be only one miscalculation or misjudg- ment away remains hidden.

Fear-Appeals

When they deem it necessary to rouse rather than lull, governments may use fear-appeals and depictions of a terrifying enemy. This practice may be a near-universal psychosocial activity. Students of myths note that all societies invent legends of evil enemy forces to increase solidarity and mobilize collective action. Bomber gaps, missile gaps, and windows of vulnerability generate fear and uncertainty and justify military spending. President Reagan's "focus of evil" speech was a patent attempt to elicit support for continuing the arms race. Such fear-appeals are most effective when they contain an element of truth. For example, during the period when the missile gap was being created and publicized, the United States lagged behind the Soviets in land-based missiles. The United States held a large lead, however, in submarine-based and cruise missiles. There is serious disagreement about whether the United States was ever in a position worse than parity.

Fear-appeals are sometimes alternated with rhetorical devices aimed at soothing and reassuring. At other times these functions are carried out simultaneously. Fear and reassurance must be kept in balance; a citizenry presented only with horror pictures might refuse to cooperate with war preparations or become so paralyzed that it ceases to function.

Abstraction and Technical Detail: The Nuclear Priesthood

A third device the government uses in its communication is abstraction and technical obfuscation. This device, in turn, aids in creating a caste of nuclear experts or priests. Government's use of arcane language, graphs, acronyms, and other insider speech makes relatively simple strategic concepts difficult to understand. Sterile or abstract terms also blunt the horror of the reality they depict. As one author stated: "The quality of universal death grows stale partly because the arguments are unnecessarily complex . . . and use terms that pointedly mute just what it is these bombs will do, which is, to start with, to kill the people one loves and nearly everyone else as well."

Technical talk has a soothing sound. The thought that someone has made a deadly subject a science comforts the listener; it implies that the problem is under control. Technical talk serves similar functions for the expert, enabling him or her to divorce himself or herself from the human consequences of nuclear warfare. Technical talk may also render effective criticisms impossible, and reinforce the audience's impression that the expert's task is esoteric and important.

Doublespeak, Weasel Words, and Lies

Government speech frequently contains language that is deceptive in various degrees. Orwell wrote of doublespeak; lawyers speak of weasel words, which enable the speaker to seem to answer a question without really doing so. When first presenting the neutron bomb to the public, the Defense Department acted and spoke as though the weapon were not a nuclear bomb. President Reagan recently explained that United States Marines in Lebanon were not engaged in "hostilities" because incoming artillery fire was not directed specifically at them, but merely at the area in which they were encamped. During the 1960s and 1970s, thousands of pounds of plutonium and uranium were discovered to be missing from nuclear sites. Despite strong circumstantial evidence that some of this was stolen, nuclear developers and agencies have repeatedly claimed that there is no evidence of theft. The SALT II agreement, which the current administration has agreed to abide by, obliges countries not to build additional fixed ICBM launchers. Asked whether a proposal to build new bases for the MX missile would not violate the Salt II agreement, the secretary of defense replied that it would not. When pressed, he explained that "a silo is not a launcher."

Doublespeak sometimes approaches self-parody, as when General William Westmoreland justified manipulation of the news on the ground that "[w]ithout censorship things can get terribly confused in the public mind." A secretary of state declared that American arms buildup is "absolutely essential to . . . hopes for meaningful arms reduction." During the early days of nuclear power, the Atomic Energy Commission (AEC) suppressed a key report showing need for caution on the ground that "[w]e thought it would be misunderstood by the public."

At times, the government has resorted to deceptive use of statistics or outright misstatements of fact to win public support or avoid criticism. When fallout from a hydrogen bomb test drifted outside the test range, the AEC chairman denied that Japanese fishermen had suffered radiation burns or that fish had been contaminated, although both were known to have happened. In making his case for increased defense spending, President Reagan recently asserted that the Soviet Union is ahead of the United States in "virtually every measure of military power." What he neglected to mention was that the United States holds a commanding lead in nuclear warheads launched from submarines, cruise missiles, and bombers, and is ahead in total deliverable warheads.

Response Mechanisms

By means of such devices as euphemism, abstraction, and doublespeak, the government fosters a worldview in which its assumptions and aims are unlikely to be seriously questioned. Because of the way government defines reality, certain thoughts do not come to mind. Through a kind of mass taboo-formation, ideas and options are placed out of bounds. In many cases, the

230   means used to attain this result are not agitational; the language is not perceived to be political.

In addition to their generalized discourse-shaping effect, government communications in the area of weaponry may acquire peculiar potency by tapping unconscious response mechanisms. These mechanisms include denial and numbness, identification with the source of danger, and submission to a strong leader. Leaders may be equally affected; the language used enables them to maintain a collective illusion of safety while denying their individual responsibility for the threat.

Denial and Numbness

One mechanism that enables individuals to deal with life-threatening events is denial. The mind cannot easily comprehend a threat so huge as nuclear holocaust; it therefore shuts it out, ceasing entirely to respond. A recent American Psychiatric Association task force found that many adults responded to the threat of nuclear annihilation by distancing, numbness, or "psychic shutdown." Children and adolescents showed a similar reaction. The government's use of technical jargon accentuates this response; one author called government publicists "hired anesthetists." Once numbness and denial set in, psycholinguistic devices like those discussed earlier help maintain these mechanisms in place.

An extreme form of denial has been observed in some nuclear workers and strategic analysts. Workers in nuclear weapons plants gave shallow responses when questioned about their work; the work was "just a job" that "pays the bills"; and weapons were "just a part of life" that will always be with us. Many workers lost themselves in technical details, or rationalized that weapons are necessary because it is human nature to be cruel and warlike. Many use drugs. Nuclear strategists who have left their positions have written that the only way they could carry out their tasks was to numb themselves, to see only numbers and symbols on a map.

Embracing the Threat

While some deal with life-threatening events by denying them, a smaller group copes with the possibility of nuclear destruction by embracing the threat. These individuals become fascinated with and absorbed in the details of strategic planning, warhead counts, and weapons systems. Robert Lifton calls this syndrome, which he purports to find in some military decision-makers and strategists, "nuclearism." The nuclearist views the bomb as akin to a deity: all-powerful, vengeful, destructive, and arbitrary. Nuclear weapons, like a god, must not be limited. As with the opposite response, numbing, the preoccupation of nuclearism disables the individual from acting constructively to improve his or her situation. Nuclearists are uncritical advocates of new weaponry: They resist questioning the need for more weapons because the weapons are self-validating.

Desire for a Strong Leader

A final response to situations of anxiety is desire for a strong leader—someone who, like a father, will protect his charges and set everything right. This desire is part of a generalized human reaction to crisis: In times of stress, one wants a strong person to take charge and reduce the stress.

This propensity facilitates development of a nuclear priesthood, a group of experts who are invested with wide-ranging powers and are beyond ordinary accountability. That the priests speak in arcane language and work in secrecy only heightens their appeal. Their isolation and special vocabulary may also encourage arbitrariness and a diminished sense of moral responsibility on their part. One ex-strategist reported that "[t]here were no people in these [fictional] 'exchanges,' only calculations. It was a curious fiction, never discussing the humans at the military installations or the industries or the cities. I guess that made it easier on the targeters in Omaha, the people there in charge of launching the missiles . . . and the analysts like me." The ex-analyst comforted himself with the thought that others above him were responsible for the human dimension of war planning. It was not until years later that he discovered, to his shock, that, like him, his superiors lived in a vague world of figures and symbols.

DIFFICULTIES WITH SELF-CORRECTION
Censorship, Secrecy, and News Management

Communications on nuclear armaments may thus have psychological impact exceeding that of most other forms of speech. The ability of weapons-talk to still or bypass rational thought processes suggests that the messages conveyed are less likely than are other communications to be challenged effectively in the marketplace of ideas. As later sections herein suggest, this observation is constitutionally and politically troublesome; remedial action may be in order.

An additional group of concerns stems from the government's power to maintain secrets and manipulate the news. The usual, and constitutionally preferable, solution to most problems of offensive speech is not censorship, but "more speech." The rationale is that in the "marketplace of ideas," the

232 evils of offensive speech will be exposed by responsive messages, and the truth will emerge. In the areas of armaments and national security, however, the marketplace may be an uncertain means of determining truth. The government's power to classify secrets severely hampers the ability of a critic to marshal an effective response. The government may classify the critic's message, preventing its dissemination entirely. Alternatively, the government may simply prevent access to the data necessary to support a contrary opinion. Both impediments undermine the effectiveness of a "more speech" solution.

Secrecy and news management have characterized the government's approach to nuclear weapons from the beginning. This approach began with the Manhattan Project, which was conceived and built in total secrecy. The press in rural New Mexico learned that top-secret installations were being built in Los Alamos, but the government forbade them to report anything. The term "nuclear energy" did not appear in the American press at all during the war years; nor did the term "uranium." After the first atomic bomb was dropped on Hiroshima, the United States government controlled all press coverage of the event. When reporters gained admission to Hiroshima and reported lingering deaths resulting from radiation disease, the occupation army ordered them expelled and they placed the city off limits. Reports of radiation poisoning were denied or explained as Japanese propaganda. The existence of censorship was itself censored; the press was not permitted even to mention the limitations placed on its coverage. Medical research and exchanges about the biological effects of nuclear explosions were not permitted; doctors worked among the victims of Hiroshima and Nagasaki unaware of what they were treating, Japanese citizens concluded that radiation illness was contagious and avoided contact with the sick.

The preoccupation with secrecy did not end with the war. Scientists who expressed reservations about nuclear weapons research were reassigned or found their testimony blocked by executive privilege. Critics found their jobs threatened; most employees feared that by discussing safety, they risked being fired. In *United States* versus *The Progressive, Inc.*, defense lawyers were prepared to introduce affidavits of leading scientists to show that any competent physicist working from public sources could have prepared the magazine's story on how to build a nuclear bomb. The government ordered the affidavits classified. The same occurred when a critic of nuclear energy wrote to the Department of Energy with questions about nuclear policies and safety: the department ordered his letter classified.

The present administration has, if anything, intensified the preoccupation with secrecy and news management that has existed since the early days of atomic power. The Reagan administration has exercised its discretion to block public access to unclassified nuclear information. Recently, the president issued a national security directive authorizing lie-detector tests to counter leaks on sensitive subjects. The administration also issued an order subjecting present and former senior government officials to lifetime prepublication review of any speeches or articles containing material that *might* be classified. The administration has excluded foreign speakers and films with points of view that deviate from its own, and has attempted to limit the scope of the Freedom of Information Act. When the National Education Association proposed a junior high school course on nuclear arms, to be prepared by the Union of Concerned Scientists, the Reagan administration accused the association of "brainwashing America's schoolchildren."

At the same time that it suppresses or discourages critical messages, the government aggressively markets its own viewpoint. The government has offered free trips and other rewards to "loyal" journalists, while creating obstacles for those with critical views. The government also provides selected reports and data to reporters who, under the pressure of deadlines, often do not have time to verify them or seek out opposing views. Government publicists attempt to reassure or frighten the public, as different policies dictate. On one occasion, the secretary of defense objected to a publication of the Arms Control and Disarmament Agency, "World Military Expenditures," as overstating the size and nature of United States and NATO defense budgets. The pressure was effective; the agency discontinued the reports, then resumed them, but with more statistics and tables and less comparative analysis.

In addition to blocking criticism, secrecy augments the power of the subconscious defense mechanisms described earlier. Secrecy and denial synergize each other. The government's use of secrecy implies that the truth would be gruesome and terrifying; the audience is almost grateful for being spared the frightening information. Secrecy can also fortify the image of the nuclear strategist, in both his own and the public's eyes, as all-powerful and above ordinary obligations of responsibility and honesty. Why was he given the extraordinary power to operate in secret if not deserving of obedience and discretion?

Agenda Setting

Even short of censorship and secrecy, government controls the content of news by working with the mass media to set social agendas. According to some communications scholars, the crucial characteristic of mass media is their capacity to shape social reality by setting the agenda for public discourse. The media may not always succeed in telling people what to think, but they are highly successful in telling them what to think about.

234   This capacity for agenda-setting can become pernicious if the media are subject to manipulation. Research in communications theory suggests that when the media construct social reality, they do so according to relatively predictable patterns. The news net cast by the media traps primarily big fish; the institutional and professional values of reporters lead them to rely heavily on legitimated institutions and high-ranking officials for their subject matter. The journalistic convention of objectivity ensures that the messages of institutional speakers get through relatively unscathed, thereby reaffirming the legitimacy of those institutions and their communications.

The news net largely determines media content. Government speech, because it emanates from legitimated institutions, is likely to be caught in the news net. Speech from unofficial sources is likely to slip through the net. The media do report the speech of a Nobel Prize winner, or the occasional mass demonstration against nuclear weaponry. These events are not caught because of their subject matter, but because public figures and mass gatherings are considered intersections in the news net; they are newsworthy in their own right. Such sporadic coverage of speech from unofficial sources cannot match the institutionalized reporting of government sources.

The government, therefore, plays an important role in determining media content and thus in setting the agenda for public discourse. As has been seen, government speech on nuclear matters is often distorted or euphemistic, and frequently untruthful. Yet the agenda-setting hypothesis suggests that such slanted communications will nevertheless have a profound effect on the way people think about nuclear matters. If this effect occurs, the government may succeed in controlling attitudes and behaviors with respect to nuclear weapons simply because it dictates the terms of debate. An individual may have an intuitive revulsion toward nuclearism, for example, but be unable to articulate opposition; the language and structure of the debate may render such beliefs unsayable.

Communications theory, then, further explains the means through which government speech on nuclear arms achieves dominance. When the government's own powers of secrecy and news management are added to the equation, government speech not only shapes the contours of the debate, but also renders opposition ineffectual. It is therefore critical that government communications dealing with nuclear weaponry and policy be held to the highest standards of probity. The next two sections examine whether this objective can be accomplished consistently with the First Amendment.

CONSTITUTIONAL STATUS OF GOVERNMENTAL SPEECH ON NUCLEAR WEAPONRY

In the American political system, government relies for its legitimacy on the consent of the governed. We are committed, at least in theory, to a political system in which vital decisions are made through a collective examination that probes the tensions, contradictions, and alternatives inherent in our life together. Any serious impairment of this process undermines a principal mechanism by which democratic government functions. Although all governments use language to some extent to enhance their own authority, this practice seems more exaggerated, and more pernicious, in connection with the arms race than it does in other contexts.

These considerations suggest that some measures to limit government dishonesty concerning armaments should be considered. A principal difficulty for any such effort is the traditional deference our society gives to free speech values. Accordingly, we examine below the extent of protection due government weapons speech. We discuss remedies that may be applied when such speech goes beyond acceptable bounds and limitations on such remedies.

Does the First Amendment Require a Remedy?

A few commentators have suggested that certain types of government speech violate the First Amendment and affirmatively call for a remedy. One commentator boldly asserts that government speech in support of controversial political premises offends an implied establishment clause in the First Amendment. Although he draws analogous support from case law, no court has adopted his theory directly. Were courts to adopt an establishment-clause approach, however, government speech on nuclear arms would be a good candidate for unconstitutionality. The types of publicity and news control described earlier pose all the principal dangers that government speech analysis seeks to avert: They promote controversial political premises, enforce orthodoxy, and threaten to drown out opposing voices and views.

A second set of considerations suggesting that government arms-race talk is unconstitutional stems from doctrines dealing with censorship and the rights of captive audiences. Ordinarily, these doctrines apply in quite different factual circumstances and have opposite effects. The First Amendment forbids government censorship of private speech. Censorship is offensive because it silences communications that the people might wish to hear and establishes

236 government as the judge of what shall be heard. Captive-audience doctrine, by contrast, allows, and perhaps mandates, government interference with private speech. In the case of government speech on nuclear arms, however, these paths converge. The government's use of psycholinguistic devices to manipulate the people on nuclear issues, coupled with its ability to control information, presents the dangers of imposed orthodoxy; such speech can become the functional equivalent of censorship. Similar considerations apply in the case of the trapped-audience comparison. The listener is bombarded with one-sided, terrifying messages on nuclear weaponry, with little opportunity to escape them. Both considerations argue for controls.

Considerations of constitutional structure supply a further ground for limiting government speech of the types described in this article. The governmental model laid out in the Constitution is a form of representative and participatory democracy. The First Amendment reflects the judgment of the framers of the Constitution that free trade in ideas is essential both to effective participation and to emergence of the ultimate good. The First Amendment, therefore, "embodies more than a commitment to free expression and communicative interchange for their own sakes; it has a structural role to play in securing and fostering our republican system of self-government."

The structural argument suggests that the First Amendment guarantees not only the right to communicate, but also the right to the information and means necessary to communicate effectively. If, however, the government is permitted to curtail the flow of information necessary to effective speech, the structural role of the First Amendment is undermined. When the government goes further, itself using powerful, distorted speech that may effectively render the listener incapable of meaningful response, it threatens impairment of popular participation in the political arena. Protection of our form of constitutional government, then, requires that government speech on nuclear arms, which has the potential effect of stilling intelligent response, be subject to restraint.

These three sets of considerations suggest that unremitting government weapons talk may constitute, in itself, a violation of the First Amendment. If so, remedies would be not merely permissible but affirmatively compelled; the only restraints would be political. The evils of government speech can be remedied by a less drastic route, however—by a finding that government speech is not per se unconstitutional, but nevertheless regulable.

Does the First Amendment Permit a Remedy?
Analytical Approaches

A sizable body of government-speech commentary argues that official speech, if not affirmatively violative of the First Amendment, is at least regulable consistently with that amendment. Courts are more likely to adopt this latter **237** position; it is less radical doctrinally, and poses fewer enforcement difficulties than the approach under which official speech is found affirmatively unconstitutional. The remainder of this article therefore evaluates weapons speech from this perspective.

Two analytical routes converge on the conclusion that government speech of certain types is constitutionally regulable. The first asserts that government, *qua* government, has no First Amendment right to speak. The second holds that government may have some such right, but this right may be restricted on a lesser showing of necessity than that applicable to private speech.

The case for nonprotection was first made more than two hundred years ago. James Madison wrote that government speech stood on a different footing from private speech, was a potential threat to representative democracy, and could be limited or censored as the people wished. His argument, albeit in less sweeping form, has been echoed by a number of current commentators, most notably Mark Yudof. Yudof asserts that government speech poses special dangers and was not intended by the framers of the Constitution to receive constitutional protection. He urges, however, that as a matter of policy only some, not all, government speech be closely regulated. Much that government wishes to say is harmless or is necessary for effective government functioning. For example, government needs to educate, to promote industry and commerce, and to marshal support for its policies.

Particular types of government speech are problematical, however. For example, the commentators agree that government has no business expending public resources on speech aimed at reelecting itself, or at creating, as opposed to effectuating, consensus. Similarly, government speech that is untruthful or misleading has little claim to protection. It has also been suggested that government speech that is so powerful as to "drown out" smaller voices, and thus coerce orthodoxy, should be toned down.

Other commentators seem to concede that the government does have some right to speak, but reason that government speech is entitled to less protection than most private speech. These writers raise virtually the same arguments as the no-protection school: Official speech is peripheral to core First Amendment values, was not intended by the framers to receive protection, and poses dangers for representative democracy. These considerations lead to the conclusion that government speech occupies a middle position in the hierarchy of First Amendment values—comparable perhaps to the status of commercial speech.

The no-protection school and the lesser-protection school come to similar conclusions: Government speech may be regulated on a lesser showing of need than that required for other categories of speech. The considerations that lead each school to this conclusion are also similar. Accordingly, the remainder of this section examines these concerns and the extent to which they arise in government speech on nuclear weaponry.

Dangers of Government Speech

The dangers that government speech theorists identify as justifying special treatment of official speech center around subversion of First Amendment values. These values fall into two groups: extrinsic values, mainly those concerned with the role of speech in democratic government; and instrinsic values of self-expression and self-realization.

"Drowning out," Falsification of Consent, and Self-Perpetuation. Concerns related to the drowning out of private voices, and to the monopoly on ideas that results, are easily and compellingly substantiated in the area under examination. The government devotes substantial resources to promoting its own viewpoints, especially with respect to defense policy. Although the actual figures are difficult to ascertain, the Pentagon probably spends more money spreading its message than do all opposing private speakers combined. In addition, the government can count on the publicity efforts of defense contractors, whose viewpoint generally coincides with its own. The result is a flood of reports, releases, films, commercials, and press conferences all promoting a single viewpoint. Faced with this publicity barrage, opposing voices operate at a marked disadvantage.

The imbalance between government's powerful voice, magnified by communications technology, and less-powerful private voices can result in *falsification of consent*. According to government-speech theorists, falsification of consent problems arise when government uses speech, not to effectuate the will of the people, but to manufacture that will without popular consent or conscious participation. The manipulative strategies described earlier plainly have the potential to falsify consent, and probably have already done so to a considerable extent. The combination of loaded messages, news manipulation, and arcane technical language, all of which trigger subconscious defense mechanisms that disable effective response, presents unique dangers for a political system based on consent. It undermines the processes by which the citizenry exercise political choice at the same time that it decreases their range of choices and dictates the terms in which those choices are understood.

For the same reasons, government speech on nuclear arms also presents dangers of self-perpetuation. As early as 1961, President Eisenhower warned of the dangers to democracy posed by a growing alliance between the military and government that would work to maintain a constant state of military readiness, high expenditures for the armed forces, and foreign policy shaped by military concerns. To some extent, Eisenhower's predictions have come true.

The exigencies of the world situation may explain this phenomenon, at least in **239** part. But the continued existence of a government attuned to military concerns may result equally from conscious propaganda and from information-control efforts by the military-industrial complex. Government speech aimed at such self-perpetuation has little claim for First Amendment protection.

Nonpolitical Values. Curtailing government weapons speech would also serve certain nonpolitical, or intrinsic, First Amendment values. On an individual level, freedom of expression promotes personal development. At a societal level, it serves a role in creating the social world. Through speech, individuals express and define themselves. Societies, too, create the world as they talk about it. Thus, speech restrictions, excessively domineering speech, or speech that dictates the terms of debate all reduce the scope of creative conversation. In so doing, they arbitrarily reduce the realm of the possible. Individuals may wish to actualize themselves by advocating new approaches to the nuclear dilemma; society may wish to engage in conversation about the same issues. To the extent that government weapons-speech impairs these possibilities, individuals and society are diminished.

Summary: Concerns Supporting Regulation

The above discussion suggests that government speech on nuclear weapons should be regulable, as a matter of either constitutional necessity or social policy, when all or many of the following concerns are present:

Concerns Dealing with Falsification of Consent. The government speech is un-remitting, monolithic, and accompanied by measures, such as secrecy and news management, that eliminate competition. The speech is calculated to trigger unconscious response mechanisms. The effect of the communication is to limit, not broaden, citizens' powers of choice on nuclear issues.

Concerns Dealing with Self-Perpetuation. The speech threatens perpetuation of government based on military spending and values.

Concerns Related to "Drowning out." The speech is persistent and powerful; other voices have little opportunity to be heard.

Concerns Based on Parallels to Trapped Audiences and Censorship. The audience has no effective means of escaping the speech and internalizing the message it conveys. The speech institutionalizes orthodoxy.

Concerns Based on Nonmarketplace Values. The speech devalues the autonomy of the listener and society and limits opportunities for growth or experimentation.

The items on this checklist should apply cumulatively. When many of the concerns are present, courts and legislatures should act to moderate the threat to democratic decision-making. When few are present, the case for intervention weakens. The identity and rank of the speaker, as well as the context of the communication, are also relevant; for example, they may be factors in the determination that certain speech is self-serving and aimed at personal or institutional aggrandizement.

FRAMING A REMEDY

Much government speech on nuclear issues presents the dangers summarized above. Remedies designed to prevent these dangers should thus be constitutionally permissible. Any remedy should be narrowly tailored to avoid undue interference with legitimate government functions and concerns. In crafting the remedy, Congress and the courts should also consider political and institutional feasibility. Three basic types of approach are possible: judicial, legislative, and shared. Because of the difficulty of the problem, and the delicacy and flexibility demanded of the solution, it seems probable that a combination of the three will be necessary.

Judicial Remedies

Judicial remedies would attempt to cure the problems of government weapons-speech without the aid of express legislation. Such approaches could be either direct or indirect. Direct approaches would be possible should the Supreme Court find certain types of government speech directly violative of the First Amendment. The remedy would take the form of an injunction against further violations. It seems unlikely, however, that the courts will conclude that government speech directly violates the First Amendment; much the same result could be achieved, without such radical doctrinal change, simply by finding it regulable.

Indirect judicial remedies would not deal head-on with the evils of nuclear propaganda. Instead, these remedies would attempt to strengthen mechanisms that enhance citizens' exercise of independent choice. Thus, courts could broaden and strengthen such doctrines as academic freedom and reporters' privilege. They could give narrow construction to rules pertaining to secrecy and executive privilege, and could resolve FOIA cases in favor of access. They could uphold, in the face of challenges, grade school and high school courses dealing with nuclear issues. Courts could also continue to mandate open forums, wherever the government is using a forum to promulgate only one perspective on nuclear arms. These approaches would lessen government's near monopoly on nuclear issues and assure that a fairer marketplace of ideas existed.

In contrast to direct judicial approaches, this indirect approach seems quite feasible. The courts would not make significant doctrinal changes; rather, they would adapt existing doctrine to new conditions. The judicial role would also be relatively nonconfrontational toward other branches of government. Thus, indirect judicial remedies would be both institutionally feasible and politically acceptable. As the examples above suggest, however, these remedies would also be quite limited in both scope and effect. Alone, they could not solve the problem of offensive government speech on nuclear arms.

Legislative Remedies

Legislative remedies could also be direct or indirect. Indirect remedies would take the form of ad hoc sanctions against the offending branch or agency. Such remedies would not be unprecedented; Congress has on several occasions responded to overzealous communications activities of government agencies by abolishing public-relations offices, cutting appropriations, or influencing the selection of personnel. There is no reason that Congress could not use the same means to curb improper speech on nuclear weaponry.

Congress could also use direct approaches, such as a federal statute (designated, perhaps, The Truth in Governmental Communications on Armaments Act) directing the executive branch to communicate truthfully and fully to Congress on all matters connected with nuclear weaponry. Specific psycholinguistic devices, such as euphemism, scare words, and misleading metaphors could be illustrated and forbidden. There is some precedent for such statutes in perjury laws and other information-forcing legislation. A more ambitious approach would extend the requirement of candor to government communications to the people at large on nuclear arms. Arguably, restrictions on government speech to the public are more defensible than restrictions on communications addressed to Congress; members of Congress may be better informed and less susceptible to manipulation than the average citizen. Some precedent for this approach exists in the form of a few federal statutes forbidding government agencies from communicating to the people in certain ways.

Shared Remedy

The final type of remedy blends judicial and nonjudicial approaches. In this approach courts would, on their own, identify categories of government propaganda and information control that most threaten democratic values. The categories set out on pages 240–242 might serve as a starting point for such a list. Within these categories, courts would insist on express agency approval for each communication. In the absence of such approval, the courts would declare the communication unlawful. By means of such "remands," courts would ensure open and advertent decisions on the dissemination of speech that threatens processes of representative government. This approach allows the courts to attack problems of government excesses directly rather than indirectly, and also to invite explicit consideration by government agencies of some of the problems posed by their own speech.

Separation of Powers

Remedies in which one branch of government coerces another to take or refrain from action raise issues of separation of powers. Separation of powers, along with related doctrines such as political question and executive privilege, generally ensure that the three branches of government do not overstep their bounds and interfere with one another's proper functions. It might be urged that direct remedies, by which the judiciary or Congress orders the executive branch to discontinue deceptive talk about armaments, violate this constitutional principle. Similarly, although the indirect remedies suggested above might not be unconstitutional, they may nevertheless be assailed as imprudent on quasi-constitutional grounds. The remainder of this section examines the impact of separation of powers principles on the remedies proposed above.

Rules limiting weapons speech could, arguably, interfere with the national defense and foreign relations functions of the executive branch. In these areas, the Constitution gives the president broad authority. Article II, Section 2 provides that the president shall serve as commander in chief of the armed forces. This power arguably encompasses communicating to the nation about military matters, including nuclear arms and strategy. The president's military powers, however, are shared with Congress, which controls the appropriations process through its authority, as stated in Article I, Section 8, to "raise and support Armies" and "to provide and maintain a Navy." Congress is also empowered "to make Rules for the Government and Regulation" of the armed forces, and "to provide for calling forth the Militia to . . . repel Invasions." It also has sole authority to declare war, a power recently reaffirmed and made specific by the War Powers Resolution of 1973, which limits presidential power to deploy troops abroad. Article I, Section 8 of the Constitution imposes a further curb on presidential authority, limiting military apropriations to a two-year period.

Presidential authority with respect to military matters is thus limited. These limits are drawn even more tightly when the president seeks to act domestically in furtherance of international military policy. In the steel seizure case, President Truman tried to seize and operate the nation's steel mills to avert strikes and assure an adequate supply of steel for the Korean War. The Supreme Court ruled his action an unconstitutional usurpation of legislative authority.

The president's military authority is further limited in areas where Congress articulates an intention to limit presidential power. In such areas, which might include publicity and communications on nuclear matters, the presidential power "is at its lowest ebb." Congress might plausibly assert an interest in accurate depiction, to both Congress and the people, of the current military situation. Shared information is a prerequisite for the exercise of Congress's shared power in military matters. The people need truthful information, as well, to form opinions on matters of war, peace, and weaponry, and to communicate these opinions to their elected representatives.

Similar limits exist with respect to the conduct of foreign affairs. Although the president has traditionally been accorded wide latitude in matters of diplomacy, he is not the sole actor in foreign affairs. The president must seek the "advice and consent" of Congress with respect to treaty-making and diplomatic appointments. Moreover, Congress retains the power of the purse, and may use it to shape presidential action in foreign affairs. Congress's authority to regulate foreign commerce may impose a similar limit; for example, when President Nixon imposed a surcharge on many articles imported into the United States, his action was declared an unconstitutional usurpation of the latter power. As in the area of military policy, the president's foreign affairs power becomes attenuated when invoked as a ground for domestic action. In the Watergate case, the Supreme Court held that the president has no inherent authority to conduct warrantless electronic surveillance within the nation's borders. It would seem, then, that the president's foreign policy power, like his power in military affairs, offers little basis for resisting reasonable rules regulating domestic communications on matters of nuclear policy.

One area where some of the broad rules and policies pertaining to presidential prerogatives have been tested, with close ties to the subject under consideration, is executive privilege. Executive privilege is generally invoked to enable the president or other high-ranking members of the executive branch to *refuse* to speak. Nevertheless the concerns raised in support of such a refusal are similar to those that might be invoked to justify dishonest or manipulative speech. Twice in the last thirty two years, the Supreme Court has confronted claims of executive privilege by a sitting president. Each time, the Court has recognized that the privilege exists, while holding that courts may determine the factual predicates that support the privilege. The courts also have the power to decide whether countervailing considerations outweigh those underlying the claim of privilege. When courts have found against the president on a claim of privilege, he has acquiesced. On the three occasions when presidents have been subpoenaed, each has complied.

244   In the most recent Supreme Court decision concerning executive privilege, *United States* versus *Nixon,* the court acknowledged the desirability of preserving the confidentiality of high-level executive conversations. The Court concluded, however, that the need to preserve the integrity of the judicial system decisively outweighed the privilege. The Nixon case arose in the context of the criminal prosecution of some of the Watergate defendants. Other cases have held that executive privilege may also have to yield in civil trials. In *Halperin* versus *Kissinger,* a federal district court held that the plaintiffs, who were suing for civil damages for the illegal wiretapping of their telephones, were entitled to take the deposition of former President Nixon.

Protection of the integrity of the political processes and congressional decision-making would seem to be an interest at least as strong as the protection of the judiciary in a criminal or civil trial. Moreover, it would seem that an executive's claim to a privilege to dissemble can rarely if ever be as strong as the claims to a privilege to remain silent that were overridden in recent cases. Consequently, considerations drawn from executive privilege would seem to pose little obstacle to rules limiting executive branch dissembling.

CONCLUSION

This article has suggested that government has systematically used deceptive, manipulative language to influence the American people on matters of nuclear strategy and weaponry. Such language is particularly effective because of the nature of the threat of nuclear destruction and the ways in which normal human minds react to that threat. Effective countercommunications are made difficult by government news management and official secrecy. The combined effect is to falsify consent and ensure perpetuation of a military-political alliance based on heavy weapons spending and a policy of nuclear deterrence.

Recent commentary has proposed that government speech may be regulated on a lesser showing of need than that required to abridge private speech. The fears that support special treatment for government speech are particularly acute in connection with nuclear weaponry. To restore the integrity of the political process and ensure full and informed debate on the vital issue of nuclear policy, Congress and the courts may—in fact they should—undertake remedial action. Narrowly tailored measures that draw on the resources of both these branches could alleviate the threat to democratic decision-making, while respecting the legitimate functions of the executive branch.

[Nat Hentoff]

16

PRESUMPTION OF GUILT

"I don't take drugs and I don't believe I have to piss in a bottle to prove I don't."
—Bob Stanley, pitcher, Boston Red Sox

"If you hang all the people, you'll get all the guilty."
—Tom T. Hall, country singer

In March 1986, Ira Glasser, executive director of the American Civil Liberties Union, sent a letter to twenty of the nation's largest labor unions inviting them to take part in a series of seminars in the fall to work out a strategy for the unions and the ACLU to protect the privacy of Americans where they work.

"Government employees and employees of private industry, railway workers and baseball players," Glasser wrote, "are being required in ever greater numbers to prove their innocence by submitting to intrusive and humiliating urine and blood tests." The seminars, he said, would deal not only with "random drug testing of people not suspected of using drugs" but also with "other violations of the right to privacy of the workplace."

As many workers can testify, privacy rights in the workplace have been eroding for a long time by means that range from management eavesdropping on employee telephone calls to placement of hidden microphones in employee washrooms in order to pick up intelligence concerning "troublemakers." What prompted Glasser's rallying cry, however, was the proclamation of an unprecedented massive and official attack on workers' privacy.

On March 2, the President's Commission on Organized Crime strongly recommended—in the name of "national security"—that all federal employees

---

246 be tested for drug use. Not particular individuals about whom some reasonable suspicion of drug abuse exists, but *all* employees. Furthermore, the commission urged all private employers who have federal contracts to begin dragnet testing of their workers. If the contractors refuse, they should be denied any further government business.

The commission went on to recommend that all private employers, not just those with federal contracts, start collecting urine samples and otherwise screen their workers concerning drug use. Peter Rodino, chairman of the House Judiciary Committee and a member of the President's Commission on Organized Crime, objected strenuously, noting that such wholesale testing "raises civil-liberties concerns." Nonsense, said Attorney General Edwin Meese, a mail-order scholar of the framers' intentions on these matters. No unlawful search and seizure is involved, Meese explained, because, "by definition, it's not an unreasonable seizure because it's something the employee consents to as a condition of employment."

In other words, when the boss tells you to pee into a bottle if you want to keep your job, you consent to that condition if you don't want to lose your job.

At the press conference with the attorney general was the chairman of the president's commission, Judge Irving Kaufman of the Second Circuit Court of Appeals. Kaufman was the judge who sent Ethel and Julius Rosenberg to the electric chair after praying earnestly for guidance, thus making God an accomplice in the execution. As the years went on, Kaufman, extremely sensitive to charges that he was the prosecutor's judge in the Rosenberg case, has developed an exceptional reputation as a defender of First Amendment rights of defendants, especially the press, against the government. But now, in the twilight of his career, Kaufman has again become the prosecutor's judge by supporting dragnet drug testing of millions of Americans.

The testing he and the majority of the commission advocate, says Kaufman, is no more an invasion of privacy than requiring any American to walk through metal detectors at an airport. However, as Tom Wicker notes in the *New York Times,* "Having one's bodily fluids forcibly and randomly inspected is substantially different from putting one's luggage through an electronic device."

What's more, the drug tests aren't even accurate. "The most commonly used urine test is notoriously unreliable," Ira Glasser noted in an ACLU statement. "It cannot identify specific drugs and it cannot distinguish between common cold medicine and illegal substances like marijuana and cocaine. The test cannot determine when someone used a particular drug or to what extent. And it cannot measure impairment of the ability to function on the job."

There are also blood tests for drugs, and they reveal much more than the government or a private employer claims to be testing for. Charles Seabrook, an unusually probing science writer, pointed out in the *Atlanta Journal & Constitution* last year that "from a single ounce of a person's blood, sophisticated computerized tests can determine, or at least strongly suggest, whether a person is predisposed to heart attacks, whether he smokes, drinks to excess, has had a venereal disease, or is epileptic, schizophrenic, or subject to depression. . . . 'Given enough blood and enough lab technicians, I could find out hundreds of things about you—what you eat, what drugs you take, even the kind of booze you drink,' says Dr. James Woodford, a forensic chemist in Atlanta, who is frequently consulted in drug-related cases."

Judge Kaufman and the attorney general may have unwittingly rendered a considerable service to the nation because their proposal has begun to focus attention on routine invasions of privacy in the workplace. A growing number of large corporations have been doing just what the President's Commission on Organized Crime is pushing.

As an index of the dragnet testing that is already in place, everyone who applies for work at United Airlines, IBM, Exxon, Du Pont, Federal Express, Lockheed, Shearson Lehman, TWA, and a good many other companies has to undergo urinalysis. Indeed, at least a quarter of the Fortune 500 companies test all applicants for drugs. Even without prodding from the president's commission, many other firms, large and small, would have joined the list. Any time management has a chance to control its work force more firmly, it seizes on that chance. Now, the notion that every worker is guilty until proven innocent also has the imprimatur of a blue-ribbon government commission that insists on regarding urinalysis and other forms of testing workers—before and after they are hired—as essential for national security.

At the ACLU seminars with labor unions to be held in the months ahead,★ the first distinction to be drawn will be between the government and private employers. Although Kaufman and Meese claim there are no constitutional problems with regard to testing public employees, case law indicates otherwise. When the State is the employer, the Fourth Amendment prohibition against unreasonable search and seizure comes into play. The Fourth Amendment requires that there be probable cause—or, in some instances, the lower standard of reasonable suspicion—that *particular* individuals may be doing or holding something illegal.

In 1984, for example, the Eighth Circuit Court of Appeals affirmed a decision granting prison guards an injunction against random urinalysis even

---

★On November 10, 1986, the ACLU and the Food and Allied Service Trade Department (FAST) of the AFL/CIO co-sponsored a one day conference in New York City entitled: "The Drug Testing Debate: Remedy or Reaction?" [Ed.]

248 though they certainly perform crucial security functions. The court ruled that for the bodily fluids of public employees to be seized there has to be an *individualized,* reasonable basis for the search.

In East Rutherford, New Jersey, last year, the school board ordered all students to undergo urine and blood testing for drugs and alcohol as part of an annual physical examination. Any student who tested positive would be suspended or expelled from school. The ACLU of New Jersey, representing five of the students, took the case to court and the rule was struck down because, said the judge, it violated each student's "legitimate expectation of privacy and personal security" under the Fourth Amendment.

Also in 1985, the school board of the Patchogue-Medford School District on Long Island decided that to be given tenure, a teacher would have to submit to a urine test to determine the presence or absence of illegal drugs. In Suffolk County Supreme Court, Justice Thomas Stark could not have been more clear in his decision declaring that the school board had acted unconstitutionally.

"The Fourth Amendment of the United States Constitution, applicable to state action through the Fourteenth . . . protects individuals from unreasonable searches of the person. The compulsory extraction of bodily fluids is a search and seizure within the meaning of the Fourth Amendment." Such a search is permissible, he added, only when there is particularized, reasonable suspicion "based on objective supportable facts."

Workers in private employment, however, do not have Fourth Amendment protections because the order to give up bodily fluids does not come from the State. Alternative sources of protection are available, however. Union contracts can include, through collective bargaining, provisions extending to workers the equivalent of First Amendment, Fourth Amendment, and other constitutional rights. Some United Auto Workers locals, for example, have won contracts with clauses that make it difficult to fire an employee for anything he says or puts on a bulletin board or wears on a T-shirt.

Until now, most workers and their unions have been slow to recognize the importance of battling for such contract clauses. It may well be that the Meese-Kaufman assault on workers' privacy may spur more collective-bargaining strategy to get language that will give workers the same rights on the job as they have on the streets and at home. As bus driver Randy Kemp of Seattle put it in *Time,* "You've got to have a search warrant to search my house. Hell, my body is a lot more sacred than my home."

Another route to protecting privacy is through state constitutions and local statutes. Some state constitutions have stronger privacy provisions than the U.S. Constitution, and if the language covers private employees, dragnet and random searches can be banned. Richard Emery, a Fourth Amendment specialist with the New York Civil Liberties Union, also points out that under

some local human-rights statutes, it is illegal to fire anyone who has a disability if that disability does not affect his job performance. Drug use can be
a disability, but not necessarily one that interferes with worker competence.
Accordingly, if a local statute includes drug dependence as a disability, and if
the worker is doing his job efficiently, he can't be fired if he fails a drug test.

More directly specific is a San Francisco ordinance—the first in the country
—that prohibits employers from administering random, dragnet blood and
urine tests. And state legislatures in California, Maine, Oregon, and Maryland
are considering bills that would limit or regulate testing of employees.

Clearly there is potential for a natural alliance between workers and civil
libertarians to educate local and state legislators and to lobby for protective
statutes. Invasion-of-privacy horror stories and realistic remedies ought to be
covered in union newspapers, general publications, and—never to be underes-
timated—letters to the editors of all kinds of papers and magazines.

For many workers, civil liberties have long seemed to be a class issue. If
you look at the composition of most ACLU affiliates and chapters, the overwhelming majority of members are lawyers, academics, enlightened business-
men, and a very few union officials. Blue-collar workers are seldom represented. The rights that have appealed most to workers are economic rights,
and they don't see the ACLU and other civil liberties organizations as being
particularly concerned with take-home pay and benefits. But when a worker
can lose his job if he won't piss into a bottle, the Fourth Amendment, at least,
becomes much less abstract, and that is why a coalition between the usual civil-
liberties activists and workers is not only plausible but potentially effective.

The possibility of protests within certain shops also exists. Job actions not
for more pay but for the right to be a free citizen at work could put some heat
on certain company officials.

Take the *Los Angeles Times*. Its editorial page has been among the most
forceful and lucid in the nation in fighting to keep the Bill of Rights in working
order. Yet, according to Daniel Jussim, writing in the ACLU's *Civil Liberties*
newsletter, "The *Los Angeles Times*, though its director of employee relations
says there's no particular drug problem at his newspaper, recently adopted a
mandatory urinalysis program 'to stay current with what other employers are
doing.' "

Imagine the impact in Los Angeles if Anthony Day, the civil libertarian
who is editor of the *Los Angeles Times*'s editorial page, were to lead a picket
line outside the paper, with such signs as:

*James Otis, Father of the Fourth Amendment, Fought British General Search War-
rants on Behalf of Working People—Not Just Publishers.*

The need for alliances to preserve what is left of privacy grows greater by
the day. Charles Seabrook writes of new tests that can "detect the presence

250   of the abnormal levels of chemicals found in patients with severe depression, schizophrenia, and manic-depression . . . that can detect chemical 'markers' that may mean a person is at high risk of developing diabetes, arthritis, or cancer . . . that can screen for more than 150 genetic diseases, including sickle-cell anemia . . . and cystic fibrosis."

Would an employer hire someone who is at risk of developing cancer? Should an employer have access to such private information?

On a more modest level, a new test developed by Werner Baumgartner, a Los Angeles chemist, bypasses such old-time procedures as requiring the random suspect to urinate into a cup or bottle. The new test uses radiation on hair and discloses not only what drugs have been taken but when they were taken, something urinalysis can't do.

As for coming attractions that verify the prescience of George Orwell: The *Washington Post* reported in mid-1984, "Researchers in academia and industry say it is now possible to envision a product that could instantaneously assess whether employees are concentrating on their jobs by analyzing their brain waves as they work."

There isn't much time left to create, in law, the best possible defenses against government and employer intrusions into privacy, including intrusions that now seem inconceivable.

[Harry G. Levine and Craig Reinarman]

17

THE POLITICS OF AMERICA'S

LATEST DRUG SCARE

In 1986 American politicians and news media went through an extraordinary antidrug frenzy. Every major newspaper, newsmagazine, and TV network carried lurid, exaggerated stories alleging that cocaine and other drug use was "taking over" cities and suburbs alike. We were told that America's youth, economic competitiveness, and even our very national security are all gravely threatened by drugs. In March, *Newsweek*'s cover story, "Kids and Cocaine," used the words "plague" and "epidemic," despite noting later that the percentage of high school seniors reporting that they had tried cocaine had increased from 16% in 1981 to only 17% in 1986. In May, NBC News told its millions of viewers that crack, a risky new crystalline form of cocaine that is smoked, "has become America's drug of choice." In fact, there is no evidence that any substantial proportion of the 22 million Americans who have tried cocaine use it in its crack form, or that crack is widely used at all outside major cities. *Readers' Digest* took out full-page ads in the *New York Times* and other major newspapers with the banner headline, "FROM MIDDLE AMERICA COME REPORTS OF TEEN PARTIES WHERE COCAINE IS SPRINKLED ON THE POPCORN." Cocaine users across America must have laughed aloud. Even if cocaine use were half as prevalent as the alarmists claimed, few if any users would waste such an expensive drug by using it in a way that would not only ruin its intended effects but make the popcorn taste terrible to boot.

An abbreviated version of this article first appeared in *The Nation* magazine as "Abusing Drug Abuse: What's Behind 'Jar Wars'" *The Nation* 244 (March 28, 1987), pp. 388–390.

252   School administrators in Hawkins, Texas, inspired by the hype and by the recommendations of Education Secretary William Bennett, announced plans to spend twenty-two dollars per student for schoolwide drug testing—four times more per pupil than Hawkins spends for library books. In October, President and Nancy Reagan hosted an antidrug television special in which they informed viewers, "This epidemic has our children's names written on it." They claimed that because drugs were "terrorizing" the country, the war on drugs was nothing less than "another war for our freedom." Presumably it was in the name of this "freedom" that his administration proposed massive urinalysis testing that would invade the privacy and encroach upon the civil rights of millions of workers and students, and subject tens of thousands of freeway travelers of certain ages and races to searches by police and, soon, by armed services personnel.

As election day approached, candidates challenged each other to urinate into specimen cups to provide chemical proof of their moral purity, clean urine presumably being a measure of fitness for high office. In a show of good faith, President Reagan and Vice President Bush led the way to the toilet, with many high-level staffers in tow. Some observers called the whole episode "jar wars." The White House drug advisor, Carlton Turner, went so far as to tell *Newsweek* that marijuana use causes homosexuality. Capping this off, Congress passed the wishfully named "Drug Free America Act." The new law provides a remarkable panoply of new drug controls, including mandatory life sentences to twenty-one-year-olds who sell a gram of cocaine to twenty-year-old friends, and gives most of its nearly two-billion-dollar appropriation to law enforcement and military agencies to wage yet another futile "war on drugs." It was quite a year.

Buried in the blizzard of drug scare stories, there were critical and dissenting reports. Articles in the *Los Angeles Times, Christian Science Monitor, The New Republic,* and a fine one in *TV Guide* ("Is TV News Hyping America's Cocaine Problem?") suggested that the extent of new and current drug abuse had been seriously exaggerated. Even *Time* magazine, in an issue with a typical scare cover, included a graph showing drug use had not risen appreciably for six years. *Time* quoted the head of the National Institute on Drug Abuse as saying: "The trend since 1979 is that people are backing off. In almost all classes of drugs, abuse among younger people has diminished." Gradually it became clear that the epidemic was one of media and political attention and not of drug abuse.

Little more than a decade ago the political climate about drugs was very different. In the early 1970s President Nixon's hand-picked National Commission on Marijuana and Drug Abuse recommended decriminalization as a policy alternative that should be considered seriously. Many states and locali-

ties eased penalties on marijuana use, without experiencing any of the horren-
dous increases in drug problems that were predicted. In 1976 President Carter
still spoke of decriminalization as a rational policy. How, then, did we find
ourselves confronted in 1986 with a wave of antidrug hysteria?

Drug scares are a recurring theme in American history. Just as red scares
scapegoat leftists, accusing them of undermining the foundations of America,
drug scares blame all kinds of social problems on the use of one chemical
substance or another. The first and most commonly scapegoated drug was
alcohol. Throughout the nineteenth century the American temperance movement persuaded tens of millions of people that alcohol was a demonic substance. Temperance leaders said that alcoholic drink was responsible for most
of the poverty, crime, violence, mental illness, moral degeneracy, broken families, lost productivity, and individual failure in industrializing America. In the
early twentieth century, prohibitionists promised that constitutional prohibition would be a panacea that would literally empty the prisons and mental
hospitals and ensure lasting economic prosperity and moral well-being.

The claims first made against alcohol were reapplied with racist imagery
in subsequent drug scares. In the 1870s California passed the first law against
smoking opium after a campaign that raised the spectre of Chinese men drug-
ging white women into sexual slavery. The law in effect enhanced police and
employer control over immigrant Chinese workers, and was only one of many
such laws supported by white workers in a political-economic context of re-
cession, unemployment, and xenophobia. During the first cocaine scare, in
another tight labor market just after the turn of the century, some southern
sheriffs claimed they had switched from .22 to .38 caliber pistols because their
old guns could not stop the "coke-crazed" black man. Such racist fears were
used by moral entrepreneurs to overcome the resistance of Southern "states'
rights" congressmen to the first federal law against cocaine and opiates.

In the depression of the 1930s, alcohol prohibition had been repealed and
the Federal Bureau of Narcotics had succeeded in criminalizing both opiate use
and medical treatment of addiction. They soon faced budget cuts and needed a
new villain, so the bureau began a crusade to popularize an image of marijuana
as a "killer weed" that made smokers, especially Mexicans, violent. By the
1970s, however, a new generation of drug warriors reversed field and claimed
that marijuana was the "drop-out drug" that was destroying the motivation
and patriotism of middle-class youth (the same generation nowadays derided
as overly ambitious and conservative yuppies).

There has often been an economic dimension to drug scares. Many large
employers in the early twentieth century supported antialcohol crusades in
order to increase worker productivity. Today, nearly half the Fortune 500 companies use blood or urine tests to screen employees and job applicants for

254 illicit drug use (far fewer look at the more prevalent problems created by licit drugs like alcohol, Valium, and tobacco). Corporations justify the tests on the grounds of efficiency and competitiveness. However, although many corporations claim they must use drug tests for cocaine to stop America's falling rate of productivity, there is clearly more to the story than that. Productivity rates began to fall in the late 1960s, long before the use of cocaine became widespread. Despite the tendency for many businesses to blame drugs for their problems, most business journals have demonstrated that falling productivity has to do with disinvestment, capital flight, poor management, obsession with short-term profitability, and the tendency to invest in mergers rather than productivity-enhancing plants and equipment. It also must be noted that such tests intimidate workers and give management surveillance over their employees' private lives. Although often construed as concern for employee welfare, many corporate approaches to drug problems also serve as means of controlling workers and giving managers an additional weapon in their battles with unions.

In January 1986, President Reagan ordered drug testing for over one million federal employees. The most optimistic and self-serving estimates of the testing industry claim "only" a 2 percent or 3 percent rate of "false positives." That means that perhaps 30,000 federal employees who do not use illicit drugs will be erroneously declared guilty, threatening their reputations and livelihoods. Everyone forced to go through the degradation of supervised urine tests will have lost their constitutional rights to privacy, to the presumption of innocence, against self-incrimination, and against unreasonable searches. The drug tests should have been instantly discredited as unconstitutional, insanely expensive, and impossibly inaccurate. Instead, they are going forward. In December 1986, news reports explained that even high-level Justice Department officials were opposed to the tests but were unwilling to speak out for fear of being branded "soft on drugs." Unions and civil libertarians who are trying to stop the tests have won most court cases thus far, but there are other battles to come. Perhaps the major obstacle faced by opponents of the drug tests is the irrational environment of public opinion created by politicians and the media.

There is a long tradition of fascination with drug horror stories in the American media. William Randolph Hearst's "yellow journalism" empire was built in part on sensationalistic tales of ruin and redemption at the hands of this or that consciousness-altering chemical. Although American journalism has in many respects made great progress since those days, the media's willingness to knowingly distort and exaggerate the nature and consequences of drug abuse in the name of circulation, "dramatic footage," and higher ratings remains intact. A classic case of this occurred in 1980 when a young reporter for the

Washington Post won a Pulitzer Prize for her story of an eight-year-old heroin addict whose mother's boyfriend was injecting him. The story flew past the *Post*'s legendary editors and the distinguished Pulitzer jurors before being exposed as concocted. An embarrassed retraction was printed and journalism's highest prize was returned. What is most telling about this sad story was that it succeeded precisely because it fit all the preconceived biases we have about evil junkies. Ironically, any junkie could have told the editors the story was a phoney. What addict in his right mind would *give* precious "junk" to a child even if he were vile enough to *want* to do so?

In addition to racism, bureaucratic self-interest, economics, and mongering by the media, drug scares always have deeper political facets as well. The increased power and legitimacy of political and cultural conservatism in the Reagan era have contributed significantly to the making of the current drug scare. The right wing has long been attracted to the issue of illicit drug use because it focuses political attention on *individual* deviance and immorality and away from structural social ills like economic inequality, injustice, and lack of meaningful roles for young people. A crusade against drug use allows conservative politicians to be law-and-order minded; it also permits them to give the appearance of caring about social ills without committing them to do or spend very much to help people. In the last ten years, New Rightists and other cultural conservatives have championed a life-style politics that is antihomosexual, antiabortion, antisex out of wedlock, antidrugs, and even anti-rock and roll. Politicians opposed to the agendas of the right have often felt obliged to give lip service to some conservative moral issues in order to retain their own political legitimacy.

Participation in the antidrug crusade of 1986 gave Democrats a way to take a strong stand on something without opposing a then very popular president. Being against illegal drugs has always been a safe issue for politicians because there are no large, powerful corporate opponents with wealthy and influential lobbies, as there are for tobacco, alcohol, pharmaceuticals, firearms, automobiles, and other dangerous products. In fact, for some Democrats, allocating more money for a war on drugs than even Reagan asked for seemed ideal; it deprived conservatives of one of their issues, and gave liberals a way of appearing more middle-of-the-road. Spending money on the drug war even gave politicians a way of saying they were doing something about minority and inner-city problems after most of them had pushed for or acquiesced in six years of crippling cuts in social programs for the poor.

By offering this critique of the latest drug scare we do not want to imply that there are no drug problems, or that all new concerns have sprung out of thin air. The percentage of people who have used cocaine once or more increased substantially from 1970 to 1980, although it has remained relatively

256 stable since. Many people certainly abuse drugs and do lasting physical or psychological damage to themselves or others. Daily use of cocaine is a very bad idea indeed: It can damage physical and mental health, ruin careers, strain personal relationships, and, except for the wealthy, exhaust personal finances. In the last two years a purer, more powerful, crystallized form of cocaine called "freebase" or "crack" has been packaged in smaller, less expensive units and sold on the street. This has made cocaine affordable for the first time for those with little money (for instance, vulnerable populations such as young people and the poor). Freebase or crack is smoked rather than snorted, thus getting more of the drug into the body more rapidly. This is an unusually risky way to use cocaine because it greatly speeds up the heart and provides an orgasmic "rush" that hastens the user's desire to repeat the experience, thus increasing the risk of psychological dependence. Everyone agrees that cocaine can be abused easily and that crack is an especially dangerous way to use it.

What is not often mentioned, though it is known by many people, is that with cocaine and marijuana, as with alcohol and Valium, there are lots of users and only a relatively small proportion of abusers. Although most users will admit that cocaine is a seductive drug and that they have known people who have seriously abused it, they will also attest to the fact that use does not *inevitably* lead to abuse. In fact, with cocaine as with other drugs, nonabusive, controlled, and "recreational" patterns of drug use are the dominant ones. According to the National Institute of Drug Abuse, some 22 million Americans have used cocaine at least once, and at least 4 or 5 million use it more regularly. As many as 60 million Americans have tried marijuana, with 30 to 40 million using it at least once a year, and 20 million of them smoking more frequently. Over 100 million people use alcohol. None of these three substances is *inherently* or automatically addicting. Although no one knows the percentage of users who abuse cocaine, we have a decade's worth of data making it clear that the vast majority of people who try it do not become addicts, end up in emergency rooms, or sell their mother's TV set for a fix. Conservatives and other antidrug warriors tend to hold that the very notion of "controlled" or "recreational" use of illicit drugs is an oxymoron. But that claim is an ideological rather than an empirical one.

A sense of perspective and proportion is missing from current discussions about drug problems. Last year there were nearly 600 deaths related to cocaine use. While this loss of life is tragic enough, it is useful to remember that almost the exact number have died since 1982 using all-terrain vehicles (three-wheeled motorized dirt bikes, which are often used by children). More important, the physical, psychological, and economic damage done by legal drugs still dwarfs the damage done by illicit drugs. For example, in 1985, *for every one cocaine-related death, there were 500 tobacco-related deaths.* Alcohol is the direct medical or physiological cause of more than 18,000 deaths a year and is a contributing factor in perhaps twice that number of fatal accidents in homes and cars. The point is not to minimize the dangers of illegal drugs; it is simply to note that the amount of physical, psychological, and economic loss associated with a drug bears absolutely no relationship to how it is categorized or controlled by American government.

Since drugs *are* dangerously abused by some people, and since enough families really *have* suffered, it is fair to ask, what is the harm in a little hysteria about drug abuse? Reasonable people may wonder, if all the *sturm und drang* against drugs saves just a few young people from the tragedies that *might* befall them, then is antidrug propaganda such a bad idea? The answer is twofold. First, drug scares are counterproductive even on their own terms. Exaggerated warnings that do not correspond with users' own experiences lead them to disregard all warnings. This happened in the 1960s when propagandistic warnings about marijuana and hallucinogens were so clearly contradicted by countless firsthand experiences with those drugs. It is likely that some current cocaine abuse developed precisely because users no longer trusted official scare stories. In public health warnings, the truth is usually scarey enough and is always the best policy. In fact, sensationalist accounts of drug abuse may actually stimulate the behavior they pretend to prevent. The *New England Journal of Medicine* recently reported research showing that the incidence of teenage suicide increased after news stories about them. Similarly, studies of drug use in the late 1960s found that the incidence of bad trips on LSD rose after the appearance of sensationalistic news reports about them. This pattern is especially likely when new and exotic drugs like crack are tried by young, inexperienced users who have not had the benefit of a user folklore that teaches them what to expect and what to watch out for. So, if there was any historical evidence that drug scares actually *worked,* really did prevent drug problems, then all the alarms might have some justification. As it stands, they not only do not help but may actually hurt.

Second, drug scares not only fail as public health policy, they divert the nation's attention and resources from more serious problems. Obscured or forgotten in all the political rhetoric and media coverage of crack use among inner-city and minority youth are the intractable social and economic problems that underlie drug abuse, and which are much more widespread—poverty, unemployment, and the prospects of life in the permanent underclass. Dealing drugs, after all, is often quite accurately perceived by poor city kids as the highest-paying job they will ever get. Liberal Democrats correctly denounced the Reagan administration's hypocrisy in declaring war on drugs and then cutting drug-education budgets. The more important point, however, is that the "just say no" administration had at every opportunity just said no to virtu-

258 ally every social program aimed at creating alternatives for inner-city young people. Unfortunately, these kids cannot "just say no" to poverty and unemployment. Like "Communists," or "outside agitators," "drug abuse" has been used as a chemical bogeyman, to be blamed for crime, rebellious youth, falling productivity, broken families, urban poverty, and lots of other social problems that have little to do with drugs and a lot to do with how our society is structured. Such public discourse is an abdication of analysis. It is, quite simply, scapegoating.

Drug scares have never been merely about drug problems, serious though they are. They are about blaming drugs for all sorts of problems people fear and fret over but cannot do much about without disturbing the underlying structural features of our society that give rise to them. This is never done, of course, because to do something about the sources of drug problems would entail tampering with aspects of our social order from which we benefit. The current scare, drawing upon old, ugly traditions in American culture and politics, is a reflection of a very conservative moment. Church and state, family and corporation seem to be out to reaffirm the symbolic order of some real or imagined moral *ancien régime,* which they imagine would make people behave in ways that better suit the powers-that-be in such master institutions. Perhaps the one good thing that *may* come out of all this hysteria over cocaine is the realization that a serious problem is being manipulated rather than addressed. There is a limit to how far hype and hyperbole can go without drawing critical attention to itself. With the legitimacy of Reaganism eroded, it may be possible to return to a public-policy discussion about drugs that is more humane, honest, and effective. What we had in 1986 was largely drug-abuse abuse.

[Athan Theoharis]

18

CONSERVATIVE POLITICS AND SURVEILLANCE: THE COLD WAR, THE REAGAN ADMINISTRATION, AND THE FBI

Concluding one of the more dramatic "spy" cases of the Cold War years, on January 21, 1950, a federal jury convicted former New Dealer Alger Hiss of two counts of perjury—based on his denial of having given classified State Department documents to an admitted Communist agent, Whittaker Chambers, in 1938. Five days later, Congressman Richard Nixon addressed the House of Representatives to commend the role of the House Committee on Un-American Activities (HUAC) in effecting Hiss's indictment and to condemn the Truman administration's unwillingness to confront this serious threat to America's internal security.

Sympathizers praised Nixon's speech. Even critics denounced it only as a partisan attempt to exploit Hiss's conviction. Both critics and supporters, however, missed Nixon's unintentional revelation of his close but covert re-

260 lationship with the FBI. For Nixon had disclosed that he had had privileged access to confidential FBI investigative files, that he had known of the FBI's confidential interview with Igor Gouzenko and of the Justice Department's prosecutive strategy of late 1948, and that HUAC had been aware, prior to subpoenaing Whittaker Chambers in August 1948, of Chambers's 1939 interview with Assistant Secretary of State Adolf Berle.

"Since December of 1948," Nixon admitted, "I have had in my possession photostatic copies of eight pages of documents in the handwriting of Mr. White which Mr. Chambers turned over to the Justice Department on November 17, 1948." (Actually, Chambers's lawyer gave them to FBI agents on December 3, 1948.) Nixon summarized the contents of this eight-page memorandum, and the full text was then reprinted in the *Congressional Record*. Nixon further disclosed that as early as 1946 Igor Gouzenko (a former Soviet embassy employee who, having defected that winter, briefed Canadian officials about Soviet espionage activities in Canada) "had been questioned by intelligence agents of the United States and had furnished information dealing with espionage activities in this country." Nixon then quoted from "a secret memorandum, dated November 25, 1945," based on the testimony of another ex-Communist, Elizabeth Bentley, "dealing with Soviet espionage in the United States and prepared by an intelligence agency [the FBI] of this Government, which was circulated among key Government departments and was made available to the President."

Developing the theme of conspiracy and subversion, Nixon pointedly questioned why the Truman administration had failed to act on this information in 1945 and 1946. Even after November 19, 1948, when Hiss's attorneys turned over to Justice Department officials typed and handwritten State Department memoranda that Chambers claimed he had received from Hiss in 1938, the administration had done nothing. Instead, the Justice Department apparently decided to discontinue the investigation of Hiss and to seek Chambers's indictment for perjury, to the intense frustration of FBI officials, notably FBI Director J. Edgar Hoover.

Nixon then took credit for thwarting the Justice Department's strategy. On December 2, 1948, HUAC subpoenaed and Chambers turned over to HUAC investigators the so-called Pumpkin Papers, microfilm copies of State Department documents dated January 1938. In the widely publicized hearings of December 6–9, 1948, HUAC portrayed these microfilm documents as confirming Hiss's espionage activities. These HUAC hearings in turn impelled the Justice Department to seek Hiss's indictment for perjury.

When commending HUAC's December 1948 hearings, Nixon impressively recounted the Justice Department's original handling of Chambers's November 1948 revelations:

I have learned from personal investigation that no agents of the Department of Justice even approached Mr. Chambers [between November 17 and December 3, 1948] let alone questioned him about the highly important evidence which he [*sic,* Hiss's attorney] had turned over [on November 19, 1948] to the Justice Department. In view of the [*Washington Daily News*] story which appeared on December 1, [1948] stating that the Justice Department was ready to drop the investigation [into Chambers's allegations about Hiss] for lack of new evidence, the only conclusion which can be drawn . . . is that it was the intention of the Department not to make an investigation unless they were forced to do so.

[HUAC] was able to force the Department to institute an investigation and [indict] . . . Hiss. . . . Even as late as December 5, members of the committee learned from an unimpeachable source that Justice Department officials before proceeding with further investigation of Mr. Hiss were considering the possibility of indicting Mr. Chambers for technical perjury due to his failure to tell the whole story when he first appeared before the committee and the grand jury.

Nixon's inadvertent revelation of the behind-the-scenes cooperative relationship between himself, HUAC, and the FBI does not disclose the scope and nature of that relationship. How extensive were FBI leaks of derogatory personal and political information to conservative congressmen and reporters during the Cold War years? Was the FBI-Nixon relationship atypical or representative? How extensively had FBI officials covertly promoted the politics of red-baiting successfully employed by conservative congressmen and reporters to discredit liberal and radical activists and further conservative political objectives? Had the FBI become so politicized, and its conduct so immune to traditional means of oversight, that bureau officials unhesitantly collaborated with the likes of HUAC and other anti-Communist activists? For Nixon's disclosure underscores that the bureau had shifted from collecting information to disseminating it, with the resultant impact on public opinion and public policy.

Nixon's revelations about the FBI's behind-the-scenes political role are revealing about one phase of FBI activities, made possible because of the absence of tight external scrutiny. Assured of secrecy, FBI officials were also emboldened to authorize "clearly illegal" (their own phrasing) investigative techniques, such as break-ins to obtain documents recording the supporters and political objectives of radical organizations. Recently released FBI documents demonstrate how, at least since 1940, high-level FBI officials blatantly circumvented legal restrictions (concomitantly devising separate filing procedures to preclude public discovery of their illegal activities). FBI officials, furthermore,

262   were not content to amass information on dissident activists. Instead, under the direction of J. Edgar Hoover and Assistant Director Louis Nichols, derogatory information from FBI files was purposefully disseminated to "friendly" reporters and congressmen.

In leaking such information, FBI officials had two complementary objectives. They sought to lend credence to the efforts of conservative activists like Congressman Richard Nixon, Senator Joseph McCarthy, HUAC, and Don Whitehead (*New York Herald-Tribune* reporter and author) to establish the "seriousness" of the internal security threat confronting American society. They further sought to neutralize potential challenges to the bureau's investigative activities and independence. FBI officials successfully dissuaded President Truman from appointing a special presidential commission in 1949 and 1950 to investigate FBI practices, and later contained the Long Subcommittee's investigation of the bureau in 1965 and 1966. Aroused by the potentially damaging revelation of illegal FBI activities during the Judith Coplon trial, FBI officials assisted in the preparation of Morris Ernst's article "Why I No Longer Fear the FBI" and, through *Reader's Digest* Senior Editor Fulton Oursler, arranged for its publication in the *Digest*'s December 1950 issue.

The FBI's resort to illegal break-ins and investigative techniques was not confined to radicals. In January 1942, for example, FBI agents illegally entered the New York City offices of the American Youth Congress (AYC) to photocopy Mrs. Eleanor Roosevelt's correspondence with AYC officials. Copies were forwarded to FBI headquarters in Washington, where Hoover ordered them "carefully reviewed & analyzed." To prevent disclosure of its activity, the bureau prepared the resultant report under a Do Not File procedure and placed the copies themselves in FBI Assistant Director Louis Nichols's unserialized Official and Confidential File.

In July 1940, and this time at the direction of President Roosevelt and Assistant Secretary of State Adolf Berle, the FBI initiated an investigation of former Republican President Herbert Hoover. Having been advised by reporter Marquis Childs that the former president and his personal secretary Lawrence Richey had allegedly "addressed certain cablegrams to former Premier Laval of France," Roosevelt directed the FBI to "determine what messages, if any, of the type were sent by Mr. Hoover and Mr. Ritchey [*sic*] and what replies were received." The FBI conducted an investigation of "trans-Atlantic communications," but "failed to disclose that any such messages were sent." Significantly, this FBI investigation—like later investigations of New Left organizations—stemmed from Herbert Hoover's opposition to administration foreign policy. As in the 1960s and 1970s, the rationale was "national security": Hoover's and Richey's alleged contacts with Laval were subject to "official inquiry" because they had "injected themselves into international entree . . . so related to the operation of the Federal Government."

Whether or not coincidentally, on November 2, 1940, the FBI also prepared a thirty-nine-page "blind memorandum" (that is, not listing the names
of sender and recipient) on labor leader John L. Lewis, who in that year had
broken with President Roosevelt over his bid for a third term and his foreign
policy toward Germany and had endorsed the candidacy of Republican presidential nominee Wendell Willkie. This November 2, 1940, report confirmed
that the FBI had followed Lewis's and the United Mine Workers' activities
closely since the 1920s and had intercepted, on April 18 and 27, 1938, at least
two of Lewis's telephone conversations with Mexican official Alejandro Car-
rillo.

This cursory review of some of the FBI's past abuses, conducted because
the scope of FBI investigations and methods employed were effectively immunized from external scrutiny, is not without contemporary relevance, given
the Reagan administration's policy priorities and congressional consideration
of FBI charter legislation. What should the proper limits be on FBI investigative authority? Should its investigations be strictly limited to violations of
federal statutes? When should FBI investigations be initiated and, in the event
no evidence of illegal activities were uncovered, when should they be terminated? How loosely should the FBI's "national security" powers be defined?
Moreover, is it reasonable to base reform on administrative discretion rather
than on tightly defined legislative prohibitions?

These are not academic questions. As recently as 1975 bureau officials misled congressional investigators about the scope of its past illegal activities. On
September 22, 1975, the Senate Select Committee on Intelligence Activities
had requested from FBI officials statistics on all "domestic security" break-ins
conducted by the bureau since 1942. Responding on September 23, 1975, FBI
officials had said that an accurate accounting could not be provided because
there was "no central index, file, or document listing surreptitious entries conducted against domestic targets" and any reconstruction would have to depend
upon "recollections of Special Agents." But FBI officials were disingenuous.
They could have provided a more detailed accounting of past FBI break-ins,
since, until July 1966, surreptitious entries authorized by FBI headquarters
were recorded "in a symbol number sensitive source index maintained in the
Intelligence Division." Furthermore, the FBI's New York field office maintained a file (despite Hoover's orders to destroy such documents every six
months) recording break-ins conducted by New York agents since 1954, and
including documents pertaining to earlier FBI break-ins. In 1975, responsible FBI officials were aware of this index and of the existence of documents
pertaining to past FBI break-ins. They could have been more responsive to
the Senate Select Committee's request for statistics. That they were not is an
important fact.

Nor was this misleading response the sole instance of FBI dissembling

264 about past break-in activities. During the period 1973–1976, the bureau also misled the House Select Committee on Intelligence Activities; a federal court (in responding to Judge Thomas Griesa's ruling on a suit brought by the Socialist Workers Party); responsible Justice Department officials (when preparing responses to court-ordered discovery motions); and the General Accounting Office (then conducting an audit of FBI investigative activities at the request of the chairman of the House Committee on the Judiciary).

Taken together, the FBI's abuses of power—whether disingenuousness during the 1970s and its investigative and political activities during the Cold War years—were possible because FBI officials had successfully immunized such operations from any meaningful external scrutiny. Lacking a legislative charter defining the scope and limits to FBI investigative authority and methods, the FBI was an agency subject to the direction of the White House and the attorney general. FBI officials, moreover, were able to circumvent effective controls by either the White House or the attorney general—either because presidents used the FBI's resources to further their own policy objectives or because attorneys general did not know or did not want to know what FBI officials were doing.

The series of dramatic revelations of past FBI abuses in the mid-1970s gave impetus to congressional demands to draft an FBI legislative charter, ending this practice of executive discretion and abuse. Reflecting the divergent priorities of liberals and conservatives, two different charter measures were drafted and introduced in 1979–1980.

The first FBI charter bill, S. 1612, was introduced on July 31, 1979, by Senator Edward Kennedy on behalf of the Carter administration. S. 1612 did not limit FBI investigations to uncovering evidence of criminal activity. It permitted a major exemption to the restrictive provisions—"except as to foreign intelligence and foreign counterintelligence investigations"—and authorized the FBI to obtain "information" as well as to ascertain whether an individual "will engage" in criminal activities. The bureau was empowered to investigate whether alleged "terrorist" activities would "influence" government policy and whether civil disorders are "threatened." The FBI was also to be given access to "third party records"—including telephone toll, insurance and credit, and bank records—and to assist other federal agencies and state and local governments without determining whether such agencies may lawfully receive such information.

Senator Paul Laxalt introduced a second FBI charter bill, S.2928, on July 2, 1980. Laxalt's bill abandoned any pretense of applying criminal standards to FBI investigations. Repeating the "foreign intelligence" and "foreign counterintelligence" exceptions, Laxalt's bill further authorized the FBI to "conduct such investigations, and collect and maintain such intelligence and information, as may be necessary for the security of the United States and its defense, and to facilitate the operations of the FBI in carrying out investigations authorized by this chapter." Under the Laxalt bill, the FBI could investigate "activity which is likely or has the potential of violating the criminal laws of the United States"; individuals and groups seeking to "influence or bring about a change in the policy of the United States or any State or subdivision thereof"; "civil disorders or threatened civil disorders or public demonstrations which have a potential for violence, disruption, or disorder"; and "terrorist activity," defined as including "influencing or retaliating against the policies or actions of the Government of the United States or of any State or political subdivision thereof or of any foreign state, by intimidation or coercion." The FBI would further be empowered to disclose "information to the private sector" if that information "relates to potential terrorist activity" or concerns individuals "seeking employment of a type in which prior criminal history would indicate that such individual's conduct would constitute a clear and present danger to his employer or to employment." Furthermore, and particularly in view of the FBI's covert relationship with HUAC and the Senate Internal Security Subcommittee during the Cold War years, the Laxalt bill authorized the bureau to "provide investigative assistance . . . to those committees of the congress for which it is authorized to conduct background investigation of staff members. . . . if the chairman of the committee requests, and the Attorney General or his designee approves, the provision." Even Alfred Regnery, an aide to Senator Laxalt, conceded that S.2928 "would theoretically leave the way open for those [recently disclosed] FBI abuses"; he offered the palliative that "we don't think those things are likely to happen again."

Neither Kennedy's nor Laxalt's bills, or amended versions of either, were enacted. Introduced in the waning months of the Carter administration, formal action on them was deferred until after the 1980 election. Then, with Republican control of the presidency and of the Senate, any impetus to drafting an FBI charter bill was abandoned.

This inaction is not surprising, given the reality that the principal beneficiary of past FBI activities, and the principal constituency supporting former FBI Director Hoover's autonomous operation of the FBI, were American conservatives. Rather than imposing legislative guidelines to govern FBI operations, conservatives opted instead for the restoration of executive discretion.

Abandoning the approach of the Laxalt bill, the Heritage Foundation (a right-wing research organization) in November 1980 released a three-thousand-page report urging the newly elected Reagan administration and the Ninety-seventh Congress to adopt a harder line toward dissident organizations and activists. Its major premise was that "individual liberties are secondary to the requirements of national security and internal civil order." Accordingly,

266 the foundation recommended reviving HUAC and the Senate Internal Security Subcommittee; rescinding Attorney General Edward Levi's March 1976 guidelines and President Carter's Executive Order 12036 of January 24, 1978, limiting bureau investigations of "terrorist" and "potentially subversive" organizations; authorizing the FBI to use "such standard intelligence techniques as wiretapping, mail covers, informants and (at least occasionally) illegal entries"; exempting intelligence agencies from the disclosure provisions of the Freedom of Information and Privacy acts; and abolishing the secret court, created under the 1978 Foreign Intelligence Surveillance Act, that reviewed and authorized all "foreign intelligence" and "foreign counterintelligence" electronic surveillance.

Although Reagan administration officials denied that presidential policies governing the intelligence agencies and internal security would follow the Heritage Foundation recommendations, the report nonetheless offers insights into the priorities of conservative Republicans for the 1980s. Not surprisingly, on December 5, 1980, the newly elected Republican majority on the Senate judiciary committee voted to revive the Internal Security Subcommittee (terminated in 1978 in reaction to the abuses of civil liberties perpetrated under the rubric of "internal security"). As an aide to the Judiciary Committee chairman, Strom Thurmond, confided, the subcommittee "could keep watch over communist activities within the United States." In a companion effort, Congressman John Ashbrook introduced two bills in January 1981: H.J.R. 18, to create a Joint Committee on Internal Security, and H.R. 14, to reestablish the House Committee on Internal Security (the former HUAC, so renamed in 1969).

Meanwhile, the Freedom of Information Act (FOIA) came under attack. In March 1981 the CIA repeated an earlier request for a legislative exemption from the FOIA's disclosure provisions. The FOIA, Deputy CIA Director Max Hugel claimed, hindered the agency's "ability to perform its vital mission" while only rarely producing information of public interest. "While we do not question the principle that U. S. citizens should have the right to know what their government is doing and has done in the past," Hugel added, "we firmly believe that an exemption should be made in the case of the CIA." Then, on May 4, 1981, Attorney General William French Smith rescinded former Attorney General Griffin Bell's May 1977 rule governing FOIA suits whereby the Department of Justice would defend in court only those exemptive claims of federal agencies in which disclosure of information would be "demonstrably harmful" to the national interest. Smith concurrently announced that the Reagan administration had initiated a formal review of the FOIA to "assess the need for legislative reform." Such a review was required, he emphasized, because of the FOIA's administrative costs and the further consequence that "informants are more reluctant to share information with U. S. intelligence agencies, . . . and other impediments to effective government are created."

The administration formally submitted its proposed amendments in October 1981. In testimony before the Senate Select Committee on Intelligence Activities, CIA Director William Casey demanded that the files of the CIA, the Defense Intelligence Agency, and the National Security Agency be totally exempted from the act. Introducing the FOIA amendments, Assistant Attorney General Jonathan Rose recommended, among other changes, increasing the fees to cover all costs for processing FOIA requests (to include as well the salaries of officials who were reviewing documents for possible deletions), limiting judicial review of "national security" claims to determining whether withholding of such information was "arbitrary or capricious," and authorizing the attorney general to withhold whole categories of information relating to "terrorism," "foreign counterintelligence," organized crime, and ongoing investigations.

In a further assault on the First Amendment, on May 8, 1981, the Reagan administration proposed the Intelligence Identification Act, which would impose jail sentences of up to ten years for those who, having access to classified information, disclosed the names of agents, and of up to three years for those not having such access, including reporters and scholars, who merely published the names, even if they had obtained them from public sources. This legislative proposal was eventually enacted into law in 1982.

After meeting with intelligence agency officials early in 1981, President Reagan also ordered a review of existing regulations governing intelligence activities, ostensibly to improve antiterrorist capabilities. In response, an interagency working group, headed by the CIA's general counsel, drafted an executive order revising many of the restrictions instituted under President Carter's Executive Order 12036 of January 24, 1978. Under this draft, intelligence agencies, including the CIA, would have been authorized to spy on American citizens within as well as outside the United States—permitting the use of electronic surveillance, break-ins, and infiltration of domestic organizations. Although Carter's order had restricted the collection of intelligence information and the use of intrusive techniques, the proposed Reagan order would authorize such practices: Section 2 of Carter's order was appropriately titled "Restrictions on Intelligence Activities" with a subcategory "Restrictions on Certain Collection Techniques," but the comparable section in the proposed Reagan order was titled "Conduct of Intelligence Activities" and the subcategory, "Use of Certain Collection Techniques." The proposed Reagan order would, inter alia, downgrade the attorney general's oversight and review roles; broaden the type of surveillance that intelligence agencies could

268 conduct when investigating "unauthorized disclosure" of intelligence information; authorize the CIA to "engage in electronic surveillance activity within the United States only for the purpose of assisting, and in coordination with, another agency" having the authority to conduct such surveillance; drop the "probable cause" standard and requirement of presidential approval for use of searches and break-ins and substitute approval by the attorney general or (with his authorization) the head of the intelligence agency; and permit the collection, storage, and dissemination of information about individuals if it is merely "believed" (in contrast to the requirement of Carter's order that it be "reasonably believed") that the person was acting on behalf of a foreign power or engaging in international terrorist or narcotics activities.

Leakage of the text of the proposed executive order to the *New York Times* on March 9, 1981, resulted in extensive publicity, mostly adverse, and forced the Reagan administration to downgrade the status of the proposed order to merely a "first draft" by a "working group" of intelligence agency officials. FBI Director William Webster, it was reported, thought that the FBI neither needed nor wanted the proposed changes, and so responsibility for these particular recommendations was attributed to lower-level intelligence officials, particularly within the CIA, and to conservative Republicans committed to unleashing the intelligence agencies. Throughout the week-long furor, the White House remained silent. Finally, on March 17, 1981, White House aide Edwin Meese told reporters that "I don't contemplate any change in the direction of loosening the reins on the CIA in domestic spying. The White House is absolutely opposed to the CIA getting into domestic spying." Meese, nonetheless, confirmed that within the next two to three weeks a new executive order on intelligence activities to combat terrorism would be issued.

The promised executive order did not materialize. In May 1981, a revised draft, written by the interagency task force, was circulated within the White House, the National Security Council (NSC), the intelligence agencies, and the congressional intelligence committees, but it was promptly opposed by the National Security Council staff. According to Reagan administration officials, National Security Adviser Richard Allen and other NSC staff complained that the second draft would not give the intelligence agencies the mandate or structural changes required to bolster their intelligence-gathering activities.

In October 1981, the Reagan administration submitted a third draft of its proposed executive order for review by the House and Senate intelligence committees. This draft gave the intelligence agencies (including the CIA) broad authority to infiltrate domestic organizations and to review bank, medical, telephone, and other personal records of American citizens and residents (specifically lifting the Carter order's ban on the CIA's conduct of "special activities" within the United States); freed intelligence agency officials from reporting possible federal crimes by their employees; authorized the agencies to conduct warrantless searches, including opening the mail, of American citizens and residents; and permitted the intelligence agencies to "cooperate with appropriate [state and local] law enforcement agencies for the purpose of protecting [their] employees, information, property, and facilities." Key congressmen and a congressional staff analysis of the order raised serious concerns about the scope of the order, but administration spokesmen undercut these criticisms by citing the provision that "nothing in this order shall be construed to authorize any activity in violation of the constitution or statute of the United States." They further asserted that the Department of Justice was currently drafting guidelines to clarify the powers of the intelligence agencies.

On December 4, 1981, President Reagan issued the new executive order 12333. In response to the congressional criticisms, Executive Order 12333 had deleted the sections permitting the CIA to infiltrate and influence domestic organizations without a warrant; freeing intelligence agency heads from reporting to the attorney general any possible federal crimes committed by their employees; affirming the president's "inherent" powers to authorize warrantless electronic surveillance; and permitting the intelligence agencies to conduct investigations within the United States into the unauthorized disclosure of classified information and sources. Nonetheless, the Reagan order radically expanded the intelligence agencies' permissible activities. They were now authorized to "conduct administrative and support activities within the United States and abroad necessary for the performance of authorized activities," as well as "such other intelligence activities as the President may from time to time direct." While their principal responsibilities were overseas, the CIA and the Defense Department intelligence agencies could conduct "counterintelligence activities" within the United States if coordinated with the FBI. In turn, the FBI was empowered to "conduct within the United States, when requested by officials of the intelligence community designated by the President, activities to collect foreign intelligence or support foreign intelligence collection requirements." The breadth of the order's definitions of "counterintelligence" and "foreign intelligence" would permit potentially broad domestic investigations. Such investigations were seemingly limited by the stipulation that they could not be undertaken "for the purpose of acquiring information concerning the domestic activities of United States persons." Other sections qualified this restriction, however, permitting the acquisition and dissemination of "information obtained in the course of a lawful foreign intelligence, counterintelligence, international narcotics or international terrorist investigation," if necessary to protect "the safety of any persons or organizations, including those who are targets, victims or hostages of international terrorist organizations"; "incidentally obtained information that *may* indicate involvement in activities that *may*

270 violate *Federal, state, local or foreign law* [emphasis added]"; and information "necessary for administrative purposes."

Reagan's executive order, in effect, authorized the FBI to resume investigating dissident political activities, thereby reversing the recent scaling down of such investigations owing first to the disclosures of abuses during congressional hearings involving the intelligence agencies of 1975–1976 and then to the restrictive "domestic security" investigative guidelines issued by Attorney General Edward Levi in March 1976. As the result of "specific taskings from the National Security Council and the Central Intelligence Agency" and the "counterintelligence" provisions of Executive Order 12333, in 1983 the FBI began interviewing individuals associated with organizations opposed to the Reagan administration's Central America policy (including religious organizations such as Sojourners or active in the Sanctuary movement). While FBI Director William Webster conceded during 1985 congressional testimony that the FBI had interviewed one hundred citizens who had traveled to Nicaragua purportedly "to see if they have any information at all that would be useful to [the FBI] in performing our counterintelligence function," FBI interviews went beyond such individuals. FBI agents also interviewed individuals who had contributed financially to organizations opposed to the Reagan administration's Central America policy—and thus whose names could only have been obtained by obtaining access to the bank records of these organizations—and a law student who had never been to Nicaragua but who had attended a discussion at his university on U.S. policy in Central America. The FBI, in addition, interviewed the landlords and employers of individuals who had visited Nicaragua, as well as those citizens who had visited the Nicaraguan embassy in the United States.

Civil libertarians have questioned whether the openness of such interviewing was intended to intimidate critics, stressing the flimsiness of the counterintelligence rationale. None of those interviewed were involved or suspected of involvement in spying activities and were not privy to information about espionage activities of foreign governments. The Reagan administration's apparent political use of the FBI is wholly consistent with another recently publicized action: Civil Rights Division attorney Mary Mann's request that the FBI check the criminal record of a black Birmingham, Alabama, city employee. Information about this employee's arrest record was accordingly turned over to the lawyer representing white plaintiffs who were challenging in court Birmingham's affirmative action plan.

Then, in a companion move, on March 7, 1983, Reagan's attorney general, William French Smith, issued new FBI "domestic security/terrorism" guidelines, rescinding those instituted in March 1976 by President Ford's attorney general, Edward Levi. Abandoning any "probable cause" standard as the basis

for initiating FBI investigations of radical activists, Smith's permissive guidelines authorized the FBI to "anticipate or prevent crime" and thus permitted
investigations of individuals whose statements "advocate criminal activity or
indicate an apparent intent to engage in crime, particularly crimes of violence."
Even more revealingly, Smith rescinded Levi's requirement that the Department of Justice "determine in writing whether continued [domestic security]
investigation is warranted." Unwilling to meet this oversight responsibility,
Smith instead made his role, and that of other responsible Department of Justice officials, discretionary, stipulating that the attorney general "may, as he
deems necessary, request the FBI to prepare a report on the status of the [do-
mestic security/terrorism] investigation."

Under President Reagan, then, a concerted effort has been made to rescind
the limited controls and required oversight instituted in the mid-1970s in reaction to the revelations of past FBI abuses. Whether the FBI has resumed
the massive surveillance and dissemination activities of the 1940s and 1950s
cannot be known; the Reagan changes invite, if not encourage, their resumption. The principal deterrent to such resumption stems not from the decisions
of an administration rhetorically committed to the rule of law and "getting
the Government off our backs" but to the mandatory disclosure provisions of
the Freedom of Information Act and the greater skepticism of congressmen
and reporters who remain committed to libertarian values and constitutional
procedures and, for these reasons, are unwilling to defer to so-called national
security rationalizations which, since the 1940s, had effectively immunized the
FBI and the White House from needed scrutiny.

[Geoffrey R. Stone]

19

THE REAGAN ADMINISTRATION,

THE FIRST AMENDMENT,

AND FBI DOMESTIC SECURITY

INVESTIGATIONS

The government undertakes domestic security investigations to obtain information on the activities of groups or individuals who may use unlawful methods to achieve their political ends. Such investigations pose a fundamental conflict for a democratic society. On the one hand, a democratic society must protect itself against unlawful acts designed to subvert the legitimate political order. The essence of self-governance is that political decisions are made through public debate and open election rather than through force, violence, and terrorism. Domestic security investigations may thus be essential to the preservation of a democratic society.

On the other hand, domestic security investigations threaten the very fabric of a democratic society. Unlike ordinary criminal investigations, which are ordinarily confined to determining who committed particular acts and terminate with the decision to prosecute or not to prosecute, domestic security investigations attempt to forestall future crimes and to gather information about the size, composition, goals, and techniques of political organizations that may not have engaged in any past criminal activity. Such investigations are thus broader, less discriminate, and more long-lasting than ordinary criminal investigations. Moreover, domestic security investigations require government officials to draw the often very fine line between dissent and subversion. The danger is that government officials, who are generally committed to the preservation of the existing order, may too readily slide—consciously or unconsciously—from the investigation of dangerous subversives to the investigation of political dissidents. How a society draws and enforces the line between subversion and dissent is a critical measure of its commitment to the freedom of speech and the democratic process.

In 1983, Attorney General William French Smith issued a new set of guidelines for FBI domestic security investigations. The Smith guidelines replaced the preexisting guidelines that had been issued by Attorney General Edward Levi in 1976. The Smith guidelines made significant changes in the standards for domestic security investigations in the United States. This paper explores the constitutional and legal implications of the Smith guidelines.

I

The issues posed by the Smith guidelines can best be understood only against the backdrop of the history of the FBI. The FBI had a less than auspicious beginning. Attorney General Charles Joseph Bonaparte first proposed the creation of a federal police force in 1907, but congressional authorization was withheld because of the widely held view that the establishment of such an agency would lead to "a general system of espionage" and would be "contradictory to the democratic principles of government." During a congressional recess in 1908, however, Attorney General Bonaparte quietly established the Bureau of Investigation within the Department of Justice. Despite vehement protest in Congress, the bureau, with the active support of President Theodore Roosevelt, survived.

In its early years, the bureau directed its energies primarily to enforcement of the Mann Act. Shortly after World War I, however, Attorney General A. Mitchell Palmer, frustrated by the bureau's inability to solve a series of apparently anarchist-inspired bombings, created the General Intelligence Division of the FBI to investigate radical and subversive activities. The GID failed to solve the bombings, but within six months it had compiled personal histories on 60,000 suspected "radicals." Before long the index grew to include more than 200,000 names.

During the Harding administration, the bureau, under the direction of William J. Burns, thrust itself still more deeply into the investigation of wobblies (members of Industrial Workers of the World) anarchists, Communists, and "subversives" generally. The bureau wiretapped at random, broke into offices, and kept tabs on personal lives. The targets were often critics of the bureau or of the Justice Department and even included several senators who may have asked too many questions.

In 1924, Attorney General Harlan Fiske Stone, determined to refocus the bureau's activities, ousted Burns and replaced him with J. Edgar Hoover. Hoover pledged that the bureau would get out of the business of investigating political views and would henceforth limit itself to its intended function of investigating federal crimes. For the next twelve years the bureau exercised considerable restraint, but with the outbreak of World War II it turned its attention once again to the investigation of political dissidents.

In a series of directives in the late 1930s, President Franklin Roosevelt, alarmed by reported attempts of foreign agents to influence domestic affairs, instructed Hoover to gather information concerning Fascist and Communist activities in the United States and to conduct investigations concerning possible espionage and sabotage. Although these directives did not expressly authorize the investigation of "subversive activities" generally, Hoover, apparently reasoning that persons opposed to the American form of government or to basic governmental policies might engage in espionage or sabotage, construed the directives as broadly mandating open-ended inquiries into "subversion." And by repeatedly misinforming a succession of careless or indifferent presidents and attorneys general as to the precise scope of the Roosevelt directives, Hoover managed for more than three decades to elicit tacit executive approval for ongoing FBI investigations of an ever-expanding class of political dissidents. From 1957 to 1974, the bureau opened investigative files on more than half a million "subversive" Americans. In the course of these investigations, the bureau, in the name of "national security," engaged in widespread wiretapping, bugging, mail-openings, and break-ins. Even more insidious was the bureau's extensive use of informers and undercover operatives to infiltrate and report on the activities and membership of "subversive" political associations ranging from the Socialist Workers Party to the NAACP to the Medical Committee for Human Rights to a Milwaukee Boy Scout troop.

Although some of these investigations were no doubt aimed at espionage, sabotage, or other federal crimes (such as violations of the Smith Act), they served other purposes as well. As early as 1939 the bureau, without statutory authorization, initiated the compilation of a Custodial Detention List containing the names of those individuals whom the bureau determined should be "apprehended and interned immediately" in the event of war. The individuals' names were derived from subscription lists of German, Italian, and Communist newspapers, membership in identified organizations, and informant and agent reports on meetings and demonstrations. Hoover counseled FBI field offices that the existence of this list and its "purpose should be entirely confidential."

COINTELPRO was the most daring of the bureau's activities. By the late 1950s, the Supreme Court had embraced restrictive interpretations of the Smith Act and the Internal Security Act of 1950, rendering them relatively ineffective in the fight against subversion. Frustrated by these decisions, and not content merely to compile extensive files on organizations and individuals viewed as threats to the nation's security, Hoover decided to take matters into his own hands. In 1956 he launched COINTELPRO, which was designed to "expose, disrupt and otherwise neutralize" dissident individuals, organizations, and movements. COINTELPRO involved the extensive use of extra-legal measures to combat domestic subversion. The bureau sent anonymous, scurrilous, and false letters to break up marriages, attempted to sow internal dissension within organizations, and informed public and private employers of the political activities and organization membership of "subversive" persons.

Although directed initially against the Communist party, the program expanded over the years to include Socialist, White Hate, Black Nationalist, and New Left targets as well. This extraordinary program was initiated without any prior executive or legislative authorization, and the very existence of COINTELPRO was a closely guarded secret, shielded from public view by a carefully crafted system of multiple filings. As was often the case in this period, the bureau's foremost concern was not with legality, but with avoiding the embarrassment of exposure. And, as with its extensive political surveillance and emergency detention programs, the FBI's COINTELPRO was officially terminated only after its existence and operation were finally revealed to the public through a series of exposés, lawsuits, and congressional investigations in the early 1970s.

A confidential document stolen in 1971 from the FBI field office in Media, Pennsylvania, gave the public its first hint of the existence of COINTEL-PRO. Watergate, however, led to most of the initial revelations. Disclosure of the "Huston Plan" and other instances of White House misuse of the bureau played a central role in the events leading to Richard Nixon's resignation in 1974. The following year, Attorney General Edward H. Levi confirmed that Hoover had maintained secret files on various public figures, that the bureau had on several occasions attempted surreptitiously to discredit its critics, and that it had gathered political intelligence on administrations of both parties.

In reaction to these and other disclosures, select committees of the House and Senate embarked upon investigations of the bureau's internal security operations, and the House Judiciary Committee asked the General Accounting Office to review FBI domestic intelligence policies and procedures. At

276 the same time, various lawsuits seeking information under the Freedom of Information Act or charging the bureau with unconstitutional or otherwise unlawful conduct brought forth further revelations.[1]

II

On April 5, 1976, the Department of Justice, under the direction of Attorney General Edward Levi, for the first time promulgated a set of public guidelines governing the initiation and scope of the FBI domestic security investigations. The Levi guidelines were designed to focus such investigations solely on possible criminal activity and to prevent the bureau from engaging in open-ended investigations of "subversives" and "dissidents" generally. The guidelines provided that domestic security investigations could be conducted only to ascertain information on the activities of groups or individuals who might commit federal crimes involving the use of force or violence.

The Levi guidelines established three distinct levels of domestic security investigations—preliminary investigations, limited investigations, and full investigations. The bureau could undertake preliminary investigations "on the basis of allegations or other information that an individual or group may be engaged in [unlawful] activities which involve or will involve the use of force or violence." The guidelines confined such investigations "to determining whether there is a factual basis for opening a full investigation." In conducting preliminary investigations, the bureau was limited to public sources of information, existing law enforcement records, and other previously established sources of information.

The Levi guidelines authorized limited investigations only if a prior preliminary investigation proved "inadequate to determine if there is a factual basis for a full investigation." The guidelines authorized the bureau to use such additional techniques as physical surveillance and personal interviews in conducting limited investigations, but expressly prohibited the use of more intrusive techniques such as mail covers, electronic surveillance, and the recruitment or placement of informants.

The guidelines authorized full investigations only "on the basis of specific and articulable facts giving reason to believe that an individual or a group is or may be engaged in [unlawful] activities which involve the use of force or violence." The guidelines provided that, in deciding whether to undertake a full investigation, the bureau should consider the "magnitude of the threatened harm," the "likelihood that it will occur," the "immediacy of the threat," and the "danger to privacy and free expression posed by a full investigation."

The Levi guidelines had a dramatic impact on the conduct of domestic secu- rity investigations. In March 1976, the FBI was conducting 4,868 domestic security investigations. In December 1981, the FBI was conducting 26 domestic security investigations. Moreover, the organizations subject to investigation in 1981, such as the FALN, the JDL, the CWP, and the Arizona Chapter of the KKK, were all clearly involved in violent criminal activity.

III

The Levi guidelines did not meet with universal acclaim. To the contrary, in a series of hearings in 1981–1982 before the Senate Judiciary Committee Subcommittee on Security and Terrorism, conservative critics sharply attacked the Levi guidelines for "crippling the ability of law enforcement personnel to do their job." The views of Senator Jeremiah Denton, the subcommittee chairperson, are illustrative: "At this time of ever increasing terrorist activity, I believe the American people need an organization that has the ability, the desire, and the understanding of the threat to see through propaganda and false colors so that the American people can be informed of the threat presented by organizations committed to the destruction of our freedoms. When I speak of a threat, I do not just mean that an organization is, or is about to be, engaged in violent criminal activity. I believe many share the view that the support groups that produce propaganda, disinformation, or 'legal assistance' may be even more dangerous than those who actually throw the bombs."[2]

Similarly, Senator John P. East, another member of the subcommittee, maintained that the Levi guidelines "have virtually destroyed an adequate internal security function in the FBI." In East's view, the "criminal standard for intelligence collection essentially misunderstands the nature of both intelligence work and the phenomenon of subversion," for the "conduct of subversion itself consists in large measure in the utilization of legal activities to undermine . . . legally established institutions." East therefore expressly called for the elimination of the criminal standard.[3]

Moreover, the subcommittee heard testimony from several expert witnesses, such as W. Mark Felt, former associate director of the FBI, Joseph A. Sizoo, president of the Society of Former Special Agents of the FBI, and John R. Simpson, director of the U.S. Secret Service, all of whom confirmed that the Levi guidelines had unduly hampered the bureau in the performance of its essential functions. To illustrate the point, these witnesses suggested that incidents such as the kidnapping of Patty Hearst, the Brink's robbery in Nyack, New York, the Greensboro shoot-out, and John W. Hinckley's attempted

278 assassination of President Reagan might all have been prevented if only the FBI had been free to pursue its intelligence operations in a more aggressive manner.

By 1982, the Levi guidelines were under direct attack both within the Reagan administration and within the bureau itself. Testifying before the Subcommittee on Security and Terrorism, FBI Director William Webster declared that the 1976 guidelines "were no longer adequate to guide us in dealing with the kinds of terrorist groups that we are confronted with today." Webster explained that "these groups are small, cohesive, and difficult to penetrate. The organizational structure is more fluid and ill-defined than that of groups that we have dealt with in the past and they often receive direct support for their criminal activities from others outside the organization." Not surprisingly, then, during the Reagan administration the number of domestic security investigations has climbed steadily from 26 in December 1981, to 38 in August 1982, to 76 in December 1982. And from 1981 to 1984, the number of agent work-years devoted to domestic security investigations increased by 600 percent.[4] As Director Webster conceded, "we have been aggressive about this in the last year or two especially, in opening investigations which in the past I suspect either prudence or the Department of Justice would have dictated otherwise."[5]

IV

On March 21, 1983, the Department of Justice, under the direction of Attorney General William French Smith, promulgated a new set of guidelines governing the initiation and scope of FBI domestic security investigations. Although the Smith guidelines did not adopt some of the more far-reaching proposals of Senators Denton and East, and were described by Director Webster as part of an "evolutionary process," they significantly altered the Levi guidelines.

First, the Smith guidelines eliminate preliminary and limited domestic security investigations. Inquiries short of a full investigation, to determine whether leads indicating specific criminal activity warrant full investigation, are now conducted under the bureau's General Crimes authority.

Second, whereas the Levi guidelines authorized a full investigation only "on the basis of specific and articulable facts giving reason to believe that an individual or a group is or may be engaged in [unlawful] activities which involve the use of force or violence," the Smith guidelines authorize a full investigation whenever the "facts or circumstances reasonably indicate that two or more persons are engaged in an enterprise for the purpose of furthering political or social goals wholly or in part through activities that involve force or violence." The Smith guidelines, in other words, eliminate the "specific and articulable facts" requirement.

Third, the Smith guidelines explicitly extend the so-called enterprise concept, which has been used in organized crime investigations, to domestic security investigations as well. The "enterprise concept" permits the FBI to cross organizational lines to investigate groups that "knowingly support" the criminal objectives of a violent group but do not themselves engage in criminal activity.

Fourth, under the Levi guidelines, the bureau tended to close investigations and terminate informant coverage whenever the violent activity of a group ceased for a period of time. On the theory that it may be difficult to redevelop informant coverage if the organization again becomes active, the Smith guidelines authorize the bureau to continue to monitor organizations that may be temporarily inactive so long as the threshold standard for investigation is satisfied.

Finally, although the Levi guidelines did not directly address this question, the Smith guidelines expressly state that when an organization advocates criminal activity, "an investigation may be warranted unless it is apparent, from the circumstances or the context in which the statements are made, that there is no prospect of harm."

Although these changes may be part of an "evolutionary process," there can be no doubt where the evolution is headed. It is headed toward a reexpansion of the FBI's authority to investigate domestic "subversion."

V

This, then, brings me to the First Amendment. To what extent, if any, does the First Amendment restrict the potential scope of domestic security investigations? To what extent, if any, do the Smith or Levi guidelines violate the First Amendment? Surprisingly, there is no clear answer, for the nexus between the First Amendment and government investigation of political organizations has rarely received direct judicial consideration.

At one level, however, the answer may be simple. All the government is doing in these investigations is investigating—it is not directly *prohibiting* anyone's expression or association. Thus, such investigations arguably do not implicate the concerns underlying the First Amendment.

The Court, however, has consistently rejected this conception of the First Amendment. In a series of decisions, the Court has held that the compelled

280 disclosure of membership in political organizations can itself violate the First Amendment. In NAACP v. *Alabama*,[6] for example, the Court invalidated as applied to the NAACP an Alabama law requiring all out-of-state corporations seeking to do business in the state to turn over certain information, including the names and addresses of its members. The Court concluded that, in the circumstances of the South in the 1950s, the disclosure of such information could have a "substantial" deterrent effect on the willingness of individuals to exercise their constitutional right to join and support the NAACP. Similarly, in *Gibson* v. *Florida Legislative Investigating Committee*,[7] the Court held that a legislative committee investigating the infiltration of Communists into various organizations could not constitutionally compel the NAACP to turn over its membership lists without a demonstration that such disclosure was necessary to serve an "overriding and compelling state interest." And in *Brown* v. *Socialist Workers '74 Campaign Committee*,[8] the Court invalidated as applied to the Socialist Workers Party the disclosure provisions of the Ohio campaign reporting law, which required every political party to report the names and addresses of all campaign contributors and recipients of campaign disbursements, because individuals might be deterred from exercising their constitutional right to associate with the SWP in light of the long history of "both governmental and private hostility toward and harassment of SWP members and supporters."[9]

In these decisions, then, the Court recognized that the "Constitution protects against the compelled disclosure of political associations and beliefs," for such "disclosures 'can seriously infringe on privacy of association and belief guaranteed by the First Amendment.'"[10] Indeed, the Court has noted that "[i]nviolability of privacy in group association may in many circumstances be indispensable to preservation of freedom of association, particularly where a group espouses dissident beliefs."[11] Thus, the "right to privacy in one's political associations and beliefs will yield only to a 'subordinating interest of the State [that is] compelling,' . . . and then only if there is a 'substantial relation between the information sought and [an] overriding and compelling state interest.'"[12]

Domestic security investigations intrude on the "privacy in group association." Indeed, under the Smith guidelines, such investigations may collect information on the target organization's members and "other persons likely to be knowingly acting in furtherance of its [possible] criminal objectives," its "finances," and its "past and future activities and goals."

It may be argued, however, that such investigations have a less severe "chilling" effect than the sort of compelled disclosure at issue in cases like *NAACP* v. *Alabama, Gibson,* and *Brown,* for domestic security investigations are "secret" operations and the information obtained is not routinely available for public inspection. Target individuals are therefore less likely to know of the "disclosure" and they have less to fear in the way of private reprisals and harassment.

The argument is unpersuasive. Even though domestic security investiga- **281**
tions are technically "secret," the members of dissident organizations surely *fear*
that they may be the targets of investigation, and the very secrecy of the investigation may thus increase the uncertainty and actually exacerbate the chilling
effect. Moreover, as the Court recognized in *Brown*, the FBI's misuse of the
information it gathered in past investigations is itself a cause for concern. And
this is so even if the information is not openly disclosed to the public and even
if the bureau has taken steps to reform. Finally, unlike the situation at issue in
most of the compelled disclosure cases, where *all* organizations were required
to disclose their membership and contributor lists, domestic security investigations are targeted at only *some* organizations, thus triggering additional First
Amendment concerns about evenhandedness and neutrality. All things considered, then, the FBI's domestic security investigations should be governed
by essentially the same standards as compelled disclosure.

How, then, do these standards apply? At the outset, it should be noted that
the Smith guidelines expressly declare that domestic security investigations are
to be conducted solely "for the purpose of preventing, detecting, or prosecuting violations of federal law," and that such investigations may not "be
based solely on activities protected by the First Amendment." Such straightforward, seemingly unambiguous declarations of principle can have significant
symbolic and even practical impact in confining the opportunities for abuse.
Standing alone, however, they cannot satisfactorily guard against the inevitable
temptation to investigate political beliefs. As history amply demonstrates, the
line between investigating political beliefs and investigating potential criminal
activity in the political realm is fuzzy at best. The bureau in 1919 was certainly
justified in investigating bombings. It no doubt thought that it was doing precisely that when it compiled dossiers on all the anarchists and radicals it could
find. In the late 1930s, the bureau was certainly justified in investigating potential espionage and sabotage. It no doubt thought that it was doing precisely that
when it gathered information on anyone even remotely suspected of having
Fascist or Communist sympathies. Particularly in times of national crisis, even
the most well-meaning of government officials may too readily make the not
wholly illogical leap from investigating crime to investigating belief. In at least
some circumstances, it is, in the end, merely a matter of degree.

To lessen the likelihood of such investigatory leaps, the Smith guidelines
provide that the bureau may conduct full domestic security investigations, as
opposed to less intrusive and more limited preliminary inquiries, only "when
the facts or circumstances reasonably indicate that two or more persons are
engaged in an enterprise for the purpose of furthering political or social goals
wholly or in part through [unlawful] activities." This is an inadequate safeguard. The "reasonably indicate" standard is vague in the extreme. Is an association's mere abstract avocacy of unlawful conduct in itself sufficient to satisfy

282 the standard? The Smith guidelines expressly suggest that such advocacy *is* sufficient "unless it is apparent, from the circumstances or the context . . . that there is no prospect of harm." This reliance on advocacy as significant evidence of danger indicates that the administration has learned little from the past. For as history demonstrates, it is not uncommon for radical organizations to use abstract advocacy as a tenet, dogma, or slogan without in fact posing a *bona fide* threat to society. Although the fact of advocacy of unlawful conduct is not irrelevant to the question of danger, it should not be accorded the special weight suggested in the Smith guidelines.

My concern is heightened by the open-ended nature of the investigations authorized by the Smith guidelines. The extension of the "enterprise concept," the elimination of the practice of terminating investigations of "inactive" organizations, and the authorization of investigations for possible *future* crimes, without regard to whether the suspected criminal activity is to take place imminently or at some uncertain time in the indefinite future, all vastly expand the potential for abuse. All three of these features should be changed.

The extension of the "enterprise concept" from the racketeering context is inappropriate. By authorizing full investigations of any person "likely to be knowingly acting in furtherance" of a target organization's unlawful objectives, the Smith guidelines invite highly intrusive inquiries into the affairs of individuals who may do nothing more than provide financial support, legal assistance, or other aid to target organizations and whose own activities are perfectly lawful and protected by the First Amendment. The cavalier assumption that what works well in the investigation of organized crime should be carried over to the more sensitive area of domestic security is simply unsupportable.

The express elimination of the prior practice of terminating investigations of "inactive" organizations is similarly problematic. This change opens the door to precisely the kind of never-ending investigations that so characterized the bureau's past excesses.

The express decision to permit investigation of possible future crimes, however, is perhaps the most troubling aspect of the guidelines, for such an open-ended authorization will enable the bureau to embark upon investigations of virtually unlimited duration despite the absence of even the suspicion of present danger. It is precisely these sorts of freewheeling investigations that are most likely once again to get the bureau into mischief. To mitigate this danger, the guidelines should be amended to permit full investigations only when, on the basis of clear and objective evidence, there is reason to believe that the organization will engage in criminal activity in the "immediate future." Although such a standard is obviously not devoid of ambiguity, it at least focuses attention upon what should be a centrally important limiting consideration. And although its use would doubtless forestall early investigation of at least some potentially dangerous organizations, this is a necessary and unavoidable trade-off if we mean seriously to avoid a repetition of the past.

Finally, I should add a word about informers. Under existing Justice Department guidelines, the FBI may employ informers in full a domestic security investigation if there is a reasonable indication that the organization may engage in unlawful conduct, the operation "appears to be an effective means of obtaining evidence or necessary information," and the operation "will be conducted with minimal intrusion consistent with the need to collect evidence or information in a timely and effective manner." These safeguards are insufficient. Infiltration of a politically oriented association should be permitted *only* when authorized by a judicial warrant premised upon a finding of "probable cause." Like a wiretap, which is of course subject to such restraints, an informer poses a severe threat to associational privacy. The suspicion that an infiltrator might be present can cast a demoralizing cloud of uncertainty and mutual distrust over the members of the association and can seriously chill their willingness to speak freely even within the confines of the organization. Moreover, infiltrators not only report on First Amendment activity, they participate in it. An informer can vote, make policy suggestions, and even serve in influential administrative and leadership positions. In light of the bureau's past inclination to use this technique indiscriminately, the probable cause and warrant requirements are essential to adequately safeguard First Amendment rights.

VI

The Reagan administration's influence on domestic security investigations is evident not only in its promulgation of the Smith guidelines, but also in the work of Reagan appointees to the federal bench. By the end of his second term of office, President Reagan will have appointed more than half of all federal judges. These appointments have for the most part been made on the basis of adherence to a narrowly defined ideology of judicial "conservatism." This ideology, and its impact on the issue of domestic security investigations, is illustrated by the 1984 decision of the United States Court of Appeals for the Seventh Circuit in *Alliance to End Repression* v. *Chicago*.[13]

In 1973, the Alliance to End Repression, the American Civil Liberties Union, and numerous other groups and individuals filed suit in federal district court in Chicago alleging that the Federal Bureau of Investigation and other state and federal defendants had violated the plaintiffs' constitutional rights

284 by conducting surveillance of their lawful political activities; compiling and maintaining dossiers on them as a result of their lawful political activities; gathering information about them by the use of unlawful break-ins, wiretaps, and informers; and disrupting and harassing their lawful political activities. Throughout the next decade, the plaintiffs conducted extensive discovery which disclosed numerous FBI abuses and substantiated many of the allegations of plaintiffs' complaint. Finally, in 1981, after "many years of 'sharply contested' litigation," the parties entered into a settlement agreement.[14] The agreement expressly barred the FBI from "conducting an investigation solely on the basis of activities protected by the First Amendment."

After the Reagan administration promulgated the Smith guidelines, the plaintiffs sought an order prohibiting the FBI in Chicago, which was subject to the settlement agreement, from implementing the provision of the Smith guidelines that explicitly authorized the FBI to initiate domestic security investigations solely on the basis of statements advocating criminal activity "unless it is apparent, from the circumstances or context in which the statements are made, that there is no prospect of harm." The plaintiffs maintained that this provision violated the settlement agreement's express prohibition of domestic security investigations initiated "solely on the basis of activities protected by the First Amendment."

The federal district court judge who had accepted the settlement agreement held that, in entering into the settlement, the parties had clearly understood that the agreement prohibited domestic security investigations based on advocacy of unlawful conduct if such advocacy is "protected by the First Amendment." To determine when such advocacy is "protected by the First Amendment," the district court turned to the Supreme Court's 1969 decision in *Brandenburg v. Ohio,*[15] which held that "the constitutional guarantees of free speech and free press do not permit a State to forbid or proscribe advocacy of the use of force or of law violation except where such advocacy is directed to inciting or producing imminent lawless action and is likely to incite or produce such action." Interpreting the settlement agreement in the light of *Brandenburg,* the district court reasoned that advocacy of law violation is "protected by the First Amendment" within the meaning of the agreement unless it "is directed to inciting or producing imminent lawless action and is likely to incite or produce such action." The district court then observed that, unlike the Levi guidelines, the Smith guidelines expressly authorize domestic security investigations on the basis of unlawful advocacy whether or not such advocacy "is directed to inciting or producing imminent lawless action" or "is likely to incite or produce such action." The district court thus concluded that the Smith guidelines expressly authorize investigations "solely on the basis of activities protected by the First Amendment" in violation of the 1981 agreement. The district court therefore enjoined the implementation of this aspect of the Smith guidelines in the Chicago area.[16] The United States Court of Appeals for the Seventh Circuit affirmed.[17]

Shortly thereafter, however, the court of appeals agreed to rehear the case *en banc*. In an opinion by Judge Richard Posner, perhaps the most brilliant and most influential of the Reagan judicial appointees, the court of appeals reversed the district court's order.[18] In reaching this result, Judge Posner expressed "doubt" that the Justice Department would have entered into the settlement agreement as construed by the district court, "for if it did, it was trifling with the public safety of the people of Chicago." Moreover, Judge Posner's "doubt" was deepened by the fact that, had the case gone to trial, the plaintiffs could "not have gotten" an injunction any broader than the one embodied in the consent decree as interpreted by the district court. Judge Posner concluded that, in such circumstances, it would be absurd to construe the agreement as assuming that the Justice Department had bargained away "the public safety of the people of Chicago" for a mere "saving of some litigation expenses."

Judge Posner was still left with the task of offering an alternative interpretation of the provision of the settlement agreement that expressly prohibited the FBI from "conducting an investigation solely on the basis of activities protected by the First Amendment." Judge Posner maintained that the *Brandenburg* standard, which was relied upon by the district court, did not define in a relevant way the circumstances in which the advocacy of unlawful conduct is "protected by the First Amendment," for *Brandenburg* dealt with criminal punishment rather than mere investigation. And although *Brandenburg* may define the circumstances in which the advocacy of unlawful conduct is "protected by the First Amendment" against criminal prohibition, it does not define the circumstances in which it is "protected" against investigation. Whether activities are "protected by the First Amendment" turns not only on the nature and value of the activities, but also on the nature of the government's interference with those activities. Having put aside *Brandenburg,* Judge Posner then construed the settlement agreement's provision prohibiting the FBI from "conducting an investigation solely on the basis of activities protected by the First Amendment" not as a prohibition of domestic security investigations based on the advocacy of unlawful conduct, but as a prohibition of investigations based on "improper" motivations—that is, as a prohibition of investigations motivated by a desire on the part of government officials to suppress constitutionally protected expression. Because the Smith guidelines did not authorize such improperly motivated investigations, Judge Posner concluded that the guidelines do not violate the settlement agreement.

Judge Posner's opinion is an unfortunate illustration of a court of appeals judge rewriting a carefully worked-out agreement in a highly sensitive area to

286 suit his own—and the administration's—ideological preferences. There are at least three things wrong with the opinion.

First, Judge Posner exaggerated the extent to which the agreement, properly construed, trifles "with the public safety of the people of Chicago." The agreement expressly distinguished between "investigations" and "inquiries," a distinction derived from the Levi guidelines. The settlement prohibited "investigations" initiated "solely on the basis of activities protected by the First Amendment." It did not prohibit mere "inquiries." The purpose of an "inquiry," of course, is to determine whether a full investigation is warranted.

Second, Judge Posner misunderstood and hence understated the advantages to the Justice Department of the settlement. The settlement was reached after almost a decade of litigation had produced endless disclosures of FBI abuse. By 1981, with the arrival of a new administration, the Justice Department wanted desperately to close the book on this unfortunate chapter in the bureau's history. A public trial would have lasted months, if not years, it would have generated countless headlines, and it would have required dozens of government officials to testify under oath to a wide range of unconstitutional actions. The Justice Department thus purchased a great deal more in the settlement than a mere "saving of some litigation expenses"—it avoided further exposure of investigative abuses and continued erosion of public confidence in the FBI. Moreover, prior to the settlement, the Justice Department and the plaintiffs engaged in extensive litigation over the scope of the informers' privilege. The Justice Department knew that a trial—with the consequent exposure of its informers—would impair the FBI's ability to recruit undercover agents in the future. The settlement avoided this embarrassment.

Third, Judge Posner's alternative interpretation of the agreement—that it prohibits only "improperly motivated" investigations based "solely on activities protected by the First Amendment"—is both naive and destructive of the essential core of the agreement. In effect, it interprets the agreement as permitting the government to launch full-scale investigations of political organizations "solely on the basis of activities protected by the First Amendment" so long as the government's motivation is not "improper." This completely misunderstands the motivations of the FBI in the past. The FBI's investigations of the Communist party, the Socialist Workers party, and the NAACP were not motivated by an "improper" desire to suppress legitimate dissent. Rather, such investigations were motivated for the most part by an honest belief that such organizations posed a genuine threat to the national interest. The real "evil" of the FBI investigations was not that they were "improperly" motivated, but that they were the product of exaggerated fears, bad judgment, and insensitivity to the value of constitutional rights. Judge Posner's opinion, which was undoubtedly "properly" motivated, reflects a similar mind-set.

The danger of terrorism is real. The FBI may and must act to combat it. But it must do so consistently with our traditions of free expression and with an awareness of past abuse. In its investigative guidelines and its judicial decisions, the Reagan administration is headed in the wrong direction.

NOTES

1. For more elaborate accounts of this history, see Frank Donner, *The Age of Surveillance* (1980); Athan Theoharis, *Spying on Americans* (1978); Senate Select Committee to Study Governmental Operations with Respect to Intelligence Activities, Final Report, Intelligence Activities and the Rights of Americans, Book II, S. Doc. No. 13133-4, 94th Cong., 2d Sess. (1976).

2. Statement of Senator Jeremiah Denton, Hearings Before the Subcommittee on Security and Terrorism of the Committee of the Judiciary of the United States Senate on The Domestic Security Investigation Guidelines, 97th Cong., 2d Sess. 4 (1982).

3. Statement of Senator John P. East, Hearings Before the Subcommittee on Security and Terrorism of the Committee on the Judiciary of the United States Senate on The Domestic Security Investigation Guidelines, 97th Cong., 2d Sess. 35–41 (1982).

4. From 1981 through 1984, the number of agent "work-years" devoted to such investigations increased as follows: 1981 (9 agent work-years); 1982 (12); 1983 (49); 1984 (53). See Federal Bureau of Investigation, 1986 Appropriate Request 49 (1985) (Testimony of William H. Webster before the House Subcommittee on Appropriations); Federal Bureau of Investigation, 1985 Appropriation Request 48 (1984) (Testimony of William H. Webster before the House Subcommittee on Appropriations); Federal Bureau of Investigation, 1984 Appropriation Request 47 (1983) (Testimony of William H. Webster before the House Subcommittee on Appropriations); Federal Bureau of Investigation, 1983 Appropriation Request 44 (1982) (Testimony of William H. Webster before the House Subcommittee on Appropriations).

5. Testimony of Hon. William H. Webster, Director, Federal Bureau of Investigation, Hearings Before the Subcommittee on Security and Terrorism of the Committee on the Judiciary of the United States Senate on The Domestic Security Guidelines, 97th Cong., 2d Sess. 8–33 (1982).

6. 357 U.S. 449 (1958).

288

7. 372 U.S. 539 (1963).

8. 459 U.S. 87 (1982).

9. *Ibid.* at 99.

10. *Buckley* v. *Valeo*, 424 U.S. 1, 64 (1976).

11. *Brown* v. *Socialist Workers '74 Campaign Committee*, 459 U.S. 87, 92 (1982), quoting *NAACP* v. *Alabama*, 357 U.S. 449, 463 (1958).

12. *Brown* v. *Socialist Workers '74 Campaign Committee*, 459 U.S. 87, 92 (1982), quoting *NAACP* v. *Alabama*, 357 U.S. 449, 463 (1958), quoting *Sweezy* v. *New Hampshire*, 354 U.S. 234, 265 (1957) (concurring opinion).

13. 742 F. 2d 1007 (7th Cir. 1984).

14. *Alliance to End Repression* v. *Chicago*, 561 F. Supp. 575, 576 (N.D. Ill. 1983).

15. 395 U.S. 444, 447 (1969).

16. *Alliance to End Repression* v. *Chicago*, 561 F. Supp. 575 (N.D. Ill. 1983).

17. *Alliance to End Repression* v. *Chicago*, 733 F. 2d 1187 (7th Cir. 1984).

18. *Alliance to End Repression* v. *Chicago*, 742 F. 2d 1007 (7th Cir. 1984) (en banc).

[Michael Ratner and Eleanor Stein]

20

THE NEW CONSPIRACY

TRIAL: PATTERNS IN FEDERAL

PROSECUTION

The conspiracy trial, once a familiar feature in the American political landscape, has returned. In the last five years, the Reagan administration, without attracting much attention, has prosecuted a series of federal political conspiracy trials reminiscent of the Nixon/Mitchell antiwar movement conspiracy prosecutions of the late 1960s and early 1970s. The current trials are characterized by broad-ranging conspiracy indictments, investigative grand juries, informants, and hostile publicity. Even when they end in acquittal or suspended sentences, these trials drain resources, tarnish reputations, and divert movements. Those that end in convictions have sent activists to jail, some of them for life.

But beyond the consequences for the individual defendants emerges a disturbing pattern that may well have broader effect. Conspiracy indictments have long been criticized for the advantages they give to prosecutors, easing the way for convictions. Under "conspiracy" one can be guilty of a crime of association and planning without actually having carried out any other criminal act. And the testimony of one coconspirator (which could be excluded as hearsay in most criminal trials) can be sufficient basis for sending someone to jail. The recent wave of federal conspiracy trials benefits from these re-

---

Excerpts of this essay were published in *Counterattack* 1 (September 1987): 3–4, 14.

290 laxed evidentiary rules. However, in addition, the Reagan Justice Department has utilized a host of newer devices—(1) preventive detention, (2) anonymous juries, (3) extraordinary courtroom security, (4) unprecedented invasions of privacy as part of FBI information gathering, and (5) motions in limine to preclude the defense's presentation of their case to the jury—which further shift the balance in favor of the prosecutor and against the accused. These tactics affect the fairness of the trials, and put in place some frightening constitutional precedents that impact on civil liberties for all of us.

In preparing this article we have focused on seven recent prosecutions in which a number of these newer devices were utilized. Probably the first was the Brink's trial—the federal RICO conspiracy trial of underground radicals and others associated with the Black Liberation Army (BLA), who were charged with the attempted robbery of a Brinks armored truck in Nyack, New York, in 1980.★ A guard and two policemen were killed during the robbery attempt. Four people were convicted in the initial federal trial and are currently serving sentences ranging from 12½ to 40 years—the maximum sentences possible for the crimes for which they were convicted. An additional five people are serving sentences on state charges stemming from the same robbery. At least ten people were jailed for civil contempt, for refusing to cooperate with the federal grand jury convened to investigate the robbery. And still others have been prosecuted for aiding the Brinks defendants, or for possessing weapons and planning prison escapes for the same group.

A second prosecution in which a number of these methods were pioneered —most notably "preventive detention"—was the 1984–1985 prosecution of the "New York Eight"—a collective of nine black radicals charged with weapons possession and conspiracy to carry out a prison escape. Primarily middle-class and well-educated, the "eight" received substantial support from the black community and were eventually acquitted of most charges after a four-month trial.

More recently, in its conspiracy prosecution of "the Ohio Seven," a number of these devices were again put to use. The Ohio Seven are white activists from predominantly working-class backgrounds, some with a long history in the anti-Vietnam War and prisoners' rights movements. They were charged with a long series of United Freedom Front bombings related to South Africa and Central America (among them a bombing of South African Airways). In a trial that ended in late March 1986, all seven were convicted of conspiracy as well as varying counts of bombing, and received sentences ranging from

---

★ The reference to the RICO conspiracy trial refers to an indictment under the terms of the Racketeer Influenced, Corrupt Organizations Act. [Ed.]

fifteen to seventy-seven years. They still face RICO charges in Boston for the same bombings, as well as bank robberies.

Also included in our survey are the Chicago trials of five Puerto Rican independentistas for "seditious conspiracy," in 1982 and 1984, and the grand juries impaneled to investigate bombings by the FALN (an armed clandestine group supporting Puerto Rican independence). More than a hundred people have been jailed for refusing to testify before these grand juries, some for periods of several years.

Most recently, these prosecutorial devices have been expanded in the government's case against "the Hartford Sixteen". The defendants—Puerto Rican independentistas—have been charged with the 1983 robbery of a Wells Fargo truck in Hartford, Connecticut. Victor Gerena—the Hartford resident and Wells Fargo employee who allegedly carried off the heist and then reportedly fled to Cuba—has become somewhat of a folk hero for the Latino community in Hartford. Over seven million dollars was stolen in the robbery, some of which was later used to purchase and distribute thousands of dollars' worth of toys to neighborhood children in Hartford and Puerto Rico on Three Kings Day. In pretrial hearings and press reports, the government has linked the defendants to a Puerto Rican "terrorist" group, "Los Macheteros" (the Machete Wielders). Nine of the sixteen have been held in "preventive detention" since their arrest in August 1985.★

Finally, although in a somewhat different vein, some of the same prosecutorial devices have been used in the government's recent "Sanctuary" investigation and trial. Sixteen religious sanctuary workers were charged with a conspiracy to smuggle, transport, and harbor illegal aliens, for their actions assisting Central American refugees. After a seven-month trial, eight of the eleven defendants who stood trial were convicted, although they were given only probationary sentences.

Except for Sanctuary, the cases we have focused on involve at least the rhetoric of political violence. Only the Sanctuary defendants have tapped popular support comparable to that given political conspiracy trials in the 1960s and early 1970s. Although some defendants, notably the New York Eight and the independentistas, have received substantial support from the black and Latin communities, on the whole the government has been able to limit these defendants' rights without meeting a great deal of outcry.

What follows is a discussion of some of the patterns that emerge from our survey of defense attorneys, media reports, Justice Department documents, trial papers, reported opinions, and defendants related to these seven cases.

★ Eight of the nine defendants originally held have now been released on bail. [Ed.]

292 Our discussion is not meant to be exhaustive, but merely illustrative of some of the dangers to which these cases point.[1]

GUILTY BEFORE TRIAL

Preventive Detention

Preventive detention means holding someone without bail, before trial, based not on what they have done, but on what they *might* do if released. The term usually calls to mind countries like South Africa, where blacks can be detained indefinitely on the mere charge that they have engaged in an act or utterance that embarrasses the state; or like Northern Ireland in the early 1970s, where the policy of "internment" allowed for the roundup and detention of all those believed to be associated with the IRA (Irish Republican Army). Less known is that here in the United States, preventive detention was written into the federal criminal justice law for the first time in October 1984 as part of the Bail Reform Act.[2]

Although directed toward major drug offenders, since its passage at least thirty-five political activists have been held without bail under its provisions. One of the first victims was Coltrane Chimurenga, one of the New York Eight defendants. Chimurenga was held in preventive detention for seven months, although his trial ended in his acquittal. Another victim of the statute, Dr. Alan Berkman, a New York physician, has been held in preventive detention since May 23, 1985, on charges of harboring and giving medical treatment to Brinks robbery fugitives, as well as on charges of weapons possession. He has since developed cancer and could not obtain adequate medical treatment in prison. At a subsequent preventive detention hearing, held to reconsider his detention without bond, the government argued that Dr. Berkman's cancer made him even more dangerous to the community, as he might carry out a suicide mission if released. The judge continued his preventive detention.

The preventive detention hearing allows the prosecutor to present witnesses and testimony as to the beliefs and associations of the accused. Such information—which would not be admissable at the actual trial—is considered grounds for detaining the defendant without bond, and also receives wide press coverage. For example, in the Hartford case, defendants were indicted for an armored car robbery in which no one was injured. At their preventive detention hearings, however, the prosecution linked them to a fatal 1982 attack on a navy bus and a 1981 bombing of National Guard fighter planes in Puerto

Rico.[3] Although the defendants have never been charged with these incidents, the press has continued to repeat these charges.

Backed by civil liberties organizations, the Hartford defendants challenged the preventive detention law in the Second Circuit Court of Appeals, which on May 2, 1986, held it unconstitutional as applied to several of the accused. Writing for the majority, Judge Jon O. Newman stated that jailing people to prevent their committing a future crime is a "police state approach," and warned of the dangers that this posed.[4] Despite this, the court refused to release the defendants on bail pending the government's appeal to the Supreme Court. Currently two of the sixteen defendants have been imprisoned for over a year. With the trial not scheduled to begin for another six months, and expected to last at least six months, these defendants could end up spending three years in jail before they are even judged guilty, or acquitted. Unfortunately, in a different case, *U.S.* v. *Salerno* (May 1987), the constitutionality of the preventive detention laws was upheld by the Supreme Court.

Anonymous Juries

Anonymous juries keep defendants from learning the names of jurors, or where they work or live. Pioneered in major drug cases to protect jurors from intimidation or retaliation by organized crime, the Reagan Justice Department has begun using this device in political trials as well. Despite the lack of evidence of actual danger to jurors in these cases, anonymous juries have been granted—and upheld by the Second Circuit—in a number of Brinks-related trials as well as the criminal contempt prosecution of Julio Rosado, for failing to testify before the Puerto Rican grand jury.[5] The effect of such juror anonymity is twofold. First, it hampers the critical jury selection process, since defendants cannot fully question jurors as to their potential prejudice or bias. Secondly, and perhaps most importantly, it communicates to jurors, even before the trial begins, that the defendants are dangerous and probably guilty.

Usually the jury is the wild card in the trial process, where the government has least control. Today, when almost one-half of the supposedly impartial federal judiciary are Reagan appointees screened for their right-wing political outlook,[6] juries are critical. Popular skepticism about the veracity of government agents threatens a Justice Department that wants convictions. For example, the Nixon administration suffered a number of defeats in political trials where juries were unwilling to believe the elaborate schemes charged by the government and their informers (for example, the acquittal of the Panther Twenty-one and Harrisburg Eight). More recently, the New York Eight jury clearly

294 rejected the government's theory that this collective of black professionals and community organizers represented a dangerous criminal conspiracy.

The Armed Courtroom

Military-style arrests and obtrusive security in and around the courtroom also add to jury perceptions, as well as the general public's that the defendants are dangerous and guilty. During the Ohio Seven trial, as many as twenty-five marshals were in the courtroom at a given point. At one point, defendants were beaten and stun-gunned when they insisted on reading their prepared statements in court. They remained dazed for several hours as a result of the electric shocks. Susan Rosenberg and Timothy Blunk, two other post-Brinks defendants, were sped back and forth to court each day through the Holland Tunnel, with a convoy of armored cars. The tunnel was closed down, and at times helicopters flew overhead.

The Hartford case, too—although it has not yet gone to trial—has already seen extraordinary security. At the defendants' first court appearance in Hartford, Connecticut, September 3, 1985, the *New York Times* reported,

> "Sharpshooters patrolled roads, police dogs sniffed the area surrounding the courthouse for bombs, and police barricades closed a downtown street. . . . All 11 suspects wore handcuffs that were locked to chains around their waists. . . . Outside the courthouse police officers armed with shotguns and tear gas rifles stood guard." [7]

The *San Juan Star* for the same day reported, "The U.S. District Courthouse was turned into a virtual armed camp. All those entering the courtroom had to pass tight security that included metal and x-ray detectors." [8] One defense lawyer was quoted as commenting, "You have a small army outside in military uniform, which would taint any prospective juror." [9]

Sensational press adds to the tense atmosphere. In an unusual step in the 1984 Chicago Puerto Rican seditious conspiracy trial, the judge allowed NBC and ABC-TV to enter the case as intervenors. The judge recognized that the media was a party in the case, that is, had a legal interest in the outcome: their concern about the "charges of domestic terrorism." While denying the networks instantaneous access to the video surveillance evidence unfolding in court, the judge promptly released these tapes during trial recesses.

Gathering Information from
Children, Church, and Home

With the continued erosion of Fourth Amendment protections against un-reasonable search and seizure, convictions become easier as information is gathered from people and places formerly considered off limits. Recalling the Orwellian image of the child spying on and reporting to authorities about his parents, children have been detained and interrogated. The children of Ohio Seven defendants Tom and Carol Manning, ages 3, 5, and 11, were held in state custody for two months following their parents' arrest, and could not even be contacted or located by attorneys. The children were initially held in police headquarters and then put into a state home in Norfolk, Virginia, where their parents had been arrested. Only when the Mannings went on a hunger strike and dozens of letters arrived from social-work and child-care organiza-tions, as well as supporters and family, were the children released to family members. While held by the state, the children were interrogated by both state and federal officials.[10] During the FBI's investigation of the Mannings, prior to their arrest, the FBI printed "Wanted" posters with the children's pictures, and contacted day-care centers and doctors' offices in three states to enlist help in finding the children.

In the Chicago seditious conspiracy case, the bulk of the government's evi-dence came from 130 hours of videotape obtained from tiny cameras hidden in the kitchens, bedrooms, and bathrooms of two Chicago apartments. The dis-trict court excluded the tapes from trial use as clearly violative of defendants' Fourth Amendment rights to privacy and freedom from unreasonable search and seizure. But on appeal, the circuit court judge, Richard Posner, a Reagan judicial appointee writing for the panel, allowed the tapes in. He admitted that judicial approval of such surveillance was unprecedented and that overuse of it would "eliminate personal privacy as understood in modern Western nations." But he allowed the tapes in on the grounds that earlier FALN actions, for which these defendants were not on trial, had cost human life.[11]

The FBI investigations in the New York Eight, Sanctuary, and Hartford cases also involved extensive electronic surveillance and use of informers. In the case of the Sanctuary investigation, two informers infiltrated and recorded hundreds of hours of conversation at Bible study classes and church meetings.

Limitations on Defenses

Many of the defendants in these cases have been forbidden to put on their defense or explain the contexts for their actions. Motivation has been ruled

296 irrelevant. A political trial tends to be a struggle between the government's portrayal of defendants as criminals without humanity or ideals, and the defendant's efforts to show that they, not the government, have both. For example, during the sixties many defendants accused of raiding draft board offices admitted their actions; yet jurors returned not guilty verdicts after hearing their "justification" or "necessity" defenses—that they believed they had a responsibility to act to call attention to an unjust and illegal war. Because such defenses can win acquittals, since the sixties conspiracy trials the government and many judges have narrowed the defense field drastically.

In a series of pretrial rulings, the Sanctuary trial judge, Earl H. Carroll, virtually precluded any such defense. The defense attorneys, under threat of contempt, could not present any testimony related to how the defendants believed their actions were legal, that is, their belief that those they sheltered were political refugees entitled to stay, or testimony as to conditions in Central America and the protections refugees are entitled to under international law. The defendants were not even allowed to testify as to their religious motivation.

Despite governmental denials, the political nature of these trials is inescapable. At the sentencing of post-Brinks defendants Susan Rosenberg and Timothy Blunk on charges of conspiracy to possess and possession of explosives and weapons, the New Jersey federal court judge excoriated them for their political motivations. "If it became necessary to do so, you'd not have the slightest hesitancy or suffer any compunction of conscious[*sic*] in robbing and murdering," he said, and suggested that the defendants read "The God that Failed,"—a book written by disillusioned ex-Communists. At the same time, however, he charged that defendants' "distorted rhetoric about this being a political trial is best described as 'hogwash.'"[12] Rosenberg and Blunk were sentenced to 58 years, on charges that usually carry an average sentence in federal court of 67.3 months, that is, about 5½ years.[13]

THE BATTERING RAM

Any one of these government tactics could seem innocuous. However, in concert in any one prosecution, they profoundly tip the scales against the defendants. Seen as an emerging pattern over a series of cases, they represent real changes in the rights guaranteed the accused.

The prosecutions assure that these defendants are convicted and given long prison sentences. But they have a wider impact as well. The Reagan administration's ideological agenda has included moving the legal system to the right:

abolishing the constitutional protections of the Warren Court and narrowing the conception of due process. The administration has complained about coddling criminals and about judicial activism. It seeks to resurrect an archaic view of the Constitution, and is setting back the clock on women's rights, affirmative action, and economic rights.

Using the court system gives a legitimacy to the Reagan repressive package which purely executive action might not carry. These cases lend themselves to this administration's purpose. With the exception of the Sanctuary case, they are not popular, nor are they accurately reported. This makes them the perfect battering ram for an assault on the justice system that has offered some protection to the accused. It is difficult to organize opposition to anonymous juries and preventive detention when they are used in trials of so-called terrorists. When a group is called "terrorist"—even if it is for a nonlethal bombing of a South African Airways building, as in the case of the Ohio Seven—even civil libertarians are less likely to care that the government is intimidating them through their children. A pattern emerges behind these prosecutions that goes beyond the borders of law enforcement: constitutional erosion, and elaboration of the terrorism scare.

The persistent waving of the terrorism flag covers up a pattern of denial of rights for political prisoners and the criminalization of people fighting for change. The terrorist label is broadly used—not only against people who profess or use violence. In the Hartford case involving a Wells Fargo robbery, those arrested were labeled terrorists with connections to Cuba. The day of the Hartford/Puerto Rico arrests, Attorney General Meese stated "the indictment is a signal to terrorists and their supporters that our response to their cowardly acts will be decisive. The goal of our terrorism program is to eliminate terrorism from our shores." [14]

Terrorism tends to be a status crime: once labeled, it is a status next to impossible to shed. Once the government achieves the isolation and criminalization of part of a movement, the stripping of its rights and the long-term imprisonment of its activists more easily follows. The press, local police forces, and terrorism experts from private think tanks provide the ideological justification for these steps.

The far right continues to pressure the administration for a more aggressive domestic counterterrorism using military methods, including covert action and preemptive strikes. In September 1984, the Heritage Foundation released the report of Samuel T. Francis, aide to the late Senator John East (R–North Carolina), urging the administration to act literally on Secretary of State Schultz's definition of terrorism: "a form of war." Heritage argues, "terrorism is a problem of national security, and not only law enforcement but also military and national security measures and agencies should be used against it." [15]

These prosecutions send a message to those who engage in action to oppose the administration's policies, even peaceful and legal action. Opposition to the inroads on civil liberties in these cases is seen as supporting terrorism. But so is simple opposition to U.S. intervention in Central America or colonialism in Puerto Rico. Recently discovered FBI documents single out organizations such as the Committee in Solidarity with the People of El Salvador (CISPES) as a target in a counterrorism investigation.[16] The effect is not only to make it difficult to support those on trial, but to illegitimize opposition.

This is a typical function of a political criminal trial. It reduces problems to those of law and order and criminalizes left-wing political ideas and action. Keeping the defendants' political justification out of a trial not only makes conviction easier but stigmatizes the movement. In the Sanctuary trial, where there was no doubt about the religious, moral, and political motivation of the defendants, they were precluded from testifying to it because of the court's *in limine* ruling. At the same time, the government was free to tell the jury that the defendants were smugglers, and introduced an informant to claim they did it for money. Whereas in most criminal trials this would have opened the door for defendants to testify as to their motivation, the judge kept it closed. In the New Jersey weapons-possession prosecution of Blunk and Rosenberg, the prosecutor submitted a list of fifty-four forbidden words or phrases: among them "Central America," "Nicaragua," "Reagan's repressive legislative package." A Puerto Rican independentista tried for seditious conspiracy in Chicago was not allowed to present testimony as to the colonial status of Puerto Rico or as to why seditious conspiracy is an "impossible crime" (since, in his view, the United States has no legitimate jurisdiction in Puerto Rico).

The government has convened broadly investigative grand juries in these cases and jailed over a hundred family members, neighbors, and political co-workers for refusing to testify. In the Puerto Rican cases, criminal contempt charges, following as much as three years' incarceration for civil contempt, added three more years to peoples' sentences, merely for refusing to give information. The threat of a subpoena and of possible criminal prosecution for contempt operates as a warning to all associated with the Puerto Rican independence movement that association alone can mean years in jail.

The extensive surveillance and information-gathering chills political activities. Speaking on the phone or in one's own house becomes risky: Children must be insulated from political discussion. The essential trust in one's friends, in political groups, and in the sanctity of the church is breaking down.

The criminalization of politics prevents the growth of a more effective, broader, and more activist left. The repressive strategies against the black liberation and anti-Vietnam War movement were only set in motion fairly late, as the Cold War ideologues belatedly realized the power these movements generated while they were looking for 1950s-style Communists. This made it difficult for the repression to work without being heavy-handed. As repressive responses to popular movements, COINTELPRO was effective but only by the use of assassination, frame-up, and dirty tricks, all of which caused public indignation when later exposed. This administration has learned from the past and is not making the same mistake. By putting these new measures into place at this stage, they will have the statutes and the judicial precedents available for the future if government policy is seriously threatened from the left.

NOTES

1. Some of the tactics we refer to have been used in recent federal as well as state conspiracy prosecutions of antinuclear protesters. We welcome correspondence from readers as to other recent cases where these tactics, or others, have been utilized.

2. For the first time under federal law, defendants may be held without bail because of "the natures and seriousness of the danger to any person or the community that would be posed by their release." See Bail Reform Act of 1984, 18 U.S.C. 3141.

3. See John Riley, "Preventive Detention Use Grows—But Is It Fair?" *New York Law Journal*, March 24, 1986, pp. 1, 32–33.

4. *U.S. v. Melendez-Carrion*, 790 F. 2d 984 (2d Cir. 1986).

5. *U.S. v. Rosado*, 728 F. 2d 89 (2d Cir. 1984).

6. Eric Effron, "Tug of War Toughens on Judicial Picks," *National Law Journal*, March 31, 1986.

7. *New York Times*, September 4, 1985.

8. *San Juan Star*, September 4, 1985.

9. *Ibid.*

10. Three children of two other "Ohio Seven" defendants, Jaan Laamen and Beshard Curzi, were also detained and interrogated following their parents' arrests.

11. *U.S. v. Torres*, 751 F. 2d 875 (7th Cir. 1984).

12. *U.S. v. Rosenberg*, (U.S.D.C. for New Jersey), sentencing transcript, May 20, 1985.

13. U.S. District Court Sentences Imposed Chart for June 1983–June 1984.

14. Quoted in UPI dispatch August 31, 1985.

15. "Dealing with Terrorists: A Better U.S. Policy Is Needed," prepared

300 by Samuel T. Francis for the Heritage Foundation, in *Backgrounder*, No. 382 (Sept. 20, 1984), p. 12.

16. Documents obtained by Movement Support Network—an antirepression project of the Center for Constitutional Rights, which monitors government misconduct—as a result of Freedom of Information Act requests to the FBI on behalf of Central America groups and activists. See also *Boston Globe*, Mar. 26, 1985, morning edition, Ross Gelbspan, "Opponents of U.S. Latin Policy Charge FBI Harassment"; see also *Dallas Morning News*, Apr. 6, 1986, front page, Christi Harlan, "The Informant Left Out in the Cold," about an FBI informant who infiltrated CISPES for several years, 1981–1984; Alfonso Chardi, *Arizona Daily Star*, Nov. 16, 1986, "Reagan Reportedly O.K.'d 50 Covert Acts" documenting a three-year operation on the part of the CIA, FBI, and NSA to monitor the activities of opponents of U.S. Central America policy and the Sanctuary movement.

[Michael McConnell and Renny Golden]

21

THE SANCTUARY MOVEMENT

Pedro, a Salvadoran refugee in sanctuary in New York was a photographer with the Salvadoran Human Rights Commission. This is his testimony:

> On my first day as photographer, the driver showed me where to search for bodies. We came upon a woman lying in the road. Villagers had covered her with cardboard. I took a picture of her face and turned to leave. The driver stopped me saying, "No, that's not how it is done. You have to document the torture." This upset me very much. She had been pregnant. Her stomach was split open. Inside her stomach the fetus had been cut out and in its place was the head of the woman's husband. Several yards away lay the body of her husband. The fetus was placed where the head should have been.
>
> That is what my job was like, day after day. I would have to put bodies together, like pieces of a puzzle. Sometimes I had to pick up the bodies of those whom I had worked with.

The Sanctuary movement was born of moral necessity when the plight of Salvadoran and Guatemalan refugees pouring across our borders confronted the religious community. The spectre of death in their own countries matches their fear of deportation from this one, as they live clandestinely in our cities in order to avoid the U.S. Immigration and Naturalization Services' (INS) mass detention and deportation of Central Americans. Of the half million Salvadorans in the United States, 32,000 have already been deported back to El Salvador where, according to an American Civil Liberties Union study, over 130 deported Salvadorans were found to have disappeared, been tortured, or killed.[1]

The religious community's covenant with the refugees led to the resurrect-

302 ing of the ancient religious tradition of sanctuary—an act currently punishable by five years in prison and a $2,000 fine for every refugee harbored. Congregations make a public declaration of sanctuary and house in their buildings or shelter under their auspices refugees fleeing the political violence of El Salvador or Guatemala. In declaring sanctuary, communities of faith are drawn into an effort to stop a major perpetrator of this suffering—the U.S. government's support of Salvadoran and Guatemalan governments that have killed over 90,000 civilians in the last five years, according to independent human rights reports.

Sanctuary has touched the lives of sisters in Concordia, Kansas, where they house twenty-five Guatemalans at a small retreat center, a working-class church in Ohio, ten university graduate student unions, the prestigious New York Riverside Church, community congregations of farmers in Iowa and synagogues in Arizona and Milwaukee. Twenty-two cities have declared sanctuary, and Governor Tony Anaya declared New Mexico a sanctuary state. The New York State Assembly passed a resolution declaring New York State a sanctuary.

Why did this happen? What was so compelling about the Sanctuary movement that attracted and emboldened so many people, even when it meant confronting U.S. law and risking fine and imprisonment?

EL PUEBLO

For the first time in this century the war victims, the people on the other end of U.S. bombs, artillery fire, and covert actions, were not an anonymous enemy that could be labeled "Vietcong" or "gooks." Instead they were Juan, José, and Albertina, Angelica and Ramon. The carnage of U.S. foreign policy arrived on our shores as living or half-living people.

Some bore the physical scars of torture or the burns from phosphorous bombs. Others could barely whisper of the atrocities they had lived through. There were also the less visible scars—the nightmares, the ache of children lost, the ulcers still not healed, arthritis from the damp ground or the wet border crossing.

They were the survivors, but they spoke for those who had not survived or for those whose survival at that very moment hung in the balance. They came as a remnant of a people making an uncertain exodus into anything but a promised land. They always remembered the people back home, not only friends and relatives but El Pueblo. In Spanish, "pueblo" connotes the poor majority who are struggling to forge a new history, and who are connected not only by blood, race, or culture but by a moral bond. That bond was the first glimpse the North American church had of the depth solidarity had taken in Central America. As refugees told their stories of both horror and resistance, the religious community was to learn more about the meaning of solidarity than it ever expected.

They came seeking refuge, speaking about their lives in Morazan, Guazapa, Chalatenango, Quiché, Huehuetenango, reminding listeners of other places and other times . . . Saigon, My Lai, Kai Sahn, or further back to Dachau and Auschwitz.

The cry of a suffering people was finally making its way north, carried by a refugee community whose presence in the United States placed before the religious community of North America a fundamental faith option: to choose sides. The assassinated Archbishop Romero had said: "Neutrality is impossible; either we support the Salvadoran people or we are accomplices in their death!"

The religious community demonstrated its support by confronting both the U.S. foreign policy responsible for supporting Guatemalan and Salvadoran militarist governments that have been driving the refugees into exodus, and the U.S. government's violation of the Refugee Act of 1980, which guarantees political asylum to any civilian fleeing persecution. Since 1980, only 3 percent of Central American refugees have gained political asylum in the United States out of nearly 30,000 applications. In 1981 and 1982, the United States deported an average of 1000 per month to El Salvador. The United States is the only country in the world that has signed the UN Protocol and still deports refugees to El Salvador and Guatemala. Of approximately 5500 Salvadorans who applied for asylum in 1981, only 2 received it. According to immigration lawyers, Salvadorans have the best case for political asylum possible and the repeated denial of their applications demonstrates the political nature of the government's attitude toward them. Said immigration lawyer Marc Van der Hout: "If they were Russian ballerinas or Romanian tennis players, they would have no problems."[2]

In such a context, sanctuary was born on March 24, 1982, when the Reverend John Fife of Tucson's Southside Presbyterian Church and five East Bay area churches in California declared themselves public sanctuaries for Central American refugees. Within four years, 310 churches, synagogues, and Quaker meetinghouses had declared public sanctuary. An underground railroad, involving 70,000 religious people, was developed to "conduct" the refugees from the border into the heartland and eastern coast of El Norte.

The first arrest of sanctuary workers occurred in February 1984 when workers from Casa Romero, a Texas refugee assistance center, were apprehended by the Border Patrol as they attempted to drive three Salvadoran refugees out of the Rio Grande Valley.

304   A year after these arrests, sixteen Arizona/Mexico workers including two priests, three nuns, and one minister, were indicted on seventy-one counts of conspiring, encouraging, and aiding illegal aliens to enter the United States by shielding, harboring, and transporting them. Forty-nine refugees were arrested and named as "illegal alien unindicted coconspirators," as well as some North Americans, three of whom refused to testify and were placed under house arrest.

Most of the evidence in the indictment was gathered through informers who, wearing bugging devices, had infiltrated church meetings. Sanctuary workers called the surveillance both a threat to civil liberties and unnecessary since the Sanctuary movement has always been open. The government also filed a motion to severely limit the kind of evidence that could be presented in the court. There could be no mention of international law, the Refugee Act of 1980, religious conviction, events in El Salvador or Guatemala, U.S. foreign policy, or stories of the refugees fleeing persecution. The defendants could not even use the word "refugee" in court.

Sister Darlene Nicgorski, who was convicted on five counts, has characterized the government's indictments as an "attempt to silence the truth by silencing refugee witnesses to atrocities. As long as the war in Central America can remain technological, clean, and distant, the reality of the people's suffering does not become real to our U.S. people."

Eight of the eleven sanctuary workers who stood trial were convicted, all receiving suspended sentences.[3] The U.S. government hopes the guilty verdict will effectively telegraph a message across the country that those who continue their involvement with the "underground railroad" will be punished.

The government failed to understand the potential of faith put to fire, finding its heart and voice in a situation not of complex intrigue, as the government claimed, but of startling simplicity and depth. With the arrests the Sanctuary movement moved closer to the persecuted church of Central America where solidarity with outcasts and the subversive poor can cost life itself. Instead of intimidation, Sanctuary was discovering the depth of solidarity and willingness to bear far more licks than the government had calculated. What does the State do to stop the church from discovering its own epiphanal depths, to harness such an unexpected political threat? Historically the powerful are unimaginably predictable. Thus the Sanctuary movement should expect more infiltration, propaganda campaigns, arrests, and imprisonment.

Although the government has not silenced the Sanctuary movement, the discouraging fact remains, however, that a jury who never heard defendant testimony (because the defense rested their case) found these religious workers criminally guilty. But that jury's dilemma may be symptomatic of the nation's malaise, a paralysis before "New Right" strident authority. The jury's legal and moral right to disregard Judge Earl Carroll's final instruction, if they so desired, was not clear to them. Instead, the jury found eight of the eleven guilty, even though some admitted later that they felt the people were morally right in what they had done. The trial, and the Sanctuary movement itself, may be instructive at a critical national moment. It may serve to alert our people that there are other options besides blind obedience, that to muster the courage to go against the popular mood of patriotic militarism and fear of the foreigner/stranger, is to become free, to reclaim our moral authority, and to gift the nation with acts of compassion and justice in a dark moment.

SANCTUARY IN THE CONTEXT OF WAR

It is impossible to understand the Tucson trial without viewing the Sanctuary movement in the context of the war in Central America. For the first two years of the movement the Justice Department refused to move against sanctuary workers. But in 1984 things changed because the movement had become effective at bringing the voices of Central American campesinos to the parish halls and church basements of heartland America.

In 1983, U.S. intervention in Central America took a more intensive form called by U.S. military strategists "low-intensity warfare." Colonel John Waghelstein, former head of U.S. advisors in El Salvador, says: "The term 'counterinsurgency' has been replaced by the less controversial 'low-intensity conflict.' . . . It is total war at the grassroots level."

This military strategy is an undeclared war that is, despite its name, intense, continuous, and deadly. It utilizes the full range of U.S. power at the economic, political, psychological, and military levels that can be escalated and shifted with incredible speed and coordination. Low only refers to the low number of U.S. troops used directly in combat and the low public visibility of this type of warfare. Total war aims at the total or near total control of the affairs of the Central American countries for the benefit of United States interests. It is total war at the grassroots level because there is no aspect of the life of the people of Central America that is not attacked.

TARGET: CIVILIANS

In "total war," civilians are the targets because the opposition forces are too elusive. It is the old counterinsurgency adage that if you cannot catch the fish

306 then you drain the sea. As Americas Watch reported in September 1985: "It is apparent from the testimony of those fleeing Guazapa over the past few years that the civilians and their means of subsistence have been the true targets of the Army in that area." This has meant daily air bombardments of civilians in the countryside.

The killing of civilians and the creation of refugees are the linchpin of total war. The elimination and/or dislocation of the population is seen as crucial to a Salvadoran (and therefore U.S.) military victory. The targeting of civilians and their means of subsistence is, of course, against the Geneva Accords and other international law governing the conduct of war. Once civilians are displaced they are captured by the Salvadoran or Guatemalan army and placed in "strategic hamlets"—guarded villages where the army can control their movements. Once under guard and dependent upon the army, the population is considered "pacified." Pacification, as in Vietnam, is designed to address neither root causes of poverty nor humanitarian emergencies. Rather, the food and medicine are used by the army to control the population and separate them from the opposition forces. The aid is used primarily for a military purpose, not a humanitarian one. U.S. economic aid and some private U.S. aid, notably from right-wing groups, come "wrapped in a counterinsurgency package," as one Salvadoran priest has called it.

Refugees fleeing El Salvador and Guatemala are not victims of random violence, people "caught in the middle" of a bloody war; they are the real targets. The killing and dislocation of the civilian population is the real purpose of the bombing campaigns. The creation of refugees is crucial in the U.S. military strategy. When those refugees happen to make it to the United States they are still targets. The U.S. government does not want them speaking here, telling the story of the bombing. So they are called economic refugees, denied asylum, and deported.

INS AND TOTAL WAR

In 1985, as the total war was moving into high gear, the U.S. government dramatically increased the Border Patrol. The Immigration and Naturalization Service has increased its surveillance of the border using helicopters and adding road blocks and sophisticated sensing devices that can detect people walking in open country. Meanwhile, INS has continued its denial of asylum to from 97 to 99 percent of Guatemalan and El Salvadoran refugees, deporting 3,026 to El Salvador in 1985, according to preliminary INS statistics. Archbishop Rivera y Damas said last November, "The authorities and members of the government of the United States have closed their doors and their hearts against the suffering of my people, unprotected in a foreign land. To return the persecuted to the source, the origin, the cause of their suffering is an act of injustice in the eyes of Christian love." The Immigration and Naturalization Service has become, therefore, the domestic extension of the total war waged against the people of Central America.

In 1986 the Salvadoran Air Force, with U.S. advisors, U.S. bombs, and U.S. surveillance, carried out massive bombings of civilians in the Guazapa Volcano and Chalatenango areas—the heaviest bombings in the history of the Americas. Archbishop Rivera y Damas of El Salvador called upon the military to stop the bombing because those areas were populated by civilians. The bombing continues.

At the same time that Salvadoran campesinos were fleeing from the laser-guided gun sights of U.S.-equipped aircraft, the criminal convictions were handed down against those who dared to stand with the "targets" of U.S. intervention. The U.S. government, surprised and alarmed by the strength of the religious resistance, has reacted with surveillance and repression of civil liberties that has evoked a church/state confrontation.

GOVERNMENT AND RIGHT-WING
OFFENSIVE

The U.S. government attack on the Sanctuary movement is an extension of the attack on the people of Central America. Its aim is to stop the movement's ability to protect refugees and influence public opinion against the administration's policies in Central America. The government has five strategies that it has used and will continue to use, probably with greater intensity in the near future. The five are: (1) indictment and prosecution; (2) harassment; (3) discreditation; (4) false use of terrorism in relation to refugees and those who support them; and (5) government-supported private anti-immigrant groups.

Indictment and prosecution are the most overt attacks, draining money and energy of the movement away from refugees and the protest of U.S. Central American policy and into legal intricacies that will take years to unravel. This attack serves to criminalize religious work and make national law the sole binding authority for human actions.

Harassment entails all the activities designed to intimidate sanctuary workers. The major form of harassment has been break-ins at over a dozen sanctuary churches where no money is taken but files are disturbed and membership lists are left on the desk. The break-ins are reminiscent of the FBI

308 COINTELPRO operations of the sixties and seventies aimed at disrupting progressive movements. Other more overt FBI investigations have occurred. Freedom of Information Act requests from some sanctuaries leave suspicions that there is an informer in the midst of the congregation. Other types of harassment have included threats, surveillance, or implied surveillance. Harassment is designed to fan fears and make the participants in the movement voluntarily limit their actions. So far it has little or no effect on the movement other than emboldening and enraging participants.

Discreditation involves the whole range of slander techniques and redbaiting intended to destroy the character and moral authority of various leaders in the Sanctuary movement. Those leaders that the right wing and government officials are attacking are those who make the connections between what the U.S. government is doing in Central America and the creation of refugees. In other words, those who are prophetic and call upon others to make those connections will be the ones under greatest attack. Reporters are quoting the government as saying that communism has infiltrated the church of Central America and now it is infiltrating the North American church, as well. Some local INS spokespeople have called Sanctuary workers "atheists." The INS charges that some members of the Sanctuary movement are "political" rather than "religious." Charges that those leaders are manipulating the movement sow distrust and are aimed at splitting the movement. It also sends the signal that if people just do charitable work and keep silent about the causes of the refugees' flight they will not be indicted.

False links with terrorism are being made against those crossing the Mexican border, arousing fears and latent racism against Hispanics in general and the Sanctuary movement in particular. This is a "spin-off" of the "terrorism" theme that has been used to discredit Libya and Nicaragua, while justifying violent actions of the United States and its allies. INS and the administration are talking about the "terrorists" coming across our southern borders and the "national security threat" that poses. Paranoia and fear of strangers (xenophobia) are escalating, labeling any dark-skinned person who doesn't speak English as a terrorist. Consider these recent events:

- The Los Angeles County Board of Supervisors pass a resolution asking the president to dispatch troops to the border.
- A suburban Tucson town council practices what they would do in a terrorist attack.
- County Sheriff Alex Perez of Harlingen, Texas, asks for M-16 submachine guns to supplement the Israeli Uzi submachine guns he received last year. "We're on the front lines of the battle, so we have to be well prepared," Perez said.

Government officials are lending support in the creation of anti-immigrant private groups. In Los Angeles, Harold Ezell, the INS western regional com-

missioner, has been instrumental in beginning a private citizens group called
Americans for Border Control. The *Los Angeles Times* said of Ezell, "Ezell has
become the immigration service's most visible figure, leading his agents on
raids . . . and crisscrossing his territory with a single, dark message: The numbers of illegal aliens crossing the border constitute an invasion that is costing
the taxpayers millions of dollars each year and slowly destroying American
society." The brochure for Americans for Border Control warns of the "appalling legacy which will be left our children and grandchildren" without stricter
border control. This overtly racist message has led several Latino community
leaders in Los Angeles to call Ezell's role in the formation of the group inappropriate and divisive. Amin David, president of the Los Amigos, an Orange
county immigrants-rights group, said that Ezell is "promoting fear" through
the use of "xenophobic rhetoric."

In Seattle a similar group, this time called Citizens for Responsible Immigration is trying to get the city council to rescind their declaration of sanctuary.
The INS director, Alan Nelson, visited Seattle recently to "commend" the
group.

ANALYZING GOVERNMENT
REACTION IN THE CONTEXT
OF NEW RIGHT STRATEGY

The arrest of sanctuary workers needs to be understood within the framework
of the Reagan administration's own stated goals in relation to the progressive
church. These goals were put forth in the Sante Fe document. This position
paper was composed by Reagan's Pre-Election Committee. Many of its points
became part of the Republican Party platform and the "Reagan doctrine" in
foreign policy. In part, it stated that:

> U.S. foreign policy must begin to counter (not react against) liberation
> theology as it is utilized in Latin America by the "liberation theology"
> clergy. The role of the church in Latin America is vital to the concept of
> political freedom. Unfortunately, Marxist-Leninist forces have utilized
> the church as a political weapon against private property and productive
> capitalism by infiltrating the religious community with ideas that are less
> Christian than Communist.[4]

The document goes on to state that the United States must use its "security
system" to meet internal and external threats posed from Central America in

310   order to "further our national interests . . . combining our arsenal of weaponry with the manpower of the Americas." Serving as a blueprint for U.S. intervention in the area, the document endorses a program of military training, as well as technological and psychological assistance to these countries. As early as 1980, Reagan's Central American strategy team referred to the Sandinista triumph as terroristic and predicted a subsequent triumph in El Salvador with "Guatemala . . . the strategic prize of Central America, adjoining as it does the vast Mexican oil fields." To prevent all this, a military security system and a propaganda campaign would be created. Thus, the Santa Fe document also proposed that:

> U.S. policy formulation must insulate itself from propaganda appearing in the general and specialized media which is inspired by forces explicitly hostile to the U.S. . . . Coverage of Latin American political reality by the U.S. media is both inadequate and displays a substantial bias favoring proponents of radical socioeconomic transformation of the less developed countries along collectivist lines.[5]

The Sante Fe statement goes on to criticize "radical activists" for lacking a deep enough understanding of the real political and economic situation of these countries, and contriving to feed a "constant stream of misinformation which abuses our friends and glorifies our enemies."[6]

U.S. government strategy in relation to the Sanctuary movement bears an uncomfortable resemblance to the Banzer Plan—named after Colonel Hugo Banzer, who took power and became the president of Bolivia in 1971. The Banzer Plan, predicated as it is on infiltration, destabilizing, and delegitimation of progressive religious movements, is effectively used against the church by the ruling groups in El Salvador and Guatemala today. The following are excerpts from the Banzer Plan:

- Never attack the church as an institution and even less the Bishops as a group. Rather attack the part of the church that is the most progressive.
- Control certain religious orders.
- The CIA has decided to intervene directly in this affair. It has promised to give us information about certain priests (personal documents, studies, friends, addresses, publications, foreign contacts). Arrests should be made in the countryside, on deserted streets late at night. Once a priest has been arrested, the minister should plant subversive material in his briefcase and, if possible, in his room or home and a weapon, preferable a high calibre pistol. Have a story prepared disgracing him before his Bishop and the public.
- By any means of public communication, publish loose, daring, compromising material in order to discredit priests and religious people who represent the progressive element in the church.

- Maintain a friendly relation with some Bishops, with certain members of the church. . . . In such a way we will assure that public opinion does not believe that there is a *systematic persecution of the church but only of a few dissident members*[7] [our emphasis].

Even though U.S. religious culture is pluralistic and shaped by a highly developed first-world society, many of the Banzer Plan strategies can be used by any government wishing to suppress a liberation process while not appearing to persecute the church.

Former CIA analyst David MacMichaels, commenting on the administration's response to the efforts of the religious community to arouse public outcry, said, "The anger that people like you, especially religious people and alternative journalists, arouse in officialdom, you have to see to believe. They totally reject, not only what you have to say if it conflicts with the official view of reality, but they question your motives, even your right to exist."[8]

Another strategy aims at creating splits and/or exploiting different perspectives within the movement. This is accomplished by discrediting one side of a different tendency, or the leaders from a side, so that witch-hunts will appear to be deserved. A group, sector, or individual is dubbed "bad" (fill in—Communist, subversive, radical, not religious) as opposed to the "good" (fill in—mainstream, institutionally grounded, pious, negotiable, naive but sincere, well-intentioned). The State Department, Elliott Abrams's office, and INS have characterized those elements within the Sanctuary movement who align with liberation theology as the "political" element who are not truly "religious."

An attempt to create splits was already made by Abrams on a National Public Radio broadcast. Abrams "understood" why so many religious people are involved in the Sanctuary movement:

> I think that many of the militants, let me put it that way, the militant activists are really just opposing American policy in El Salvador. I think they mislead many churchgoers around the country and others in human rights groups around the country thinking that there is some horrendous 1930's type situation and that if they don't act thousands will die by the end of the week. I've seen some of the material that is handed out by organizers to people in churches. It's horrendously misleading stuff. It's the kind of stuff that would lead any sensible person who read it to jump into the sanctuary movement. But what I would like to say to people involved in the movement is have you gone to see your congressman and senator, have you made it an issue in the re-election campaign, have you exhausted every possible way of addressing this issue in a democratic country before you take the law into your own hands? Because I think

the answer is that they sure haven't. This is just a matter of casual law breaking.[9]

Abrams is correct in stating that the Sanctuary movement has understood their support of refugees to be an inevitable political act. In spite of attempts at intimidating religious people by labeling their motivations as political and not religious, the ploy has not been successful. Chicago Sanctuary worker Mary Ann Corley spoke directly to both the government's efforts to divide and the internal debate within the movement.

> Liberation without charity is only a power struggle. Charity without liberation is only self-serving peitism. But when charity is truly effective it acts to stop the deprivation of charity, entering a struggle for liberation. When we quote Matthew 25 claiming before courts our moral duty to feed the hungry, clothe the naked, shelter the homeless, will we risk challenging the root causes of people's hunger, nakedness, and homelessness? Will we name that cause (for example, U.S. foreign policy) and act to change it even if in so doing we do not fit the government's definition of religious? If not, our "charity" will remain unbiblical, ahistorical pietism aimed at ministering to timeless refugees who are without concrete historical, political, moral claims on our lives.

POSSIBLE GOVERNMENT RESPONSE

If the government calculates that current penalties are not stiff enough to deter resistance, one obvious tactic would be to levy heavier sentences, a tactic currently in use against peace activists involved in direct actions aimed at dysfunctioning production or use of nuclear weaponry (e.g., Ploughshares I and II). But the last and most ominous government weapon that could be aimed at the Sanctuary movement would be to call for a federal grand jury. FBI operatives would thus be offered a legal excuse for investigations based on their need to serve subpoenas to potential grand jury defendants. This tactic was used against domestic resistance groups during the Vietnam era.

Historically, grand juries were used by our ancestors to protect the accused from government intimidation. But now they are used as a form of inquisitional intimidation against the accused and in support of government power. If a special grand jury is called the government will have a net capable of sweeping in prey. (It doesn't matter that the Sanctuary movement's actions have always been public.) Such grand jury probes become fishing expeditions to gather in anyone tangentially connected with a movement. The intent of such expeditions is much less fact-finding than it is intimidation and disruption. Since an aura of illegitimacy and betrayal is created when anyone agrees to testify before a grand jury, investigations of this sort represent an insidious attempt, under the guise of "justice," to create informers.

The governing board of the National Council of Churches adopted a resolution on grand jury abuse which said in part:

> It is the governing board's conviction [that] the use of the grand jury's powers as an instrument of investigative support of law enforcement, rather than as an evaluator . . . of evidence already gathered is a distortion of its already quasi-judicial function. The use of the grand jury's powers to harass and pursue political dissidents is a departure from its proper constitutional function and is a great threat to public order, lawful governments and true domestic security.[10]

Congress has never given the FBI subpoena powers, yet agents today routinely threaten uncooperative persons with subpoenas from a grand jury, and often indeed serve such subpoenas upon them.

In spite of the National Council of Churches' denunciation of the use of grand juries for the purpose of political repression, there is no assurance they will not be used against the Sanctuary movement. In refusing to cooperate in such a probe, members of the Sanctuary movement would sustain moral leadership, and faithfulness to a God, not of law but of people, especially the disenfranchised. The cost of this discipleship, however, would be high, both personally and collectively.

CONCLUSION

The fact that communities of religious people did reach across race and class barriers to accept into sanctuary indigenous campesinos, is significant, especially since it was not primarily an act of charity but one of protest. At root, what the congregations defied was not one immigration law, but a whole pattern of exploitation based on race and class, that the United States began in 1823 with the Monroe Doctrine and upheld through thirty-six invasions of Latin America in the last eighty-five years. That is why this movement appears so dangerous to the government and enlivening to the religious community. It might even be called a revival, an awakening in the life of the interfaith community that has given new historical commitment to the faith and new credi-

314 bility to religion, even to those who had long been skeptical of the "church." Whether this points to a new era of faithfulness, mirroring the grass-roots resurgence of the church in Latin America, will depend upon how far the movement takes this beginning act of solidarity and how willing it is to wield its faith against the Goliath of national security.

NOTES

1. *New York Times*, January 19, 1985.

2. Gary MacEoin and Nivita Riley, *No Promised Land: American Refugee Policy and the Rule of Law* (Boston: Oxfam, 1982), p. 41.

3. The certainty of their deportation was confirmed as 1984 immigration statistics were released. In 1984, the U.S. government only approved .4 percent of political asylum applications from Guatemalans. That was the same year that Amnesty International called the Guatemalan government one of the worst violators of human rights in the world. For Salvadorans the United States refused 97.5 percent of the applications for political asylum during 1984.

4. Committee of Sante Fe, "A New Inter-American Policy for the Eighties" (Washington: Council for Inter American Security, 1980).

5. *Ibid.*, Sante Fe Committee.

6. *Ibid.*

7. William O'Malley, *The Voice of Blood* (New York: Orbis, 1980), p. 46.

8. David MacMichaels, "Calling the Bluff," *Crucible of Hope* (Washington: Sojourners, Fall 1984), p. 43.

9. Elliott Abrams, "All Things Considered," National Public Radio, April 19, 1984.

10. Richard Gillett, "Jailing Grand Jury Resisters: Implications for Church Activists," *The Christian Century* (September 26, 1984).

[Jamie Kalven]

22

THE REAGAN ADMINISTRATION

AND THE FEDERAL JUDICIARY

President Reagan's most enduring legacy may well prove to be his impact on the federal courts and hence on the future course of constitutional law. He has made three appointments to the Supreme Court—Sandra Day O'Connor, Antonin Scalia and Anthony Kennedy—and has elevated Justice William Rehnquist to the chief justiceship. Yet this is only the most visible dimension of a larger phenomenon. By the end of his second term he is expected to have appointed *the majority* of the federal judges in active service. Never before has a president appointed so many judges. Never before have the criteria of selection been so narrowly ideological. And never before have those criteria been applied in so disciplined and unrelenting a fashion.

Administration spokesmen argue that the president is simply doing what others before him have done. All presidents, so the argument runs, have sought to select ideologically compatible judicial nominees. This argument has some force. There is indeed a sense in which Reagan is doing what others have done. Only more so. And the difference in degree amounts to a qualitative difference. In the past, the judicial selection process had the saving grace of messiness. A multiplicity of interests and values played through it and ensured

This essay is a revised and combined version of two essays that originally appeared in *The Nation*: "Robert Bork and the Constitution," October 1, 1983, pp. 262–268, and "Round Two For Judge Bork," June 16, 1984, pp. 731–734. Reprinted by permission of the author and the publishers. Judge Bork's reply to Kalven, which is quoted in this essay, was originally published in the February 1984 issue of the *A.B.A. Journal*. Bork's reply is reprinted with permission from the *A.B.A. Journal*, "The Lawyer's Magazine."

316 a certain mix in the pool of judges appointed. The Reagan selection process, by contrast, is unprecedented in its unwavering clarity of purpose, its narrowly ideological criteria, and its single-minded diligence.

Some of President Reagan's early appointments disarmed criticism. Those selected were distinguished not only by their right-wing views but also by their intellectual credentials—men like Scalia and Richard Posner of the University of Chicago Law School, Robert Bork and Ralph Winter of the Yale Law School. Over time, however, as the number of appointments has mounted, the quality of the appointees—as assessed by generally accepted standards of the profession—has declined sharply. It seems that the pool of those at once sufficiently reactionary and unimpeachably qualified is small. The administration will gladly appoint a competent ideologue, if one can be found, but forced to choose between competence and ideological purity, will opt for the latter. Again and again it has jettisoned other values—even minimal competence— in pursuit of its goal of a federal judiciary dominated by judges committed to the Reagan constitutional agenda.

What is that agenda? The president and Attorney General Meese have not been shy about spelling out particulars: Do away with various procedural protections for criminal defendants—above all, *Miranda v. Arizona,* the decision holding that police must inform suspects of their rights to remain silent and to have a lawyer present during questioning; overrule *Roe v. Wade,* the abortion decision; eliminate affirmative action; relax standards with respect to race and sex discrimination; ease the separation between church and state; and reduce the access of citizens to the courts to challenge government action.

Beyond such particulars, the attorney general in a series of public statements has promoted a blueprint for overhauling the foundations of our constitutional system. In the name of fidelity to "the original intentions" of the framers, he has advocated canons of interpretation so crabbed and narrow they would largely empty the Constitution of enforceable meaning. He has challenged the doctrine of "incorporation" under which certain constitutional guarantees— such as the First Amendment—are applied to the states as well as to the federal government. And he has restated a truism—that the supreme law of the land is the Constitution, not the Supreme Court's interpretations of it—in such a way as to leave the impression he was inviting officials and citizens to defy decisions with which they disagree.

Taken together, the statements of the president, the attorney general and other administration spokesmen evoke a vision of a constitutional order in which government power would be largely unrestrained. This is a radical vision. Yet, ironically, its advocates enjoy a rhetorical advantage: Their radical program is cast in the idiom of conservatism; their activism, in the idiom of restraint. Their position can be stated simply. It is clear and coherent. It has the ring of common sense: The Constitution means what those who wrote it intended it to mean; the role of judges is limited to enforcing that meaning; **317** if they go beyond that role, they usurp the legislative function and write their own personal preferences into law. The counterargument cannot be put so cleanly; nor can it easily be pitched at the level of generality congenial to the mass media. Debate must be joined at the level of specific issues and concrete historical experience.

That is precisely what happened in the course of the great controversy provoked by President Reagan's nomination of Judge Robert Bork to the Supreme Court. The Bork nomination became the focus of sustained public debate over the merits of the Reagan-Meese constitutional vision. And the emphatic rejection of the nomination must be seen, in part, as a repudiation of that vision.

We thus stand at a fascinating juncture. Measured by the number of judges named, the administration's effort to effect a constitutional counter-revolution by means of the appointment power is far advanced. Yet the Bork episode demonstrates the depth of resistance—in the legal profession, the academy, and the public—to the substance of the Reagan-Meese constitutional agenda. The interplay between these tendencies is likely to determine the course of constitutional law in coming years.

I wrote the following study of Judge Bork's First Amendment views several years before he was nominated to the Supreme Court. It was published as two separate articles; the second was occasioned by his response to the first. Its original function—to raise the alarm about Bork—has, needless to say, been rendered obsolete by events. Yet it is, I hope, of more than purely historical interest. Read today, after the avalanche of debate and commentary loosed by the Bork episode, this isolated exchange between a judge and one of his critics may help make clear what all the fuss was about.

ROBERT BORK AND THE CONSTITUTION

I

A new struggle for intellectual dominance in constitutional theory is under way at this moment. The struggle is about the duty of judges with respect to the Constitution. It is taking place out of public sight, in a sense, because it is carried on almost entirely in the law schools and in the law reviews. But that doesn't mean it won't affect our entire polity in the years ahead. The ideas that win hegemony there will govern the profession, including judges, for at least a generation and perhaps more.

—Judge Robert Bork
National Review
September 17, 1982

318   The struggle to which Judge Bork refers is the latest chapter in the perennial American debate over the place of judicial review in a democratic polity. That debate is, at bottom, a dispute over the role of constitutional values in American life, and it is now at a critical juncture. It is possible that the ideas of Robert Bork—and a small group of like-minded legal theorists—will soon achieve dominance in constitutional law.

This is not because of any impending triumph in the intellectual sphere but rather because President Reagan has elevated a number of the most forceful of those theorists—men who combine, in unnerving degree, reactionary views and professional competence—to the federal bench. There is every reason to expect that, given the opportunity, he will follow the same course in making appointments to the Supreme Court, thereby determining the shape of the Court for the rest of the century.

Prediction in these matters is, of course, tricky, but several things are clear. Three of the nine members of the Court are 75 years of age or older. The justices farthest to the right are also the youngest. In view of the present alignments on the Court, even a single appointment could have great impact; depending on whom he or she replaces, the next appointee may represent the decisive vote on a wide range of issues. Two or three vacancies—and at least that many can be expected during the remainder of the Reagan presidency—could produce a solid right-wing majority of justices with the skill, the energy, and the unified vision to remake constitutional law.

Robert Bork is the most prominent of the legal scholars Reagan has named to the federal appeals court. And his name has long been rumored to be at the top of the list of candidates for the next Supreme Court vacancy. It is hard to imagine how Reagan could, for his purposes, do better. Bork is best known outside legal circles as the man who executed President Nixon's order to fire Watergate special prosecutor Archibald Cox, but apart from that blemish, his professional credentials are impeccable: Yale law professor, solicitor general in the Nixon and Ford administrations, judge on the United States Court of Appeals for the District of Columbia Circuit. And he is more than just a reliable conservative vote. He is an intellectual force, a formidable and uncompromising advocate of an approach to constitutional interpretation that would severely restrict the role of the federal judiciary—and of constitutional values —in our public life.

The fullest expression of Bork's philosophy is a 1971 article in the *Indiana Law Journal*, "Neutral Principles and Some First Amendment Problems," in which he sets forth his general approach and then, by way of illustration, applies it to the First Amendment. The result is one of the most restrictive theories of freedom of speech ever advanced. After sketching his stance on constitutional interpretation, I want to consider his First Amendment analysis in some detail, for it is at the level of concrete application that one can most **319** clearly see what is at stake in the debate over constitutional theory.

Bork's point of departure is the familiar conservative complaint that the federal judiciary has exceeded its legitimate authority within our democratic system. His argument goes like this:

The federal courts—above all, the Supreme Court—have usurped the legislative function. In the guise of interpreting broad constitutional language, judges have substituted their personal preferences for those of the majority as expressed in law. If such "judicial imperialism" is to be curbed, we must insist that judges decide constitutional cases in accordance with "neutral principles." Those principles must be neutral not only in the sense of being defined in general terms and applied evenhandedly; they must also be neutral *in derivation*— that is, they must reflect the intentions of the framers of the Constitution insofar as those intentions can be inferred from the text, the history of its adoption, and "their fair implications." There is no place in constitutional adjudication for value judgments by the Court; its proper role, its only role, is to implement the value judgments of the Constitution's framers. When the Court strikes down legislation on any other basis, it abuses its power and invades the domain of democratic choice.

In other words, where the text and the historical record do not unambiguously yield the meaning of a constitutional provision—and this will be true in varying degrees of all but the most specific provisions—the articulation of constitutional values is beyond the competence of the courts. The Constitution speaks of broad values like equality and liberty, but judges who attempt to give concrete meaning to such general concepts without clear and specific guidance from the text or history overstep their proper role: "There is no principled way in which anyone can define the spheres in which liberty is required and the spheres in which equality is required. These are matters of morality, of judgment, of prudence. They belong, therefore, to the political community."

Bork's point is not simply that the farther judges move from the text, the greater the risk of error becomes. It is that they will inevitably err, will inevitably impose their own values: "Where constitutional materials do not clearly specify the value to be preferred, *there is no principled way to prefer any claimed human value to any other*" [emphasis added].

Here we touch upon the source of the hard-edged clarity of Bork's vision, the source of both its rhetorical power and its essential poverty—a moral skepticism so profound that it renders weightless everything in the Constitution that is not specifically nailed down. Bork rejects the possibility of moral knowledge; for him, all questions of value reduce down to matters of preference. That is the premise on which his approach to constitutional adjudication—and, presumably, to all moral and political questions—rests. Viewed

320 through this prism, the only legitimate source of constitutional meaning is the framers' intentions; any other line of inquiry into the meaning of a constitutional value can yield only an expression of the judge's personal preferences.

In short, in Bork's view, constitutional values have no independent reality apart from what can be gleaned from the text and the historical record, and they make no claims upon us. In a passing gibe at the Equal Protection Clause —the textual basis of the egalitarian legacy of the Warren Court and a primary target of his argument—he offers what he calls the "Equal Gratification Clause," the principle that where the Constitution does not provide specific direction, there is no way "to decide that one man's gratifications are more deserving of respect than another's or that one form of gratification is more worthy than another." In other words, some like equality, some like pistachio ice cream, and there is no principled way to distinguish between these "gratifications."

If one grants Bork's central premise, if one shares the nihilism that informs his approach, then his severe conclusions follow. If, however, one believes in the possibility of moral knowledge, if one believes that our understanding of constitutional values can be deepened by experience and advanced by moral inquiry, then one must reject his stance as profoundly illogical and intolerably wasteful. For it is precisely the most central constitutional values that, by virtue of their generality and scope, are rendered unsuitable for judicial enforcement and so are surrendered to the will of the majority. The net result of his argument is to convert broad public values into matters of private taste.

This perverse constitutional alchemy can be observed when Bork turns to the First Amendment. It becomes clear that what animates his approach is not his stated concern with "neutral principles" but his underlying moral skepticism. And its impact is devastating. In a world in which everything is a matter of taste, the only way he can see to practice fidelity to a constitutional provision—the only way he can see to guard it against misinterpretation—is to empty it of meaning.

Contemporary First Amendment doctrine—even its most ardent aficionados would concede—is messy. It is various and complex; it defies succinct summary. Bork's thesis, by contrast, is the soul of simplicity and clarity:

> Constitutional protection should be accorded only to speech that is explicitly political. There is no basis for judicial intervention to protect any other form of expression, be it scientific, literary or that variety of expression we call obscene or pornographic. Moreover, within that category of speech we ordinarily call political, there should be no constitutional obstruction to laws making criminal any speech that advocates forcible overthrow of the government or the violation of any law.

One must pause to absorb the full import of those confident words. We **321** are accustomed to thinking of First Amendment protection as a general rule subject to a few limited exceptions. But Bork asserts that government power to regulate expression should be the general rule, and constitutional protection the exception. Consider all that he would banish from the domain of the First Amendment: art, science, philosophy, literature—all expression, all communication between human beings, that is not "explicitly political." And within that category he would deny protection to the advocacy of revolution and the violation of any law. In other words, the only speech courts may protect is that which is explicitly political in character and not too radical in its conclusions.

Bork arrives at this pinched and ungenerous reading of the First Amendment by way of a brisk exercise in the "neutral derivation" of constitutional meaning: Although neither the text of the amendment nor the history of its adoption provides much guidance as to its meaning, the governmental structure established by the Constitution does. Representative democracy is "a form of government that is meaningless without open and vigorous debate about officials and their policies." Hence "even if there were no first amendment," freedom for "explicitly political" speech "could and should be inferred." And despite the fact that there *is* a First Amendment, no more can properly be inferred. The sole end served by the amendment, he argues, quoting a famous opinion of Justice Louis Brandeis, is the "discovery and spread of political truth."

Few would dispute the proposition that the First Amendment protects political speech, but does that exhaust its meaning? Are there no other constitutional rationales for freedom of speech besides facilitating the democratic process? Bork insists there are not. The rationale for constitutional protection, he argues, must be *unique* to speech; otherwise, there is no neutral basis on which to protect speech but not to protect the various forms of conduct that serve the same ends. It follows that benefits often attributed to free speech—such as "the development of the faculties of the individual" and "the happiness to be derived from engaging in the activity"—do not provide acceptable rationales for First Amendment protection: "An individual may develop his faculties or derive pleasure from trading on the stock market, following his profession as a river port pilot, working as a barmaid, engaging in sexual activity, playing tennis, rigging prices or in any of thousands of other endeavors." Thus, a judge "cannot, on neutral grounds, choose to protect speech that has only these functions more than he protects any other claimed freedom."

This is sophistry. The fact that playing tennis and reading Shakespeare, rigging prices and writing a poem, all contribute to personal happiness and self-development does not mean that there is no constitutional basis for distinguishing between them. Indeed, the framers of the First Amendment made such a distinction when they explicitly and without qualification provided constitutional protection for *speech* as distinct from conduct. Such protection has traditionally been understood to reflect a perception that, while speech may serve the same ends as various forms of conduct, it does so without generating the adverse effects that may attend other activities, and further that it is especially vulnerable to unwarranted suppression and hence in need of special protection.

Perhaps the First Amendment *should* be limited to speech that contributes to the political process, but it is hardly a sufficient argument for that proposition simply to reject other rationales for protection on the ground that they do not satisfy the artificial requirement that the ends served by the First Amendment be unique to speech. This requirement is little more than a logical trick. And one might well ask whether even the speech Bork would protect can really be said to satisfy it: Do not various forms of conduct convey political messages and thereby serve the same ends as political speech?

In any case, it is not necessary to assert other rationales for First Amendment protection in order to challenge Bork's theory. It can be criticized on its own terms. Indeed, the really startling thing about the theory is how poorly it serves the sole function he ascribes to the First Amendment: protection of speech that contributes to the democratic process. In this respect, the theory confounds indignation. It is hard to know whether to be more disturbed by all that he is prepared to sacrifice in the name of democracy or by his insensitivity to the requirements of democracy. Perhaps both reactions amount to much the same thing. For his conception of democracy is dictated by his moral skepticism and is untouched by any other values or aspirations. It is a vision not of vigorous self-government but of blunt majoritarianism as the appropriate institutional response to a world in which all is preference.

As conceived by Bork, the great public debate under the First Amendment is a gray, impoverished affair. His theory would produce a bizarre divorce of political discourse from its social and cultural foundations. Many—perhaps most—political issues cannot be discussed fully and intelligently without drawing on other bodies of thought. The artistic, literary, and scientific speech Bork would exclude from First Amendment protection is often integral to the debate over a public issue. Moreover, works of an artistic, literary, or scientific character may inform our understanding of political matters and deepen the judgment we bring to our responsibilities as citizens.

It is instructive to contrast Bork's theory with that of Alexander Meiklejohn, the great proponent of the principle that the First Amendment is intended to serve the ideal of self-government. There is an obvious kinship between their theories. Both derive the meaning of the First Amendment from its relationship to democratic government; both distinguish between speech that is concerned with public matters and speech that is not. Yet they reach widely divergent conclusions as to the scope of the First Amendment.

When Meiklejohn first articulated his theory in the late 1940s, it appeared that his category of "public"—and hence protected—speech was almost as narrow as Bork's category of "explicitly political" speech. But in response to criticism that his theory left much speech of undeniable public value unprotected, he ultimately broadened the category of protected speech to include not only public discussion of public issues but also education, philosophy, science, literature, and art. The people "need novels and dramas and paintings and poems," he wrote, "because they will be called on to vote." That concession may, as some have argued, have damaged the coherence of Meiklejohn's theory. It also testified to his good sense.

Bork, by contrast, stands his ground. While acknowledging that "the publication of a novel like *Ulysses*" may contribute to the formation of "attitudes that ultimately affect politics," he insists that there is no neutral basis under the First Amendment for a judge to distinguish between censorship of the novel and "regulations of economic activity, control of entry into a trade, laws about sexual behavior, marriage and the like," for those activities too may contribute to the formation of political attitudes.

The upshot is that under his theory, speech that serves the function he ascribes to the First Amendment—speech that is political, albeit implicitly or indirectly—would be denied protection. Such speech may shape our perceptions of the world, of human nature, of political arrangements; it may touch our politics at the deepest level. Yet Bork would cede it to the domain of the censor in order to guard against the threat to democracy posed by allowing judges the latitude to distinguish under the First Amendment between, say, the suppression of *King Lear* and a restriction on the sale of underwater real estate.

At this juncture we can see one of the major ways in which Bork's philosophy affects his approach in practice. Confronted by the need to define the scope of constitutionally protected activity—by the need to draw lines—he is compelled by his moral skepticism to do so in terms so narrow that they amount to a surrender of the particular activity to the will of the majority. Thus he can agree that a novel like *Ulysses* advances the ends of the First Amendment, but his moral skepticism prevents him from drawing a line that would protect it—a problem he resolves by excluding all literature from protection. This strange dynamic reaches its climax with his argument that advocacy of the violent overthrow of the government or of the violation of any law should be categorically excluded from First Amendment protection. Here, the speech he surrenders to censorship is not merely valuable within the terms of his theory; it is essential.

324   The keynote of his argument is a perverse misreading of the phrase he borrowed from Brandeis to describe the end served by the First Amendment: the "discovery and spread of political truth." He turns classic free-speech rhetoric inside out and defines "political truth" as "what the majority thinks it is at any given moment." "It has no unchanging content," he writes, "but refers to the temporary outcomes of the democratic process. Political truth is what the majority decides it wants today." It follows that advocacy of forcible overthrow of the government—speech that calls for a minority to seize control of the state —"is not political speech because it violates constitutional truths about process and because it is not aimed at a new definition of political truth by a legislative majority." Hence there is no constitutional basis for judicial intervention to protect it. Similarly, advocacy of law violation falls outside the protection of the First Amendment because it is "a call to set aside the results that political speech has produced."

Two basic issues are implicated in this tidy logical exercise. The first is posed by civil disobedience. Typically, the advocacy of this form of law violation is an *appeal* to democratic processes, not a rejection of them. Bork does not address—or even acknowledge—the problems this creates for his argument. Under his theory, would a speech by Martin Luther King, Jr., advocating sit-ins at segregated facilities have been denied the protection of the First Amendment? I am not sure that this is an intended implication of the theory, but there is nothing in the *Indiana Law Journal* article that bars such a reading.

Civil disobedience aside, the primary issue is posed by the advocacy of political doctrines that call for the use of violence and lawlessness as political tactics. This has been the central issue of political speech in the American experience. It has elicited some of the most profound judicial reflections on the meaning of freedom of speech, and it has occasioned a series of cases, from World War I to the present, that provide rich material for understanding the dynamics of dissent in a free society.

Bork largely ignores that body of experience and analysis. Sweeping aside a half-century of doctrinal development, he argues that the law in this area should be built on two decisions of the 1920s—*Gitlow* v. *New York* and *Whitney* v. *California*—in which the Supreme Court upheld convictions for speech that in general terms and without evident effect advocated revolutionary action. Today these decisions are remembered chiefly because they prompted an eloquent dissenting opinion (*Gitlow*) and a concurrence in the spirit of dissent (*Whitney*) by Justices Holmes and Brandeis on behalf of the proposition that speech may be constitutionally suppressed only if it produces "a clear and present danger" of law violation.

It is from those opinions rather than from the majority opinions that the law in this area has grown. Bork acknowledges their power. Holmes and Brandeis were, he writes, "rhetoricians of extraordinary potency, and their rhetoric retains the power, almost half a century later, to swamp analysis, to persuade, almost to command assent." He does not, however, submit to that power. Had he sat on the Court in the 1920s, he would have joined the majority in holding that it is constitutional for a state to outlaw the advocacy of violent overthrow, no matter how general and remote from action such advocacy might be. Crisply dismissing the development of First Amendment doctrine since *Gitlow* and *Whitney,* he asserts that the majority opinions in those cases have never been "discredited, or even met, on intellectual grounds." Intended to provoke, these words have their desired effect. Why, indeed, should we protect the advocacy of force and the violation of law?

The answer rests on a premise Bork claims to share, namely that "no society in which seditious libel, the criticism of public officials, is a crime can call itself free and democratic." This principle has not always been securely anchored in American law; through much of our history the constitutional status of seditious libel was unsettled. It was only in 1964, in *New York Times* v. *Sullivan,* that the Supreme Court unequivocally declared that the abrasive criticism of government that in other times and places has been punished as seditious libel could not in America be made a crime. This follows, Justice William Brennan wrote for the unanimous Court, from "a profound national commitment to the principle that debate on public issues should be uninhibited, robust, and wide-open."

Bork writes in similar, if less eloquent, terms. Indeed, he places this principle at the center of his theory. Yet he refuses to acknowledge its implications for the issue of subversive advocacy. He flatly declares such advocacy to be of "no political value within a republican system of government," as though the withdrawal of constitutional protection from this category of speech would have no implications for the speech that, by his own account, is essential to democracy: criticism of government officials and policies. But subversive advocacy does not take place in a vacuum; it occurs in a political context and is invariably part of a larger political critique. Thus, to draw the line beyond which such advocacy becomes criminal is also to determine the limits of permissible criticism of government. My father, Harry Kalven, Jr., a legal scholar who wrote widely about the First Amendment, once framed the issue this way:

> If a man is seriously enough at odds with the society to advocate violent overthrow, his speech has utility not because advocating violence is useful but because the premises underlying his call to action should be heard. He says something more than "Revolt! Revolt!" He advances premises in support of that conclusion. And those premises are worth

protecting, for they are likely to incorporate serious and radical criticism of the society and the government. . . . [T]here is a fundamental tension between the principle that seditious libel cannot be proscribed by law and the common sense of stopping free speech at the boundary of incitement to crime. The accommodation between these two notions is perhaps the central issue for the American tradition of free speech.

By categorically excluding subversive advocacy from constitutional protection, Bork denies the existence of this problem—or, at any rate, denies that it falls within the province of the courts. His position is that such speech is somehow rendered unworthy of protection by the speaker's hostility toward democracy. But he never explains why this should override our need as self-governing citizens to hear the speaker's criticisms and to consider his or her arguments. Thus again, Bork's theory, while invoking the democratic ideal, promotes a stunted view of the responsibilities and requirements of citizenship in a democracy.

The prevailing approach to subversive advocacy, which grows out of the Holmes-Brandeis dissents, has sought to reach an accommodation between the necessity of protecting radical criticism of the government and the claims of public order by drawing the constitutional line at the point at which advocacy merges with criminal action—the point beyond which the remedy of counter-speech is no longer available. The current standard, articulated in *Brandenburg* v. *Ohio* in 1969, is that the government may forbid the advocacy of force and lawlessness only "where such advocacy is directed to inciting or producing imminent lawless action and is likely to incite or produce such action."

The importance of this stringent standard resides not only in the protection it affords the most radical speech but also in the "breathing space" it provides for criticism of the government that stops well short of the line. Without such a secure margin, many potential critics would be silenced by fear and uncertainty. By drawing the boundaries of permissible advocacy at the last possible moment and with the greatest possible clarity, the Court has sought to ensure a spacious forum for vigorous debate about public issues.

In Bork's view, by contrast, it is the *government* that needs breathing space: It may constitutionally claim the power to silence the least whisper of sedition. That is the meaning of a passage from the majority opinion in *Gitlow,* which he quotes and endorses without qualification:

A single revolutionary spark may kindle a fire that, smoldering for a time, may burst into a sweeping and destructive conflagration. It cannot be said that the state is acting arbitrarily or unreasonably when in the exercise of its judgment as to the measures necessary to protect the public peace and safety, it seeks to extinguish the spark without waiting until it has enkindled the flame or blazed into conflagration. . . . It may, in the exercise of its judgment, suppress the threatened danger in its incipiency.

Note the fragility of the political system evoked by that imagery. Surely a system so delicate cannot tolerate much free speech. Note too the boundless logic that supports the suppression of threats of disorder in their "incipiency." If the political order is so vulnerable that all subversive advocacy must be prohibited, no matter how general and remote from action, no matter how deeply embedded in serious political criticism, then surely it is only prudent to take the next step and curtail abrasive criticism of the government that is not joined to explicit advocacy. After all, such speech is likely to breed disrespect and contempt, which may in turn lead to acts of resistance and lawlessness. And so on. . . . Thus it is that in times of tension governments, if unrestrained, tend to read the threat of disorder and subversion into virtually all challenging criticism.

The constitutional standard set forth in *Brandenburg* is intended to restrain that tendency. But Bork insists that any such standard is "improper" because "it erects a barrier to legislative rule where none should exist." The irony here, the ultimate absurdity of his argument, is that he sees an intolerable threat to democracy if judges are allowed to set standards to protect the speech he calls essential to democracy—criticism of government—but he apparently sees no danger to democracy if the task of defining the limits of tolerance for such criticism is left to the government officials criticized.

This then is where his theory comes to rest. Having radically reduced the scope of the First Amendment on the ground that it protects only explicitly political speech, he greatly restricts the ability of judges to intervene on behalf of the speech that nominally remains within its protection. His singular achievement is to have fashioned a theory of freedom of speech under which most of the speech men have historically been moved to suppress would be left exposed to the will of the majority. His argument completed, the First Amendment stands all but empty: a principle—a neutral principle—which would not be offended if the clamor of "uninhibited, robust, and wide-open" public debate about the myriad things that matter to human beings was drowned out, in Brandeis's grim phrase, by "silence coerced by law."

Bork closes the article in which he presents his blueprint for overhauling First Amendment doctrine by characterizing his arguments as "tentative and exploratory." Dare we hope that Judge—and perhaps Justice—Bork will disavow the ideas advanced by Professor Bork? Is there a chance that he will prove susceptible to what my father used to call the "charisma" of the First Amendment—its power to recruit patient inquiry and generous interpretation from the judges charged with its protection?

Perhaps. But I doubt it. Bork's views on the First Amendment are an ex-

328 pression of a general stance toward constitutional adjudication that is anything but "tentative and exploratory," and that his every utterance about constitutional theory reaffirms. This stance is cast in the attractive idiom of neutral principles, but as I have tried to show, it is animated by a moral skepticism which is deeply alien to the way most Americans, including many conservatives, think about law, justice, and the Constitution. Having seen the impact his approach would have on the First Amendment tradition, a relatively settled area of constitutional law, it is not hard to imagine how it would affect more controversial and fragile constitutional traditions. For as Bork's First Amendment analysis shows, his deafness to the moral resonance of constitutional values leads inexorably to the triumph of majoritarianism over all else. It debases—trivializes—the Constitution. And it is a threat to our most basic freedoms.

II

Last fall in these pages I examined the constitutional philosophy of Robert H. Bork, a judge on the U.S. Court of Appeals for the District of Columbia. I took as my text a 1971 law review article in which Judge Bork—at the time a professor at Yale Law School—set forth his general approach to constitutional interpretation and then applied it to the First Amendment. He did not respond directly, but when an item about my article appeared in the December issue of the *American Bar Association Journal*, his response was swift and sharp. Apparently he was prepared to leave the readers of *The Nation* in a fog of uncorrected error about his views, but not the 340,000 lawyers who receive the *A.B.A. Journal*.

The offending item, titled "Here Comes Attila the Hun of the Constitution," appeared in a column called "Browser," which presents short, chatty summaries of recent articles thought to be of interest to the bar. Judge Bork's reply, in the February issue [reprinted here with the *A.B.A. Journal*'s permission], began:

> It is unfortunate that the Browser department . . . should choose to summarize my constitutional philosophy as presented in the *Nation* (not the *New Republic* as you suppose.★ There is a difference.). The *Nation* piece, by Jamie Kalven, in turn purports to state my views entirely on the basis of a 13-year-old article. It is one thing for a column to digest articles from other publications in which a writer states his views. It is quite another to repeat, without checking, what another writer reports to be the views

★ The *A.B.A. Journal* had cited *The New Republic* rather than *The Nation*.

of a third person. The Browser piece commits that journalistic sin and then compounds it by adding its own Attila-the-Hun characterization to what Mr. Kalven actually wrote. Perhaps your writer thinks the matter humorous, but a number of readers are likely to suppose that reporting contained in the official publication of the American Bar Association would be accurate.

I sympathize. The column collapses a long, complex argument into a few paragraphs. It imparts to that argument a somewhat *ad hominem* flavor. And the title is deplorable: it is not only insulting to Judge Bork; it misses the point of my article. Bork is dangerous not because he is some sort of wild man. He is dangerous because he is a persuasive champion of an approach to constitutional adjudication that is powerfully coherent, appeals to common sense, and would, in practice, largely empty various central constitutional values of judicially enforceable meaning.

To see clearly the perverse dynamic that underlies the surface plausibility of Bork's theory, it is necessary to engage his ideas at the level of application. That is why Bork's "Neutral Principles and Some First Amendment Problems," in the Fall 1971 *Indiana Law Journal*, is of such interest. This "13-year-old article" remains his central statement on constitutional law. Often cited by his admirers, it is part of the canon of right-wing constitutional scholarship. Most important, it offers his own account of what his approach would mean in practice for one highly valued constitutional tradition.

The article's thesis is that the proper role of judges is to decide cases in light of "neutral principles" that reflect the intentions of the framers of the Constitution insofar as those intentions can be inferred from the text, the history of its adoption, and "their fair implications." When judges go beyond those sources in interpreting a constitutional provision, argues Bork, they have only their personal preferences to guide them. And in a democracy, it is intolerable that the preference of judges should exercise a veto over the preferences of the majority.

Applied to the First Amendment, Bork's mode of interpretation yields the principle that the amendment's sole function is to protect speech that contributes to democracy. He proceeds from that premise to a set of startlingly narrow conclusions: First Amendment protection should be limited to "explicitly political" speech; there is no constitutional basis for protecting any other form of expression; and within the category of political speech there should be no constitutional bar to the suppression of "any speech that advocates forcible overthrow of the government or the violation of any law."

In his *A.B.A. Journal* reply, Judge Bork, having dealt with the "Browser," turns to my analysis of his First Amendment theory:

As it happens, Jamie Kalven's summary of my views is both out of date and seriously mistaken. I do not think, for example, that First Amendment protection should apply only to speech that is explicitly political. Even in 1971, I stated that my views were tentative and based on an attempt to apply Prof. Herbert Wechsler's concept of neutral principles. As the result of the responses of scholars to my article, I have long since concluded that many other forms of discourse, such as moral and scientific debate, are central to democratic government and deserve protection. I have repeatedly stated this position in my classes. I continue to think that obscenity and pornography do not fit this rationale for protection.

It is good news indeed that Judge Bork has in some respects broadened his view of the scope of the First Amendment. But how was one outside the halls of Yale Law School to know? Surely it is beyond the pale of civilized discourse to answer one's critics by implying that they cut class!

The fact is that the 1971 article remains the central statement of his First Amendment views. So far as I have been able to determine, he has published nothing prior to his *A.B.A. Journal* reply that in any way disavows or revises it. Moreover, in the course of my research last year, I informed Judge Bork, via one of his law clerks, that I was working on an article on the First Amendment theory he advanced in 1971, and requested copies of two more recent statements by him which had not yet been published: a lecture on the First Amendment delivered in 1979 at the University of Michigan Law School, and an essay that was to appear in a forthcoming book on the role of the judiciary in America. His clerk wrote back, explaining why I could not see either piece and adding: "On behalf of Judge Bork, I am sorry that we could not assist you more in your First Amendment study. I hope that the pieces Judge Bork has already published on the subject will suffice for your work." But his published work on the First Amendment *is* the 1971 article; there is virtually nothing else. Thus, notified that a study of his First Amendment views was in the works, Judge Bork, in effect, referred me to the article he now characterizes as "out of date." Under the circumstances, I find it hard to accept his implication that it was somehow underhanded of me to take seriously what he wrote in 1971.

There is perhaps a lesson here about the risk one runs in a society committed to uninhibited, robust, and wide-open debate when one does not publicly respond to criticism of ideas one has urged on one's fellow citizens. In any case, had Judge Bork at any time over the last thirteen years publicly acknowledged that he had been moved by "the responses of scholars" to revise his First Amendment theory, I certainly would not have misreported his current views on the constitutional status of nonpolitical forms of speech, such as moral and scientific debate.

In the interest of avoiding any further misunderstandings and embarrassments, I would like to ask Judge Bork which portions of the First Amendment theory he advanced in 1971 he still stands by. Are we to understand that he continues to subscribe to that which he does not explicitly disavow in his *A.B.A. Journal* reply? Specifically, is artistic expression—literature, art, film, and so on—embraced within the "many other forms of discourse, such as moral and scientific debate," that he now believes the First Amendment ought to protect? Or does he perhaps find it necessary to exclude all artistic expression from protection in order to get at "obscenity and pornography"?

And what are his current views on speech that advocates forcible overthrow of the government or violation of the law? In 1971 he argued that all such advocacy, no matter how general or remote from criminal action, could constitutionally be suppressed. To my mind, this is the most dangerous part of his theory, and a substantial part of my article was devoted to refuting it. Yet his *A.B.A. Journal* reply fails to mention the point. How are we to interpret that silence?

The closing, and most heated, passage in Judge Bork's reply is addressed to my use of the term "moral skepticism" to characterize the premise underlying his approach to constitutional adjudication:

> More serious, however, is the wholly fallacious statement [by Mr. Kalven] that my view of neutral principles in constitutional adjudication is "animated by moral skepticism." Here, the *Journal* is betrayed by Mr. Kalven's unaccountable inability to understand what he reads. I believe in moral values and moral choice, and I, in common with the vast majority of men and women, live my life that way. It is absurd that an irresponsible allegation should require me to state that. My article argues that a judge has no means of demonstrating that his moral views about forms of human gratification are superior to the views of others. For that reason, a judge has no warrant, where the Constitution is silent, to force *his* morality upon a legislature that has made a different moral assessment. To suggest, on the basis of that argument, that I reject the "possibility of moral knowledge" is nonsense, and vicious nonsense at that.
>
> Your writer obviously did not take the necessary 30 minutes to look at my article or the necessary five minutes to call me. He should have. It is no light matter to make public assertions about another person's moral views. It is astounding that the *Journal*, of all publications, should display such a light-hearted disregard for truth and reputation.

Judge Bork has defended himself against an allegation I never made. He appears to have been moved to do so by a misunderstanding of the term "moral

332   skepticism." The term as I used it referred not to his character but to his philosophical assumptions. I did not mean to imply that he is amoral or unprincipled or without personal scruples. Moral skepticism is not skepticism about morality. It refers, rather, to the philosophical position that there is no way to demonstrate the correctness—or, for that matter, the wrongness—of particular moral judgments. That is what I understand Judge Bork to be saying, albeit in a rather opaque way, when he writes, "A judge has no means of demonstrating that his moral views about forms of human gratification are superior to the views of others."

It follows, he argues, that "a judge has no warrant, where the Constitution is silent, to force *his* morality upon a legislature that had made a different moral assessment." But the issue is not what to do when the Constitution is *silent*. It is what to do when the Constitution speaks loudly and distinctly but in broad generalities: equal protection, due process, cruel and unusual punishment, freedom of speech, and so on.

In the name of fidelity to the Constitution, Judge Bork would, in effect, bar judges from undertaking the interpretive effort that such broad provisions, by their nature, demand. Constitutional values, he insists, are enforceable by the courts only to the extent that the text and legislative history yield clear and specific guidance as to their meaning. Beyond that they are matters of preference, of taste, and as such should be left to the political process. Because the more open-ended the provisions, the less specific and unambiguous is the guidance afforded by the text and history, the effect of Bork's approach would be largely to surrender various central constitutional values to the will of the majority.

Argument at this level of generality takes one only so far. My point is that the clarity of Bork's vision is less the product of what he sees than of what he does not see. Something essential is missing. I have called that absence "moral skepticism"; perhaps another name would be more apt. In any case, it is at the level of particulars that the absence becomes palpable—nowhere more so than in his treatment, in the 1971 article, of the issue posed by advocacy of forcible overthrow of the government or violation of the law.

Central to First Amendment doctrine is the principle that seditious libel, the criticism of government, cannot be made a crime. Given this premise, which Bork says he accepts, government efforts to suppress advocacy of force and of law violation pose an issue that goes to the heart of the First Amendment. For the call to criminal action does not stand alone; it is typically part of a larger political critique. Hence, to set the boundaries of permissible advocacy is to delineate the point beyond which criticism of government may be constitutionally suppressed.

It has fallen to the judiciary, as the institutional guardian of First Amendment freedoms, to decide when the government may legally suppress advocacy. The best-known device for this purpose has been the "clear and present danger" test; and the current standard, articulated in *Brandenburg* v. *Ohio* in 1969, is "incitement to imminent lawless action." Whatever the precise phrasing of the legal formula, a consensus has emerged in American law about the underlying principle: Our constitutional commitment to vigorous and unrestrained debate of public issues demands the maximum protection for subversive advocacy consistent with public order.

This is not a theoretical matter. It is an insight born of experience. We can fix with some precision the cost in political freedom and the constriction of public debate that result when courts cede to government the power to suppress all such advocacy. We know that in times of stress the government tends to construe dissent as subversion and to punish seditious libel under the name of illegal advocacy. That is the lesson bequeathed by the series of decisions handed down during and immediately after World War I, in which the Supreme Court held that advocacy of force and law-breaking could be suppressed without regard to its proximity to criminal action. And it is a lesson that was renewed and enlarged by the decisions of the 1950s—decisions like *Dennis* v. *United States* (1951), which affirmed the convictions under the Smith Act of Communist Party leaders for, in effect, conspiring to organize a political party for the purpose of advocating revolution at some future time.

The tradition of freedom of political speech we enjoy today issues from a repudiation of those decisions—from a deep, widely shared sense that they were fundamentally at odds with the First Amendment, that they were *wrong*. Judge Bork, writing in 1971, does not share this view. The advocacy of force and of law violation, he writes, "has no political value within a republican system of government." He expresses agreement with the majority opinion in *Gitlow* v. *New York,* the culminating decision in the World War I era series of cases. And his only complaint about *Dennis* appears to be that in justifying its decision, the Court felt compelled to restate the clear-and-present-danger test in such a way as to eliminate its stringency, thereby bringing the teaching of Marxist doctrine within its terms. In his view, the proper course would have been to dispense with the test altogether, since any such standard "erects a barrier to legislative rule where none should exist."

Thus a theory that starts from the premise that the First Amendment's purpose is to protect the essential democratic freedom to criticize government ends by leaving the task of defining the limits of permissible criticism to the government officials criticized. This is an absurd outcome—a telling illustration of the general tendency of Bork's approach, in defiance of both logic and experience, to subordinate essential constitutional values to the preferences of the majority.

334   But, then, perhaps the passage of time and "the responses of scholars" have moved him to change his mind. What, I wonder, has Professor Bork been telling his students in recent years about the issue posed by the advocacy of force and of law violation? And what, given the opportunity, will Judge— perhaps Justice—Bork tell us all about the extent of our freedom to criticize our government and to dissent from its policies? ★

★ See pages 24–25 for a brief analysis of Judge Bork's testimony on *Brandenburg* during the confirmation hearings held by the Senate Judiciary Committee.

[Martin Garbus]

23

THE SHARON VERDICT:

WRONG CASE, WRONG PLACE,

WRONG RESULT

The press's reaction to the verdict in *Ariel Sharon* v. *Time Inc.* was astonishing. The *New York Times* proudly proclaimed that it affirmed "the law's special protections for a free press" and demonstrated that the Constitution "plainly aims to protect and promote fearless reporting and debate." The *Washington Post* wrote that the decision upheld the Supreme Court's purpose in protecting free speech. Various First Amendment lawyers and media executives said the outcome of the case proved that juries are capable of determining if public officials should recover damages in libel suits. The consensus was that all is well with the First Amendment; we can breathe a sigh of relief.

On the contrary. The Sharon verdict proves that public officials who claim they have been libeled by a critical story should not be permitted to sue. *Time* and General Ariel Sharon each claim that the other lost, but the loser was the public. If cases like Sharon's continue to be allowed to go to trial, the public will be deprived of critical information about matters of public controversy.

Twenty-one years ago, in the watershed case of *New York Times* v. *Sullivan,* the Supreme Court held that to prove libel, a public official must establish that

Reprinted from *The Nation* 240 (February 16, 1985), pp. 161, 176, 178–179, by permission of the author and the publishers.

the statements about him had been published with "actual malice"—that is, with knowledge that they were false or in reckless disregard of the truth. But the *Sullivan* rule has failed to protect the press adequately. There has been an explosion of lawsuits against the media; juries have awarded large damages (since 1980 there have been more than twenty cases in which damages exceeded $1 million); and the high legal costs incurred by defendants have been a warning to others, inducing self-censorship and reducing the flow of information to the public.

Sharon's suit, that of General William Westmoreland against CBS, and all the other actions brought by public officials are not attempts by individuals to win restitution for personal wrongs. They are attempts to vindicate their political positions and their conduct in office—to rewrite history. Whether Sharon or the political coalition he represented bore responsibility for the Beirut massacres should not be determined in a U.S. court. The Founding Fathers never intended America's courts to be used to settle political questions, especially those of another country.

To make his point, General Sharon pounced on a minor error in *Time*'s story about the final report of Israel's Kahan Commission. The commission had found the general "indirectly responsible" for the killing of several hundred Palestinians living in the Sabra and Shatila refugee camps. David Halevy, *Time*'s correspondent in Jerusalem, testified under oath that several confidential sources told him that Sharon had a more direct involvement in planning the massacres. Midway through the trial, the magazine conceded that it had erred in reporting that allegations of Sharon's complicity appeared in the secret Appendix B of the commission's report, but that was an inconsequential mistake, one small detail in a single paragraph that was part of a long, devastatingly accurate story. Nevertheless, two of six jury members at first believed that *Time* was guilty of malice, that Halevy was "out to get" Sharon. If the jury foreman hadn't argued them out of that view, *Time* might not have been acquitted.

To be fair, the jury had an impossible task. In his meticulous sixty-six-page charge, Judge Abraham D. Sofaer asked them to determine not if *they* thought the key paragraph was defamatory or false but if "the average reader" would think so. They were asked to evaluate the "state of mind" of the senior editor who wrote the article, the state of mind of the numerous people who edited it, and also what *Time*'s words implied to the average reader. Those questions were difficult enough, but the jurors were also expected to ascertain who was responsible for massacres that occurred in Lebanon more than two years earlier. Make no mistake about it: That was the key issue they had to resolve, for if they believed Sharon was responsible, they would find *Time*'s story accurate.

On the question of malice, the jurors were instructed by Judge Sofaer to determine if *Time* had "exaggerated" the facts or "fabricated" them. They spent a total of forty-two hours poring over one paragraph. If a dozen writers spent the same amount of time attempting to come up with a description of Sharon's involvement, they each would produce many different versions, some that could be construed as exaggerations or distortions.

Twenty pages of the judge's charge were devoted to defining malice. Reading them is a painful experience. Although I have been a practicing lawyer for twenty-five years, specializing in libel law, I am not sure that I could apply the charge to the facts, and I am certain that a jury could not. Most of us understand malice as meaning ill will, spite, or hostility. That is not how the Supreme Court defined it in the *Sullivan* case. A reporter can love the person he is writing about and still be found guilty of malice; he can hate the person and be found innocent. The jurors in this case were understandably confused about the concept of malice. Richard Zug, the jury foreman, said they entered the malice stage of the deliberations with "almost all of us in the question-mark category." That is too fragile a reed to support a free press.

The Sharon verdict does not increase one's confidence in the ability of even a properly instructed jury to comprehend present libel law. Moreover, people outside the profession have little idea how difficult it is for the media to establish and report the truth. Publishers bring out hundreds of books; television news programs present thousands of facts; newspapers publish complex stories under relentless deadlines. Reporters and writers are expected to locate the ultimate truth in a welter of controversial facts and charges. By definition, the stories most in need of protection by the First Amendment—those that expose wrongdoing or criticize the powerful—are the most likely to provoke litigation. The only way a publisher or news organization can be sure it will not be sued is not to publish controversial articles or books. The operative work is "controversial." Thus the chief effect of the recent flood of libel judgments has not been greater accuracy in the media but greater timidity. Free speech has been curtailed; the flow of information to the public has been diminished.

The most serious impact has been on investigative journalism, which has decreased in recent years. Most investigative reporting is antiestablishment. Although portrayed as leftist in origin, the scope is much greater. Journalists seek to reveal corruption in City Hall, to expose official lies about foreign policies, to uncover double-dealing in Washington. It is no surprise that expensive libel suits are often backed by conservative elements, which tend to support the power structure. Indeed, the media has become a prime target of the right —witness Senator Jesse Helms's call for a conservative takeover of CBS—and libel suits are a favorite instrument to attack it. Both Sharon and Westmoreland represent a specific political viewpoint. In Sharon's case, it is the rightist

338 forces in Israel who support his political comeback; in Westmoreland's, it is conservatives in this country who hold that the Vietnam War was lost because of opposition on the home front.

Libel suits inhibit journalists by making them excessively cautious about finding and revealing the facts. Obviously, they should base their reporting on the facts, but sometimes all the facts are not available because a government or a corporation refuses to divulge them. In such cases, journalists should be free to make inferences about public issues. During the Nixon administration, the speculation and hunches of newspaper reporters led to the Watergate exposés. Skepticism about official statements on the progress of the Vietnam War drove the press to smoke out the facts that turned the public against the war. When the secret policies of the government were revealed in the Pentagon Papers, many of the journalists' inferences were proved correct.

Reporters frequently rely on evidence that would not hold up in court— and that is proper. Take, for example, Strobe Talbott's *Deadly Gambits*, which describes secret arms negotiation talks in the Reagan administration, and Carl Bernstein and Bob Woodward's *All the President's Men*, which describes the events that led up to Watergate. Those books were pieced together by authors who were not at critical meetings; they were often based on fragmentary information and confidential sources. So long as authors explain their methodology and let their readers know the limitations of their research and sources, they should be permitted to draw even wrong conclusions without the threat of a libel suit hanging over them.

As the Supreme Court recognized long ago, in *Board of Education* v. *Barnette*, "compulsory unification of opinion achieves only the unanimity of the graveyard." As Professor Lawrence Tribe of Harvard Law School put it, the genius of the First Amendment is its recognition that more speech is the cure for misleading speech. All that government may demand is that the dialogue be expanded, not that the offending remark be stopped or that the publisher be shut down.

Self-censorship often arrives insidiously. Editors, executives, and attorneys who check manuscripts for libel problems are frequently evaluated on their ability to avoid lawsuits. The criterion for deciding to print a controversial article becomes not whether the company could successfully defend a libel suit; it is whether the plaintiff could keep it alive and force the company to bear the expense and burden of frivolous litigation. If the latter seems likely, the natural tendency is not to publish.

Publishers routinely deny that they kill articles because of the risk of libel, but the chilling effect is well known to lawyers who work with the media. Publishers who once asked me whether the target of an article could win a lawsuit now simply ask, Will he sue? More and more, I see unflattering adjectives removed, incisive analyses of people and events watered down, risky projects dropped.

Similar experiences are reported by other attorneys when libel issues are discussed. At a board meeting of the American Civil Liberties Union, a number of case histories of libel suits that led to self-censorship were analyzed. One publishing house canceled the second printing of a book and the paperback edition after being hit with a libel suit that was eventually shown to have no legal basis.

Those who sue for libel are usually large corporations or wealthy individuals—not cranks or ordinary people. Few attorneys will take a libel case on a contingency-fee basis. Lawyers for the networks and major publishers know how to run up litigation costs to try to drive the plaintiff from the courthouse. It is people like the owners of Rancho LaCosta resort, currently suing *Penthouse*—they claim they were wrongly identified as being connected with organized crime—who can afford to pay the fees lawyers usually demand to take on the likes of *Penthouse*. *Time* spent more than $1 million on its defense against Sharon; *Penthouse* has spent more than $20 million in the ten-year LaCosta suit.

One reason for the rash of libel suits and claims in the last few years is a more general litigation frenzy. It has encouraged individuals who fancy themselves defamed to peddle their grievances to groups (usually on the right) that will underwrite their expenses. Widespread negative feelings about the press have infiltrated the jury room, resulting in megaverdicts in libel suits. Juries have great discretion in deciding the merits of such cases and the amount of money to award.

After trying hundreds of cases before juries, I've learned that they are ruled by emotion. As a result, I am skeptical when I hear jurors give their rationales for a verdict. The jurors in the Sharon case were under great pressure to appear objective and meticulous; in the post-trial interviews they gave the impression that they had engaged in a dispassionate search for the truth. But some of their remarks revealed the prejudices that had erupted in the jury room. Why, for example, did the jurors feel obligated to state, "Certain *Time* employees, particularly correspondent David Halevy, acted negligently and carelessly in reporting and verifying the information"? Who asked them? Why did juror Patricia DeLoatch say, in justifying the statement, "We didn't want *Time* to think they're so lily white that they don't make mistakes"?

Justice Hugo L. Black, in his opinion in the *Sullivan* case, wrote, "I doubt that a country can live in freedom where its people can be made to suffer physically or financially for criticizing their government, its actions, or its officials."

340 His doubt does not appear to be uppermost in the minds of the majority of the American people, today's journalists, or Supreme Court justices. As a result the media continues to operate in a state of siege. Our Founding Fathers' vision of a free and vigorous press is in danger of being destroyed. Fidelity to their visionary document, the Constitution, requires that public officials be barred from bringing libel suits.

[Walter Schneir and Miriam Schneir]

24

BEYOND WESTMORELAND:

THE RIGHT'S ATTACK ON THE

PRESS

The outcome of the Westmoreland trial is a gain for America—the America of the Constitution and the Bill of Rights. But for the political movement that funded and supported it, the case is merely a lost battle. The New Right's war against the mass media continues unabated, and that outcome is still in doubt.

In their quest for political power, the energetic and ambitious leaders of the New Right (many of whom now call themselves "conservative populists") regard the media as a formidable barrier. The problem, as they see it, is that the media is controlled by liberals, who are their natural enemies. The leaders' animus toward the media appears to be shared by their foot soldiers, the millions of "social conservatives" concentrated in the Sun Belt and the Midwest, who support a "pro-family" agenda and respond favorably to appeals for patriotism and a strong national defense.

Central to the thinking of the movement is the idea that the media is now the dominant force in America. Patrick Buchanan, the president's director of communications, argued in 1977 that the main obstacle to the victory of conservative forces in this country was not the Democratic party but the liberal

Reprinted from *The Nation* 240 (March 30, 1985), pp. 361–367 by permission of the authors and the publishers.

342 media. Kevin Phillips, one of the right's most admired theorists, maintains that the old political parties have "lost their logic." He says, "Effective communications are replacing party organizations as the key to political success." It follows then that to take power—as opposed to winning an election—the right must capture the liberal media, lock, stock, and barrel.

Phillips and other New Right social critics lean heavily on the theory of elites propounded by the early twentieth-century sociologists Vilfredo Pareto and Gaetano Mosca, who, not coincidentally—since elite theory counters the concept of class conflict—strongly influenced the young Mussolini and early Italian Fascism. New Right analysis, following another line trod by Italian Fascism, claims a unity of interest among "producers": business, labor, and agriculture. "The basic economic and political split in America today," according to William A. Rusher, publisher of *National Review*, "is no longer between 'business and labor' but between 'producers and non-producers.'"

Among the nonproducers are the print and electronic media, part of a "verbalist" elite that battens on the hide of the hard-working producers. Rusher believes this unjust situation should not be permitted. So does Samuel T. Francis, a former policy analyst for the Heritage Foundation and a legislative assistant to North Carolina Senator John East. He cites the media as one of those "power preserves of the entrenched elite whose values and interests are hostile to the traditional American ethos and which is a parasitical tumor on the body of Middle America. These structures should be leveled."

Although the New Right believes that the presidency will continue to be held by conservatives, they see liberals clinging to control of the all-powerful media. In this situation, they sometimes regard the First Amendment as a weapon used by their enemies. How to convince people that the First Amendment is not sacrosanct? The New Right has already broached that touchy subject.

An article by Kevin Phillips in *Human Events* on January 13, 1973, was titled "Is the First Amendment Obsolete?" To which Phillips answered "Yes," noting, "'The Public's right to know' is a code for the Manhattan Adversary Culture's desire to wrap the 1st Amendment around its attack on the politicians, government and institutions of Middle America."

Two years later, in a book titled *Mediacracy*, Phillips pursued the argument: "The Bill of Rights is hardly a static legal concept . . . perhaps the First Amendment may undergo a shifting interpretation . . . to reflect the new status of the communications industry. The media may be forced into the status of utilities regulated to provide access."

Phillips gave no specific details as to how the media was to be "regulated." But in 1981 some extraordinary suggestions were offered by James L. Tyson in *Target America: The Influence of Communist Propaganda on U.S. Media*. Tyson, who lists as his past affiliations the Office of Strategic Services (precursor to the Central Intelligence Agency), Time-Life International, and I.B.M. World Trade Corporation, proposes that a government official be stationed at each of the three major television networks to check news stories for fairness and accuracy. The networks have "become so powerful in opinion formation that national survival demands some assurance that they will not be free to disseminate the misinformation and distortions that have occurred in recent years," he writes. "In a word, TV news has become much too important a matter to be left to TV newsmen."

As a "solution to this problem," Tyson offers what he terms a preliminary recommendation. He would "require an ombudsman for each major network . . . appointed by an independent outside body such as the FCC." This individual would see that the Fairness Doctrine is adhered to and would insure that the networks follow "expert advice" on issues like "the neutron bomb, nuclear power, or our policy in Indo-China."

Several New Right groups, including the American Security Council and the National Strategy Information Center, assisted Tyson with his research. But what gives his book the imprimatur of the New Right is the endorsement of Reed Irvine, the movement's preeminent media maven. When we called to request material on media bias from a number of well-known New Right organizations—among them, the Heritage Foundation, the National Journalism Center, and the Conservative Caucus—we were informed in each instance that the person to see was Reed Irvine.

Irvine is chair of Accuracy in Media (AIM), a self-described media watchdog, and editor of the semimonthly newsletter "AIM Report." AIM's national advisory board included Clare Boothe Luce, Eugene Lyons, Professor Frank N. Trager, former Treasury Secretary William E. Simon, industrialist and Heritage trustee Robert H. Krieble, and Midge Decter, also a Heritage trustee and executive director of the Committee for the Free World. Funding comes from a core group of right-wing foundations (such as Scaife and Coors) and also from many large corporations, including Mobil Oil.

Although, to the best of our knowledge, Irvine has never discussed *Target America* during his appearances on national television (now made with increasing frequency), it is fair to say that he endorses the ideas in the book. He assisted Tyson with the research, wrote the preface, hired Tyson for the "AIM Report" staff, reprinted a paperback edition of the work, offers the book free to subscribers of the newsletter, and at a CBS annual stockholders' meeting proposed that the corporation drop Walter Cronkite from its board of directors and replace him with James Tyson.

Tyson's thesis is that the Russians are pursuing "a massive secret propaganda campaign" carried out by at least four thousand journalist-agents stationed in

344 the United States. To identify those operatives and their assistants he urges investigations of "Communist propaganda activities in the United States" by the Federal Bureau of Investigation and House and Senate internal security committees. Meanwhile, he has devised a clever "balance sheet" method for smoking out "Communist agents in the media." Passing Tyson's loyalty test is no simple matter; telling the truth will not do the trick. An investigative reporter whose work is accurate but does not include what Tyson judges to be "anti-Communist truths" is, he declares, "as suspect as those whose output consists totally of falsehoods." In the preface to *Target America*, Irvine asserts: "Tyson documents what so many have only surmised. This country is the target of a massive and frighteningly successful war of words inspired by governments that despise and fear freedom and aided by a host of witting and unwitting helpers."

How much support is there in the New Right for a return to the investigative techniques of the McCarthyite 1950s? Tyson merely echoes the 1981 Heritage Foundation report to President Reagan, *Mandate for Leadership*, which urged the reactivation of internal security probes by the FBI and Congress, and noted, "Individual liberties are secondary to the requirement of national security and internal civil order." Moral compunctions will not inhibit a new McCarthyism. Richard Viguerie, the genius of New-Right direct-mail politics and the publisher of *Conservative Digest*, recalls that during his student days his heroes were "the two Macs"—General Douglas MacArthur and Senator Joseph McCarthy. And Kevin Phillips, in his 1982 book, *Post-Conservative America*, blandly projects an America in which "increased surveillance would crack down on . . . extreme political dissidents."

Another current plan that would stifle debate on public issues should be mentioned. The Reagan administration is attempting to stretch the draconian Espionage Act to cover leaks to the media by government employees. When a Navy Department employee sent photographs of a Soviet ship to a British publication, the Justice Department obtained an indictment for espionage against him, and that indictment was upheld by a federal district court judge in Baltimore. As if in tandem, a former high-level CIA official, George Carver, has been calling publicly for legislation to permit the Espionage Act's use against federal employees who disclose classified information to journalists. Carver, now with Georgetown University's right-wing Center for Strategic and International Studies, characterizes this suggested change as "fine-tuning."

These far-reaching proposals for an end run around the First Amendment by some "regulatory" mechanism, for McCarthyite probes of newspeople and for expanded use of the Espionage Act are still unrealized, so the New Right's antimedia shock troops have had to rely on a variety of lesser weapons and hope those will have a cumulative effect.

Reed Irvine, for example, harasses the networks by enlisting his supporters **345** in letter-writing campaigns to media corporate executives and advertisers. "AIM Report" has a circulation of about thirty thousand, and Irvine reaches thousands of others through his syndicated newspaper column and his five-day-a-week radio commentary, *Media Monitor.* He also buys shares in media corporations so he can attend stockholders' meetings and introduce resolutions. In addition, AIM maintains an active speakers' bureau and sponsors conferences.

In the past few years AIM has campaigned against television programs critical of Agent Orange, Nestlé's infant formula, nuclear power, J. Edgar Hoover, Senator McCarthy, Anastasio Somoza, and the present Guatemalan government. Other objects of its ire have included stories considered favorable to the Nicaraguan revolution, the nuclear freeze, and Jane Fonda and her film *The China Syndrome* ("an anti-free enterprise movie"). CBS and its correspondents Mike Wallace, Dan Rather, and Bill Moyers are frequent targets of Irvine's invective. In 1975 he wrote: "At least some of the blood shed by South Vietnamese when Saigon fell to Communist aggressors last April belongs on the hands of the Columbia Broadcast Corporation. CBS' biased news . . . proved influential in turning public sentiment against the war effort."

When that article was reprinted in Viguerie's *Conservative Digest,* it was accompanied by a photograph of Walter Cronkite, with the caption: "Walter Cronkite and his fellow CBS newsmen deserve at least some of the blame for the fall of South Vietnam."

About a decade ago AIM and the American Security Council each began filing complaints against the networks with the Federal Communications Commission under the Fairness Doctrine, seeking license revocation or other sanctions. They met with no success. The advent of the Reagan administration and the appointment of conservatives to the FCC raised their hopes. What followed, however, was a split between conservatives who genuinely wanted less government regulation, and so favored abolition of the Fairness Doctrine, and those, like Irvine, who tend to think in hard-boiled *Realpolitik* terms. After FCC chair Mark Fowler rejected one of Irvine's petitions, Irvine wrote with obvious contempt that the conservatives on the FCC were giving "the liberals who dominate the big electronic media just what they want. They seem to be doing this because they are ideological purists."

Another New Right organization, the American Legal Foundation (ALF), established in 1980, has also been assiduously filing Fairness Doctrine complaints—including one against CBS for the documentary on General William Westmoreland. When the CIA filed its precedent-setting FCC complaint against ABC *World News Tonight,* the ALF offered a supporting petition. The ALF describes itself as "the only pro-free enterprise, public interest law cen-

346 ter in the nation that devotes all of its activities and resources solely toward fighting media bias."

Aside from posing threats to the licenses of the broadcasters, the FCC complaints serve as a focus for antimedia publicity campaigns that may have an even more intimidating effect. The ALF was part of such a campaign prior to the screening of ABC's film about nuclear war, *The Day After*. Later the ALF's general counsel, Michael P. McDonald, claimed, "If ALF and other conservative organizations hadn't been involved in the whole *Day After* brouhaha, I don't think we would have seen the viewpoint segment that aired afterwards, which was a fairly conservative panel."

While continuing to file FCC complaints, the foundation is also investing heavily in libel suits, and it has organized a Libel Prosecution Resource Center to aid "media victims." In a recent interview, McDonald said that he was disappointed about the outcome of the Westmoreland case but that his organization would continue to support libel prosecution against the media. "I think we'll be seeing some additional big cases," he said. "There are some pending right now." He mentioned Senator Paul Laxalt's libel suit against a California newspaper group.

Many in the New Right would like to see more suits by public officials against the media, and regard the Supreme Court's 1964 decision in *New York Times* v. *Sullivan* as the principal impediment to that goal. In that decision the Court—to encourage vigorous debate on public issues—made it difficult for officials to win libel actions. In the past year the New Right has been sharpening its knives for *Sullivan*. McDonald has said: "We believe *New York Times* v. *Sullivan* destroyed 180 years of libel law. . . . The media is being afforded too much protection." Another opponent of *Sullivan* is Leslie Lenkowsky, who was staff director of the Smith Richardson Foundation when it helped fund the Westmoreland case. Interviewed before the trial began by Connie Bruck for *The American Lawyer*, Lenkowsky said he hoped the case would have two long-range effects: a change in the malice standard of *Sullivan* and the demise of CBS Reports, the division of CBS News responsible for the Westmoreland documentary.

The strongest attack on *Sullivan* came in three advertisements placed by Mobil in the *New York Times*, the *Washington Post*, and many other leading dailies. The ad that appeared on October 18, 1984, suggested that if the Supreme Court did not "redefine" the libel standard applied to public officials, such officials should be provided "government-financed" libel insurance that would pay for suits against critics. It also solicited contributions to assist the Westmoreland defense. Recently a number of those opposed to *Sullivan* joined forces to produce a monograph titled "*New York Times* v. *Sullivan*: An Obstacle to Enlightened Public Discourse and Government Responsiveness to the

People." Written by Bruce E. Fein, a lawyer with the conservative American
Enterprise Institute, it was published by the American Legal Foundation and
has a preface by McDonald and an introduction by Herbert Schmertz, vice
president for public affairs of Mobil.

The New Right's latest project against the media is the ploy of Senator Jesse
Helms to gain control of CBS through stock purchases. In January a new organization called Fairness in Media, based in Raleigh, North Carolina, mailed
nearly a million letters to conservatives throughout the country. The letter,
which is signed by Helms, begins: "For years good Americans like you have
asked President Reagan and me what can be done to combat the flagrant bias in
the liberal news media. At last there's an answer to that question." The answer:
recipients should vote the CBS stock they purchase or already own "to take
control of that network . . . to elect a new Board of Directors . . . committed
to ending liberal media bias." As evidence of CBS's offending policies, the letter cites a *TV Guide* study that found CBS "the most anti-Reagan network,"
a Bill Moyers program "that made it appear that President Reagan's policies
were hurting the poor," and CBS News's misleading coverage of the Tet offensive. The letter implies that during the Vietnam War the media was General
Vo Nguyen Giap's "greatest weapon in defeating America."

Although Helms is unlikely to gain control of CBS, he cannot be dismissed
lightly. He has a huge following among the New Right rank and file and
is said to have presidential ambitions. During his twelve years in the Senate
he has built a personal political empire, which includes six nonprofit educational foundations and a political action committee, the National Congressional Club, which is the largest in the country. When we called Fairness in
Media headquarters, a spokesman told us the response to the mailing has been
"tremendous." CBS lawyers have counterattacked with a lawsuit charging
improper political activities by tax-exempt organizations. Meanwhile, since
Helms's original announcement, the price of CBS stock has risen sharply.

Recently Ted Turner, chair of Cable News Network and Turner Broadcasting Systems, announced that he was seeking to buy CBS. For several years
Turner, whose headquarters is in Atlanta, has made no secret of his desire to
buy a network, but Wall Street observers do not believe he has sufficient funds,
unless he has some big-money backers in the wings. Although a spokesman
for Turner denied any connection with the Helms action, *The New York Times*
reported, "Turner has met in recent weeks with representatives of Fairness in
Media."

Turner's links with the New Right are not generally known. Last June the
National Conservative Foundation, an offshoot of John T. (Terry) Dolan's
National Conservative Political Action Committee (NCPAC), sponsored a
conference in Washington on The Conservative Movement and the Media. It

348 was a true gathering of the faithful, and speakers included Richard Viguerie, Representative Newt Gingrich, Reed Irvine, and Dolan, a founder of the New Right. Dolan pondered the question "Why is the American media pro-Soviet?" and observed that there probably were "active Soviet agents" in American journalism. The keynote speaker in this select company was none other than the man who now seeks to buy CBS, Ted Turner. He told the audience that the networks are "the greatest enemies America ever had" and repeated a charge he had made on previous occasions—that broadcast executives are "guilty of treason."*

On January 26, 1982, three days after the CBS documentary "The Uncounted Enemy: A Vietnam Deception" was shown, General Westmoreland appeared at a press conference at the Army-Navy Club near the Pentagon to denounce the network. Flanked by ex-CIA officials, former diplomats, and retired military officers, Westmoreland inveighed against the "notorious reporter, Mike Wallace," who had tried to prosecute him in "a star-chamber procedure with distorted, false and specious information, plain lies, derived by sinister deception." The accusations against him, he declared, constituted "a preposterous hoax and will not go unanswered."

Shortly afterward, Irvine, whom Westmoreland had contacted in advance of the broadcast, devoted his newsletter to a strident attack on CBS. Under the headline "CBS Should Fire Mike Wallace," Irvine wrote that the documentary was a "disgraceful example of the atrocious journalism practiced" by CBS News. He suggested the motive behind it: "CBS is smarting under the charge that they and others in the media helped cause our defeat in Vietnam."

Soon, another stalwart of the right came galloping in hot pursuit of CBS. The May 29, 1982, issue of Walter Annenberg's *TV Guide* ran a highly unusual twelve-page cover story titled "Anatomy of a Smear: How CBS News Broke the Rules and 'Got' General Westmoreland." Using unedited transcripts of interviews that were leaked to *TV Guide* by a CBS Deep Throat, the magazine accused CBS News, producer George Crile, and Mike Wallace of numerous serious violations of journalistic standards. The fact that Annenberg is a long-time right-winger and a close friend and supporter of Ronald Reagan made some members of the press skeptical about the magazine's objectivity. *News-*

---

*However, by summer 1985 New Right critics were expressing reservations about Turner because of his sudden involvement with what *Human Events* described as a "liberal do-good organization" and also with a group that promotes citizen exchanges between the United States and over forty nations—including the Soviet Union! According to *Human Events*, the latter "little-known organization based in Atlanta" strongly backed Turner's bid to take over CBS. Ironically, as CBS, NBC, and ABC have cut back their TV news division budgets over the past few years, the coverage accorded some major events—for example, the Iran-Contra hearings—by Turner's Cable News Network (CNN) has been superior to that of the three major networks.

week questioned whether *TV Guide* was a suitably "neutral forum" for such **349**
an investigation, given Annenberg's conservative background and his declared
opposition to "adversary journalism."

But at the time the *TV Guide* article appeared, CBS News had a new president, Van Gordon Sauter. Faced with the exposé, Sauter responded by an-
nouncing that he had commissioned an investigation of the documentary by
network executive Burton Benjamin. The harshly critical "Benjamin Report"
was released in summary form in July 1982 and stated that the makers of the
documentary had committed mistakes in procedure and violations of CBS
News guidelines—though both Benjamin and Sauter affirmed that they supported "the substance of the broadcast."

It is easy to understand why New Right ideologues would have thought
the Westmoreland affair had all the makings of a perfect antimedia project—
their most ambitious one to date. Thus, some time before the fall of 1982, an
individual named Richard Larry approached Washington attorney Dan Burt,
president of the Capital Legal Foundation. Larry is a trusted agent of Richard
Mellon Scaife, the great-grandson of the founder of the Mellon banking fortune and one of the principal moneybags of the New Right movement. If Burt
would fight CBS on behalf of Westmoreland, Larry proposed, Scaife would
help pay for the suit. That secret arrangement was not disclosed until after the
suit ended. Burt has now revealed that Scaife contributed well over $2 million
to Capital Legal (more than 70 percent of the cost of the litigation), which
suggests that the trial might more aptly be titled *Richard Mellon Scaife* v. *CBS*.
(Other major backers were the Smith Richardson and the John M. Olin foundations.)

That little has been written about Scaife is not for lack of journalistic enterprise. He has come into his own only since the early 1970s and goes to great
lengths to avoid publicity. The most useful elucidation of his political financing
activities is an article in the *Columbia Journalism Review* by Karen Rothmyer,
a former *Wall Street Journal* reporter who teaches at the Columbia School of
Journalism. Based on public and private financial records, Rothmyer's 1981
story estimated that Scaife's charitable foundations already had granted $100
million and were continuing to contribute heavily to a variety of conservative,
neoconservative and especially New Right organizations. (Both Accuracy in
Media and *The Public Interest*, a magazine run by Irving Kristol and Nathan
Glazer, are funded in part by Scaife.) Moreover, Scaife has been particularly
influential as a source of seed money for such organizations as the Committee
for the Free World, the Institute for Foreign Policy Analysis, the Institute for
Contemporary Studies, the Media Institute, and the Heritage Foundation. All
this bespeaks a good deal of political sophistication.

Rothmyer was never able to discuss her findings with Scaife. Although she

350   repeatedly requested an interview, he repeatedly refused. She finally cornered him at an exclusive club in Boston one evening and shot a question at him: "Mr. Scaife, could you explain why you give so much money to the New Right?" He responded, "You fucking Communist cunt, get out of here."

Scaife is also known to have provided seed money for the National Legal Center for the Public Interest and six affiliates, one of which was the Capital Legal Foundation. Other benefactors of this New Right legal network were the Coors and Fluor families, both closely identified with conservative causes. In 1977, when Capital Legal was incorporated, its board included Leslie Burgess, a vice president of the Fluor Corporation; Peter J. Fluor, president of Texas Crude and a major stockholder of Fluor; and associates of two leading conservative organizations, the American Enterprise Institute and the Media Institute.

In 1980 Dan Burt left a lucrative private law practice (he had an office in Al Khobar, Saudi Arabia, where Fluor Arabian has headquarters) to become president of the Capital Legal Foundation. That same year Scaife commissioned Michael Horowitz to study conservative public-interest law firms. Horowitz concluded they were too stereotypically pro-business to capture the sympathy of many Americans. Burt may have followed this advice, or perhaps he had a natural affinity for playing the kind of role recommended by Horowitz. He severed the foundation's ties to the National Legal Center and publicly criticized his erstwhile counterparts. He began to tell interviewers that his firm practiced a new breed of public-interest law. It was for the little guy rather than big business and was more libertarian than conservative. Nevertheless, his connections to the right do not appear to have suffered as a result of his apostasy. He developed a working relationship with Senators Paul Laxalt, Orrin Hatch, and Edward Zorinsky; he was accorded the honor of a long interview in the John Birch Society's newsletter, "Review of the News"; and his big-business, New Right board of directors was virtually unchanged. Moreover, Capital Legal's budget tripled between 1980 and 1982, with much of the money still coming from Scaife.

In spite of—or perhaps because of—his independent stance, Burt and his foundation were chosen by Scaife to handle the Westmoreland suit. At a press conference attended by Burt on September 13, 1982, the general announced that on that day the Capital Legal Foundation had filed a $120 million libel suit against CBS on his behalf.

Soon after, Reed Irvine solicited donations for a Westmoreland legal fund (he later said he did this at Burt's request). He also sent out a nationwide mailing of a letter signed by Westmoreland, blasting CBS and appealing for contributions to AIM. In addition, Irvine ran a three-quarter-page advertisement in the *Washington Times* for AIM and the Tyson book, with a photograph of

Westmoreland in full military dress, captioned: "General Westmoreland wrote that 'Accuracy in Media did a fantastic job of exposing the dishonest smear job that CBS perpetrated. Everyone should read the AIM Report.'"

In late January 1983, CBS News president Sauter told a meeting of journalists in Philadelphia that the Westmoreland libel suit "has become a rallying point for people who seek to use it as an instrument for damaging the image, spirit and aggressiveness of the news media." Westmoreland, he added, "is merely the point man in their search-and-destroy mission." A CBS spokesman identified AIM and the American Legal Foundation as the "people" Sauter had had in mind.

Burt struck back sharply in the press, insisting that Capital Legal followed no particular political philosophy and that he had tried to distance himself from AIM and the American Legal Foundation. He was quoted as saying, "Sure, there are crazy groups on the right, but what can I do?" Irvine later reported in his newsletter that Burt had refused $41,000 that AIM had raised for the suit, and commented bitterly: "He apparently decided that the case might in some way be jeopardized if Accuracy in Media was in any way connected with it. He said that he would not want to run the risk of being accused of carrying out an anti-media crusade." That the dispute was tactical, not substantive, however, is suggested by the fact that in May, Irvine could announce to his readers that AIM had received a new contribution of $100,000 from Richard Mellon Scaife —the *éminence grise* of the Westmoreland case.

After AIM ran the ad with Westmoreland's picture a second time, Capital Legal released a letter the general had written Irvine. The letter disclaimed any animosity toward the press. "The ad, by implication, could give the reader the impression that my fight is with the media," Westmoreland wrote. "It is not! It is with CBS over a specific issue. Your ad adds fuel to the frequent allegations by some that my case is a right-wing effort to 'get' the press."

Forgotten by nearly everyone was that some years earlier the general had not hesitated to associate himself with AIM's criticisms of the media. In 1978 he had been the principal speaker at an AIM conference in Arlington, Virginia, that was also addressed by William Rusher and Patrick Buchanan. In a rambling but combative talk, Westmoreland did not go so far in his condemnation of the press as many in the New Right have, but he charged that journalists in Vietnam were "abusive, arrogant and hypocritical," that Americans had been "masterfully manipulated by Hanoi and Moscow," and that the public's "false perception" that Tet was a victory for the Communists was "directly attributable to inaccurate reporting." He declared, "If the media can create a defeat of our armies on the battlefield, they can also eventually defeat the viability of our system."

As the trial date neared, Burt—despite one slip when he exclaimed, "We

352 are about to see the dismantling of a major news network"—sounded more and more like a benign professor of journalistic ethics. He managed to focus the press on such matters as media responsibility and the right of an old man to preserve his reputation. Although a few stories made passing reference to Capital Legal's New Right funding, Burt largely succeeded in diverting attention from the motives of those who were paying Westmoreland's legal fees and the political significance of the case. Instead, the media turned on itself in a paroxysm of self-criticism. On the eve of the testimony of the first witness, *Newsweek* bore a picture of Westmoreland on its cover and a story inside with the headline "The Media in the Dock: Scrutiny of the making of a TV documentary highlights shortcomings throughout the news business."

But for Burt the party ended when the trial began.

To win his case, he had to prove that the documentary's statements about the general were false and were made with "malice"—that is, with knowledge they were false or with reckless disregard for the truth. George Crile, the producer of "The Uncounted Enemy," was one witness from whom Burt confidently expected he could extract testimony showing malice, but his examination of Crile was a disaster. Expected by some to become the scapegoat of the entire affair, Crile saved himself by coolly demonstrating that he was extraordinarily knowledgeable about the subject. He came across as a serious, well-informed journalist, who had done impressive research.

Burt's last chance to undermine Crile's testimony and prove malice was Ira Klein, a former CBS employee. Burt had stressed the importance of Klein's testimony to his case in his opening statement to the jury:

> Crile fabricated his story with the help of a film editor . . . [who] complained to Crile time and again about the way he was making the broadcast. . . . That film editor, Ira Klein, the man who physically made the broadcast, you will see testify at this trial as a witness for General Westmoreland. He will describe how Crile created "The Uncounted Enemy: A Vietnam Deception" with reckless disregard for the truth.

CBS attorney David Boies delivered the *coup de grace* to Westmoreland's case when he cross-examined Klein. This was the man who had been airily giving his "expert" opinions on alleged distortions in the broadcast for the previous three years. First, Boies forced Klein to admit that he had told a reporter that Crile was a "social pervert" and was "devious and slimy" (tape recordings of those conversations were available). Then he proceeded:

Q.: During the preparation of the broadcast, did you attend any of the interviews of people that were being interviewed?

A.: No.

Q.: Were you aware that Mr. Crile and Mr. [Sam] Adams and others associated with the broadcast took notes of interviews that they conducted in preparation for the broadcast, interviews that were not filmed interviews?

A.: Not that I'm aware of.

. . .

Q.: During the preparation of the broadcast, did you ever read any Army or CIA documents?

A.: Not that I can recall.

. . .

Q.: Did you ever review any order of battle documents?

A.: No.

. . .

Q.: There has been some testimony here about the Pike Committee. Were you aware during the preparation of the broadcast what the Pike Committee was?

A.: No.

By then, reporters in the courtroom were turning to one another incredulously. The questioning went on and on, accompanied by the refrain "No. . . . Not that I can recall," until Ira Klein finally stepped from the witness stand naked as a jaybird.

At that point, even before Boies began what would be a powerful "truth" defense, Burt already lost. And as witness after witness confirmed the documentary's charges, culminating with the testimony of officers who had served with Westmoreland, the journalistic misdeeds uncovered with so much fanfare paled by comparison. However misguided, they clearly had been committed in the service of entertainment, not to distort the facts. The Westmoreland case revealed itself finally as a striking example of that politics that denies or invents reality.

Let us be charitable and grant that some of those in the New Right have boarded an express train whose destination they do not know. But most of the first-class passengers are cognizant of where they are headed. In his 1982 book, Kevin Phillips discusses fundamental alterations in our government that leave no doubt about the direction of his thinking. Although he calls his model state parliamentary, it in no way resembles a true parliamentary system, which em-

354 phasizes party responsibility. Instead, Congress would be reduced to an arm of an imperial presidency, with congressional leaders serving in the Cabinet and the two-party system merged into a single-party coalition. Also, the jurisdiction of the federal courts would be cut back. All this, he assures us, could be accomplished without changing the Constitution. As for the media, presumably he still favors his earlier suggestion that it be regulated by the federal government.

According to Senator East's legislative assistant Samuel Francis, the "best known characteristic" of the New Right is its rejection of "abstract universalism," with its emphasis on the "brotherhood of man" and "egalitarianism." Replacing these, the New Right will stress "a Domestic Ethic that centers on the family, the neighborhood and local community, the church, and the nation." A primary value will be "the duty of work," which may result in "a more harmonious relationship between employer and worker." His remarks remind one that in 1940, when the French Republic became the collaborationist Vichy dictatorship, its coins changed also, with "liberty, equality, fraternity" replaced by "work, family, country." The New Right clearly feels far more comfortable with that triptych than with such "abstract universalism" as "a decent respect for the opinions of mankind" or "all men are created equal."

We should by no means regard the New Right movement with any sense of inevitability. Events are moving rapidly. In the next four years the New Right could field its own presidential candidate—Helms, for example—in the Republican party, or it could be a powerful third party movement. Or it may overreach itself, peak and decline. William Rusher has admitted, "Any development that revives and inflames the old division between haves and have-nots in the producing segment of the society could quickly disrupt the [New Right] coalition." With a blue-collar and lower-middle-class constituency, the New Right quails before class consciousness and conflict as vampires recoil from sunlight or a crucifix.

Meanwhile, right-wing harassment of the mass media will continue and, although greater journalistic accuracy is a blessing to be desired and striven for, neither accuracy, nor fairness, nor conciliation will end these attacks. Averting our eyes from what is happening will not make it go away. Above all, this is not the time for a failure of nerve.

[Louis Wolf]

25

INACCURACY IN MEDIA:

ACCURACY IN MEDIA REWRITES

THE NEWS AND HISTORY

We are not for hire," says Murray Baron, president of the controversial group Accuracy in Media (AIM). The Washington-based organization loftily touts itself as "America's only citizen's watchdog of the news media," a mission it pursues with reactionary zeal. Its chairman, Reed Irvine, has picked fights with nearly every major media outlet in the United States, claiming they have strayed from AIM's alleged cause of media "accuracy," "balance," and "fairness."

During 1975, in one of his rare candid moments, Irvine acknowledged that "almost anything you say in a few words isn't going to be the whole truth of the matter." In AIM's own case, though, Irvine's rhetoric and tactics give his game away. He and his group work tirelessly to convince the public there is a creeping Red menace in much of the U.S. media. Their mass mailing fund-raiser reads, "Help us combat the disinformation and false propaganda that is permeating our media."

Reprinted from *Covert Action Information Bulletin* 21 (Spring 1984), pp. 24–38, by permission of the author and the publishers.

Its beginnings were modest. With a reported initial capital of two hundred dollars, AIM was formed in September 1969, and incorporated in June 1971. The original national advisory board included, until his death in 1971, former Secretary of State Dean Acheson. The trio that signed the incorporation document comprised John K. McLean, an investment broker and past publisher of the little-known *Underground Conservative*; Abraham H. Kalish, who worked from 1949 to 1958 with the U.S. Information Agency and from 1958 to 1971 at the U.S. Army's Defense Intelligence School; and Reed Irvine.

Reed John Irvine was born in 1922 to Mormon parents in Salt Lake City, Utah, and attended college in Utah and Colorado. During World War II, he served in the Marine Corps as a Japanese language officer in the Pacific, and after the war, from 1946 to 1948, he worked for the War Department as a member of the U.S. Occupation Forces in Japan. After brief academic stays in Washington State and Colorado, he ultimately received a bachelor of literature degree from St. Catherine's Society, part of Oxford University in the United Kingdom. His thesis topic was telling—"Unemployed Labour as a Pressure Group in Great Britain: 1919–39." In 1951, Irvine returned to the United States and was hired as an economist by the Federal Reserve System; there he spent what two former co-workers informed CAIB was an undistinguished quarter century.

In its early years, AIM was run by Abraham Kalish, who worked for a hundred dollars a year attending press conferences or badgering individual journalists. He cut a bizarre figure in Washington in his fluorescent bow ties, loudly colored shirts, and lizard-skin shoes. In 1971, when Kalish was not rehired at his Defense Intelligence School job, he gradually moved toward a career, albeit unsuccessful, in local politics. Irvine then assumed a larger, more influential role in the workings of the group, while, at first, he still held his Federal Reserve job.

Irvine's new influence was seen as a positive change by foundation and corporate donors. AIM's 1971 tax return showed expenditures of $5,047.14 and a net worth of $1,364.57. Then, in 1972, the return reflected a tenfold rise in total expenses to $51,430.72. There was no looking back.

AIM'S LEADING LIGHTS

An examination of the roster of past and present officers, directors, and members of the national advisory board confirms AIM's sharp rightward tangent, belying its claim to be nonpartisan or, for that matter, its asserted accuracy, **357** balance, or fairness.

Murray Baron, AIM associate since 1972 and president since 1976, has made his living since the 1930s first as a union official with the International Brotherhood of Teamsters in New Jersey, and then as a labor and industrial relations consultant to various U.S. and overseas corporations. He was a trustee of Freedom House, the right-wing counterpart to Amnesty International; a member of the CIA-funded Citizens Committee for a Free Cuba, and of the archconservative Committee of One Million, a defense appropriations lobby; and a cofounder of the CIA-sponsored Citizens Committee for Peace with Freedom in Vietnam. In exchange for the many introductions he has made to AIM of various right-wing and corporate supporters, Baron receives a finder's fee of a thousand dollars a month.

Vice president Wilson C. Lucom, a longtime anticommunist trooper, is best known for his disinformation campaign during the early 1970s against the president of Chile, Salvador Allende. Lucom collaborated closely with right-wing New York public relations entrepreneur Marvin Liebman who, according to a court statement filed by the Department of Justice, received funds from Chile's United Nations mission to publish *Chile la Verdad* (Chile the Truth), an openly anti-Allende propaganda sheet distributed throughout the United States. After the Chilean embassy was mysteriously robbed in May 1972, a number of people whose names were on the embassy's mailing list suddenly began receiving the Lucom publication, and a Justice Department subpoena was issued against him. The subpoena was later withdrawn when pressures were exerted on the Nixon White House by International Telephone & Telegraph, the CIA, and others who had vested interests in the anti-Allende propaganda that Lucom and Liebman were grinding out.

AIM cofounder and communications director since 1974, Bernard Yoh was born in Shanghai, China, and emigrated to the United States in 1947. He was a personal advisor in counterinsurgency techniques to former South Vietnamese puppet president Ngo Dinh Diem from 1955 to 1962, serving under CIA's infamous General Edward Geary Lansdale. Yoh participated in covert missions into North Vietnam. He takes personal credit for creating the Sea Swallows, an elite paramilitary and intelligence-gathering unit in the Vietnamese Delta region; he was in fact the conduit through which CIA funds for the program were passed. At least one of their prisoners is known to have died under interrogation, in Yoh's presence. Though Yoh is now generally considered a has-been by agency stalwarts, he still collaborates with Washington-area right-wing Vietnamese exiles, sometimes providing them AIM office space for their meetings. He even discussed with one U.S.-trained Vietnamese munitions officer a proposed 1981 training session in fabrication of homemade explosive

358   devices, ostensibly for use in some Third World country. Yoh was an advisor to Spanish dictator Generalissimo Francisco Franco and to the Philippine and South Korean governments, and has provided similar services to other governments in Asia, Latin America, and Europe. Yoh once even bragged of having designed a machine gun for the Pentagon. He lectured for some years at the Air War College in Alabama on counterinsurgency and psychological warfare, skills that enhance his current AIM position. He was active in arranging the November 1983 visit to Washington by Holden Roberto, leader of the largely superfluous Angolan antigovernment group, FNLA. Like Jonas Savimbi and his UNITA, Roberto has depended upon South African and CIA backing in military campaigns trying to overthrow the Angolan government. Yoh helped circulate a four-page letter from Roberto to a number of senators, asking for material and for abolition of the 1976 Clark Amendment, which prohibits CIA covert activities against Angola.

Board member Elbridge Durbrow joined the State Department in 1930, subsequently holding diplomatic posts in Poland, Romania, the U.S.S.R., Italy, Portugal, and Malaysia, and was ambassador to Vietnam from 1957 to 1961. Before retiring in 1968, he left the diplomatic field to serve as advisor to the commander of Maxwell Air Force Base in Alabama. In 1971, he became director of the Freedom Studies Center set up by the far-right American Security Council and the now defunct Institute of American Studies. Now eighty-one, Durbrow still keeps a hand in AIM affairs.

Other AIM advisory board members include:

- Marx Lewis, a former trade-union official, who claims he has been fighting communism since 1917. At eighty-five, he is still engaged in that preoccupation as chairman of the Council for the Defense of Freedom (formerly the Council Against Communist Aggression, established in 1951). This organization sends mass mailings to public libraries, universities, media outlets, and various government agencies, and it also lobbies Congress. CDF publishes and distributes, jointly with AIM, a free weekly eight-page sensationalist tabloid called *The Washington Inquirer*. (Some readers unwittingly pay a $20 or $30 annual subscription.) Not surprisingly, at least ten individuals associated with Accuracy in Media, including Murray Baron, Reed Irvine, *Inquirer* editor Wilson Lucom, and Bernard Yoh, sit on CDF's national board and national committee.

- Retired Admiral Thomas H. Moorer, former chief of naval operations and Joint Chiefs of Staff chairman during the Nixon administration. He was a Nixon and Kissinger loyalist viewed by his Pentagon colleagues as a superhawk, especially while a member of Kissinger's top-level "40 Committee," overseeing the multifaceted and most secret operations of the intelligence apparatus, particularly the key covert actions against Vietnam, Cambodia, Laos, and Chile.

- Retired Marine Corps General Lewis W. Walt.
- Retired Rear Admiral William Chamberlain Mott, former special assistant to the Joint Chiefs of Staff chairmen, and now president of the avowedly conservative Washington-based Capital Legal Foundation. Mott is also vice president of Trager's National Strategy Information Center.
- William E. Simon, former Treasury secretary and energy czar in the Nixon and Ford administrations; Heritage Foundation trustee; and wealthy funder of right-wing causes, in part via the John N. Olin Foundation, of which he has been president since 1977. Called the "Billy Graham of capitalism" by a columnist, Simon has personal assets reportedly well over $20 million and owns a stable of racehorses. He worked in and was a major contributor to Ronald Reagan's 1980 presidential campaign. One immediate reward was his appointment as president of the U.S. Olympic Committee.
- Dr. William Yandell Elliott, onetime Harvard University government professor who was on the National Security Council's planning board and was a trustee of Radio Liberty, long sponsored by the CIA.
- Dr. Eugene P. Wigner, eighty-one-year-old Hungarian-born recipient of the 1963 Nobel Prize for physics, advisor to the Atomic Energy Commission for over ten years, chairman since at least 1976 of the International Conference on the Unity of the Sciences, a front organization of Reverend Sun Myung Moon, activist on behalf of pronuclear and fallout-shelter lobbies.
- Dr. Frederick Seitz, president of Rockefeller University in New York City, former vice-chairman of the Pentagon's Defense Science Board, executive committee chairman of the newly formed pronuclear New York–based Scientists and Engineers for Secure Energy, Inc., busily involved since the mid-1970s with Rev. Moon's probes to establish credibility in the science field.
- Dr. Harry David Gideonse, once chancellor at the New School of Social Research and chairman of the Freedom House board of directors.

WHO BANKROLLS AIM?

It is evident from the professional experience and political composition of the flock clustered around AIM that these people mean business and such business costs big money. As noted earlier, the fortunes of the organization began to improve in 1972. Then, for several years, the annual budget was in the $60,000 to $100,000 range. In 1977, it exceeded $200,000; in 1979 it was up to about $513,000; and by 1981, the budget had risen sharply to over $1.1 million. Knowledgeable sources have told CAIB that the current annual budget is over $1.5 million.

Part of the difficulty in assessing AIM's funding arises from the wall of secrecy they attempt to maintain around this aspect of the operation, particularly the identity of major donors. Their statistics on the number of subscribers to the twice-monthly AIM *Report* vary. In 1981, AIM's direct-mail sales pitch claimed the figure was "over 30,000." But in a November 1982 Denver speech, Irvine offered a lower, 25,000 figure, and currently, they say, they print between 30,000 and 40,000 copies per issue, depending on the topics covered. In any event, many copies are given away free.

In an interview with CAIB, Elizabeth Doherty of the National Council of Better Business Bureaus in Arlington, Virginia, stated categorically that Accuracy in Media does not meet two specific bureau standards. First, AIM's audits are conducted only on a cash basis, not on the required accrual basis, a practice she said "is not in accordance with generally accepted accounting procedures." Also, the audits do not break down into categories sufficient to verify actual expenses. Thus far, despite three letters from the Better Business Bureau requesting AIM's 1983 audit, Ms. Doherty said AIM has not even replied. Further, bureau standards for nonprofit organizations stipulate that no more than 20 percent of the board members should receive compensation. In AIM's case, three of the twelve board members receive payment from AIM.

AIM rewards its largest benefactors with a seat on its national advisory board. Shelby Cullom Davis has been a successful New York investment banker since 1947, except from 1969 to 1975, when he was U.S. ambassador to Switzerland. He joined AIM's board in 1972, and sits on the boards of the Heritage Foundation and the anti-union National Right to Work Foundation, to both of which his personal foundation also contributes generous sums. Examination of Davis's New York foundation tax returns reveals the high level of support for AIM. Between November 1975 and February 1983, his recorded AIM contributions, all tax-deductible, totaled a whopping $448,000.

Robert H. Krieble, chairman of the board and chief executive officer of the Loctite Corporation in Connecticut, which manufactures paints, sealants, and industrial machinery, has made substantial contributions to AIM since 1978. He received more than the usual national advisory board seat; Murray Baron and Reed Irvine purchased two hundred shares of Loctite Corporation common stock, worth about ten thousand dollars.

AIM contributor and board member Henry Salvatori is the founder and retired head of Western Geophysical Company, a Houston-based Litton Industries subsidiary specializing in seismic petroleum exploration by over 120 crews with 4,000 employees in Latin America, Africa, and Europe. Salvatori has for years been involved with various far-right organizations having an international and/or strategic thrust.

Karl Robin Bendetsen, who during World War II commanded Japanese internment camps in the United States, is a lawyer. He retired in 1972 as chairman of the Connecticut-based Champion International Corporation. Owning 3.5 million acres of prime timberlands and more than one hundred plants in eighteen states, Champion still pays Bendetsen over ten thousand dollars monthly in benefits. He retired during a price-fixing controversy after which Champion was forced by the government to pay $47 million in damages and fines. Bendetsen has made frequent large donations to AIM.

Sir James Michael Goldsmith, fifty-one-year-old right-wing British industrialist, is publisher of the French magazine *L'Express*, and the subject of numerous lawsuits in Britain arising out of his multifaceted financial enterprises, many of which have reportedly nibbled at the fringes of Her Majesty's monetary laws. (See CAIB Number 13 on Goldsmith's Guatemalan oil dealings with former CIA Deputy Director Vernon Walters.)

Reed Irvine proudly announced (AIM Report, April [A] 1984) that a man who wished to remain anonymous had written a check for $100,000 to launch an "endowment fund" so AIM could have "some permanent income." Irvine added ambitiously, "We would welcome bequests. . . . You may also wish to consider donating assets while you are still alive and arranging to receive the income from those assets as long as you live. There are tax advantages in this procedure and we can advise you on it if you are interested."

Perhaps the most significant spoke in AIM's wheel of fortune is Richard Mellon Scaife. The Scaife Family Charitable Trusts doled out a $150,000 grant to AIM in January 1982, according to *Group Research Report*, which monitors the right wing in the United States. Most recently, according to the AIM Report (March [B] 1984), Scaife's Carthage Foundation gave $50,000. Altogether, Scaife has steered approximately $433,000 to AIM since 1977. Based in Pittsburgh, Scaife is, at fifty-one, a very busy philanthropist and kingpin of both Old Right and New Right media projects. He was a willing partner with the CIA in creating and maintaining the agency's London-based propaganda front, Forum World Features, until it was exposed in 1975 by European and American journalists. If ever the CIA wanted to channel financial assistance to Reed Irvine and company, the chances are better than even that laundryman Scaife would be in a position to supply the soap.

Since 1973, assorted conservative causes and institutions have received a grand total of over $37 million from Scaife's foundations. The $150,000 grant to AIM is to our knowledge the largest ever bestowed upon it. (The best in-depth work on Scaife is "Citizen Scaife," by Karen Rothmyer, *Columbia Journalism Review*, July/August 1981.)

362 BUTTERING UP THE BOARDROOMS

There is a correlation between some of the issues AIM takes up in the AIM *Report*, letters to newspapers or TV editors by Irvine and others, and some of the corporate money it receives. *Soho News* (July 15, 1981) revealed the first hard facts on the funding AIM was receiving from the oil companies. A Mobil Oil spokesman confirmed that the company doled out $10,000 to AIM in both 1980 and 1981, and at least $20,000 has been given since by the company. Irvine took up Mobil's case with the media on several occasions. In June 1980, he wrote to the board chairman of RCA, which owns NBC, claiming the network was guilty of an "anti-business" leaning, and unabashedly setting forth what must have been Mobil's own bottom line: "One solution would be to permit businesses such as Mobil to air opinion programs." In June 1981, at AIM's annual meeting, *Mobil Oil* was given an AIM award praising the firm for its hard-hitting television and newspaper advertising offensive, concluding that "corporations need not be timid."

Bernard Yoh admitted in 1981 that Mobil was at the top of AIM's corporate donor list. The same year, the Texaco Philanthropic Foundation gave AIM $7,000 for what it called "unrestricted support" and has given more since. Exxon, Chevron, Getty, and Phillips have also contributed substantially, as have a number of smaller oil exploration firms.

Irvine and friends like to project a populist image of themselves as advocates for the common people against what AIM calls "the media Goliath." In February 1976, during a gasoline price crisis, NBC's New York City affiliate aired a five-part series on the issue. In April, beneath the headline, "NBC Zaps the Oil Companies," AIM *Report* said the program showed an "antipathy toward business." Highlighting statements by Mobil and Exxon, AIM bleated that the oil companies, which it called "victims," should be given a right of reply under the fairness doctrine.

In August 1982, Bill Moyers did a two-part investigative story on the CBS-TV Evening News about the use in New York and Florida of the pesticide Temik, manufactured by Union Carbide. In a long letter to CBS president Van Gordon Sauter, Irvine acknowledged that Union Carbide had stopped selling Temik in New York when contaminated ground water was discovered on Long Island, but accepted at face value Union Carbide's claim that Florida soil conditions were different and that Temik decomposed there before getting into the ground water. AIM simply red-baited the two State University of New York scientists who had discussed on camera the ill effects of Temik, railing about their being members of the progressive organization Science for the People, and ignoring their scientific evidence.

Irvine's letter to CBS was liberally sprinkled with Union Carbide's posi-

tion on every aspect of the story, including the company's own alleged scientific data attempting to show that Moyers was out to get the company and the
orange growers. What emerges more clearly from the letter is that Irvine was
out to get Moyers. Though he did not respond directly at the time, Moyers
spoke candidly in 1983, saying Irvine "is to accuracy in media what Cleopatra
was to chastity on the Nile."

The negative utility of AIM's material was also illustrated after *Philadelphia Inquirer* reporters won a Pulitzer Prize for an April 1977 four-part series
on the police brutality rampant in the city at the time. Much of what happened in the stories had appeared in television news footage graphically showing police beating and kicking defenseless citizens, nearly all of whom were
black. Nevertheless, Irvine produced an impassioned but highly questionable
acquittal of the Philadelphia police (AIM *Report*, August [II] 1978), predictably
blaming the newspaper for reporting the story the way it did. Mayor Frank
Rizzo bought a hundred copies of the *Report* and put together a press packet to
argue that the newspaper was misguided and his police force humane.

AIM RECOLORS AGENT ORANGE

In Vietnam and Laos, thousands of mothers are today bearing stillborn and
monstrously deformed babies with two heads, with limbs growing from abnormal parts of the body, eyes facing inward, and so on (see CAIB Number
17). In the United States, over twenty thousand Vietnam veterans have filed
disability claims because of the effects they believe resulted from exposure to
Agent Orange and other defoliants that the U.S. sprayed in Indochina. These
include birth defects, liver failure, testicular cancer, skin diseases, tumors, bone
deterioration, hearing and memory loss, headaches, speech impediment, and
personality change. In frustration and fear, ninety thousand Vietnam veterans
have signed the computerized Veterans Administration "Agent Orange Reg-
istry" for medical screening. Most recently, even the conservative American
Legion has come down firmly on the side of the veterans, trying to press the
government to deal forthrightly with the issue.

AIM has ignored all these developments; instead, AIM *Report* and *The
Washington Inquirer* have featured several denunciations of the widespread questions about Agent Orange. An AIM-sponsored February 1983 luncheon meeting in Washington starred retired Air Force Colonel Charlie Hubbs, who was
involved in Operation Ranch Hand, the Air Force program that drenched the
rice paddies, forests, streams, and people of Vietnam with 12 million gallons
of Agent Orange. He claimed that in Vietnam, he would "slurp the stuff to

364 demonstrate its harmlessness," and that his crews were often "doused thoroughly" with the defoliant.

Two years earlier, the April 1981 AIM *Report* glibly dismissed "the Agent Orange scare." The *Report* also reiterated attacks, first made in 1974 and 1978, against a February 1974 *New York Times* article by scientific reporter Richard Severo about the effects of U.S. defoliation on Vietnam's environment. Based on a study by the National Academy of Sciences which suggested it would take one hundred years for the forests to recover, the report was branded by AIM "the study that never was" simply because it was a draft leaked to the *Times*.

Irvine responded to four other Agent Orange articles written by Severo in May 1979 and March 1981, saying some "were constructed in a way that was bound to spread fear and suspicion," while others were not "balanced" and created a "gross distortion." "The *New York Times* has a long record of misinforming its readers" about Agent Orange, Irvine insisted. He finally admitted he "got help from the VA" in his critique. The Veterans Administration actually assisted him in research and in writing the AIM *Report*, which they then purchased and sent out to the media under the VA letterhead and, for months, it was handed to veterans applying at VA offices for Agent Orange–related disability status.

AIM's partiality on this issue was further demonstrated in October 1983 when Reed Irvine spoke to the twenty ninth annual meeting of the Southern Agricultural Chemicals Association. Asserting that it was the media, not the chemical industry that was polluting our society, Irvine told his listeners that Agent Orange was good for agriculture and the lumber industry. Suggestions to the contrary in the media, he told his happy audience, have been part of a large propaganda and disinformation campaign. SACA members not already funding AIM were told they should do so and thereby "fight the media."

A medical study of Operation Ranch Hand pilots just released by the Air Force concedes a statistically significant number of birth defects, infant deaths, skin cancers, circulation problems, and liver disorders. The *Washington Inquirer* (March 2, 1984) immediately twisted the study's conclusions to fit AIM's recurrent theme, using the headline: "Agent Orange Exonerated."

AIM DISINFORMATION

In full-page newspaper advertisements for the 1981 book by AIM employee James L. Tyson, Jr., titled *Target America: The Influence of Communist Propaganda on U.S. Media*, readers were asked to ponder: "Did the Kremlin cook up that story you read in this morning's paper? . . . Are you reading what your Soviet enemies want you to read?" The *Chicago Tribune* called the book "witless and unpersuasive." Undiscouraged, AIM reissued the book in 1983 in condensed form as a paperback.

Reed Irvine's preoccupation with the creeping Communist menace is legendary. In February 1983, as a conference on "The Lessons of Vietnam" was convening at the University of California, he branded former *New York Times* correspondent and author Harrison Salisbury a "purveyor of disinformation" for the views he expressed about the American role in Vietnam. Irvine's colleague Cliff Kincaid accused Don Luce, former volunteer aid worker in Vietnam and longtime peace advocate, of fabricating "the false story" about Vietnamese prisoners being held in what became known as "tiger cages." It was false to Kincaid despite photographs of the cages by Luce and a member of Congress, and documents proving that the small cages were designed and built under Pentagon contract. Luce was also credited by AIM with undermining the rule of the Shah of Iran, helping "pave the way" for the Ayatollah Khomeini, simply because he had visited Teheran shortly before the Shah was finally deposed, and published a trenchant article on his trip.

Three days after the Korean Air Lines Flight 007 was shot down, *Washington Post* writer Michael Getler wrote a story citing government and private sources that suggested U.S. intelligence involvement. (See CAIB Number 20 for a lengthy analysis of the incident.) Irvine shot off a letter to the *Washington Times* snidely suggesting that Getler "seems to have planted ideas in the head of the Russians," even though the Soviet news agency had stated that the Korean plane was used "to attain special intelligence aims" the day before Getler's article appeared. Getler scolded Irvine, saying the "planted ideas" allegation was "an ugly, incorrect, ideological smear not befitting someone who is supposed to be concerned with accuracy in media."

One of Irvine's more bizarre observations, still heard today in his speeches, is to blame the media for the Watergate scandal, claiming it caused the American military defeat in Indochina and the deaths of thousands of Americans, Vietnamese, Cambodians, and Laotians.

One CBS executive said Irvine and AIM are "specialists in tunnel vision." This was personified in a letter Irvine wrote to the *Washington Post* (July 24, 1982) about Walter Cronkite, who, he had previously implied, was serving the Communist cause by some of his CBS evening news reportage. Stating that he wanted to avoid any impression that he was fingering Cronkite as a communist "dupe" or worse, he then proceeded to do just that. He claimed that "two distinguished journalists" (more than likely Arnaud de Borchgrave and Robert Moss, who are incessantly quoted by AIM) told him that "any correspondent who spends any length of time in Moscow and comes away not

366 expressing revulsion for the Communist system must be suspected of having been recruited." Cronkite was the CBS Moscow bureau chief from 1946 to 1948.

Like J. Edgar Hoover, Jesse Helms, and a half-dozen right-wing groups, AIM believes Martin Luther King, Jr. was part of the grand Communist conspiracy rather than a fighter for civil rights and justice. In February 1981, Irvine applied to the Department of Justice for the FBI's massive collection of tape recordings of wiretaps of King's home and office telephones. Conscious of the potential for widespread negative reaction against the FBI and Reagan, the FBI has thus far not released them to Irvine.

The World Anti-Communist League recently disclosed in its newsletter that its "psychological warfare committee" had met with Irvine. WACL is an association of extreme "professional" anticommunists, widely reported to have long-standing links to Latin American death squads.

To gain a grasp of the methodologies used by Accuracy in Media, it is helpful to examine two major news themes to which it has given a high profile and where its activities were critically important.

THE RE-ASSASSINATION OF LETELIER AND MOFFITT

On September 21, 1976, the explosion that shook Washington's Sheridan Circle was heard around the world. Exiled Chilean diplomat Orlando Letelier and his assistant Ronni Karpen Moffitt were killed by a bomb in their car as they drove to work.

Two months later, Jack Anderson and Les Whitten wrote a nationally syndicated column, the first link in a chain of disinformation calculated to discredit Letelier and the cause of freedom in Chile, while deflecting attention from the dastardly crime itself. Anderson and Whitten had been leaked some papers purportedly from Letelier's briefcase. The documents, translated and analyzed, were delivered to them by members of the Association of Former Intelligence Officers (AFIO). Anderson and Whitten have since publicly admitted that they never questioned the documents or the motives of the leakers. Instead, they rushed to press with a story alleging that letters in the briefcase from Salvador Allende's daughter, Beatriz, who was living in exile in Cuba, "prove" Letelier was on a Cuban payroll. The funds sent to Letelier and mentioned in Beatriz Allende's letters came in fact from the Popular Unity coalition and were funds that had been raised in Western Europe from religious, trade union,

and democratic forces throughout the world which condemned the violent, **367**
CIA-engineered overthrow of Chile's duly elected government.

The disinformation campaign that followed depended upon a consciously
repeated misinterpretation and mistranslation of the documents. Reed Irvine
began by writing congratulatory letters to the more than four hundred newspapers that carried the Anderson-Whitten column. Others in the tight circle of
columnists who simultaneously began receiving packets of the alleged briefcase contents put them right into the media hopper. They included Irvine;
William F. Buckley, Jr., publisher of *National Review*, and Jeffrey Hart, one
of its columnists; *Washington Star* veteran Jeremiah O'Leary, later with the
National Security Council under Alexander Haig, and now with the *Washington Times*; Ralph de Toledano, a longtime media asset of J. Edgar Hoover
and for many years close friend and confidante of former high CIA operative
and AFIO founder David Atlee Phillips, who headed the agency's destabiliza-
tion team against Chile; Robert Moss, who lived and worked in Chile, and
wrote with CIA help the anti-Allende book, "Chile's Marxist Experiment,"
which was financed by the CIA and given away free by the Chilean embassy
in Washington; and conservative syndicated columnists Rowland Evans and
Robert Novak. On top of this media blitz, right-wing Congressman Larry
McDonald (D-Georgia) placed the letters in the *Congressional Record* in July
1977.

Though not on the leak list, *Washington Post* reporter Lee Lescaze scruti-
nized the documents closely (they were generally "available" in Washington),
and judged that the allegations based upon them in the columns "followed the
darkest possible interpretation of the scanty material." Finally, on December
13, 1978, the federal prosecutor, Eugene Propper, put on record in a court
hearing that the FBI "had gone over the briefcase papers carefully and found
no evidence Letelier is or ever has been an intelligence asset of the Cuban Government."

Reed Irvine was not deterred from his chosen course. Insisting that Letelier
was a Cuban agent, he charged an FBI cover-up, and asked his readers, "Now
the question is, will the media tell the truth about Letelier even if the FBI
won't?" (AIM *Report*, October [1] 1980). When the *Boston Globe* wrote a story
skeptical of the AIM interpretation of the documents, Irvine wrote them, insisting on "corrections." When the *Globe* refused, Irvine crossed the street and
placed an advertisement in the *Boston Herald American*, an abrasive act in media
circles.

AIM's access to what, after all, was government evidence in a murder case,
was surprising. Even as the document packets were widely dispersed to chosen
right-wing media personalities, Orlando Letelier's widow, Isabel, was unable
to obtain the briefcase contents for many months, and then only after repeated

368 demands from her lawyer. Irvine bragged in October 1980 that AIM "has had copies of many of the documents found in Letelier's briefcase since early 1977," as well as his appointment diary and address book, "a copy of which we have long had." His devotion to "accuracy" has led him to write more than fifty-five separate stories on the case since 1976, more than any other single topic since AIM's founding. He and other members of the circle to whom the documents were leaked in the first place continue to this day dragging out their weary and spent disinformation fraud, each time hoping to kill Orlando Letelier and Ronni Moffitt once more.

THE RAY BONNER OPERATION

Whenever the major media come up with a hard story on U.S. military or intelligence agency operations, at home or abroad, AIM cries "disinformation." Witness AIM's treatment of Ray Bonner, the *New York Times* correspondent formerly based in El Salvador. Bonner had been reporting consistently on deepening U.S. involvement there, on the heinous activities of the death squads, and about bloody wholesale massacres perpetrated by U.S.-trained armed forces and police. His penetrating coverage helped him develop sources that no other journalist on the scene could command. According to Reed Irvine, Bonner was "worth a division to the communists in Central America."

On January 11, 1982, the *Times* published Bonner's front-page account of the presence of U.S. Special Forces personnel during the brutal torture by Salvadoran soldiers of persons accused of being guerrillas, based on an extensive interview by Bonner with Carlos Antonio Gomez Montano, a twenty-one-year-old Salvadoran army deserter present during the tortures. (See CAIB Number 16 for selections from an interview with Gomez.)

Other articles by Bonner dealt with the controversial 1982 election, the virtual gutting by the Roberto D'Aubuisson regime of the then already shallow land-reform program, and the widespread corruption in the government and armed forces fed in large part by the massive influx of American aid being diverted into the hands of a few ministers and generals.

Accuracy in Media quickly took Bonner on, issuing six different stories in the first half of 1982, denigrating him and accusing him of "conveying guerrilla propaganda." The nature of AIM's research became apparent, however, when it disclosed (AIM *Report*, July [II] 1982) that the fifty-one articles written by Bonner in the *New York Times* from January to June 1982 had been "analyzed" for AIM by Daniel James, described by AIM as "an author, editor, foreign correspondent and lecturer who has specialized in Latin America, Communism, and Soviet affairs for three decades."

James, the former managing editor of the right-wing magazine *The New Leader*, had acknowledged his CIA ties in a *New York Times* interview on December 25, 1977. He lived for many years in Mexico and said that in 1968 he was acquainted with Winston MacKinley Scott, a CIA veteran since 1950 who at the time was CIA chief of station in Mexico City. James told *Times* reporter John Crewdson of asking Scott for "anything that they could get for me or help me with," and affirmed, "I did get information from them." According to a CIA official quoted by Crewdson, the agency had given James "material and background" for what at the time was called a "translation" of Che Guevara's diary.

James's analysis of Bonner concludes: "[O]ne of his main objectives was to discredit the government and the military forces that were standing in the way of a communist takeover of El Salvador." The Irvine-James line on Bonner portrayed his news sources as "discredited," though they were consistently acceptable to Bonner's superiors in New York, who must necessarily be sticklers about so-called leftist sources. AIM read treachery into the fact that the majority of Bonner's sources were not identified in his stories, although the life expectancy of Salvadoreans who speak on the record of massacres by the military, of election irregularities, or of official corruption definitely tends to be on the low side. (And, as noted above, Irvine's attack on Walter Cronkite, for example, also cited unidentified sources.)

Bonner himself earned a top spot on a "death list" of journalists circulated around San Salvador by one of the many busy death squads there. But although some on the list abruptly left the country, he decided to remain. Irvine and AIM feign skepticism when they refer to " 'death squads' whatever they may be." (AIM *Report*, November [I] 1982). Have they queried the surviving relatives of the thousands of victims in any one of fifteen U.S.-supported countries where death squads ply their murderous trade?

The unremitting anti-Bonner campaign finally achieved its goal. Hundreds of AIM *Report* readers did what Irvine exhorted them to do, writing to the *New York Times* and its advertisers to complain about Bonner. In June 1982, Murray Baron and Reed Irvine got *Times* executives Arthur Ochs Sulzberger and Sydney Gruson to meet with them about Bonner. The meeting came on the heels of a public statement in San Salvador by Ambassador Deane Hinton that Bonner "does not hide the fact that he's engaged in advocacy journalism." If the statement sounded familiar to AIM *Report* readers, it was no coincidence. CAIB learned that Irvine had gone to considerable lengths to deliver AIM's views on Bonner to Hinton and other U.S. officials in San Salvador and Washington.

In October, after more cries from Irvine of "disinformation" and "advocacy journalism," and more streams of AIM-generated letters about Bonner, the *Times* had had enough. Irvine gloated when he announced: "Here is some

370 good news. You can quit writing Mr. Sulzberger at the *New York Times* about Raymond Bonner. Bonner is no longer the correspondent for the *Times* in Central America." (AIM *Report*, October [II] 1982). Claiming Bonner's was merely a normal personnel transfer, the *Times* front office pushed him back to the business desk. Recently, due no doubt to the ever-expanding U.S. role in the region and to his singular knowledge of the situation in El Salvador, Bonner has been assigned intermittently to part of the Central America beat.

OTHER AIM ATTACKS

It is not surprising, therefore, that the Reagan administration actively collaborates with AIM in trying to counter what the media say about U.S. involvement in Central America. In April and May 1983, for example, CBS showed reports of the murder, torture, and disappearance of doctors, nurses, and other public health personnel in El Salvador. AIM worked closely with at least three Agency for International Development staffers to produce an October "AIM Research Report" titled "CBS Distorts the Medical Situation in El Salvador."

AIM was jubilant about the U.S. invasion of Grenada. Though even President Reagan first called it an invasion, later renaming it a "rescue operation," Reed Irvine took his cue early on terming the operation a "rescue mission," a "liberation," and a "firm action," yet slipping once in an AIM *Report* by calling it "the American invasion." Perhaps the most telling aspect of Irvine's Grenada stance was his support for the administration policy of keeping the media from reporting until more than two days after the invasion began. Irvine impugned dishonorable motives to NBC's John Chancellor and CBS's Dan Rather for their pointed criticisms of the policy, even suggesting that many journalists verge on being traitorous. Hence, it is no wonder that AIM's newest gimmick is a red white and blue bumper sticker, available for a dollar, which AIM calls a "work of beauty." It reads: "GRENADA—MEDIA DEFEAT." Apparently, to AIM, the best media is no media at all.

AIM's style is often marked by sensationalism, as in these AIM *Report* headlines: "CBS Undermines Central America" about the September 1, 1982, documentary, "Guatemala," in which reporter Ed Rabel showed the effects of government-sponsored terror on the population of that country. AIM claimed that the CBS documentary pulled the wool over the eyes of the American people.

"Soviet Terror Links in Lebanon" and "Lies About Lebanon" related to Israel's June 1982 invasion and aerial bombing, with AIM charging that the media coverage was distorted and that the Israelis had captured PLO documents proving Soviet support for terrorism in Lebanon. This disinformation, reported on by AIM, was similar to the discredited El Salvador "White Paper" of the State Department. The "documents" were given by the Israeli embassy in Washington to AIM's sister publication, the *Washington Inquirer*, though refused to CAIB by the Israelis, when requested.

AIM also asserted vociferously that the full-page ads in major newspapers condemning "Death and Devastation in Lebanon . . . terror bombings, with consistent death and dreadful injury among the most vulnerable of the civilian population—women and children, the elderly and the ailing" were part of what they called "The PLO Disinformation Campaign." Irvine disputed a UPI story from Beirut about Israel's use of antipersonnel phosphorus shells, which described the incredible agony of victims. He called the report "inflammatory." AIM then quoted unidentified Israeli authorities as saying phosphorus shells have long been used by armies as "markers" for artillery strikes and are not antipersonnel weapons. Irvine soon had to print a correction, however—which he does rarely—after retired U.S. Army officers wrote to AIM saying the Israelis were lying. Yet Irvine had willingly disseminated the lie despite television coverage showing phosphorus in use against heavily populated West Beirut.

Other AIM topics have included "The Bulgarian-KGB Plot," "The Journal's Kwitny Never Quits," "NBC Airs Soviet Propaganda." "Bill Moyers Plays Left Field," "Donahue Indoctrinates the Housewives," "Who's Behind the Freeze?" and "ABC Smears J. Edgar Hoover."

A source close to Accuracy in Media has shared with CAIB a very curious AIM internal document. It is an outline of the priority of themes, in both the domestic and foreign spheres, which AIM should feature in its publications and speech-making. Though undated, it appears to have been written in early 1979, and demonstrates that AIM's program works along specific theme lines. Perhaps it is no coincidence that the CIA's own media and propaganda operations (see extensively documented article by Fred Landis in CAIB Number 16 on the agency's media thrust to destabilize Chile under Salvador Allende, Jamaica under Michael Manley, and present day Nicaragua) are also conducted along selected theme lines.

In January 1983, a reliable CAIB source, while visiting AIM's offices in downtown Washington, heard an employee answer the phone, ask if a certain person was in the office, and be told, "He's not here. He had to drive out to the CIA for a pickup." Real journalists don't generally go to the CIA except for an occasional "briefing," and then only under very special arrangements. It was obvious this wasn't a briefing at all, but a trip to the CIA to pick up something for AIM, perhaps a story or a "lead" for the next AIM *Report* or *Washington Inquirer*.

Despite its many revelations, the Senate Select Committee on Intelligence under the late Senator Frank Church barely scratched the surface with its voluminous reports on the activities of the CIA, the National Security Agency, military intelligence, the FBI, and the IRS. The sordid history of the CIA's secret interventions around the world was discussed only in very broad and imprecise generalities. While the Church committee studied in depth the CIA's covert role in eight different countries, a deal was struck whereby the CIA would accede to the release of the volume on Chile if the other seven reports were kept secret. Yet even before the body had been established, Jack Anderson had written a column (November 5, 1974) discussing a confidential Library of Congress study on the CIA in Chile that had reached his desk. Anderson cited the government's "secret economic war" against Chile, stating correctly that "the policy amounted to financial strangulation."

AIM then went to bat, as it frequently does, for the CIA. Asserting that both the Library of Congress and Anderson were "in error," AIM blamed Chile's pre-coup difficulties on Allende's "mismanagement." On February 18, 1975, AIM placed a full-page ad ("The Post-Anderson Cover-Up") in the *Washington Post*, with a rehash of the familiar myths about Chile.

A frequent AIM tactic is to purchase small amounts of stock in the major print and electronic media organizations, to attend stockholder meetings, and to stage confrontations with corporate officers. This provides lively copy for the next AIM *Report*, with the suggestion that David has stood up to Goliath. On April 18, 1984, Irvine attended the CBS shareholders' annual meeting in Philadelphia, at which he nominated AIM's James Tyson to replace Walter Cronkite on the board of directors. Irvine later sadly related that Tyson was "nosed out" by Cronkite.

AIM's stockholder tactics have not always been legal. In April 1975, they spent nearly $13,000 on a *Wall Street Journal* advertisement urging CBS and RCA stockholders to vote for AIM resolutions. The Securities and Exchange Commission informed AIM that this amounted to an illegal effort to secure proxies and, furthermore, that the ad itself was misleading. AIM had to agree it would abide by a court order not to violate SEC's proxy rules again, and would return all the $15 donations people had sent in response to the ad.

In February 1983, perhaps mindful of the 1975 episode, the SEC rejected AIM's request for the inclusion of two proposals in CBS proxy notices sent to stockholders in advance of the annual meetings. AIM's proposals related to the $120 million suit by retired General William Westmoreland arising out of a January 1982 CBS program, "The Uncounted Enemy: A Vietnam Deception." AIM actively raised money for Westmoreland's defense, and their administrative appeal of the SEC's decision was denied. Though Irvine blustered at the time that AIM would challenge the SEC ruling in court, no suit was filed.

In March 1984, Reed Irvine declared to his readers that AIM had been given "a substantial gift of RCA stock." He continued, "We will be happy to sell any AIM member as little as a single share to qualify you to attend the RCA [NBC] annual meeting," on May 1. When reached for comment by CAIB, a senior SEC official observed that the statement was "rather irregular," and its legality "may warrant an investigation by our enforcement branch."

In April 1975, during the last days of the Vietnam War, Vice President Nelson Rockefeller and Senator Barry Goldwater were on a flight together to attend the funeral of Taiwanese ruler Chiang Kai-shek. Rockefeller told Goldwater of a comment to him by an unnamed journalist that the KGB had infiltrated the offices of a number of senators. Goldwater repeated this on a television program, adding confidently though mistakenly that Rockefeller would include it in his imminent report on CIA domestic activities. AIM rushed into print with it. Then, the vice president—not known for being soft on communism—protested in a letter to Irvine, "I have no evidence whatsoever that there is any truth to the story." Nevertheless, Irvine forged ahead with two more articles repeating the story, never mentioning the letter from Rockefeller.

While Rockefeller wasn't convinced there was a Communist under every congressional desk or manipulating every journalist's pen, AIM remains certain. In Bernard Yoh's own words, "What's wrong with McCarthyism?" (*Fairfield County Advocate*, Connecticut, November 23, 1983) Yoh stated recently in Fresno, California, that the *Los Angeles Times* is left-wing, whereas the avowedly conservative Manchester, New Hampshire, *Union-Leader* is the best newspaper in the country.

THE GIVEAWAY DERBY

A prominent feature of the AIM operation is their use of various gimmicks to build their audience. They place expensive full-page advertisements in newspapers with coupons soliciting money and subscriptions; the ads, they claim, pay for themselves. AIM also sends out computerized mailings to various right-wing lists.

Irvine sends out a weekly syndicated column, "Accuracy in Media," to about one hundred small-town newspapers around the country for a token one dollar each. Irvine and friends began in July 1978 to produce a daily taped three-minute radio broadside echoing AIM *Report* and *Washington Inquirer*

374   called "Media Monitor," presently aired on some eighty stations in the United States, provided free to them by AIM "as a public service." The program was originally created by Irvine and Lester Kinsolving, a caustic Washington-based media personality who was once expelled by the organization of journalists covering the State Department because he accepted South African and Rhodesian funds for trips there. He parted ways with AIM in 1980 following better financial and political bargaining. The radio tapes are now coproduced with Cliff Kincaid, now in the number-two editorial position at the right-wing *Human Events*, which President Reagan once called his favorite newspaper.

Since 1976, AIM has sponsored at least six conferences to project the organization's ideological views of media coverage, urging its corporate donors then to assert themselves in the media, and bestowing awards on those journalists it agrees with most. The conferences bear aggressive, alarmist titles, AIM trademarks: "The Media and the Present Danger" (1979), "Confrontation PR" (1981), "Biting the Hands That Feed Them" (1983), and "The Media: Whose Side Are They On?" (1983). This last-mentioned gathering, held in Houston, cost $18,000. The theme of still another conference, held in San Diego in June 1984, was "Media Wars: Battleground of Ideas."

AIM'S TEAMSTER TIES

Reed Irvine announced in December 1980 that an organization called the Allied Educational Foundation had given AIM a $50,000 grant to send "top-drawer" AIM speakers around the United States free of cost. In both 1982 and 1983 it gave $125,000 to AIM, and, in 1984 gave at least $100,000 (see appendix 1).

Such big money has been a boon to the work of AIM. The grants represent a masterstroke of AIM President Murray Baron. He laid the groundwork for it by contacting his old friend and union crony, George D. Barasch, who became administrator of the foundation. Barasch, born in 1910, has on different occasions stated he was born in the Soviet Union, France, and the United States. He was past president of the Allied Trades Council and former secretary-treasurer of Teamsters Local 815 in New Jersey, which covers Teamster members in the warehousing, drug, and chemical industries in New York and New Jersey.

Barasch's past is not untainted. In 1965 Senator John McClellan's Subcommittee on Investigations charged him and several Teamster associates with having misappropriated almost $5 million in union and welfare pension funds. The monies had been shifted by Barasch to shadow corporations in the United States, Puerto Rico, and Liberia run by him and his brother-in-law. When

Barasch suddenly retired during the McClellan inquiry, investigators estimated **375** his income from these dealings at almost $800,000. In the June and July 1965 hearings, Barasch invoked the Fifth Amendment several hundred times, even when asked what his occupation was.

CAIB asked the Allied Educational Foundation, in Englewood Cliffs, New Jersey, for some clarifications. An employee, Joe McCarthy, was cordial but not very communicative. He said that Barasch is "a sort of consultant" to the foundation trustees, whom he refused to name. He did say they comprised a former U.S. Marine Corps general, a National Guard member, an attorney, and a professor. He described the organization as "a charitable educational foundation" which "works on anything that violates the Constitution," but wouldn't explain what kinds of violations he was referring to. He stressed that the Allied Educational Foundation "has no direct connection with Accuracy in Media," a statement directly contradicted in AIM literature and mailings.

The installation of Jackie Presser, fifty-eight, as Teamsters president has undoubtedly been helpful to AIM. CAIB was told by two highly knowledgeable sources that Accuracy in Media already functions in part as "a Teamster public relations front."

CAIB has also learned that AIM president Murray Baron worked directly with Jackie Presser during the 1950s and 1960s, a period during which the union was riddled with organized-crime figures. Where do Murray Baron and Reed Irvine fit into the scheme of things with Presser at his new half-million dollar post? Though there are AIM issues and themes of little interest to the Teamsters, some, such as the public relations battle on behalf of Big Oil interests, ought logically to have great significance to the union, because of the bearing these developments have upon future retail petroleum prices in the United States.

It was Jackie Presser's spirited speech before the Teamsters' 1980 executive board meeting that delivered to Ronald Reagan his sole major trade-union endorsement. Reagan was quoted as saying: "I will not forget what he meant to our campaign." On August 1983, according to the *Washington Post*, White House counsel Fred Fielding warned the administration to keep "an arms-length relationship" with the three-hundred-pound Presser because the Labor Department was examining his involvement in a Cleveland embezzlement scandal. Nevertheless, even as an associate remarked that Presser "should have been in jail dozens of times," the White House continued to maintain what one official calls "cozy" ties to him. Particularly timely is Presser's public expression of support for Reagan's Central America policies. Presser took time out from other Teamster duties last September to write a piece for the *Washington Inquirer* urging that Congress should be "getting behind the President's program" in El Salvador.

In July 1982, the *Washington Times*, owned by Rev. Sun Myung Moon's Unification Church, announced it was sending invitations to some two hundred editors and journalists throughout the United States to attend the October "World Media Conference" in Seoul, South Korea, all expenses paid, including those of spouses. This was the fifth such meeting organized and financed by Moon and his growing empire. Only about a dozen of the U.S. invitees accepted, including Reed Irvine and fellow AIMers Allan Brownfeld and Peter Beckmann.

The gathering, with an agenda on disinformation and media control, was addressed by Reverend Moon and by his deputy and high KCIA operative Bo Hi Pak, by defeated Vietnamese strongman Nguyen Cao Ky, by retired U.S. Navy commander Lloyd Bucher, and by retired U.S. Army general John Singlaub.

The AIM-Moonie links go considerably deeper than attendance at this conference. Dan Holdgreiwe, a dedicated Moonie who was associate editor of the defunct Moon paper, *The Rising Tide*, is now managing editor of the *Washington Inquirer*, which shares offices with AIM. Reed Irvine also has a regular column in the Moon-owned *Washington Times*.

In an analysis of the New Right, the Republican party's semiliberal Ripon Society quoted Unification Church official Jeremiah Schnee saying that Moon's *"Project Volunteer"* is one channel whereby the Moonies "work closely" with AIM (Ripon Forum, January 1983). Bernard Yoh denied Ripon's charge that AIM receives volunteers or "low-cost workers" from the Moon organization. However, two AIM national advisory board members, defense hard-liner Dr. Eugene P. Wigner and academic ethics theorist Dr. Frederick Seitz, have worked on Moon international conferences and with known front organizations since at least 1976.

The current editor of the *Washington Times*, James R. Whelan, who says he is not a Moon church member, was the *Inquirer* publisher in 1979. From 1977 to 1980 he was vice president and editorial director of the Michigan-based newspaper conglomerate Panax Corporation, then owned by John Peter McGoff, who sold it in 1982 to Richard Mellon Scaife. McGoff, who sits on the *Washington Times* nine-member editorial advisory board, solicited for and used huge sums of South African money in 1974 in efforts to purchase a number of major U.S. newspapers, including an unsuccessful bid to obtain the now-expired *Washington Star*.

Since 1978, the Justice Department has been investigating McGoff's clandestine dealings with the South Africans, but little is expected on that front in light of Reagan's South Africa policy. The majority of McGoff's political activity is conducted in seclusion and secrecy. Most surprising, therefore, was his open sponsorship in 1979 of the *Washington Weekly*, listing his name as publisher on the masthead alongside "contributors" Reed Irvine and Ronald Reagan.

CONCLUSION

Whether viewed from Accuracy in Media's own narrow perspectives and priorities or from an independent, impartial standpoint, AIM has achieved a substantial impact both upon its limited following and upon the print and electronic media that it targets with perpetual intensity. In light of the varied data compiled in this report, several questions need to be asked of Reed Irvine, Murray Baron, and their major benefactors. Are they more interested in accuracy in the media or in coercing media to propagate a one-sided presentation of the news ideologically acceptable to AIM? Is AIM so wedded to its large corporate and philanthropic donors that its daily work has to a large degree turned into performing propaganda tasks that serve the donors' vested political and/or financial interests? Does AIM consider itself a judge or a jury of the media, or both?

In March 1981, National Public Radio aired a spoof, an attempt to guess how a speech supporting certain Reagan policies might sound. True to form, Irvine lashed out at NPR. The then NPR president, Frank Mankiewicz, replied that Irvine is "a hatchet man for his own brand of radicalism. . . . You have to wonder what Reed Irvine would have said about Will Rogers, who made fun of Congress and the president every day. Will Rogers never met a man he didn't like. But then I guess Will never met Reed Irvine."

APPENDIX I

WHO FEATHERS AIM'S NEST

Fundamental to an analysis of the program and personalities involved in Accuracy in Media is a grasp of who pays for it. CAIB spent several months examining Internal Revenue Service filings, foundation records, interviewing some corporate and foundation officers, and reviewing and double-checking information from sources both close to and inside AIM. Although by no means comprehensive, the following is a compilation of the data available to CAIB on AIM's funding, representing perhaps two-thirds of the total funding.

Foundations and Corporations	Contributions Known Given to AIM
• Allied Educational Foundation and/or Union Mutual Foundation—Englewood Cliffs, New Jersey (date and place of founding unknown) [including grants from George D. Barasch—see text]	$550,000 since 1978
• Shelby Cullom Davis Foundation—New York City (incorporated 1962 in New York)	448,000 since 1975
• Scaife Family Charitable Trusts and/or Carthage Foundation—Pittsburgh (incorporated 1964 in Pennsylvania)	433,000 since 1977
• Adolph Coors Foundation—Denver (incorporated 1964 in Pennsylvania)	130,000 since 1978
• Parker Foundation—San Antonio (incorporated 1957 in Texas)	103,000 since 1978

380 • Loctite Corporation—Newington, Connecticut   91,000 (including stocks) since 1978

• Henry and Grace Salvatori Foundation—Los Angeles (incorporated 1960 in California)   73,000 (including stock sale proceeds) since 1976

• Schultz Foundation—Clifton, New Jersey (incorporated 1966 in Delaware)   65,550 since 1976

• O'Donnell Foundation—Dallas (incorporated 1957 in Texas) $65,000 since 1979

• Dodge Jones Foundation—Abilene (incorporated 1954 in Texas)   55,000 since 1978

• American Financial Corporation Foundation—Cincinnati (founded 1971 in Ohio)   50,000 since 1980

• Mobil Foundation, Inc.—New York City (incorporated 1965 in New York)   40,000 since 1978

• [Maurice H.] Stans Foundation—Pasadena, California (incorporated 1945 in Illinois)   38,000 since 1979

• American Continental Corporation—Phoenix, Arizona   25,000 since 1981

• Thomas J. Lipton Foundation, Inc.—Englewood Cliffs, New Jersey (incorporated 1962 in Delaware)   24,000 since 1980

• Horizon Oil and Gas Company—Dallas, Texas   22,000 since 1979

• Milliken Foundation—New York City. (founded 1945 in New York as the Deering-Milliken Foundation)   20,500 since 1975

• Texaco Philanthropic Foundation, Inc.—New York City (incorporated 1979 in Delaware)   15,500 since 1980

• Grand Union Company—Elmwood Park, New Jersey (French-owned)   15,000 in 1982

• DeWitt Wallace Fund, Inc.—New York City (incorporated 1965 in New York)   12,600 between 1976 and 1981

• Gordon Fund—New York City (established 1954 in New York)   8,500 between 1976 and 1981

• Henderson Foundation—Boston (founded 1947 in Massachusetts)   8,000 between 1976 and 1980

• Goodyear Tire and Rubber Company—Akron, Ohio   7,500 in 1980

• E. L. Craig Foundation—Joplin, Missouri (incorporated 1960 in Missouri)   6,000 since 1980

- Henderson Foundation—Marshalltown, Iowa (date and place of founding unknown)   5,000 since 1980   **381**
- Champion Spark Plug Company—Toledo, Ohio $4,000 in 1981
- Earle M. and Margaret Peters Trust—Pittsburgh (founded 1953 in Pennsylvania)   4,700 during 1980 and 1981
- Sidney Frohman Foundation—Sandusky, Ohio (founded 1952 in Ohio)   3,500 between 1976 and 1982
- Texas Educational Association—Fort Worth (founded 1949 in Texas)   3,000 between 1978 and 1980
- Lawrence Fertig Foundation, Inc.—New York City (founded 1956 in New York)   2,550 between 1976 and 1980, 1983
- Ingersoll Foundation—Rockford, Illinois (founded 1948 in Illinois)   2,550 in 1982
- Grace Jones Richardson Testamentary Trust—Greensboro, North Carolina (founded in Connecticut) [and]
- H. Smith Richardson Charitable Trust—Greensboro (founded 1976 in North Carolina)   2,400 between 1979 and 1981
- Reader's Digest Foundation—Pleasantville, New York (founded 1938 in New York)   2,100 during 1981 and 1982
- Inman-Riverdale Foundation—Inman, South Carolina (incorporated 1946 in South Carolina)   2,000 since 1982
- J. B. Reynolds foundation—Kansas City, Missouri (incorporated 1961 in Missouri)   2,000 during 1981 and 1982
- Sanford Foundation—Nashville (founded 1964 in Tennessee)   1,800 since 1976
- Barbara Perkins Foundation—Los Angeles (date and place of founding unknown)   1,750 since 1978
- Harsco Corporation Fund—Camp Hill, Pennsylvania (founded 1956 in Pennsylvania)   1,600 between 1980 and 1982
- Ox Hollow Foundation, Inc.—New York City (incorporated 1965 in New York)   1,500 during 1976, 1977, 1980
- Schlitz Foundation—Milwaukee (founded 1942 in Wisconsin, dissolved 1982)   1,300 in 1981
- Citcorp [owner of Citibank]—New York City $1,000 in 1983
- Coleman Foundation—Chicago (founded 1953 in Illinois)   1,000 in 1975

Total $2,449,850★

★ Including $100,000 anonymous contribution, 1984.

382 Other Corporations That Have Given Substantial Contributions to AIM Include:

- Exxon USA • Getty Oil • Phillips Petroleum • Chevron (owned by Standard Oil Company of California) • Sun Oil Company • Union Carbide • IBM • Pepsico • American Medical Association • Dresser Industries, Inc. • Bethlehem Steel Corporation • Kaiser Aluminum & Chemical Corporation • Quaker Oats Company • U-Haul Company International • Panax Corporation (see text about John P. McGoff).

Some Major Individual Contributors to AIM:
- Richard M. Nixon—former president.
- Spiro T. Agnew—controversial former vice president under Nixon, indicted for illegal transactions in his home state, Maryland.
- Walter H. Annenberg—multimillionaire, publisher of *TV Guide* and the horseracing paper, *Daily Racing Form*, close and loyal confidante-friend of Presidents Nixon and Reagan.
- Charles G. "Bebe" Rebozo—Key Biscayne, Florida, banker, reportedly one of Nixon's closest friends whose yacht served as a frequent refuge during Watergate, alleged to have Mafia links by way of his extensive interests in the Resorts International gambling empire and his dealings with international fugitive Robert Vesco.
- William E. Simon—millionaire financier and investments lawyer-consultant, and former U.S. Treasury secretary.
- William Joseph Casey—CIA Director, millionaire, contributed to AIM since 1976 including most recently in December 1983 on a "private" basis via his Long Island, New York estate.
- Sir James Michael Goldsmith—see text.
- Karl Robin Bendetsen—see text.
- Maurice H. Stans—76, business consultant in Los Angeles, former Commerce secretary under Nixon, finance chairman of the infamous CREEP (Committee to Re-elect the President) that was implicated in the Watergate scandal.
- Edward Wyllis Scripps II—board chairman of Scripps League of Newspapers (where he has been since 1931), a director of the Inter-American Press Foundation (see CAIB Numbers 7 and 10), lives in Charlottesville, Virginia, with a home in Nassau.
- David Packard—cofounder and chairman of the electronics and minicomputer giant, Hewlett-Packard, former secretary of defense under Nixon.
- James G. Schneider—savings and loan executive in Illinois, delegate to Republican national conventions in 1976 and 1980.

- Willard Carlisle Butcher—chairman of the Chase Manhattan Bank where he **383** has been since 1947, trustee of the American Enterprise Institute think tank, a director of the multinational corporation, ASARCO.
- William and Ellen Clayton St. John Garwood—at 88 he is still a lawyer, a former Texas State Supreme Court judge.
- Dr. Edward Teller—Hungarian-born physicist known as the "Father of the H-Bomb," former member of the president's Foreign Intelligence Advisory Board.
- Henry H. Hurt—Maryland insurance agent, 76, long-standing follower of Reverend Sun Myung Moon, admitted to the *Wall Street Journal* (February 3, 1982) that he fronted for the Moon-owned U.S. Foods Corporation in McLean, Virginia. In a November 18, 1976, letter to Moon's closest associate, Colonel Bo Hi Pak, published in a congressional report, Hurt wrote, "The Leader [Moon] is the spiritual and financial strength." Still a board member of the Moon front group, the Korean Cultural and Freedom Foundation, Inc., Hurt told CAIB he is "an enthusiastic supporter" of AIM. He also said that in past years, he has given "hundreds of thousands" of dollars to various conservative organizations.
- Harold W. Siebens—president of Worldoil (Panama), lives in Toronto and Nassau.

APPENDIX II

REED RUSHES IN

There is probably nothing Reed Irvine does for AIM with greater speed than to jump to the defense of the U.S. intelligence apparatus. When the Church committee published in 1975–1976 its study of some of the abuses of the U.S. intelligence complex, AIM's pages brimmed over with attempts to discredit Senator Church, the committee, and its findings.

AIM blames the CIA's problems on the few former operatives who have left the agency and have become publicly critical of its past and present activities. These include Philip Agee, John Stockwell, Ralph McGehee, and Victor Marchetti. As for the FBI, Irvine has published frequent articles extolling the memory of J. Edgar Hoover, whose forty-eight years at the bureau under ten presidents remain extremely controversial, even by the most charitable assessments of past and present FBI officials. AIM *Report* articles have included titles such as "ABC Smears J. Edgar Hoover," "NBC to Savage J. Edgar Hoover," and "NBC Trashes J. Edgar Hoover."

Irvine's single-minded vindication of the intelligence agencies goes beyond the pages of the AIM *Report*. He speaks often at CIA and FBI alumni meetings, including the Central Intelligence Retirees Association, the Committee to Help the FBI, and, most recently, at the October 1983 Society of Former Special Agents of the FBI convention in Denver.

CAIB has learned that in November 1983, AIM typed up, had printed, and mailed out, under the society's own blue letterhead, a letter to four hundred major corporations on AIM's priority list of major advertisers. The recipients were targeted in hopes of getting them to withhold advertising from programming that is in the least critical of U.S. intelligence agencies or that examines any public domestic or foreign-policy issue in a manner that is not consistent with AIM's well-varnished viewpoint.

SELECTED BIBLIOGRAPHY

This bibliography is arranged topically and, generally speaking, follows the organization of the book. Although this collection does not contain an essay on polygraph testing, I have included a section on this topic. Mandatory lie-detector tests, which are notoriously unreliable, are required by some government agencies and, indeed, by some private corporations. They are intrusive, of course, and provide still another angle of vision in analyzing the fear, anxiety, and repression that currently grip our society.

CENSORSHIP, SECRECY, AND INFORMATION MANAGEMENT

Berman, Larry. *The Office of Management and Budget and the Presidency, 1921–1979* Princeton, N.J.: Princeton University Press, 1979.

Brownstein, Ronald, and Nina Easton. *Reagan's Ruling Class* New York: Pantheon, 1982.

Burnham, David. "Government Restricting Flow of Information." *Our Right to Know* (Winter 1983): 14.

Cannon, Terry. "Reviving McCarthyism in Washington." *Political Affairs* 60 (October 1981): 20.

Chartrand, Robert L. *Information Policy and Technology Issues: Public Laws of the 99th Congress.* Washington, D.C.: Congressional Research Service, 1987.

Claybrook, Joan, *et al. Reagan on the Road: The Crash of the U.S. Auto Safety Program.* Washington, D.C.: Public Citizen, 1982.

Cook, Blanche, and Gerald Markowitz. "History in Shreds/Freedom of Information Act." *Radical History Review* 26 (October 1982): 173–179.

Dorsen, Norman, and Stephen Gillers, eds. *None of Your Business: Government Secrecy in America.* New York: Viking, 1974.

388 FOI Service Center. *How to Use the Federal* FOI *Act*. New York: FOIA, Inc., 1984.

Galnoor, Itzhak, ed. *Government Secrecy in Democracies*. New York: New York University Press, 1977.

Glasser, Ira. "Case for New FOIA Bill." *The Nation* 238 (June 2, 1984): 669.

Gordon, Michael R. "A Fight over Government Information." *New York Times* (Jan. 6, 1987).

Greenhause, Linda. "Justices Grant CIA Wide Discretion on Secrecy." *New York Times* (April 17, 1985).

Greider, William. *The Education of David Stockman and Other Americans*. New York: Dutton, 1981.

Grosscup, Barry. "Gutting the Right to Know." *The Progressive* 46 (February 1982): 14.

Heatherly, Charles, ed. *Mandate for Leadership*. Washington, D.C.: Heritage Foundation, 1982.

Hendricks, Evan. *Former Secrets*. Washington, D.C.: Campaign for Political Rights, 1982.

Horton, Forest W. *Understanding U.S. Information Policy: The Infrastructure Handbook*. 4 vols. Washington: Information Management Press, 1982.

Lardner, George, Jr. "When in Doubt, Classify." *Washington Post National Weekly Edition* (May 20, 1985).

Lewis, Anthony. "The Right to Scrutinize Government: Toward a First Amendment Theory of Accountability." *University of Miami Law Review* 34 (July 1980): 793–806.

Lewy, Guenther. "Can Democracy Keep Secrets?" *Policy Review* (Heritage Foundation) 26 (Fall 1933): 17.

Lyman, Francesca. "Locking Up Federal Files." *Environmental Action* 13 (July 1981): 22.

Mackenzie, Angus. *Sabotaging the Dissident Press*. New York: Basic Books, 1982.

———. "CIA, Congress Draw FOIA Curtain." *Mediafile* 5 (November 1984): 4.

Melnick, Daniel, *et al. Recent Changes in the Federal Statistical Programs: An Overview of the President's Budget for FY 83 and Analysis of the Depts. of Energy, Labor, and the Bureau of the Census*. Washington: Congressional Research Service, 1982.

Middleton, Drew. "Barring Reporters from the Battlefield." *New York Times Magazine* (February 5, 1984).

Morrison, A. "Supreme Court and F.O.I.A." *The Nation* 239 (September 29, 1984), 287.

National Academy of Sciences, National Academy of Engineering. *Scientific Communication and National Security*. A report prepared by the Panel on

Scientific Communications and National Security. Washington, D.C.: National Academy of Sciences, 1982.

National Commission on Libraries and Information Science. *Public Sector/Private Sector Interaction in Providing Information Services.* Report. Washington, D.C.: National Commission on Libraries and Information Science, 1982.

National Technical Information Service. *Improving Government Resources Management: A Status Report.* Washington, D.C.: National Technical Information Service, 1983.

O'Reilly, James T. "Who's on First: The Role of the Office of Management and Budget in Federal Information Policy." *Journal of Legislation* (Winter 1983), 95–118.

Palmer, John L., and Isabel V. Sawhill, eds. *The Reagan Experience.* New York: Urban Institute Press, 1982.

Pell, Eve. "Putting the Squeeze on Information." *Rights and Bill of Rights Journal* 3 (July 1985): 12.

Relyea, Harold C., *et al. The Presidency and Information Policy.* New York: Center for the Study of the Presidency, 1981.

Savas, Emanuel S. *Privatizing the Public Sector.* Chatham, N.J.: Chatham House, 1982.

Schuman, Patricia A. "Information Justice: A Review of the NCLIS Task Force Report: Public/Private Sector Interaction in Providing Information Services." *Library Journal* 107 (June 1, 1982), 1060–1066.

Simon, Philip. *Reagan in the Workplace: Unraveling the Health and Safety Net.* New York: Center for Responsive Law, 1983.

Spake, Amanda, and Lisa Weiman. "Closing Files/Will FOIA be Saved?" *Mother Jones* 7 (February 1982): 26.

Tolchin, Susan J., and Martin Tolchin. *Dismantling America: The Rush to Deregulate.* New York: Oxford, 1983.

U.S. Congress. House. Committee on Energy and Congress. Subcommittee on Telecommunications, Consumer Protection, and Finance. *Broadcast Regulation: Quantifying the Public Interest Standard.* Hearing. 98th Cong., 1st sess., May 24, 1983.

——— . Committee on Energy and Commerce. *Contempt of Congress: Proceedings Against Interior Secretary James G. Watt.* Report. 97th Cong., 2nd sess., September 30, 1983.

——— . Committee on Government Operations. *A Citizen's Guide on How to Use the Freedom of Information Act and Privacy Act in Requesting Government Documents.* 13th Report. 98th Cong., 1st sess., November 2, 1977.

——— . Committee on Government Operations. *Administration Proposal Threatens First Amendment Rights of Government Grantees and Contractors.* Hearing. 98th Cong., 1st sess., May 4, 1983.

U.S. Congress. Committee on Government Operations. *Executive Order on*

Security Classification. Hearings. 97th Cong., 2nd sess., March 10 and May 5, 1981.

————. Committee on Government Operations. *Federal Statistics and Statistical Policy*. Hearing. 97th Cong., 2nd sess., June 3, 1982.

————. Committee on Government Operations. *Freedom of Information Act Oversight*. Hearings. 97th Cong., 1st sess., July 14, 15, and 16, 1981.

————. Committee on Government Operations. *Reorganization and Budget Cutbacks May Jeopardize the Future of the Nation's Statistical System*. 34th report. 97th Cong., 2nd sess., September 30, 1982.

————. Committee on Government Operations. *Government Provision of Information Services in Competition with the Private Sector*. Hearing. 97th Cong., 2nd sess., February 25, 1982.

————. Committee on Government Operations. *Security Classification Policy and Executive Order 12356*. Report. 97th Cong., 2nd sess., August 12, 1982.

————. Committee on Government Operations. *Who Cares About Privacy? Oversight of the Privacy Act of 1974 by the Office of Management and Budget and Congress*. 8th report. 98th Cong., 1st sess., November 1, 1983.

————. Committee on Post Office and Civil Service. *Impact of Budget Cuts on Federal Statistical Programs*. Hearing. 97th Cong., 2nd sess., March 16, 1983.

U.S. Congress. Senate. Committee on Governmental Affairs. *Implementation of the Paperwork Act of 1980*. Hearing. 97th Cong., 2nd sess., April 14, 1982.

————. Committee on Governmental Affairs. *Oversight of the Paperwork Reduction Act of 1980*. Hearing. 98th Cong., 1st sess., May 6, 1983.

U.S. Office of Management and Budget. *Information Collection Budget of the United States Government, Fiscal Year 1984*. Washington: U.S. Government Printing Office, 1983.

————. *Paperwork and Red Tape: New Perspectives, New Directions. A Report to the President and the Congress*. Washington: U.S. Government Printing Office, 1978.

THE SAMUEL LORING MORISON CASE

"Administration Says Lie Detector Use, Prosecutions Aimed at Halting Spying, Not Publication of Leaked Information; But are Trials of Journalists in Offing?" *News, Media & The Law* 14 (Fall–Winter 1985): 7–8.

"A Real Spy Scandal." *Penthouse* (June 1986): 94–95.

Church, George J. "Plugging the Leak of Secrets." *Time* (January 28, 1985): 45–46.

Cockburn, Alexander. "The Day of the Jackboot." *The Nation* 239 (November 2, 1985): 431.

"Do Loose Lips Sink Ships?" *The New Republic* 193 (November 18, 1985), editorial page.

Edgar, Harold, and Benno C. Schmidt, Jr. "The Espionage Statutes and Publication of Defense Information." *Columbia Law Review* 73 (May 1973): 929–1087.

———. "Curtis-Wright Comes Home: Executive Power and National Security Secrecy." *Harvard Civil Rights–Civil Liberties Law Review* 21 (Summer 1986): 351–408.

Garbus, Martin. "New Dangers to Press Freedom." *Publishers Weekly* 228 (December 20, 1985): 27–29.

Halperin, Morton. "A U.S. Official Secrets Act?" *Washington Post* (February 24, 1985).

Hentoff, Nat. "The Case of the Unlikely Spy." *The Progressive* 50 (February 1986): 22–24.

"It Isn't Spying." Editorial in *New York Times* (March 4, 1985).

Lardner, George, Jr. "Editors Favor Exemption from Espionage Laws." *The Washington Post* (May 3, 1986).

Powe, Scot. "Espionage, Leaks and the First Amendment." *Bulletin of the Atomic Scientists* 42 (June–July 1986): 8–10.

"Report of the Interdepartmental Group on Unauthorized Disclosure of Classified Information." (March 31, 1982). ("The Willard Report," produced by a group of U.S. government officials chaired by Richard K. Willard of the U.S. Justice Department; obtained from the Justice Department, Civil Division, using the Federal Freedom of Information Act.)

"Safeguarding National Security Information." National Security Decision Directive-84 (NSDD-84) Washington, D.C.: U.S. Government Printing Office (March 11, 1983).

Ungar, Sanford. *The Papers and the Papers.* New York, Dutton: 1972.

U.S. Congress. House. *Espionage Laws and Leaks: Hearings Before the Subcommittee on Legislation of the House Permanent Select Committee on Intelligence.* 96th Congress, 1st sess., 1979.

U.S. Congress. Senate. *National Security Secrets and the Administration of Justice: Report of the Senate Select Committee on Intelligence.* 95th Cong., 2nd sess., 1978.

392 NATIONAL SECURITY AND SEDITIOUS LIBEL

The relevant court cases are:

Abrams v. *United States*, 250 U.S. 616, 624 (1919) (Holmes, J., dissenting).
Debs v. *United States*, 249 U.S. 211 (1919).
Dennis v. *United States*, 341 U.S. 494 (1951).
Frohwerk v. *United States*, 249 U.S. 204 (1919).
Haig v. *Agee*, 453 U.S. 280 (1981).
Near v. *Minnesota*, 283 U.S. 697 (1931).
New York Times Co. v. *Sullivan*, 376 U.S. 254 (1964).
Schenck v. *United States*, 249 U.S. 47 (1919).
Snepp v. *United States*, 444 U.S. 507 (1980).
United States v. *Marchetti*, 466 F. 2d 1309 (4th Cir. 1972).
United States v. *The Progressive, Inc.*, 467 F. Supp. 990 (W.D. Wis. 1979).
Whitney v. *California*, 274 U.S. 357 (1927).

See also:

Blackstone, Sir William. *Commentaries on the Laws of England*. Chicago: University of Chicago Press, 1979.
Chafee, Zechariah. *Free Speech in the United States*. Cambridge: Harvard University Press, 1948.
Hamburger, Phillip. "The Development of the Law of Seditious Libel and the Control of the Press. *Stanford Law Review* 37 (Fall 1985): 661–765.
Morland, Howard. "The H-Bomb Secret: How We Got It, Why We're Telling It." *The Progressive* 70 (November 1979): p. 14.
Siebert, Frederick. *Freedom of the Press in England, 1476–1776: The Rise and Decline of Government Control*. Ann Arbor: University of Michigan Press, 1965.
Stephen, Sir James Fitzjames. *A History of the Criminal Law of England*, London, 1883.

IDEOLOGICAL EXCLUSION: McCARRAN-WALTER ACT

"Agee Loses Passport Case." *Guardian* 33 (July 8, 1981): 6.
Fuentes, Carlos. "Closing the Gates." *Rights and Bill of Rights Journal* 17 (December 1984): 3.

Holton, Arthur C. "Abuses in the Lara Case." Letter to the editors of the *New York Times* (January 24, 1987).

Howe, Marvin. "U.S. Denial of Visas to Foreigners Because of Politics: The Battle Heats Up." *New York Times* (July 28, 1985).

J.C. "Cold War Revisited." *Common Cause* 11 (September 1985): 10.

"McCarran Redux." *The Nation* 234 (June 19, 1982): 737.

McGregor, Matt. "Poet/Writer Randall Fights to Remain in the U.S." *Willimantic Chronicle* (Connecticut) (April 1, 1986).

Mathias, Charles McC., Jr. "A Purity Test We Don't Need." *Washington Post National Weekly Edition* (January 27, 1986).

Miner, A. Ebert. "McCarran Act/50's Relic in the 80's." *In These Times* 7 (April 20, 1983): 5

"Patricia Danilov." *The Nation* 243 (November 1, 1986): 428–429.

Ring, Harry. "Supreme Court Curbs Right to Travel." *The Militant* 45 (July 10, 1981): 24.

Sangree, Suzanne. "Love It or Keep It Out: Fighting Visa Denials." *Guild Notes* 13 (December 1984): 4.

Shipler, David K. "Seeing Visa Denials as Plan to Manipulate Debate." *New York Times* (November 12, 1986).

"State Dept. Denies Devlin Visa." *Militant* 47 (June 17, 1983): 6.

"Undesirable Alien?" *The Hartford Advocate* (March 24, 1986).

"U.S. to Critics/Keep Out." *The Nation* 238 (April 28, 1984): 497.

"Visas Denied to Activists." *Guardian* 34 (June 9, 1982): 6.

"Why Fear Foreigners' Free Speech?" *New York Times* editorial (November 13, 1986).

"Writer Facing Deportation Denies She Is a Communist." *The Hartford Courant* (March 19, 1986).

THE USIA: THE POLITICIZATION OF INTERNATIONAL EDUCATIONAL AND CULTURAL AFFAIRS PROGRAMS

"American Propanganda Machine." Editorial in *The Hartford Courant* (September 28, 1982).

Arndt, Richard T. "The Fulbright Program and U.S. Foreign Relations, 1946–1986." *OAH Newsletter* 15 (May 1986): 24–26.

Aufderheide, Pat. "America's Channel." *In These Times* 9 (November 13–19, 1985): 12–13.

Bachrach, Judy. "Wicked Business." *Rolling Stone* 19 (February 2, 1984): 30–35.

394 Curry, Richard O. "Prepared Statement of Richard Curry." SHAFR *Newsletter* 16 (September 1985): 6–12.

Fulbright, J. William. *The Two Americas*. Storrs, Conn.: University of Connecticut Press, 1966.

Gardner, Richard N. "Selling American in the Marketplace of Ideas. *New York Times* (March 20, 1983).

Grande, William Leo. "Through the Looking Glass: The Kissinger Report on Central America." *World Policy Journal* 1 (Winter 1984): 252–284.

Greenway, Sally. "America's Constricted 'Voice.'" *New York Times* (March 19, 1984).

"Information Officials Destroyed Records on Blacklisted Speakers." *New York Times* (February 26, 1984).

Keogh, Rosemary. "Professor Says USIA is 'Discredited.'" *The Hartford Courant* (March 5, 1984).

Kurtz, Howard. "Hill Rejects Nominee for USIA." *Washington Post* (May 16, 1984).

———. "Testimony at Senate Panel Hearing Conflicts Sharply on USIA Blacklist." *Washington Post* (April 6, 1984).

Lewis, Neil A. "Wick is Surviving the Criticism." *New York Times* (June 26, 1985).

Madison, Christopher. "Under Wick, the USIA Has a Bigger Budget, New Digs and an Image Problem." *National Journal* 16 (June 9, 1984): 1134–1138.

Neal, Fred W. "Reaganizing Scholars." *New York Times* (March 9, 1983).

Pear, Robert. "Information Agency Turns Down Official's Request for Transcripts." *New York Times* (February 28, 1984).

Richburg, Keith B. "Reagan's College Aid for the Needy—From Central America." *Washington Post National Weekly Edition* (July 22, 1985).

Rosenblum, Jonathan. "The Origins of the Blacklist: The USIA Today," *The New Republic* 194 (July 9, 1984): 7–9.

Safire, William. "Big Brother Triumphs." *New York Times* (February 3, 1984).

Southerland, Daniel. "The Puzzling Mr. Wick." *Foreign Service Journal* 61 (January 1984): 24–30.

Stapen, Candyce. "Radio Free Reagan." *Washington Journalism Review* 6 (1984): 10–11.

Taylor, Stuart, Jr. "Court Backs 'Propaganda' Label for 3 Canadian Films." *New York Times* (April 29, 1987).

"The Cold War Lives." *The Capital Times* (Madison, Wisconsin) (March 6, 1984).

"The USIA's Nasty Little Lists." Editorial in the *San Francisco Examiner* (February 20, 1984).

U.S. Congress. The House/Senate Conference Report on the Foreign Relations Authorization Act, Fiscal Years 1986 and 1987. Public Document 99-240.

U.S. House. Foreign Affairs Committee, Report on the State Department and the USIA *et al* Authorization Bill, Fiscal Years 1984 and 1985. Public Document 98-130.

———. Hearings Before the Subcommittee on International Operations on Oversight of the U.S. Information Agency. 98 Cong., 2nd sess., May 10 and 15, 1984.

———. Hearings Before the Subcommittee on International Operations on Oversight of the U.S. Information Agency. Addendum 98 Cong., 2nd sess., May 10 and 15, 1984.

"USIA's Little List." Editorial in *New York Times* (Feb. 20, 1984).

Weintraub, Bernard. "Profile of Charles Z. Wick." *New York Times* (Aug. 11, 1983).

DISINFORMATION, DOUBLESPEAK, AND DECEIT

"ACLU Condemns U.S. Government Secret Disinformation Plan." *The People's Rights* 4 (October–November 1986): 6.

Baker, Russell. "Words of Lead." *Quarterly Review of Doublespeak* 11 (1985): 6.

Beady, Reed. *Contra Terror in Nicaragua: Report of a Fact-finding Mission*, September 1984–January 1985. Boston: South End press, 1985.

Bennett, James R. "Page One Sensationalism and the Libyan 'Hit Team.'" *Newspaper Research Journal* 4 (Fall 1982): 34–38.

Bernstein, Carl. "Reagan at Reel II." *The New Republic* 192 (1985): 20–25.

Blumenthal, Sidney. "Trading Places." *The New Republic* 191 (1984): 14–16.

Bonner, Raymond. *Weakness and Deceit: U.S. Policy and El Salvador.* New York: New York Times Books, 1984.

Borosage, Robert, and Peter Kornbloh. "Behind Reagan's Propaganda Blitz: The Smear Nicaragua Campaign." *The Nation* 240 (April 13, 1985): 423–424.

Brodhead, Frank, Howard Friel, and Edward S. Herman. "The 'Bulgarian Connection' Revisited." *Covert Action Information Bulletin* 23 (Spring 1985): 3–38.

———. "The KGB Plot to Assassinate the Pope: A Case Study in Free-World Disinformation." *Covert Action Information Bulletin* 19 (Spring–Summer 1983): 13–24.

Butterfield, Fox. "Boston U. Focuses on Disinformation." *New York Times* (Nov. 18, 1986).

Chomsky, Noam. "Crimes by Victims Are Called Terrorism." *In These Times* 9 (July 24–August 6, 1985): 17.

396   Cockburn, Alexander. "Reagan and the Art of Lying." *In These Times* 9 (October 15–21, 1986): 17.

"DIA Report Shows Reagan Lies About Nicaragua." *Counterspy* 8 (1983): 10–11.

Green, Mark, and Gail MacCall. *There He Goes Again: Ronald Reagan's Reign of Error*. New York: Pantheon, 1983.

Herman, Edward S. *The Real Terror Network: Terrorism in Fact and Propaganda*. Boston: South End Press, 1982.

Herman, Edward S., and Frank Brodhead. *The Rise and Fall of the Bulgarian Connection*. New York: Sheridan Square, 1986.

Hollyday, Joyce, ed. *Crucible of Hope*. Washington, D.C.: Sojourners, 1984.

Institute for Policy Studies. *In Contempt of Congress: The Reagan Record of Deceit and Illegality on Central America*. Washington: Institute for Policy Studies, 1985.

Johnstone, Diana. "Rome's Verdict: A Qualified Acquittal." *In These Times* 10 (April 16–22, 1986): 9, 15.

Kenworthy, Elton. "Grenada as Theater." *World Policy Journal* 1 (Spring 1984): 635–651.

Lusane, Clarence. "Grenada, Airport '83: Reagan's Big Lie." *Covert Action Information Bulletin* 19 (Spring–Summer 1983): 29–32.

McConnell, Jeff. "Libyan Witch-Hunt: The War at Home." *Counterspy* 6 (1982): 31–40.

McDowell, Edwin. "Soviet Defector Accused of Fabrications in Book." *New York Times* (July 1, 1985).

McGehee, Ralph W. *Deadly Deceits: My 25 Years in the CIA*. New York: Sheridan Square, 1983.

McMahan, Jeff. *Reagan and the World: Imperial Policy and the New Cold War*. New York: Monthly Review, 1985.

Massing, Michael. "About Face on El Salvador." *Columbia Journalism Review* 22 (November–December 1983): 42–50.

Naureckas, Jim. "Spy Scandal May Not be Coincidence." *In These Times* 11 (April 22–28, 1987): 2.

Ridgeway, James. "Home is Where the Covert Action Is." *The Village Voice* (December 16, 1986).

"Ronald Reagan: The Movie." Sixty Minutes. New York, CBS Television Network (Dec. 15, 1985).

"Soviet 'Spy Dust' Now Determined to be Harmless, Noncarcenogenic." *The Hartford Courant* (February 15, 1986).

Tagliabue, John. "Rome Prosecutor Urges Acquittal of 3 Bulgarians." *New York Times* (February 28, 1986).

"Terrorism and Punishment." Editorial on bombing of Libya in *The Hartford Courant* (February 15, 1986).

"The World Court and the Right to Know." *The Nation* 240 (February 16, 1985): 175.

Thompson, E. P. "Look Who's Really Behind Star Wars." *The Nation* 248 (1986): 233–238.

PSYCHOLINGUISTIC MANIPULATION: THE LANGUAGE OF THE NUCLEAR ARMS RACE

Allen v. *United States.* 588 F. Supp. (D. Utah 1984), 247, 403.

American Psychiatric Association. Task Force Rep. 20. *Psychosocial Aspects of Nuclear Developments.* Washington, D.C.: American Psychiatric Association, 1982.

Blackaby, Frank. "World Arsenals 1982." *Bulletin of Atomic Scientists* 38 (June 1982).

Bonner-Lyons v. *School Commission.* 480 F. 2d 442 (1st Cir. 1973).

Brandenburg v. *Ohio.* 395 U.S. 444 (1969).

Champlin, Charles. "Build-Down: It Has a Nice Ring to It." *Quarterly Review of Doublespeak* 10 (1984): 5–6.

"Doublespeak: Telling It Like It Isn't." *Time* (December 5, 1977): 33.

Emerson, Thomas I. *The System of Freedom of Expression.* New York: Random House, 1970.

Hilgartner, Stephen, Richard C. Bell, and Rory O'Connor. *Nukespeak, Nuclear Language, Visions, and Mindset.* San Francisco: Sierra Club Books, 1982.

Kamenshine, Robert D. "The First Amendment's Implied Political Establishment Clause." *California Law Review* 67 (1979): 1104.

Lifton, Robert J., and Richard Falk. *Indefensible Weapons.* New York: Basic Books, 1982.

McCombs, Maxwell E., and Donald L. Shaw. "The Agenda-Setting Function of Mass Media." *Public Opinion Quarterly* 36 (1972): 176.

Mack, John E. "Psychosocial Effects of the Nuclear Arms Race." *Bulletin Atomic Scientists* 37 (1981).

New York Times v. *United States,* 403 U.S. 713 (1971).

Orwell, George. *1984.* New York: New American Library edition, 1981.

Shiffrin, Steven. "Government Speech." *UCLA Law Review* 27 (1980): 565.

Stanson v. *Mott,* 17 Cal. 3d 206, 551 p.2d 1. 130 *California Rptr.* (1976): 697.

Yudof, Mark G. *When Government Speaks.* Berkeley: University of California Press, 1983.

398   Ziegler, Edward H., Jr. "Government Speech and the Constitution: The Limits of Official Partisanship." *Boston College Law Review* 21 (1980): 578.

DRUG TESTING

"ACLU Fights 'Drug Hysteria' Laws." *Civil Liberties* 358 (Summer–Fall 1986): 7.

Becker, Howard S. "The Marijuana Tax Act of 1937." In his *Outsiders: Studies in the Sociology of Deviance*. London: Free Press, 1963.

———. "History, Culture and Subjective Experience: An Exploration of the Social Bases of Drug-Induced Experiences." *Journal of Health and Social Behavior* 8 (1967).

Bernstein, Arnold, and Henry Lennard. "Drugs, Doctors, and Junkies." *Society* 10 (1973): 14–25.

Brecher, E. M., and the editors of *Consumer Reports*. *Licit and Illicit Drugs*. Boston: Little, Brown, 1972.

"CCLU Proposes Legislation to Curb Arbitrary Drug Testing." *The People's Rights* 4 (October–November 1986): 2.

Cooke, Janet. "Young Addict's World One of Hard Drugs, Fast Money." *Washington Post* (October 1, 1980).

"Customs Workers Drug Test Declared Unconstitutional." *Willimantic Chronicle* (Connecticut) (November 13, 1986).

Diamond, Edwin, Frank Accosta, and Leslie-Jean Thornton. "Is TV News Hyping America's Cocaine Problem?" *TV Guide* (February 7, 1987).

Dickson, Donald. "Bureaucracy and Morality." *Social Problems* 16 (1968): 143–156.

"Drug Testing in the Workplace." *Civil Liberties* 357 (Spring 1986): 5.

Duster, Troy. *The Legislation of Morality*. New York: Free Press, 1970.

Fink, David. "Bill Would Limit Random Drug Testing." *The Hartford Courant* (April 18, 1987).

Frank, Jennifer. "Breaker Madness: The Truth About Drug Testing." *Northeast Magazine* (April 26, 1987): 28–33.

Goldstein, Richard. "The War on Drugs: Wrong Target, Wrong Approach." *In These Times* 10 (October 8–14, 1986): 12–13.

Gould, Madelyn S., and David Shaffer. "The Impact of Suicide in Television Movies: Evidence of Imitation." *New England Journal of Medicine* (September 11, 1986).

"The Great Drug Testing Debate." *Civil Liberties* 357 (Spring 1986): 4.

Grinspoon, Lester, and James Bakalar. *Cocaine: A Drug and its Social Evolution*. Cambridge, Mass.: Harvard University Press, 1976.

Hansen, Hugh J., Samuel P. Caudill, and Joe D. Boone. "Crisis in Drug **399**
Testing: Results of CDC Blind Study." *Journal of the American Medical
Association* 253 (1985).

Harvey, Barbara. "What You Should Know About Drug Testing." *Labor Notes*
80 (October 1985): 10.

Havemann, Judith. "Who Said Federal Workers Couldn't Be Fired For Using
Drugs?" *Washington Post National Weekly Edition* (December 15, 1986).

Helmer, John. *Drugs and Minority Oppression.* New York: Seabury, 1975.

Himmelstein, Jerome. *The Strange Career of Marijuana: From Killer Weed to
Drop-Out Drug.* Westport, Conn.: Greenwood, 1983.

Johnston, Lloyd D., P. M. O'Malley, and J. G. Bachman. *Drug Use Among
High School Students, College Students, and Other Young Adults: National
Trends Through 1985.* Ann Arbor, Mich.: Institute for Social Research,
1986.

Jussim, Daniel. "Drug Testing Fails Constitutional Examination." *Civil Liberties* 46 (Winter 1986): 5.

Levine, Harry-Gene. "The Alcohol Problem in America: From Temperance
to Alcoholism." *British Journal of Addiction* 79 (1984): 109–119.

Marx, Garry T. "The Company Is Watching You Everywhere." *New York
Times* (February 15, 1987).

Morgan, John P. "Problems of Mass Screening for Misused Drugs." *Journal of
Psychoactive Drugs* 16 (1984): 305–317.

Morgan, Patricia. "The Legislation of Drug Law: Economic Crisis and Social
Control." *Journal of Drug Issues* 8 (1978): 53–62.

Musto, David. *The American Disease: Origins of Narcotics Controls.* New Haven,
Conn.: Yale University Press, 1973.

Newsweek: "A Question of Privacy: Drug Tests Raise a Host of Constitutional
Issues" (September 29, 1986).

———. "Reagan Aide: "Pot Can Make You Gay" (October 27, 1986).

New York Times. "Agency Takes Steps for Partly Banning All-Terrain Vehicles"
(January 27, 1987).

Olsen, Steve, with Dean R. Gerstein. *Alcohol in America: Taking Action to
Prevent Abuse.* Washington, D.C.: National Academy Press, 1975.

Perry, Steve. "The Grand Delusion." *In These Times* 11 (October 15–21, 1986):
13–14.

Phillips, David P., and Lundie L. Carstensen. "Clustering of Teenage Sui-
cides after Television News Stories about Suicide." *New England Journal
of Medicine* (September 11, 1986).

Reinarman, Craig. "Moral Entrepreneurs and Political Economy: Historical
and Ethnographic Notes on the Construction of the Cocaine Menace."
Contemporary Crises 3 (1979): 225–254.

———, *et al.* "Scapegoating and Social Control in the Construction of a Public

Problem." In *Research on Law, Deviance, and Social Control*. Edited by Steven Spitzen and Andrew Scull. Westport, Conn.: JAI Press, 1987.

Silverman, Milton, and Phillip Lee. *Pills, Politics, and Profits*. Berkeley, University of California Press, 1974.

Steinbrook, Robert. "Medical Editor Lambasts Drug Testing." *The Hartford Courant* (Dec. 6, 1986).

Time. "Battling the Enemy Within: Companies Fight to Drive Illegal Drugs out of the Workplace" (March 17, 1986).

U.S. Congress. Public Law 99-570, Anti-Drug Abuse Act of 1986.

Williams, Lena. "Reagan Drug Testing Plan to Start Despite Court Rulings Opposing It." *New York Times* (November 29, 1986).

Zinberg, Norman E. *Drug, Set, and Setting: The Basis for Controlled Intoxicant Use*. New Haven: Yale University Press, 1984.

THE FBI AND DOMESTIC SURVEILLANCE

Cook, Fred J. *The FBI Nobody Knows*. San Diego: Pyramid, 1964.

Donner, Frank J. *The Age of Surveillance*. New York: Knopf, 1980.

Elliff, John. *The Reform of FBI Intelligence Operations*. Princeton: Princeton University Press, 1979.

Felt, W. Mark. *The FBI Pyramid: From the Inside*. New York: Putnam, 1979.

Garrow, David. *The FBI and Martin Luther King, Jr.* New York: Penguin, 1981.

Giller, Stephen, ed. *Investigating the FBI* New York: Doubleday, 1973.

"Governmental Investigations of the Exercise of First Amendment Rights." Note. *Minnesota Law Review* 60 (1976): 1257.

Levine, Howard, and Dennis Bernstein. "Congress Probes FBI Scare Tactics." *In These Times* 11 (April 22–28, 1986): 3.

Lowenthal, Max. *The Federal Bureau of Investigation*. Westport, Conn.: Greenwood, 1950.

Morgan, Richard. *Domestic Intelligence: Monitoring Dissent in America*. Austin: University of Texas Press, 1980.

O'Reilly, Kenneth. *Hoover and the UnAmericans*. Philadelphia: Temple University Press, 1983.

Overstreet, Harry, and Bonaro Overstreet. *The FBI in Our Open Society*. New York: Norton, 1969.

Powers, Richard. *G-Men*. Carbondale: Southern Illinois University Press, 1983.

Senate Select Committee to Study Governmental Operations with Respect to Intelligence Activities, Final Report. *Intelligence Activities and the Rights of Americans*. 94th Cong., 2nd sess., 1976.

Stone, Geoffrey, Louis Seidman, Cass Sunstein, and Mark Tushnet, *Constitu-* **401**
tional Law 1306–1321*. Boston: Little, Brown, 1986.
Sullivan, William. *The Bureau: My Thirty Years in Hoover's FBI*. New York:
Norton, 1982.
Symposium. "National Security and Civil Liberties." *Cornell Law Review* 69
(April 1984).
Theoharis, Athan. *Spying on Americans: Political Surveillance from Hoover to the
Huston Plan*. Philadelphia: Temple University Press, 1978.
————, ed. *Beyond the Hiss Case: The FBI, Congress and the Cold War*. Phila-
delphia: Temple University Press, 1982.
Tully, Andrew. *Inside the FBI*. New York: McGraw-Hill, 1980.
Whitehead, Don. *The FBI Story*. New York: Random House, 1956.
Wise, David. *The American Police State*. New York: Random House, 1976.

CONSPIRACY TRIALS

"An American Gulag?—Summary Arrest and Emergency Detention of Politi-
cal Dissidents In The United States." *Columbia Human Rights Law Review*
10 (1978).
Bunyan, Tony. "The Police Against the People." *Race and Class* (1981–1982):
153–170.
Donner, Frank J. *The Age of Surveillance*. New York: Random House, 1980.
Gans, Donna. "N.Y. Eight Plus: A Question of Conspiracy, But Whose?"
Overthrow 7 (Summer 1985): 10, 15, 19.
Gombossy, George. "Use of Wells Fargo Wiretaps Attacked." *The Hartford
Courant* (January 15, 1987).
————. "Court Ruling Could Mean Release of Defendants in Wells Fargo
Case." *The Hartford Courant* (November 21, 1986).
Halperin, Morton, et al. *The Lawless State: The Crimes of the U.S. Intelligence
Agencies*. New York: Penguin, 1976.
Kircheimer, Otto. *Political Justice*. Westport, Conn.: Greenwood, 1961.
Ola, Akinshju. "N.Y. 8+ Sees No Black Conspiracy." *Guardian* 37 (August
21, 1985): 6.
"State Acts to Jail New York 8 Before Trial." *Guild Notes* 9 (Winter 1985): 5.
Tuohy, Lynne. "2 Wells Fargo Defendants Stay in Prison; Bond Denied." *The
Hartford Courant* (December 23, 1986).
Wise, David. *The American Police State*. New York: Random House, 1976.

Armstrong, Robert, and Janet Shenk. *El Salvador: The Face of Revolution*. Boston: South End Press, 1982.

Barr, Tom, and Deb Preusch. *The Central America Fact Book*. New York: Grove, 1986.

Bernstein, Dennis. "Sanctuary: Disorder in the Courts." *In These Times* 10 (December 25, 1985): 6–8.

————, and Connie Blitt. "Defense Gambles, Rests Case Before Presenting It." *In These Times* 10 (March 26–April 1, 1986): 7–8.

Berryman, Phillip. *Inside Central America*. New York: Pantheon, 1985.

————. *Religious Roots of Rebellion*. Maryknoll, N.Y.: Orbis, 1984.

Blau, Ignatius. *This Ground is Holy*. (Methuen, N.J.: Paulist Press, 1985).

Blitt, Connie. "Sanctuary Churches Sue U.S. for Bugging Worship." *In These Times* 10 (January 29, 1986): 9.

Bosniak, Lindie. "Crackdown on Sanctuary." *North American Congress on Latin America* 18 (May 1984): 4–7.

Elbert-Minor, Allan. "The Politics of Asylum." *The Progressive* 49 (August 1985): 23.

Golden, Renny, and Michael McConnell. *Sanctuary: The New Underground Railroad*. Maryknoll, N.Y., Orbis, 1986.

Harding, Vincent. *There Is a River: The Black Struggle for Freedom in America*. New York: Harcourt, Brace, 1983.

Institute for Policy Studies. *Changing Course: Blueprint for Peace in Central America and the Caribbean*, 1984.

Kohn, Alfie. "The Return of Cointelpro?" *The Nation* 242 (January 25, 1986): 74–76.

Lernoux, Penny. *Cry of the People*. New York: Penguin, 1980.

MacEoin, Gary. *Sanctuary*. Albany: Harrow, 1985.

Nairn, Allain. "Assault on Sanctuary." *The Progressive* 49 (August 1985): 20.

Ovryn, Rachel. "Targeting the Sanctuary Movement." *Covert Action Information Bulletin* 24 (Summer 1985): 12.

Paterson, Kent. "N.M. Governor Declares State a Sanctuary." *Guardian* 38 (April 23, 1986): 4.

Pearce, Jenny. *Under the Eagle*. Boston: South End Press, 1981.

Tolan, Sandy, and Carol Ann Bassett. "Informers in the Sanctuary Movement." *The Nation* 240 (July 20, 27, 1985): 40–44.

THE REAGAN ADMINISTRATION AND THE COURTS

Abramson, Jill. "Right Place at the Right Time." *The American Lawyer* 8 (June 1986).

Barret, Paul M. "Constitutional Construction: How to Build a Supreme Court." *The Washington Monthly* 17 (December 1985): 45–49.

Berger, Raoul. "Justice Brennan is Wrong." *The Washington Post National Weekly Edition* (November 11, 1985).

Blumenthal, Sidney. "They May Be Meese's Founding Fathers, But They're Not Mine." *Washington Post National Weekly Edition* (November 18, 1985).

Bodine, Laurence, and Richard G. Wilry. "Q and A with the Attorney General." *American Bar Association Journal* 71 (July 1985): 44–48.

Brennan, William J., Jr. "Guaranteeing Individual Liberty." *USA Today* 115 (September 1986): 40–42.

"Brennan Opposes Legal View Urged by Administration." *New York Times* (October 13, 1985).

Caplan, Lincoln. "If This Is Judicial Restraint, Let's Hope They Never Let Loose." *Washington Post National Weekly Edition* (February 3, 1986).

Cole, David, and Jules Lobel. "Meese Founders on Founders' Values." *In These Times* 10 (January 22, 1986): 12.

Commager, Henry Steele. "Constitution and Original Intent." *Center Magazine* 19 (November–December, 1986): 4–17.

D'Souza, Dinesh. "Original Intent Jurisprudence." *Center Magazine* 19 (November–December 1986): 61.

Dworkin, Ronald. "Reagan's Justice." *New York Review of Books* (November 8, 1984).

———, and Grover Reese II. "Reagan's Justice: An Exchange." *New York Review of Books* (February 14, 1985).

Gelb, Leslie. "U.S. Will Ask Court to Reverse Abortion Ruling." *New York Times* (July 15, 1985).

Glasser, Ira. "Edwin Van Winkle: Awake Again." *Washington Post National Weekly Edition* (December 2, 1985).

Goldman, Sheldon. "Reaganizing the Judiciary: the First Term Appointments," *Judicature: The Journal of the American Judicature Society* (April–May 1985).

Hentoff, Nat. "So Long, Miranda." *Washington Post National Weekly Edition* (April 22, 1985).

Hundley, Kris. "Overthrowing the Constitution." *The Hartford Advocate* (September 18, 1985).

404 Jenkins, John A. "Mr. Power: Attorney General Edwin Meese." *New York Times Magazine* (October 12, 1986).

Judis, John B. "The Constitution as Doormat, Part IV." *In These Times* 10 (October 1, 1986): 5.

"Justice Brennan Dissents." *Washington Post* (October 15, 1985).

"Justice Senses 'Arrogance' in Recent Attacks." *Washington Post* (October 13, 1985).

Kaufman, Irving. "What Did the Founding Fathers Intend?" *New York Times Magazine* (February 23, 1986).

Kurtz, Howard, and Mary Thornton. "Edwin Meese's Justice." *Washington Post National Weekly Edition* (September 9, 1985).

Lewis, Anthony. "Mr. Meese's Petard." *New York Times* (November 4, 1985).

Meese, Edwin III. "The Tulane Speech: What I Meant." *Washington Post National Weekly Edition* (December 1, 1986).

———. "A Dissent from Edwin Meese." *Time* 128 (September 15, 1986): 8.

———. "Interpreting the Constitution." *USA Today* 115 (September 19, 1986): 36–39.

"Meese Hits Judicial Activism." *Washington Post* (November 16, 1985).

"Mr. Meese and His New Vision of the Constitution." *New York Times* (October 17, 1985).

Navasky, Victor. "Ronald Reagan and the Supremes." *Esquire Magazine* (April 1987).

Rakove, Jack N. "Mr. Meese, Meet Mr. Madison." *Atlantic Monthly* 258 (December 1986): 77–82.

Rebell, Michael A. "Judicial Activism/Court's New Role." *Social Policy* 12 (Spring 1982): 24.

"The Rehnquist Court Open For Business." *Civil Liberties* 356 (Summer–Fall 1986): 1–3.

Riordan, Donald P. "Slow Death of Habeas Corpus." *Guild Notes* 6 (September 1982): 4.

Rose, Turner. "Rehnquist: Is a 'Brilliant Legal Mind' Enough?" *Washington Post National Weekly Edition* (September 8, 1986).

Schwartz, Herman. "A Constitutional Shell Game: 'Meese's Original Intent.'" *The Nation* 241 (December 7, 1985).

———. "Reagan Packs the Federal Judiciary." *The Nation* 242 (June 14, 1986).

———. "Rehnquist's America." *The Nation* 243 (August 16–23, 1986).

———. "The Reagan Judges." *The Nation* (June 14, 1986).

Shenon, Philip. "Meese Pushing to Reinterpret the Constitution." *Maine Sunday Telegram* (October 20, 1985).

Singer, Howie. "Meese's Gunning for Miranda Backfires." *In These Times* 11 (March 25–31, 1987): 3.

"Stevens Rebuts Meese's Criticism of High Court." *Washington Post* (October 26, 1985).

Strossen, Nadine. "No State Shall Abridge: In Defense of the Incorporation Doctrine." *Civil Liberties* 356 (Summer–Fall, 1986): 5.

Sundquist, James L. *Constitutional Reform and Effective Government.* Washington, D.C.: Brookings Institute, 1986.

Taylor, Stuart, Jr. "Meese and the Supreme Court: He Deals with Critics by Softening His Remarks." *New York Times* (November 19, 1986).

———. "Who's Right About the Constitution?: Meese v. Brennan." *The New Republic* 194 (January 6–13, 1986): 17–21.

———. "Meese in Bar Group Speech, Criticizes High Court." *New York Times* (July 10, 1985).

———. "Meese and His Candor." *New York Times* (August 3, 1985).

Tribe, Laurence H. *God Save This Honorable Court: How the Choice of Supreme Court Justices Shapes Our History.* New York: Random House, 1985.

MEDIA MANIPULATION

Berlet, Chip. "Ominous Clouds for Press Rights." *Alternative Media* 12 (Spring 1981): 17.

Bradlee, Benjamin C. "The Press Is Not Reckless About National Security." *Washington Post National Weekly Edition* (June 23, 1986).

Cleghorn, Reese. "Reagan's New Bypass Operations: The White House News Service and Interviews by Satellite." *Washington Journalism Review* 7 (1985): 17–20.

DeFrank, Thomas M. "Fine-Tuning the White House Press Conference." *Washington Journalism Review* 4 (1982): 27–29.

Fields, Howard. "The White House Versus the News Media." *Television/Radio Age* 32 (November 26, 1984): 44–46.

Friel, Howard. "Media Manipulation/Covert Propaganda." *Covert Action Information Bulletin* 21 (Spring 1984): 14.

Kornbluth, Josh. "Stopping the Press." *In These Times* 6 (March 24, 1982): 4.

"Lashing Out at NBC." Editorial in *The Hartford Courant* (May 11, 1986).

Peterzell, Jay. "The Government Shuts Up: The Reagan Administration's Stonewalling Reporters." *Columbia Journalism Review* (July–August 1982): 31.

———. "Can the CIA Spook the Press?" *Columbia Journalism Review* (September–October 1986): 29–34.

PLP. "Who's Saying What We're Hearing." *Industrial Worker* 81 (April 1984): 8.

406   Reporters Committee for Freedom of the Press. *The Reagan Administration and the News Media*. Washington, D.C.: Reporters Committee for Freedom of the Press, March 1986.

THE MEDIA: SELF-CENSORSHIP

Armstrong, David. "Ten Stories the Media Didn't Tell." *Guardian* 35 (June 1, 1983): 2.

Bonner, Raymond. "A One-Sided Press." *The Nation* 239 (December 8, 1984): . 604.

Brown, Les. "Reagan and the Unseen Network." *Channels* 1 (October–November 1981): 17–18.

Cockburn, Alexander. "Collapse of the Free Press." *The Nation* 240 (March 9, 1985): 262–263.

David, Michael, and Pat Aufderheide. "All the President's Media." *Channels* 5 (1985): 20–24.

Dowie, Mark. "How ABC Spikes the News." *Mother Jones* 10 (November 1985): 33.

"The Hush Is In." *The Nation* 37 (November 12, 1983): 452.

Mackenzie, Angus. "Press Fails to Report Reagan Censorship." *Overthrow* 7 (April 1985): 5.

Millman, Joel. "Reagan's Reporters." *The Progressive* 48 (October 1984): 20.

Parenti, Michael. *Inventing Reality: The Politics of the Mass Media*. New York: St. Martin's, 1986.

Sheinfield, Lois P. "Washington vs. the Right to Know." *The Nation* 239 (April 13, 1985): 426–427.

LIBEL AND THE MEDIA

Adler, Renata. *Reckless Regard*. New York: Knopf, 1986.

Ashby, Steven. "History Will Not Absolve Sharon." *Guardian* 37 (January 23, 1985): 23.

Bezanson, Randall P. "Libel Law and the Press: Setting the Record Straight." *Iowa Law Review* 71 (October 1985).

Cockburn, Alexander. "CBS Surrenders." *The Nation* 240 (March 2, 1985): 228.

Cranberg, G. "Fanning the Fire: The Media's Role in Libel Litigation." *Iowa Law Review* 71 (October 1985).

Denniston, Lyle. "The Supreme Court Strikes Off in a New Direction in Libel Law, Exposing Media and Non-Media Defendants to Greater Risk." *California Law Review* 6 (January 1986): 38–42.

George, Nina. "Sharon Trial Outcome: 'A Moral Whitewash.'" *Guardian* 37 (February 6, 1985): 5.

"Libel Award Upset as Appeals Court Defends Investigative Reporting." *The Hartford Courant* (March 14, 1987).

"Ruling Could Add to News Media Libel Woes." *The Hartford Courant* (June 27, 1985).

Shannon, William V. "'Scoop' Revisited: Time, CBS and Libel." *Washington Post National Weekly Edition* (December 1, 1986).

Solowski, J. "The Study and the Libel Plaintiff: Who Sues for Libel." *Iowa Law Review* 71 (October 1985).

Taylor, Stuart, Jr. "High Court Upsets Libel Law That Helped Some Who Sued." *New York Times* (April 22, 1986).

"Truth and Libel." *The Nation* 243 (November 1, 1986): 427.

BEYOND WESTMORELAND: THE RIGHT'S ATTACK ON THE PRESS

Accuracy in Media Advertisements. *Washington Times* (January 14, 1983), and (July 21, 1983).

"Accuracy in Media Sues FCC on Fairness." *Human Events* (January 6, 1973): 3.

AIM *Reports* 1975–1985. See especially April 1975, May 1978, November (II) 1979, October (I) 1981, January (II) 1982, February (I) 1982, March (I) 1982, August (I) 1982, April (B) 1983, May (B) 1983, August (A) 1983, May (A) 1984.

American Security Council and FCC. *Conservative Digest* 1 (July 1975) 3.

Blodgett, Nancy. "The Ralph Naders of the Right." *American Bar Association Journal* 70 (May 1984): 71–75.

Bottomore, T. B. *Elites and Society.* Middlesex, England: Pelican, 1966.

Boyer, Peter J. "CBS-Westmoreland Dispute Heats Up." *Los Angeles Times* (January 31, 1983).

———. "Photo, Ad Anger Westmoreland." *Los Angeles Times* (July 26, 1983).

Bruck, Connie. "The Mea Culpa Defense." *The American Lawyer* (September 1983): 82–90.

Buchanan, Patrick J. "Does Big Business Deserve Our Support?" *Conservative Digest* 1 (April, 1977): 6–11.

408 "CBS Expands Its Suit Against Media Group." *New York Times* (February 28, 1985): C22.

"CBS Should Fire Mike Wallace." *AIM Report* (February (I) 1982).

Crawford, Alan. *Thunder on the Right*. New Haven: Yale University Press, 1980.

DeGrand, Alexander. *Italian Fascism: Its Origins and Development*. Lincoln: University of Nebraska Press, 1982.

Drew, Elizabeth. "Jesse Helms." *The New Yorker* (July 20, 1981): 78–94.

"FCC Votes Against Fairness." *AIM Report* (October (I) 1981).

Fein, Bruce E. *New York Times v. Sullivan: An Obstacle to Enlightened Public Discourse and Government Responsiveness to the People*. New York: American Legal Foundation, 1984.

Flaherty, Francis J. "Right-Wing Firms Pick Up Steam." *The National Law Journal* (May 23, 1983).

Francis, Samuel T. "Message from MARS." In *The New Right Papers*. Edited by Robert W. Whitaker. New York: St. Martin's, 1982.

Heritage Foundation. *Mandate for Leadership*. Washington, D.C.: Heritage Foundation, 1981.

Houck, Oliver A. "With Charity for All." *The Yale Law Journal* 93 (July 1984): 1454–1514; see especially 1506–1514.

"How Conservatives Can Get Control of CBS." *Human Events* (January 26, 1985): 1.

Jenkins, John A. "The Right's Tough." *TWA Ambassador* (January 1985): 50–54.

Jones, Alex S. "Organizations Aid Officials Who Believe They Were Defamed." *New York Times* (October 16, 1984): B4.

Kaiser, Charles. "Who Broke the Rules?" *Newsweek* (June 14, 1982).

Kowet, Don, and Sally Bedell. "Anatomy of a Smear: How CBS Broke the Rules and 'Got' General Westmoreland." *TV Guide* (May 29, 1982).

Lardner, George, Jr. "Pittsburgh Millionaire Financed Westmoreland Suit Against CBS: Scaife, of New Right Causes, Paid Much of $3 Million Tab." *Washington Post* (February 28, 1985).

Larsen, Jonathan Z. "The Battle of Black Rock: General Westmoreland's Guerrilla War With CBS." *New York* magazine (October 24, 1983): 40–53.

"Legal Group Hits Media Distortion and Error." *Washington Times* (March 9, 1984): 4C.

Lewis, Anthony. "*New York Times* v. *Sullivan* Reconsidered: Time to Return to 'The Central Meaning of the First Amendment.'" *Columbia Law Review* 83 (April 1983): 603–625.

———. "The Sullivan Case." *The New Yorker* (November 5, 1984): 52–95.

McDonald, Michael P. Interview, *Washington Times* (March 9, 1984): 4C.

"The Media in the Dock." *Newsweek* (October 22, 1984): 66–72.

Merry, Robert W. "The Populists Are Coming." *Conservative Digest* (October 1975): 52.

Mobil Advertisements. The *New York Times* Op-Ed Page (October 18, 1984, December 6, 1984).

Mohr, Charles. "The Press: How to Use It or Lose It." *New York Times* (June 28, 1984).

"Newsmakers Can't Be News Censors." *New York Times* editorial (January 16, 1985): A22.

New York Times v. *Sullivan*. 376 U.S. 254, *Supreme Court Reporter* 84 (1964): 710.

Phillips, Kevin P. "Is the First Amendment Obsolete?" *Human Events* (January 13, 1973): 37.

———. *Mediacracy: American Parties and Politics in the Communications Age*. Garden City, N.Y.: Doubleday, 1975: v, 30–31, and 207–208.

———. *Post-Conservative America*. New York: Random House, 1982.

Randolph, Eleanor. "Four Words Felled Lawsuit Against CBS, Attorney Explains Decision." *Washington Post* (February 28, 1985).

Rasky, Susan F. "Ted Turner Is Said to Plan Bid for CBS-TV." *New York Times* (March 1, 1985): 1.

Rees, John. "The Right Public Interest Lawyer, Dan Burt, An Exclusive Interview With the Conservative Lawyer Who Heads The Capital Legal Foundation and Battles the Left." *The Review of the News* (John Birch Society) (January 27, 1982): 39–52.

Rothmyer, Karen. "Citizen Scaife." *Columbia Journalism Review* (July–August, 1981): 41–50.

Rusher, William A. *The Making of the New Majority Party*. New York: Greenhill Publishers, 1975.

———. "The New Elite That Must Be Curbed." *Conservative Digest* 1 (September 1975): 26.

Rusher, William A. "The New Right: Past and Prospects." In *The New Right Papers*. Edited by Robert W. Whitaker. New York: St. Martin's, 1982: 22.

Saloma, John III. *Ominous Politics*. New York: Hill and Wang, 1984.

Schneir, Walter, ed. *Vietnam: A Documentary Collection, Westmoreland v. CBS on Microfiche*. With printed *Guide to the Westmoreland-CBS Microfiche Collection*. New York, Clearwater Publishing Company: 1985.

Schneir, Walter, and Miriam Schneir. "The Uncounted Vietcong: How the Military Cooked the Books." *The Nation* (May 12, 1984): 570–576.

———. "On Libel and Officials." *The New York Times* Op-Ed Page, November 18, 1984: E25.

410 Shales, Tom. "The 'Smear' Controversy; TV Guide, CBS and 'The Uncounted Enemy.'" *Washington Post* (May 27, 1982).

————. "CBS Lavish Apologia, and the Chill after the 'Vietnam' Inquest." *Washington Post* (July 19, 1982).

————. "Takeover Talk: All Eyes on CBS." *Washington Post* (March 4, 1985).

Smith, Sally Bedell. "Conservatives Seeking Stock of CBS to Alter 'Liberal Bias.'" *New York Times* (January 11, 1985): B4.

————. "CBS Stock in Jump; Turner Statement." *New York Times* (March 2, 1985): 33.

————. "CBS to Subpoena Ted Turner in Suit." *New York Times* (March 6, 1985): D4.

"Three Conservative 'Public Interest' Groups Turn to Libel Litigation." *Libel Defense Resource Center Bulletin* (July 15, 1983).

Tyson, James L. *Target America: The Influence of Communist Propaganda on U.S. Media.* Washington: Regnery, 1981.

Viguerie, Richard A. *The New Right: We're Ready to Lead.* New York, Viguerie, 1981.

————. *Current Biography* (1983): 427–430.

————. "The State of the Union, A Populist View." *Vital Speeches of the Day* (May 15, 1984): 474–480.

"Westmoreland Rips Reporting on War." *AIM Report* (May 1978).

Whitaker, Robert W., ed. *The New Right Papers.* New York: St. Martin's, 1982.

ACCURACY IN MEDIA

"Accuracy in Media." *Covert Action Information Bulletin* 12 (April 1981): 46.

"AIM Warriors in Court: Fighting White Justice." *Open Road* 17 (Winter 1984): 7.

Berlet, Chip. "The Big Liars are Back in Town." *Alternative Media* 13 (Fall 1981): 9–12.

Frahm, Robert A. "Student Spies on Academic Watchdogs." *The Hartford Courant* (January 1, 1986).

Healy, Timothy S. "Academic Thought Police Would Wreck Idea of a University." *The Hartford Courant* (December 23, 1985).

Massing, Michael. "The Rise and Decline of Accuracy in Media." *The Nation* 24 (September 13, 1986): 200–214.

Wolfe, Allan. "Ignorance as Public Policy." *The Nation* 234 (April 3, 1982): 385.

————. "The Real Aim is Ideological." *The Nation* 243 (September 13, 1986): 215–219.

Halperin, Morton. "How to Stop the Sale of Secrets: Don't Go For Easy Solutions." *New York Times* (July 22, 1985).

Jussim, David. "The Polygraph Comes to School." *Civil Liberties* 18 (Summer–Fall, 1986): 7.

Kirkpatrick, Jeane J. "Polygraphs? No." *Washington Post National Weekly Edition* (January 13, 1986).

"Lie Test Order Is Relaxed: Reagan Leaves Decisions up to His Cabinet." *The Hartford Courant* (December 22, 1985).

U.S. Congress, Office of Technology Assessment. *Scientific Validity of Polygraph Testing, A Technical Memorandum.* Washington, D.C.: USAPO, 1983.

Index